Count Me In

A Professional's
Guide To
Blackjack

by Al Simon

Order this book online at www.trafford.com
or email orders@trafford.com

Most Trafford titles are also available at major online book retailers.

© Copyright 2005, 2011 Al Simon.
All rights reserved. No part of this publication may be reproduced, stored in a retrieval
system, or transmitted, in any form or by any means, electronic, mechanical, photocopying,
recording, or otherwise, without the written prior permission of the author.

Author Credits: Also wrote The Think Tank, The Poker player's Bible

Printed in the United States of America.

ISBN: 978-1-4269-7590-5 (sc)
ISBN: 978-1-4269-7591-2 (e)

Trafford rev. 07/20/2011

 www.trafford.com

North America & international
toll-free: 1 888 232 4444 (USA & Canada)
phone: 250 383 6864 ♦ fax: 812 355 4082

Table of Contents

Count Me In

Introduction

Every so often someone will come up to me and tell me that he will be either going to Las Vegas, or some other city offering gaming, or he will just be passing through one that does. They invariably ask if there are any tips that I can offer them that will help their stay to be a tad more profitable. I always tell them, "If you want to lose less money don't gamble, unless you have grasped the fundamentals of card counting."

Knowledge of gaming is therefore something that will benefit you at some time in your life, whether it is immediately, or some time in the distant future. Knowing what to do when that time comes, and what to expect when you arrive at some gaming "Mecca" will be a real asset. Taking charge of a situation rather than merely being a voyeur, watching from the sidelines, will help you take a bite out of one of those "forbidden apples of life." Playing with confidence is the key.

Risking money and yet not gambling seems like a tough sell, but that is precisely what I am attempting to do in this book. It explores a basic introductory counting system, whereby the player can put the risk that is built into the game right back on to the laps of the casinos, where it rightfully belongs.

I will give you a guided tour to various casinos around the world, giving you tips and tricks that have been used on me, as well as by me, some with great effect. You will be privy to an assortment of antics used by people, and definitions as to what they are.

The book is a factual rendering of events as they illustrate the evolution of a "wide-eyed" tourist into a seasoned blackjack player, showing ways to minimize the risk. It is liberally interspersed with political barbs and philosophical humor to enhance the pleasure of the read.

I hope you enjoy it.

Introduction

This book is dedicated to my daughter Alana, and my two boys, Beau and Dylan.

A special thanks also goes out to my nephew James Simon for the hours of yeoman work put in to the formatting of Count Me In. Acknowledgements are also extended to Zoltan K. for his countless hours spent in editing the manuscript.

Chapter one: The Neophyte

I was sweating like all hell, and was praying that no moisture showed on my forehead. I fashioned my face into the stoic glare of the poker players I'd seen playing for those enormous stakes at Binion's Horseshoe in downtown Las Vegas.

I had just made the biggest bet of the trip; it was 2 bets at $300 a piece in a single deck game at Harrah's casino located in Lake Tahoe. The count was running at a plus four with about half of the deck spent, playing heads up with the dealer, the true count was hovering at approximately plus eight. The dealer yelled out "CHECKS PLAY," alerting the floor man that escalation in betting behavior had just occurred. He nodded his head in approval and the deal continued. I looked down in horror to see that the dealer was proudly displaying an ace. She said "insurance," at which time I picked up my first hand and saw that I had been dealt a 16. I then picked up my second hand and saw that I had a 15. In disgust I foolishly waved off the insurance bet and mercifully she didn't have the blackjack, thus saving me a further $300.

I was trying to remember what I had read a few weeks before, on when to stop hitting against an ace. I was sure that I wasn't to hit against an ace in a plus eight situation when the player has 16, but wasn't sure as to the number for 15.

Thus I squirmed inside; the anxiety was gut wrenching. I knew I had placed an over bet, but the book I read advised a maximum bet. Again forgetting the rule of thumb "NO BET LARGER THAN 3% OF YOUR BANKROLL." My naiveté at having a count of 8 in a single deck game caused a memory block.

The dealer prodded my hand as if to awaken me from my slumber. Still I kept searching my memory for the hitting strategy of 15 against the dealer's ace. After what seemed to be an eternity she poked my chips again stirring me to action. I took a deep breath and motioned for a card on the 15. As if in slow motion she pulled the card off the deck and placed it down. It was a five. I figured the card under the dealers ace to be a zero valued card, that is a seven, eight or a nine due to the high count, calculating a loss with the 16 and at worst a tie on the 20. You can imagine my relief when the dealer turned up a five and hit it with two face cards.

After that session, I redeemed my markers, (a marker is a promise to pay, like a check, it is redeemable at your bank and signed by yourself at the table when requesting chips from the casino) and proceeded back to my room to check the hitting strategy charts. Once I returned, I opened up the book and there it was in black and white, "YOU CAN EXPECT TO MAKE MORE MONEY IF YOU DON'T HIT THE 15 AT A PLUS FIVE OR HIGHER AGAINST THE ACE." So I could thank my lucky stars that I didn't break.

It was my first trip to the Tahoe area and, would you believe, my first time experimenting with counting cards. I knew that I would have to employ an aggressive strategy to counter the huge fluctuations of what some people describe as "LUCK" that is intrinsic to blackjack, and there obviously offering an edge to the house.

This card counting business was a huge leap from "basic strategy." This strategy is a plan devised by highly skilled mathematicians, some of whom are card counters, on when to hit and when to stand given the value of the dealer's up card. These computations are worked out on high-speed computers using millions of plays. The basic strategy method assumes that the count is always at zero. Naturally the deck's value fluctuates with the turn of each card, because each card is assigned a value whether it is minus, a plus, or a zero. For example let's assume that we have twelve facing a dealer's two and the count is 8. This means that there will be 8 more ten-valued cards and aces turned up before the count is again at zero. Armed with this knowledge the play is to not take a card. At zero on the other hand, the play is to hit.

Never mind basic strategy, some folks enter a casino without the slightest idea of how the game works. I know because I was one of those people.

My history with the game of blackjack started out innocently enough with a whirlwind vacation that dates all the way back to January 1970. That's when I first set eyes on Las Vegas.

This city, which was to become such a vital part of my life was much smaller in those days. Back then the Tropicana Hotel was the start of the "Strip" from the South end of town with the occasional hotel cropping up until you reached Flamingo Avenue. That's where the real strip began. The downtown area was far busier back then. It had a certain allure, perhaps even a western flavor to it. That's the part of town that I enjoyed the most; free drinks and free food, what more could a dude on a tight budget ask for. My accommodation was an old 1967 Dodge panel truck, affectionately referred to as the "Blue Goose."

One morning I awoke and went to wash up at one of the local casinos, the Mint I think it was called. I decided to try my luck at a blackjack table over a cup of coffee, an awfully silly thing to do not knowing even the basics of the game. I would split threes against tens double down stiffs against stiffs, in short I did all the silly things that novices do. And so it followed that I lasted just a few short hours at the one-dollar table. It was obvious to me that all the freebies offered did after all come at a high cost. I decided to high tail it out of town before the city chewed up what was left of my meager allowance.

I headed immediately for Tucson, then through Texas and into the Florida panhandle. The weather there was much to my liking, the Floridians used to say, with the connivance of their state's tourist agency that "it was just another day in Paradise." After about three weeks my money was running low, so I headed back to the cold North and Calgary.

But alas, the lure of Las Vegas couldn't be shrugged off so easily. A few years later, my brother Kevin and a good friend of mine called Jerry K., a.k.a. "The Panama Kid," did the Florida run. Jerry got his moniker because he had a habit of sporting a floppy rimmed Panama hat. This time we went straight down through to Chicago and south again with the "Blue Goose." As it turned out we received a three day stay at the Fontainebleau Hotel in Miami Beach for gratis, and all one had to do was to listen to a land sale proposal on one of their local swamps. Jerry also had a coupon for a similar venture but this time in Las Vegas at the Thunderbird Motel. In that caper they were trying to sell some sand, which was conveniently subdivided into lots. As a point of interest had we gambled our money on those properties, most of it worthless at the time, we would be very well off today.

The Neophyte

Jerry was quite the pool player. We never had to buy a round of drinks during our entire stay in Florida. Our table was always full of beer from kindly strangers trying and failing to beat our eagle-eyed champion. Often I would intercede and ask the contestants to play for burgers, hot dogs or other nourishment.

At times during the day we would make the journey to Key Biscayne to bask on the pristine beaches offered there. The Eddie Rickenbacker Causeway linked Miami to Key Biscayne and on the causeway itself we would occasionally stop, watching the big ocean liners moored at the Port of Miami. We would wonder what it would be like to be rich enough to afford excursions like that, to be pampered like those on the "Love Boat."

After enjoying paradise in Florida for three weeks we decided to travel west instead of north not only because the weather had turned bitterly cold on the return route, but also because the "The Panama Kid," and his pool expertise, had allowed us to keep our expenses to about one hundred dollars per week apiece. This saving allowed us the luxury of not having to brave the horrible weather in our path.

So off we drove with coupon in hand to Vegas. The route there was more like a clip from a war documentary than anything else. The South had just experienced a freak blast of cold weather, which turned the rain to ice as soon as it hit the asphalt. As a consequence cars, buses and jack-knifed trucks littered the ditches. Service stations were crammed full of stranded motorists, but on we went, riding the crown of the road. It might be interesting to note here that in the south roads used to be built with a crown to dissipate the enormous water load that accumulates during a cloud burst in a state like Louisiana for instance. Sometimes we would fall off the crown and start sliding toward a bayou only to deflect off a guardrail getting catapulted back to the top.

After the long and arduous trek we could see the lights of Las Vegas in the distance just past Boulder. We pulled to the side of the road to get caught up on some much needed sleep.

When we awoke the frost seemed to be an eighth of an inch thick on the windows. We brought the cold front all the way back to Nevada.

We made our way downtown to get cleaned up and enjoy the famous 99-cent Las Vegas breakfast of steak and eggs. Boy maybe it's just me but those steaks sure were quite chewy, but for a trio of hungry guys they went down just fine and were very filling. After breakfast we went to the Thunderbird Motel to activate the coupons. It was snowing by then and I guess the promoter had warm weather and sunshine in his presentation so he was a no show. The motel did however honor the stay, but for only two nights. My thoughts were that in two days the storm that was raging just to the north of us would have abated enough for us to have an uneventful return trip.

After cleaning up we went down town to test our luck. Jerry started playing the five-cent slots. My brother, the more practical one amongst us, went to play poker; as for me I just sat around having the occasional cocktail. Due to boredom more than anything else I thought that I would give that old blackjack game one more try. True to form I was a loser again. The game was unbeatable, or so I thought then. I was another $100 bucks in the hole and dick all to show for it. At this point we scoured the town for pool halls to utilize Panama's skills but to no avail. All the bars that we encountered had slot machines, not only on their perimeter, but also on the bars themselves. Go figure, this was not a pool playing town in the early seventies.

We managed to put in our two days and made our way out of Vegas. But due to the bad weather persisting in and around Montana and Idaho we decided to go home via Vancouver to visit some friends. This route was destined to take us through Reno.

Highway 93 North travels through a few interesting towns, one of which is Tonopah. Stopping for a beer at a local watering hole we started eying up a BJ table that had one spot open. Slowly sipping our beer we concocted a plan to try to recoup some of our previous losses. We pooled $100 and put into motion a plot that would have one of us go to the table, place the cash on a square saying "money play." We did this because we saw someone do exactly that in Las Vegas and we thought it sounded cool. My brother was nominated to do the honors only because he was the senior member of our party, and perhaps the wisest.

It was a dollar table and the five people playing there were betting one or two dollars a hand. The table limit was $200 so it was quite a thing when Kevin walked over to the table, and laid the money down reciting the little jingle "money play." The dealer looked at the floor man. He nodded to her giving the okay to go ahead with the deal.

The Neophyte

When I think about it we must have looked terribly green for the guy to nod the play, I wish I could have that same look now. The hand was dealt, and like a father who is trying to dissuade his son from doing something bad by slapping his hand, the dealer turned up a two card twenty-one. This is truly a devils game I thought, how could anyone enjoy this kind of cash enema? Why do people play this game? It seemed to be totally one sided.

We slithered out of the casino bar (because it was embarrassing to be seen as losers) and we continued our journey.

About 20 or 30 miles from Reno we saw a sign for the Mustang Ranch. Wow the world famous Mustang Ranch brothel that we used to read about in magazines such as Playboy and joke about among ourselves. Visiting Reno was of course the last thing on our minds. In fact the state of Nevada was looking less and less inviting with every stop. Why not pay the Mustang Ranch a visit; at least we could say that we were there.

After making a dangerous u-turn across a divided hi-way, we turned into what looked like a bunch of trailers parked abutting on one another making what appeared to be an enormous complex. After abandoning our truck in the parking lot we wandered inside. There to greet us were twenty or thirty women standing in a semi circle in front of us. Now, I had never been with a prostitute before so all this was not only very new, but also very embarrassing. The madam welcomed us to the ranch, told us where the bar was and instructed us to make ourselves right at home. Well home was never like this especially after the madam told the girls to introduce themselves; all the seasons were represented, with the months of the year, and a few days of the week thrown in for good measure. "Hi, I'm June. Hi, I'm April. Hi, I'm Tuesday. Hi, I'm Autumn," and so on. By this time I was glowing red and just wanted to get the hell out of there. So I reached out grabbing the nearest girl who led me to her room.

Once inside I breathed a sigh of relief, as I was out of the awkward psychological spotlight. My lady of choice proceeded to list off the menu. I chose "the half and half." The price was $75, because I enjoy negotiating I offered $50. To my great surprise she accepted. So now there was no turning back. I handed over the money and she put it into her dresser. She then pulled out a bucket from her closet and asked me to strip, I promptly obeyed her request. She then applied something that smelled like disinfectant and washed me thoroughly. Then she proceeded to clean herself right in front of me. Cleanliness, now that was something that I could appreciate.

With the business transaction complete, I proceeded to the lobby to meet my buddies. They were not there yet so I picked up a magazine and started to read. New clients were showing up every few minutes, subjected to the same welcome as we were. That was too much for me, so I decided to wait for them in the trusty old truck.

What seemed to be about a half an hour later they finally showed up, first Panama, then my brother. I started the truck and headed straight to Reno. Along the way we shared stories of our recent carnal adventure. Would you believe that Jerry's lady claimed to have fallen head over heels in love with him and was "heart-broken" to see him leave (as long as he still had some money that is). My brother on the other hand had quite a little party with his selection. He hired the services of not one, but three ladies at the same time. So this was the other legalized fringe business in the state of Nevada.

The Mustang Ranch has since been closed, and the owner, Joe Conforte, who I must say ran a very clean business, is on the lam living in either Brazil, or in Italy avoiding prosecution, or perhaps better put, persecution by the IRS.

We arrived in Reno quite late and we were also tired. We decided to crash in the parking lot of a downtown hotel appropriately named the Sundowner.

Morning greeted us with hunger pangs and a bad taste in our mouths. We entered the Sundowner to freshen up and get a bite to eat. I just can't get used to those steak and eggs, the meat is mostly grizzle. Alas, our 21 luck was as distasteful as the meal. So we voted to depart as dismal victims of this captivating game.

Leaving Reno I felt that I had been totally exorcised of the black-jack sickness forever. I felt that the game was totally stacked in the casino's favor. To quote the "extremely" reverend Martin Luther King, "I am free, free, thank God I am free at last." I felt that I had rid myself of the urge of trying to make money from anything other than "honest work." Fat "chance" of that.

Chapter two: Turning the Corner

" You want to go to Vegas! Are you nuts?" I can't stand that town. That place has cost me hundreds of dollars. The place was built for suckers." My new girlfriend, Linda, had never been to Vegas and wanted to take in some shows. "Look Al", she said, "You don't have to gamble just because you're in Vegas, we can check out the sights, go to a few shows and just kick back for a couple of days."

Actually that idea was totally logical. Hey, what was I made of anyway? I mean, couldn't I go somewhere and refrain from doing some activity that I found abhorrent anyway? This was after all 1976, three years since the last encounter with that dreaded town. I wasn't about to tell anyone that I was as scared as hell to ever go into another casino. Hell, maybe scared was too soft a word. Every time I even thought of going into one I felt like crapping my drawers. I just didn't get off on the atmosphere, the smoke, the endless din of the machines surrendering their treasures, the drunks and the degenerates, gambling their last dollar. The stale smell of a years worth of whiskey engrained into the carpets especially in the downtown casinos. That wasn't even taking into consideration the loathing that I felt surrendering my hard earned pay at the tables, all in the name of entertainment. Little did I know how rapidly things were about to change?

Upon our arrival we made reservations to see the late show that evening at the Tropicana. The Folies Bergere, a typical grand revue, with all the gusto of Las Vegas, promised a buffet of bare tits and pleasant curves from some of the best looking babes from all over the country. Hmm, perhaps my earlier protests were a bit hasty.

Next we made the obligatory trip to Hoover Dam, advertised as the eighth wonder of the world. This awe-inspiring structure was built for forty million dollars. As they say on the tour, the environmental impact study alone would be twice that figure in the present day. The project was started in 1931 and completed four years later in 1935 costing the lives of 112 workers. Southern Nevada receives 25 percent of its power from that dam, and Las Vegas gets the lion's share of that. Needless to say Las Vegas would be a shadow of what it is today if not for that dam.

Once in the hotel, making our way to the show room, we couldn't help notice the beautiful stained glass domed ceiling above the main gaming area. This gave a cathedral-like ambiance to the place. There a donation made wouldn't disturb the soul at all, but would instead soothe it, or lull it into the realization that the wager lost, in some mysterious way, was in fact going to a beneficial cause. And truely the cause was a beneficial one, taken from the management's point of view of course.

We finally reached the show line that deliberately meandered through the casino, past the gaming tables and the slot machines. The fact that the management planned this route would become apparent in due course. Neither Linda nor I were the classic "wait in line, grin and bear it" types; we had to be either doing something or going somewhere. She asked if she could try her luck at one of the many machines that was vacant along our extended route, while I kept our place in line. "Go for it" I said.

In the distance I could see a line forming with about five or six people in it, and the sign said "Invited Guests Only." It was that short line, "short circuiting" the multitude, that was receiving our envied glances. Now that was for me, but how does one become an invited guest?

I decided to engage the couple behind me in conversation and steered our discussion to the subject of that short line way up in front of us. It turned out that they were from the Las Vegas area and happily gave me the information that I asked for. To be in that special line, you had to gamble for a large and predetermined minimum amount of money within a specific time. Of course there was cooperation with other casinos and they would take referrals from them to accommodate a "valued guest." I guess we were doomed to languish with the masses in these serpentine lines for there was no way you could ever get me close to another table.

Linda came back to our plebian procession after about fifteen or twenty minutes, poorer fifteen or twenty dollars. Now we knew why these machines formed a shore or a haven for this river of sheeple. Some get sheared before they go in, some get sheared after, but it's truly unbelievable how many of us get trimmed at this interim "fleecing zone," setting us up for grand shearing to come.

Finally, we are the next to be seated and the maitre de asks where would be our preference. I tell him, quite naively, that a couple of seats with a view of the stage area would be appreciated. He nervously stands around for about thirty seconds while I chat with Linda. Clearing his throat, he just stood there rocking on his feet. At last, exasperated, he said, "Come with me please." We followed him to the second tier close to one side of the show room, the worst possible seats that you can imagine. A table that looks like a two by twelve with legs with a sheet draped over it and four people sitting on either side. To compound matters we were stationed at the end and had to jostle constantly to get a view of the stage.

The waiter took our order of the customary two drinks that accompanied the 25-dollar entry fee. Then on with the show, and I must say that it was very enjoyable. Pretty ladies parading around with enormous head plumes propped up from their shoulders weighing possibly 25 pounds or more. The dancers were magnificent and so were the singers. The topless girls however were a distraction, albeit a welcome one.

During a backdrop change a young magician, just starting out, made his appearance. His name was Lance Burton. His routine of lit cigarettes emanating from who knows where was awe-inspiring. I suppose the fluidity of his movements is what really impressed me the most. He was young, confident and totally composed. He had playing cards flying all over the stage mixed with pigeons drawn from virtually mid air. I had the opportunity to see him again a few years ago and his act had changed little, but he was every bit the showman and a credit to his craft.

The Folies then resumed, and after a terrific performance came to a crescendo. The entire cast was singing and parading on stage in front of the live band located in the pit. Then it was all over. We stood up and gave them a much-deserved applause and started to file out.

After the show we realized, we should have self-parked our car eliminating the annoying wait for the parking valet to fetch our vehicle. We went back to the hotel and called it a night.

About six am I found I couldn't sleep, so I quietly showered up and went down to the gift shop for the morning paper. Browsing around I came across some "How to" books on playing blackjack, craps and roulette. Leafing through a volume on blackjack, I noticed that the author advises no hitting against a dealers stiff card, if the value of your cards were fourteen or more. A stiff, by the way, is when the dealer displays a card that requires at least a one card hit to make his hand, i.e. a two, three, four, five and a six. At some casinos a soft seventeen is not a hit but a six is still considered to be a "stiff" because there are only four aces per deck that can make that hand into a contending one, that is to say one that doesn't have to be hit. Armed with this new revelation I decided to forego the morning read and apply this sliver of newfound knowledge at the gaming table.

Sitting down at a one-dollar table I promptly cashed in a fifty-dollar bill and received the corresponding amount in casino chips. After playing for about 45 minutes I realized that I was only one dollar shy of the amount I had initially started with, and this was due to the tip that was given to the cocktail lady.

To say that I was impressed would have been an understatement. I returned post haste to the gift shop, buying the book on blackjack. Studying it upstairs in our room I noticed that I could have further enhanced my game by hitting against a dealer's two and three if the cards that were displayed on my side of the table were no greater than twelve.

By now Linda was awake and puttering around. I asked her if she cared to go for some breakfast, she eagerly agreed but wanted some time to put on her face. In that case I told her to come down when she was ready and that I would be playing blackjack at one of the one-dollar tables. "Thought you couldn't stand the game," she said. I told her that I had been down stairs for a bit playing while she slept and that it was the first time that I had broken even. "I hope you don't blame me when you lose all your money." She felt a pang of guilt for coxing me down to the gambling "Mecca" of the world and didn't want to be held responsible for my fall. I assured her that she should in no way harbor any guilt, as I was only passing time at a low limit table.

By this time I knew that a player could get any kind of free drink for a mere tip. Knowing this I stepped up to the plate and offered to buy her favorite morning drink, a Spanish coffee when she finally joined me at the table.

We were intent on finishing our drinks before we trotted off to breakfast so I kept playing. In the ten minutes while she was standing behind me I couldn't lose a hand. To my amazement, I ended the session being twenty-five dollars up. For the first time ever I was on the positive side of the ledger. That made me hunger for more than food.

After breakfast we went downtown to the Horseshoe to see their world famous million-dollar display and posed for a picture. This was almost a compulsory thing to do during any visit to the downtown. The photos were free; the trade off was that while you waited, usually an hour, you would probably gamble. And gamble we did.

Linda said that she would strike out on her own to the slot machines, entertaining herself there rather than watch me play blackjack.

Here I was in one of the most famous gambling halls in the world and also the one that proved to be my nemesis years before, naturally I wanted to reap my revenge. I was about to elevate my minimum bet from one dollar to two dollars, not because I wanted to but because the one-dollar tables were all full. I proceeded to put a $50 bill on the table and received the chips. The first hand out I got a blackjack and the dealer was showing an ace. The fellow next to me, trying to be helpful, advised me to take even money. (A tie with the dealer is not a loss as a result you get paid two to one on the insurance, which amounts to even money). I said then as I often say now, "I want everything that's coming to me." This usually invokes a smirk from the dealer or player and even some laughter if the dealer turns up a blackjack. As it turned out I got paid one and a half times my bet. The player with the helpful advice sheepishly admitted that in that case it was the right thing to do. If you don't count cards it is unadvisable to take the insurance bet or even money, which amounts to the same thing, if you also have a two card 21.

Playing for another half an hour and attaining a modest profit I cashed out and fetched Linda. She was still cranking on some slot machine and in the hole about ten dollars. I talked her into cutting her loses and going next door to the Mint hotel where they had a live lounge act featuring none other than a counterfeit Elvis. We picked up the pictures that we had posed for and went next door.

Now Elvis was still alive in 1976 so impersonations of "The King" were not as rampant as they are now. I read somewhere that there were a total of 67 Elvis impersonators in the entire world at the time of his death on August 16, 1977. Now, of course, places like Las

Vegas host Elvis impersonator conventions and when they are in town the white capes and chromed glasses can be found everywhere as thousands of them descend on the city.

We bought a drink and settled down to watch some of the performance. You couldn't believe the thunderous welcome that the "caped one" received. He made his entrance in his white suit with chrome studs saying, "Thank you, thank you very much ladies and gentlemen."

He sang some "oldie goldies" like Heartbreak Hotel, Hound Dog, All Shook Up and Love Me Tender. I thought my eyes were deceiving me when three or four women, obviously enamored, approached the stage and started swooning, perhaps imaging themselves to be the object of his song. Now don't get me wrong, I thought he did a terrific job shaking and grinding his hips, curling his lips and emulating "The King's" antics, but when he wiped his fore head with one of his many scarves, and threw it to one of these mesmerized ladies, I nearly choked on my drink. We promptly left the lounge for the more sane area of the casino.

My gal went to try her luck at one of the slot machines and I to the, by now, more familiar surroundings of the blackjack tables. Sitting down at one of the two-dollar tables I started to play. Flat betting the minimum for several decks caused me to lose ten dollars after which I was joined by, what I perceived to be then, a high roller. He motioned to the pit boss. When she arrived he asked her for a $500 marker. She placed a chip on the table called a lamer with the number 500 on it for the benefit of the overhead camera, and the dealer proceeded to give him $500 in chips. The pit attendant and the player were engaged in a conversation while he was betting $25 per hand. His bets seemed to me to be fairly steep earning from me my naive respect, although he lost every bet he placed in the first deck. After the dealer had reshuffled I made a twenty after hitting my hand with several small cards against the dealers ten. He had to stay put on a seventeen and the dealer flipped over his card exposing a three. This he hit with a three and a four giving him a twenty, tying me, but beating him.

He stopped his casual chat with the pit lady and looked at me and said "I don't think he can do that forever," placing a $200 bet. I too raised my bet to five dollars, maybe as an endorsement for his bravado. Wow! He got a blackjack and I a nineteen with the dealer breaking his hand. After that I structured my betting around his. When he bet $25 I would bet two, when he bet $50 I would bet four and so on increasing my bet in two dollar increments, once even "stepping out," making a $20 bet, and winning it with a blackjack. What a terrific high that was. After about 25 minutes of dominating the play we suffered a string of loses ending our temporary partnership. He called back his marker and walked away with about a thousand dollars in chips. I too cashed in, registering a healthy $200 in profits and walked away singing to myself the famous Jackie Gleason phrase of "how sweet it is." Indeed money won is twice as sweet as money earned.

But how did this "high roller" know when to bet big and when to bet small? The answer would take a few years longer but would manifest itself very clearly. He was a card counter, one of many that I was to meet. A diabolical breed of people that would send a chill up a casino's cash flow.

Linda won about thirty dollars. Being quite content with our selves we broke off the play and went back to our hotel.

It was getting close to supper when we made our way to Circus Circus to enjoy a few drinks and in general just to hang out. I sat at a blackjack table to get our drinks and play a couple of hands. After a few rounds of play there was an announcement that some sort of juggling event was to take place under the main tent. My girlfriend went to see the show while I played. After about ten minutes the ring announcer said, "Ladies and gentlemen, if I can direct your attention to the center ring, you are about to witness a death defying aerial performance by the Blow sisters." At hearing this, the dealer immediately said, "Hey, now there is a performance that I wouldn't mind seeing myself."

Being a ho-hum session, the high light being the dealer's much appreciated little joke, I decided to leave, find Linda and grab a bite to eat at one of their coffee shops.

After supper we went to our room for some R and R, showered up and were ready for the next gala show at the Stardust Hotel and casino, called the Lido de Paris. This show had been acclaimed as more spectacular than the original from France.

As advertised the show was very satisfying and done in a totally professional manner with gorgeous gals taking the center stage. Did you know that scientists recently discovered that viewing pretty girls in skimpy attire, for most males, had a reaction similar to drugs, putting them into a euphoric state; now that's the drug for me, no hangovers and no illegalities. Driving under the influence would be highly recommended due to the mellow state one is left with, thus reducing road rage.

After the show, we went for a drink at one of the more than convenient twenty-one tables located in the main pit. I sat down at a single deck, two-dollar table that was dealing a face up game, as usual I cashed in my patented $50 bill. Receiving our drinks I played about five minutes until an older gentleman sat down at the table getting a $1000 marker. He was, as I found out later, on a junket (junkets are usually arranged by agents commissioned by various casinos to bring in guests to play at the hotel, getting reimbursed on a per head basis), his minimum bet was one hundred dollars, because he asked for black chips only. His large play affected me more than my small play affected him. He had fifteen once against a dealer's ten, playing two hands and he didn't hit. I pointed at my poultry sixteen and asked, "Would you hit that?" His reply was, "Not at this time." He was correct, as the dealer was stiffed, the next card breaking him. I won my five bucks, he his $400. I then proceeded to cash out because I didn't want to make some silly mistake that might cost him considerable damage. In retrospect this was a sentiment that could only be attributed to the most novice of players because the table was yielding it's treasures to the both of us anyway. What I did with my hand really doesn't alter the outcome of the game in the long run.

We watched for a while as he succeeded in drawing a large crowd behind himself due to several large stacks of hundreds that were now accumulating. He was by this time betting as high as $500 per hand and seemed to be really enjoying himself.

In a Capitalistic society that they claim we have in North America, money is the lifeblood of the system. Like a gladiator in an arena this champion was inflicting some heavy blows on his opponent. Like the blood sports of old, the underdog received the sympathy of the crowd. You didn't have to be an expert to realize that the casino was deeply worried at this monetary blood letting. The pit crew was on the phone to who knows who and literally biting their nails. These monetary wounds drained the table so badly that a transfusion was taking place in front of our eyes. The pit had just received a fill of black chips to replace that which had been lost. So on it went until this "warrior" lost three or four hands and cashed out.

Turning the Corner

The following morning I repeated the same routine; morning coffee at the blackjack table, waking up Linda after and then deciding where to eat breakfast. This time we opted for the Silver Slipper Casino. Straight to the gaming table we went and put our order in for her Spanish coffee. I played at a table with four people and got extremely lucky amassing $100 in just a few minutes. The lady next to me advised me to "sandbag" a couple of those bigger chips (sandbagging means to hide or take something off the table when no one is looking, so as not to draw attention to yourself). I kind of looked at her in a quizzical way wondering, why? I mean I was proud of my winnings and wanted to display them to the world or to whoever else was interested. Would a hunter want his trophy mounted in his garage, or more rather in his den. The answer was obvious, so I disregarded her request and told her that in any event we would be leaving for breakfast in a short while. She whispered to me that the pit crew was watching the game intensely and that I might be kicked out for betting too aggressively. I was in utter disbelief. Just yesterday, I watched a guy take thousands off the table and today barely $100 ahead I should pocket some chips to make it seem that I am not ahead that much. I thought to myself, "What long ears you have." She must have sensed that I thought of her as a paranoid ass because she added that, "They think that you are counting cards." Imagine that, someone even thinking that I could be capable of counting cards has to be totally bizarre. I would be hard pressed to provide the cards that I was dealt on the previous hand let alone the flow of cards throughout the entire deck. Quite frankly my memory was atrocious. I was under the impression that one had to have a photographic memory or someone who had recall abilities that far surpassed mine. These were the delusions of the game that haunted me in those early days.

Leaving the Silver Slipper and walking out the front we noticed a 1957 Thunderbird on display. It was absolutely beautiful and was to be won playing at those slot machines advertising the car. Often casinos use these older classics because sometimes the jackpots won't be hit for years on end. This relieves them of the chore of replacing the cars to be won on a yearly basis. At closer inspection however, we gasped in horror viewing a key scratch from the headlight to the taillight, all along the driver's side. What low life could be capable of such a thing? This was the type of crime that merits a beating with a shoe to whoever did it. Was it perhaps that they lost money and were in some way exacting revenge, or was it because they could never own such a magnificent piece and marred it's beauty out of envy. In either case this incident, in no small way, determined my choice of cars for a period some time in the future.

We drove downtown to just look around and to get a better feel of the inner core, We noticed a lot of pawn shops there with jewelry for sale at bargain prices, no doubt sold by some poor saps who gambled away all their money and couldn't make it home otherwise. Going a couple of blocks passed Fremont, proceeding North on Las Vegas Blvd. is highly unadvisable on foot. Lower forms of life can be readily detected. Drug use is rampant in this area and so is prostitution although both are illegal in Clarke County.

Later, returning to our room, we readied ourselves for supper and one last show. We agreed on the Riviera Hotel, so across the street we went.

At the restaurant Linda ordered a salad, and I the New York steak, hoping that it was not the same cut as the breakfast one. "Damn! Where do they get that meat? It's full of sinew; it's chewy and quite tasteless. Like there is no amount of A-1 or HP sauce that could give that chunk of meat any taste and if it does it will taste like the sauce." Hey I get it; maybe that's the main idea. Perhaps no one has ever complained about the taste. Due to this everyone cranks out the same product, dousing it with the above sauces removes the bland taste of the steak. I like millions before me somehow managed to get it down and leave.

By then it was show time, and we were escorted to cramped quarters in the Versailles room. The show featured Liza Minnelli with a mixture of comedy, magic and other first-rate entertainment used as fill ins during back drop changes. Today the Riviera features the show "Splash." Certainly one of the best variety shows on the strip.

After the performance we went straight home so as to be well rested for our last hectic day in that great city. I had come to enjoy the lights, the glitter and the dazzle of the casino environment. What a difference a couple of days, and a little winning can make.

The next morning as was my habit, I went down for a coffee at the 21 table. This time I was more aware of the people standing behind the dealer. Of course they had no concerns with me whatsoever for two reasons. First, I was at a two-dollar table varying my bet maybe five times. The second, and most important reason, was that I was losing. That's right, just when I thought that I was getting the hang of this game I realized that my coffee had cost me about ten dollars.

This was to be our last day in town so we had planned to get a lot of things in at the last minute. We had a bite to eat and got packed for a one o'clock check out. We drove back downtown to "Glitter Gulch." This was a figure of speech attributed to the locals, an expression that I personally never heard any of them use.

We wandered through an array of hotels; one of my favorites was the Four Queens. It seemed to be a popular hangout packed to the brim with noisy patrons. The Golden Nugget, just West of the Queens, seemed to have a western flair. On display was the largest nugget ever found in the California gold rush days. Along the western route there are some minor casinos, and then you reach the Union Plaza. It was named after a whistle stop of the Union Pacific Rail system in the vicinity.

Our time in Vegas passed quickly. Before I knew it we were on the plane back with our mandatory bottle of Canadian Club whiskey.

I couldn't stop thinking about the immense strides that I had taken in learning about the game of blackjack. After all, I was up over $300. For the first time ever I came away a winner. The lady that I had met back at the Silver Slipper had mentioned something about card counting. But I thought it must be very difficult to master, or everyone would be using the method. Well as things started to unfold, I couldn't have been more mistaken.

Chapter Three: Getting Serious

By 1980 I was doing very well in the real estate business. Money was easy to come by, and just as easily lost. You might say I had progressed into the big league of gambling with multi thousands hinging on one deal, or perhaps better put hinging on the whims of a corporation, or an extremely well healed individual.

Like any other business that I was involved in, I was most comfortable with a hands on approach, in other words I not only sold but also bought real estate. Many people that I associated with in the business were also like-minded. Because of our high volume in sales we had a lot of mortgage companies, banks and other interesting people paying us visits. These parties informed us of their latest inducements, rates and terms. Occasionally they would even spring for lunch.

As it happened one day Dennis B. showed up at the office, and chatted up some salesmen that were present regarding a junket he was hosting that was to leave for Las Vegas. The added bonus was two tickets for the much-advertised bout between Roberto Duran and Sugar Ray Leonard. He had left his card with one of the guys, so I promptly gave him a call. He told me that the junket was to the Dunes Hotel leaving in two weeks time. The main requirement was an established line of credit at the hotel for $10,000. Also required was a play per day, of the four-day stay, of three to four hours at a $25 minimum bet. If I agreed to these terms the flight, room, food and beverages plus hotel shows were to be covered by the casino for a party of two.

By this time I was seeing a new girl by the name of Carla. We had been dating for about two months, and I had really taken a shine to her. I phoned her up to see if she would like to escort me on a trip to Vegas for an extended weekend. I told her that she would have to take the Friday off, as our flight would depart on Thursday evening. She said that she would love to go but would have to see if she could book off for that one day.

Getting Serious

Calgary in those days was a vibrant city with a booming economy and a rosy outlook for the future. People worked a lot of overtime to keep the town running on a smooth and even keel. It wasn't at all certain that she could get the extra day off. Luck indeed seemed to smile on us as she was granted the leave.

Upon learning the good news I called Dennis, and told him that we would be interested in going but that I felt somewhat out of my league. He assured me that most of the people that were going were generally in the same boat as me. If I wanted to go on trips that were fully paid for, or in casino lingo, "fully comped," that I might as well, sooner rather than later, get used to the idea. He also added that if I did not meet the casino's requirements, the most serious consequence would be that I would never be invited back as their valued guest again.

This seemed to be a win win situation, therefore I decided to give Dennis the go ahead. He took the information on my bank, account number, branch and so forth, to insure that I wasn't a street person I suppose, and that was it. A few days later he delivered the airline tickets and answered all my questions. He assured me that I didn't need any immediate cash; I could use my markers by cashing in their corresponding value in chips at the casino cage. He shook my hand, wished me good luck and left.

So away we went on the big "yellow banana." Back in the early eighties, Hughes Air had a direct flight from Calgary to Las Vegas at least once a day. Howard Hughes, who was a brilliant businessman, wanted to parlay his recent hotel acquisitions by offering direct flights from Canadian centers to the gaming "capital" of the world. All his aircraft were painted an unmistakable and unforgettable bright yellow.

On arrival we went to the VIP hotel check-in and found that our room wouldn't be ready for another hour. The staff was very courteous and understanding, suppling us with an unlimited comp voucher for their lounge on the top level of the hotel.

At the lounge we sat down and ordered the real fancy drinks. You know the type, the ones that have the little umbrellas in them. After several of these we ordered appetizers, Oysters Rockafeller and oysters on the half shell. When we were done, the waiter presented us with the bill, I then handed him the comp and signed it; the bill came to $50. I reached into my pocket and pulled out the only American currency that I had, two dollars. I silently cursed myself for not going to the bank, withdrawing at least $100 to cover my butt in case of an emergency before boarding the flight. I apologized and told him the problem, assuring him that the tips would be better in the future. The person was Filipino and perhaps didn't understand my English. He asked in a rather rude tone whether there was something wrong with the service. Thinking that he was trying to intimidate us, because we were still dressed in our traveling attire, like lightning I grabbed the two dollars from his hand and went about two inches from his face telling him, in no uncertain terms, that the service wasn't bad but ended up grating on our nerves. We returned many times after that incident during our trip to sit at the bar drinking and joking with the bartenders. And just to drive the point home, while he was there, pouting, we made sure that whoever was serving us were well rewarded.

We were greatly impressed by the enormity of our room. It was well appointed. The management even went to the trouble of placing a gift hamper, which included two bottles of wine, one red and the other white. Well this was a far cry from the accommodations that I had been used to. We proceeded to open a bottle of red to get into the swing of things.

Later I went down stairs to address my cash problem. I went straight to the blackjack pit and put down the card that was supplied to us by the hotel check-in on a 25-dollar table. The dealer yelled out "marker," and went ahead and dealt to everyone but me. The floor man came over and asked me how much I wanted. I told him $1000. He returned back to his desk and called the casino cage. In no time he returned to the table and placed a $1000 lamer on it. The dealer then gave me eight black and eight green chips.

Not only was this the first time sitting at a $25 table, it was also the first time playing at a shoe with six decks. A shoe is a receptacle used to carry more than two decks, with a cut card placed about one and a half decks from the back in a six-deck shoe. Multi decks were incorporated into the game to dissuade card counting.

I placed a green $25 chip in the square and the dealer began dealing. I was stiffed with a nine and a seven. I then hit and broke. I did this two more times and mercifully the cut card came out, signaling a reshuffle. Once shuffled the six-decks were cut by a person at first base, then the decks were placed back into the shoe, and the deal was resumed. My first bet netted me a blackjack and I thought to myself, "boy it would have been nice to have made a larger bet." So foolishly

Getting Serious

I raised my bet and got stiffed once more. The chap at first base was also stiffed and called out "surrender." He had also made a 50 bet so the dealer took half of it leaving him with twenty-five dollars. I too followed his initiative, surrendering my sixteen. On all surrenders you lose half your bet.

Now nowhere in the pamphlet that I purchased years ago at the Westward Ho had it so much as mentioned late surrender or early surrender for that matter. I was covering new ground you might say, unfortunately for me at the highest stakes that I had ever played with in my entire life. I continued playing till the end of the shoe and at a staggering loss of about of about $200. I had done what I originally had set out to do, that is get some currency so as we could circulate around town freely. I took the $800 worth of chips and returned to my room to contemplate my strategy in light of the new surrender rule. I have since learned that when it comes to late surrender, unless you are a card counter, don't use it. Obviously if a person surrendered all his stiffs the casino would grind him down in no time flat, that's how I became the recipient of a $200 loss.

As a result of this "rethink" session, the new strategy was to not surrender the twelve, thirteen or fourteen, but only the fifteen and sixteen. The problem with this procedure was that for instance, hitting a sixteen against a seven, assuming of course that you didn't break, would usually render the dealer's seven harmless, relatively speaking. But at the other end of the spectrum, if you don't hit your sixteen against the seven you might as well surrender, because it is the most dangerous card that a dealer can have if you are stiffed. Let me explain this a little further. There are sixteen ten-valued cards and four aces in each deck that make the seven immediately dangerous. There are also four deuces, four threes and four fours that making a total of 32 cards out of 52 to insure that the dealer has as good hand. That is about a 60% chance that your stiff is a hypothetical loser against the seven. Now 50/50 is a gamble, so giving away 10% is unadvisable.

Taking stalk of a new situation always seemed to have a calming effect on me and filled me with more confidence. With cash in my pocket and a pretty red head with her arms locked in mine, made the coming battle seemed insignificant.

We took a stroll across the street to Caesar's Palace, which was the venue for the fight. The entire structure seemed to ooze of wealth. The fountain, situated in front of the building, seemed to be more than 50 yards in length. The atmosphere inside the building was electrifying. There in the main pit we saw many $100 tables and even one displaying a $500 minimum sign. On the way to the "sports book" we passed the Spanish Steps, a classy restaurant next to the Ah'So Japanese Steak House. Across from there you could catch sight of the heaving breasts on the carved talisman, part and parcel of the ornate prow on Cleopatra's Barge. It was fashioned in the form of a naked lady, undulating erotically, up and down, as the big vessel swayed. I wondered if I could ever afford to eat in a fancy place like that. All the while there were beautiful waitresses dressed in skimpy attire, adorned with long hair pieces, Roman style of course, prancing around the tables delivering drinks.

The short walk had whet our appetites so we decided to go back to our hotel and try out the Sultans Tent, a fancy restaurant which lended itself readily to the Arabian theme of the hotel, featuring twelve violinists that went from table to table serenading the patrons. We walked up to the host and introduced ourselves. He eyed me up and down and asked, "Do you have a suit jacket?" Of course the reply was no, as we had assumed this to be a very casual trip. He said that we couldn't gain entry unless I wore a jacket. "Damn," I thought to myself, "another banana peel that I just slipped on." Then he said not to worry, he had some spares in the cloakroom just for this kind of emergency. He brought one out that looked like a dressy overcoat, the shoulder pads going half down my arms and the sleeves nearly touching my knees. Carla burst out laughing. I said that there was no way I could possibly eat with this "one size fits all" tux. By this time the maitre de was also smiling, saying that all I would have to do is to walk to the table, at which time I could remove it.

Well you can imagine the looks that I got; coming across like a hobo wrapped in a size 52 tux around my size 40 frame. I later found out that I wasn't the only one to be paraded to a table in this fashion. A chap came up to me after supper and said that the jacket looked better on me than it did him. The staff must have a contest to see who can be dressed to look the most ridiculous.

Upon arriving at our table off came the "loaner" with a huge sigh of relief. We at once were given the wine list and offered a few suggestions. As this was a comp I just looked at the price, choosing the most expensive one on the menu. It was the Chateau Neuf De Pape at $75 a bottle. The waiter returned with our wine in short order and poured me a sampling. That was the best tasting red that I have ever had. The waiter then took our order. We both opted for the lobster tails and then he left.

We were sipping our wine, noticing the musicians nearing our table. Then, all of a sudden, they were there. They were just about to start when I asked, "Could you play the Hungarian Rhapsody for us." Now I didn't happen to choose that piece, originally composed by Liszt, because I am Hungarian, I chose it because it was a lively tune, sure to pick up the pace. It was a piece that starts out slowly, gradually increases in tempo, reaching a level so that even the most tin eared listener couldn't resist tapping their feet. I must say that they did a first class rendition of it, earning kudos from us, and a round of applause from several of the other patrons. I gave them a ten-dollar tip and they departed to the next table.

The food came and we rapidly devoured it. When the waiter asked if we cared for desert, I instead asked for the wine menu again because I noticed a very expensive champagne in it. After all, now is the time to try those cost prohibitive items when the price is right. The Champagne in question was the Dom Perignon at a whopping $90 a bottle. We drank it down rapidly and asked for the bill. Wow, it came to $250, thank God it was a freebie. I signed the bill, left a $30 gratuity and departed. Looking back at the seat you could see the borrowed jacket still perched on the back of the chair, hanging there like a curtain.

We felt rather tired after the hectic day and decided to call it a night, forgoing the show for another evening.

In the morning I got up early and phoned room service ordering up a breakfast fit for a king and a queen. This was going to be a great surprise for Carla as she never had breakfast in bed before, and for that matter neither had I.

About ten or fifteen minutes later there was a gentle knock on the door. I motioned to the waiter to set the table quietly, so as not to disturb the lady. I went over to Carla's bedside gently rousing her. She looked at the table noticing the array of goodies awaiting her pleasure, complete with flowers and a newspaper, compliments of the Dunes Hotel. This was a class act and available to all invited guests willing to risk their money at casino play. The problem was that I liked the perks but was hesitant to take risks to be "worthy" of the special treatment.

After breakfast, I went down to try my luck at the tables while Carla was getting ready. Once more I sat down at a $25 table and asked for a $1000 marker. The floor man promptly returned instructing the dealer to give me the necessary chips.

Things didn't gel the way they were supposed to; I was down $300 in short order and found myself craving a break.

Carla showed up about an hour later. I cashed out and went to the bar to treat her to a Spanish coffee and to relax a bit. We had a few laughs with the bartender for about an hour and then left to check out the MGM Grand, which was directly across from our hotel. It seemed to be quite fancy, but certainly not up to the caliber of Caesar's Palace, in fact I wouldn't have traded it for the Dunes, although the Dunes was much older. We walked by the 21 pit and even though I was tempted to play, I resisted the urge because of my obligation to play a set number of hours a day at where we were staying.

Every casino has a central theme, and at the MGM it was the famous movie stars of yore with the roaring lion as its symbol. You could even have your picture taken posing with this beast for a mere ten bucks.

In the back of the casino they had a huge jai alai court. Jai alai, I suppose, is the Spanish version of racket ball, except for a few major changes. The court, or "cancha," was enormous for one. Instead of rackets the players had these huge curved and hollowed banana shaped receptacles that the player wears like a glove. They were made of a reed like material, tightly woven to make it extremely tough. An orb, the size of a billiard ball, is then hurled against a concrete wall. The opponent must grab the ball in this "glove" and throw it back without letting it go past him. Because of the curvature of the receptacles the player, at times, hurl the ball back at speeds exceeding 100 MPH. This of course not only makes it a game of extreme reflex, but also very dangerous.

Walking out of the MGM we strolled next door to the Aladdin Hotel. Their theme was the Ali Baba and the forty thieves thing. Turbans and shoes that made a u-turn at the toes were the dress of the employees. My dad used to tell me that the bend was put into the shoes of the Arabian Knights to facilitate the wearer when he went to the bathroom. When you're a child you are gullible and I thought then that that would indeed be the perfect grip when confronted with the ordeal of the "Greek Toilet." I would spend a lot of time at this hotel in the future, but back then my only impression of it was as a big place, with a total lack of personality.

By now it was 6:00 pm. The match between Duran and Leonard was slated to start at 8:00 pm. We rushed back to get our tickets and prepare to go. There was a line up that took a half an hour to subside. We finally received our vouchers and to my surprise they were $200 a piece. "Boy," I thought "they must be pretty good seats for that price." With all the rushing around and waiting, we didn't have time to go to a restaurant so instead we went to the Oasis. This was an addition built on to the Dunes. There we grabbed a hot dog and a beer each, after which we crossed the street to Caesars.

There were ticket scalpers near the entrance to Caesar's Palace trying to sell their over priced products, but to no avail. Their $300 tickets were selling for $100. So I get the picture. A couple of weeks before the fight, the hotel was offered several hundred tickets for next to nothing because the gate receipts for the fight were quite low and the promoter didn't want to have the TV crews panning a half empty arena. The casinos benefit by luring boxing fans for a fight, and us chumps chance losing thousands, and generally do.

To add to the mix, these scalpers had a fist full of tickets in their palms which led me to believe that they were either employees of the promoter or that the tickets were given to them on consignment, to sell what they could at whatever price they could, to elevate the audiences numbers. Naturally the tickets couldn't just be given away because something for nothing is worth nothing. The old capitalistic axiom of supply and demand had been invoked.

Entering the arena, which was outdoors, we took our position about half way up the south end. Man what lousy seats, but after all they were only $200. We sat down in the middle of the match, which preceded the main event. After that bout there were the usual introductions of the people sitting at ring side, people like Ali, Forman, Stallone plus a host of other dignitaries and invited hotel guests. Then Michael Buffer introduced the two fighters. "In this corner RRRRoBERRRRTOOoo DURAAaannn and in this corner Sugar Ray LEONNNNAAAaaard." Then his classic pre fight line of "Let's get ready to rumblllllllle." Believe it or not this guy gets paid about a million a year to fly around to important fights and introduce the boxers. You have to give him credit though, he seems to get the Latino sounding names out dialect perfect. Actually I don't know if he really does but I have never heard anyone complaining about his pronunciations.

The match started and the sparse crowd was brought to its feet with a flurry from Leonard. Behind us there was a separate match being fought by what looks to be a Hispanic and a black man. Hmm, we feel like we are ringside VIPs without the fanfare of televised introductions. The match that we are witnessing in the bleachers seems more interesting because these combatants were hurling racial epithets like "mutha f**ken Spick" and f**cking Neeger." This battle is brought to a rapid conclusion by security and they are quickly removed. We can view other fights breaking out sporadically throughout the arena being handled with equally high efficiency. I guess one doesn't see this kind of ruckus on television because TV is politically correct by design, but incorrect by nature.

The fight drew to an end with Leonard being declared the winner. Filing out we are witness to the spicy language used by the racial cousins of the main event combatants. Oh well, that's what happens when you sell tickets for a few dollars, you end up getting a few rowdies.

Running back to the Dunes at about 9:30 I made reservations for the midnight show, then we settled down to our favorite bar to enjoy some cocktails. The show that we were going to see was called the Casino de Paris and was to be staged at the Casino de Paris show room. I also knew that we didn't have to stand in that line meandering through the casino, because now we would be treated like VIPS and be shown to our seats from the "invited guest's line."

It was nearly show time so I signed the bar tab to the room, left a tip and made our way to the show. The line had dwindled a lot because the curtain was to be raised shortly and there was no line whatever at the VIP side. We ascended the few steps to where the maitre de was standing. He asked us our names and, as if recognizing an old friend, he said, "Yes of course, here we have you seated in the front." He snapped his fingers to get the attention of a waiter to usher us to our seats. All the while the people that we had just cut off, just as I had viewed the VIPs at the Tropicana hotel years before, viewed us enviously.

Once the waiter arrived he said, "Show Mr. and Mrs. Simon to their seats." The waiter then ushered us to the front, but the seats were far too cramped. I looked up and saw two or three booths that were vacant and asked if we could be seated there instead. "I don't know, those are reserved," the waiter replied. "How much to get us into those seats," I asked? He turned around, with his back to me, and put his hand behind him, palm open. I caught the play immediately and slipped him a ten spot. Bringing his hand back to the front, he looked down quickly and said this way please. He took us to a booth, one that had a commanding view of the stage, and well worth the ten dollars.

The show started as the waiter was taking our order for a bottle of champagne. He returned quickly, decanted the bottle and disappeared. The show was great, lavishly adorned with the prettiest girls around. Their other assets as well, deserve some mention. Their breasts were seemingly perfect, little wonder as Las Vegas was the breast alteration capitol of North America.

I ordered another bottle of champagne knowing that I didn't have to drive and just stopped to reflect. "So this is how the other half lived, not a lot of worries, making lots of money they could afford to gamble, having the casino reciprocate. At the same time they were pampered and spoiled, yeah this is the life for me alright." But for me I had to work like a dog to earn my money. Somehow I just had to figure out a way to get the royal treatment without the worry of losing money. I was behind in gaming time at the tables and knew that I would have to make it up tomorrow. The thought of that prospect put a damper on the rest of the evening although I didn't show it.

The show was coming to an end and all those lovely babes were parading their nudity in front of us. The costumes, the beautiful faces, those jiggling orbs all presented themselves as a buffet for our eyes, a buffet that I am sure has in the past been responsible for launching a 1000 cold showers. And then it was over.

We sipped what remained of our champagne, chatting while the crowd subsided, and then we too left. It was close to 2:00am and I was tired. Knowing that I had a long day ahead of me gave me cause for concern. Knowing that I had my work cut out for me gave me the jitters. Straight to our room we went with our arms around each other's waist. On the way up in the elevator she thanked me for a wonderful evening and gave me a long sensuous kiss.

In the morning I ordered another sumptuous meal from room service, this time a bagel with lox, cream cheese with capers for me, and Eggs Benedict for Carla. This was delivered promptly with a carafe of fresh coffee, a jug of fresh squeezed orange juice, along with fresh flowers and the morning paper. Classy or what? She was thrilled waking up in the morning with all this wonderful fare at her fingertips. This certainly beat stalking the buffets around town and ferreting out the cheapest meals. But alas all this came with a price and after a shower and a shave I was off to do my penance at the black jack tables. Carla went off to do her pennance window shopping.

Gambling is the only currency accepted at any casino. Who can forget that great Walt Disney classic "Pinocchio?" The scene where Lampwick and our wooden hero go to Pleasure Island for an evening of unbridled fun and entertainment only to be made into donkeys at the end. Like Pinocchio we are all manipulated with strings, some that are visible, some that aren't, and like our little puppet with the woodenhead, we sometimes veer off course. Only a traumatic experience can bring a person back to the realization that to have total control over one's self is the height of freedom. Freedom is the power to be able to divorce yourself from those forces, no matter how subtle, that attempt to sway you from a certain decision.

This was my frame of mind. I was determined that the casino wasn't going to make a jackass out of me. Yeah I was on Pleasure Island all right, but I was determined not to be penned up with those immortal words ringing in my brain, "You had your fun, now you must pay."

Finding an empty table in the morning is usually quite easy as most of the revelers are still in bed, or nursing a hang over. I got to the tables at about 8:00 am and you could nearly detect an echo. I put down my player card and said "marker please." The dealer summoned the floor man and I had $1000 in front of me before the end of the shuffle. The first fifteen minutes of play were a total disaster. I was down $350 until another person sat down at first base. Then, as if by a miracle, everything changed and I, after an hour of play, had almost won back the $350 that I had previously lost. The other player had won about a $1000, then cashed out and left. That is exactly what I should have done, because as soon as he left the loses returned. Although I was playing with a lot more caution than previously, I was still down $200 after twenty minutes, so I moved to a different table. I fared no better at the new one; after thirty minutes I was down a further $200.

Later joining a table with some older gents, I noticed that they had a considerable amount of chips in front of them. I bid them a good morning and sat down. I lost the first couple of hands and then a crisp wind seemed to blow away the black cloud that was perched on top of my head. I not only recouped the $100 that I lost at my previous session, but gained back the $200 lost from the session before that.

An hour had passed and I saw Carla making her way through the casino. She carried with her two shopping bags filled with the booty of her raid at one of the more than convenient shopping malls. She was happy and the recent upturn in my fortunes made me happy as well. I cashed in my chips and we went up to our room.

Later in the afternoon we took a cab downtown to see the sights. First stop was the Horseshoe to get our photos taken in front of the million-dollar display. We then drifted around town marveling at the glitter. Carla didn't care for the ambiance, so we picked up our pictures at the Horseshoe and made our way back to the Dunes. Really, it's at night that one should take in the downtown area; its bright lights make it come alive. At night you can read a newspaper standing on the street just as well as you could in the daylight. The night also hides the seedier nature of the downtown area; the Junkies and the drunks hitting you up for their next drink, or the hooker propositioning you for her next "trick." These blend into the night by the very nature of their "darker" pursuits.

Back at the hotel I made reservations for the other great restaurant called "The Dome of the Sea." We were on the casino floor by 7:15 and with Carla there for good luck, I sat down at a table. The play for just under an hour nets me a loss of $200. "Unlucky in cards and lucky in love" was an adage that I kept repeating to myself as we walked hand in hand to the "Dome." I vowed to vengefully consume with that evening's meal, more than the $200 that I just lost.

At the Dome of the Sea there was a large fountain area with flowing water cascading down its rocks. Surrounding the fountain was water and in it a little moving platform with a huge harp placed on it. On this platform a mermaid, complete but for the tail, would play the harp as it coursed through the water. It was actually a very interesting feature but on one spot on the platforms route there seemed to be some hidden obstacle on the rail under the water, because when it went over these, our pretty mermaid would nearly lose the harp and indeed had to fight to maintain her balance. On one circuit her soft music was interrupted with a broad grin from her pretty face as the harp did its own unrehearsed version of "rock and roll."

The meal came just as we were putting the finishing touches on our bottle of wine, so we ordered another. How wonderful it was not to worry about a bill and just have whatever you desired. The meal was just as good as the Sultan's Tent. They obviously shared the same kitchen. After the meal we again declined desert and instead ordered a bottle of the Dom Pérignon. Actually the Dom Pérignon wasn't the best champagne that I had ever tasted, but it was certainly the most expensive. We received our bill and this time it was over $300. The $40 tip was more than what I would usually spend on a dinner for two with a modest half bottle of wine. Oh what sweet revenge for wiping out at the blackjack table.

We carefully swayed out on to the casino floor and thought we should try a nightcap of blackjack to recoup some of those previous losses. Within fifteen minutes that had to end because even using basic strategy required a certain amount of concentration. So I would have to wait till I slept off the liquid refreshments that we had ingested. On the way up to the room I had time to reflect at how lucky I was not to be poorer for that round of experience. Never indulge in drink after the midnight hour when playing for money.

The morning came early, about 7:00am. I needed to get in some serious play because our flight was to leave in the afternoon and I had only put in five hours according to my calculations. I approached a table, put my player card down and ordered a coffee. No markers were necessary as I had cash on me this time. With the shuffle over the deal started. I was dealt a loser, the next hand was a winner, and on it went for about an hour. Being down about a $100 I cashed in my chips and went upstairs to see if my gal was getting hungry.

She was just starting to get up as I opened the door and she came over and gave me a big hug saying, "Hey I forgot to thank you properly for a great time yesterday." By the time the thanking was over I had worked up a man-sized appetite. We were both inclined to order up rather than to go to a restaurant. You might say that we were getting used to this new life style.

Another sumptuous meal arrived at our door and I let the waiter in to set it up. It looked fabulous as usual and that made me wonder whether or not she might be as grateful for breakfast as she was for supper.

After eating, we showered, packed our things, and got everything ready for the trip home. We went down stairs just to hang out for a while at the bar. We met a couple from New York and they told us that they had lost $6000 since they came. I just couldn't fathom those kinds of losses over a few turns of the cards and what really seemed odd is that they were still jovial. They told us that they get to Vegas on a regular basis, usually ending up losing money and only on a couple of occasions had they made any.

Well that did it. If I had any desire to go back and try to redeem myself, those folks from New York doused that flicker of hope with their icy words. Trying to console myself I said, "Okay, I dumped about $800, but the fare must have been $500 for the both of us and the food and beverages must have been worth at least $300." This was of course rough cowboy figuring, Calgary style. "So they never invite me back again, I can go whenever I want on my own without the pressure of the big bet."

So those were the terms that we left Vegas on. Before leaving I redeemed my markers with a check from my bank for $3000 US. I kept the rest of the money on me in a faint hope that somehow they might infer that I had lost it gaming.

All the paper work done, and the bags collected, we flew back to Calgary on our colorful banana.

Two weeks later I got a call from Dennis B., the junketeer, asking if I would like to go to Tahoe in a few weeks. I politely decline and ask him about the ramifications of not playing enough hours at the tables at the Dunes. Much to my surprise they had told him that I was only one or two hours short. In light of the fight that weekend that was perfectly understandable and that I would be accepted back as a welcomed guest at any time in the future. I guessed that by leaving the table a lot, the clock that is used to calculate your time spent there keeps ticking, and when you leave the table for good, unless the floor person is right there, he or she will register your absence only when they actually notice that you have left.

I mentioned to Dennis that although I wouldn't be interested in going to Lake Tahoe on his up coming trip, I would however be interested in going to Monte Carlo if they offered such a junket. He said that they do go there once a year and would keep me informed.

And that, I thought, would be the last time that I would hear about junkets, or for that matter from Dennis B.

Chapter Four: Shaky First Steps

"Hey Al, you're wanted on the phone." "Who is it," I asked? "A guy by the name of Dennis," she said while sipping her coffee. Carla and I were living together by this time, and I was puzzled because the only Dennis I knew was Dennis W., and Carla also knew him well. I took the extension; it was Dennis B. of last year's junket fame. He informed me that they were going to Monte Carlo in a month and asked if I wanted to be included. Well this really perked up my ears. He had apparently put a notation by my name concerning my desire to go there. The reason he called so early was in case we needed passports or other documentation to facilitate the trip. This truly showed foresight on Dennis's part, because although I had my passport, Carla needed to get hers, and she could do that in plenty of time.

He explained to me that this trip would be different from the one before. I had to deposit $20,000 US at the cage of Lowe's Hotel and Casino. I also had to purchase the tickets for the flight to Monte Carlo, with the ticket costs to be reimbursed when we left. The junket was for one-week, and would take place right after the famous Monte Carlo formula one rally. I guessed that the Lowe's hotel expected vacancies just after the race, resulting in a SOS to junketeers around the world.

For myself time off was not a huge accomplishment, as I was still in the real estate industry, the time was April 1981, and the "Great Recession" was just starting to take its toll. For Carla it was a different matter, as a wage earner she couldn't leave her company in a lurch, and had to ask for a week off. She was gung ho to go and see the Europe that many of us can only dream about. You can imagine what a broad smile she had on her face when she informed me that she was cleared for "take off."

The next day, I phoned Dennis and let him know the trip was on. He said he would set up the reservations right away, bring over the confirmations, and get us all the necessary brochures, hotel information and casino rules for invited guests.

So we were really going to Monte Carlo, the capitol and the only city in the microstate of Monaco. As a boy that country fascinated me because of its array of unique stamps, famous not only for their color and design, but also for their unusual shapes. They featured triangles, double triangles, squares and huge rectangles. This city state, I was later to learn, had another industry, and that was gaming, which supplied the monetary grease to lubricate the ship of state. The few thousand legal residents paid no taxes.

For North Americans this country was put on the map with the wedding of Prince Rainier to one of the most beautiful daughters of America, Grace Kelly, in April of 1956. Her natural poise, Nordic beauty and charm captivated, not only me, a mere ten year old, but also an entire world of moviegoers. We were all saddened to see her leave public life, but at the same time elated to know that she was taking a huge step from princess of the silver screen to Princess of Monaco.

There would be a further bonus to our trip to Monte Carlo. I had a good friend stationed on Corsica in the French Foreign Legion whom I haven't seen for over a year. Perhaps I could coax him into taking a few days leave, kill two birds with one stone as they say; have a rip roaring visit and hopefully win some money too.

My passport was still valid so it was only a matter of getting one for Carla. This was done in just over a week. I arranged a flight with Air Canada for $1200 apiece taking us from Calgary to Frankfurt, and from there to Nice France. I then withdrew $20,000 US in the form of a bank draft and we were pretty much ready for "blastoff."

We arrived at the airport in Calgary, boarded our flight. There I noticed the grandmother of a dear friend of mine sitting in a seat very close to ours; a tough old Transylvanian who I affectionately called Ilonka nanny. She had looked after my friend Edward and I on summer excursions in the late 50s. She was just as surprised to see me, as I was seeing her. She told me that she was going to Hungary to celebrate her one-hundredth birthday. Imagine that, a one hundred year old globetrotter getting around with very little assistance. Now that's "True Grit."

The onboard meal arrived about an hour into the flight and after that we ordered a cocktail. Mine was handled uneventfully, but the stewardess fumbled Carla's, and it landed in her lap. After much apologizing the drinks were furnished to us at a swift pace, and need-less to say they were free. I went back to see Ilonka nanny, and there she was, sleeping like a baby. I covered her with a blanket, as she had done for me, so many years ago.

Landing in Frankfurt we wished the old lady a happy birthday with many more to come. Sadly, that was the last time I saw her. She died at the ripe old age of 103.

Our flight from Calgary was a little late, so we had to hurry to the next gate to make our connection with Lufthansa to Nice. Just making it before the last boarding call, we plopped into our seats, totally exhausted.

Oh boy, twenty minutes after take off my stomach started to rum-ble. I hurried to the washroom. Just before sitting down, I felt a thud that caused the aircraft to lurch in one direction, and then after another thud it lurched in the opposite direction. The pilot immedi-ately ordered everyone back to their seats in anticipation of even stronger turbulence. Well, once the call of nature is upon us nothing can loosen us from her embrace. I had to stay in the "lurching loo" and weather the storm. The plane started bucking and I was tossed around quite violently. I grabbed the faucet to avoid being thrown from my seat but the jarring movement of the aircraft was enough to cause dramatic lateral motions. Stretching my arms to maintain bal-ance I inadvertently exposed my ribs to a severe pounding. Finally, done my business I washed my hands. All the while the cabinets were creaking and groaning from the strain of the enormous force of the turbulence. I clawed my way out and down the aisle only to witness the look of amazement on the ashen faces of my fellow passengers who had also endured a similar ordeal. Into my seat, and snapping the buckle, I was safe at last.

We landed at the Nice International airport; disheveled physically and mentally. Since France is the fashion capitol of the world, we must have stood out like a cactus on the prairies. Carla's dress had a huge stain from a spilt drink and she was in a tangled state of "all overness." We didn't have time to groom ourselves properly due to the time constraints of our connecting flight, so here we were two urchins in Nirvana. It was in this condition that we decided to take the ride to Monte Carlo and hob knob with the filthy rich.

Exiting the airport building, as luck would have it, our prearranged limo was not there. So here we go again. The hotel was about 30 kilometers away, the cab fare was sure to be steep, and I was stuck with not a French franc to my name. So it was a taxi that took us along the serpentine route to Monaco.

The Cote D'Azur is breathtaking, with beautiful colors emanating from the azure tinted sea. Then finally, beautiful Monte Carlo came into view. We drove through well-planned streets till we came to a plaza, turned right, and there it was, the world famous Grand Casino. We then followed a road full of hairpin turns, down a steep hill until we reached the Loew's Hotel.

I dashed into the hotel, found the VIP check-in line and told them of the transportation difficulties; they immediately got the cash I needed to cover the unexpected fare and tip.

We dragged our butts inside. The clerk took one look at our shoddy appearance and said, "Maybe you want to just rest for the remainder of the evening." Well, I guess more people than ourselves go through similar ordeals, because they seemed to understand our situation. The bellhop then took us to a luxurious ocean side suite with a balcony, complete with table chairs and a million dollar view.

Our accommodations were very elegant. A tray of cheese, various Melba styled breads along with sweets, nuts, fruits, and wine had been thoughtfully placed on the table. The fragrance of fresh cut flowers emanated from a vase full of assorted colored roses on the writing desk. Our mini bar was full of various liquors, sodas, snack foods and oysters, again for our free consumption as junketeers.

Carla made us a drink and we took the tray of food outside to enjoy an unbelievable panoramic view of our surroundings. The air was clean, the seas were gentle; it seemed that we had been placed into paradise. I picked up a strawberry nearly the size of my fist and took a bite. Without a doubt it was the best strawberry that I had ever tasted, the melons too had a sweetness that perhaps only the European soil alone can create. Next, we decanted the wine and found it to be typically French and pleasant tasting. After finishing half the bottle we couldn't decide if we were intoxicated from the beverage or from our surroundings; probably from both.

We were brought back to reality with the high-pitched sound of a jet engine racing toward the open sea. We looked up and saw a sleek Mirage fighter and from the Fleur De Lies design on the fuselage, we realized it was French. Later we discovered that the French Air Force also has a military base on Corsica. The island is the birthplace of the great Napoleon Bonaparte.

I phoned my buddy in the French Legion. He was unavailable so I left a message at his Captain's office for him to call me at my hotel room, just in case he was able to take some time off. I had planned to treat him like a king; it would have been a welcome relief after the Spartan lifestyle that he was living for the past year.

The trip had been an exhausting affair, and our eyes were getting weary. We went for a nap to shake off some of the accumulated jet lag before supper.

Waking up at 6:30 pm I noticed that it was still daylight. With a nudge I roused Carla from her slumber. After that brief power nap we were awake, and feeling fresh again.

I read a note on top of the refrigerator, it said that as invited guests we were entitled to eat at any restaurant but one, the real fancy one, the La Truffe. The hotel would invite aggressive players at their own discretion to that special eatery but even those, only once per junket. I am sure that everyone got the invitation anyway; I guess it was the hotels way of making you feel extremely special when you received it. I wonder if anyone was ever refused. Reading on I noticed another caveat, bottles of rye, scotch, bourbon and rum can be ordered by room service but they would be supercharged at $50 per bottle. I suppose too many people had used those bottles as their single allowable bottle on their return trip through Canada Customs. After reviewing all the restaurants that the hotel had to offer, our evening plan was to take in the dinner show at the Folies Russes. Carla made the necessary reservations.

Because we were older and wiser due to our previous experiences in Vegas, we strode up to the maitre de's station, Carla with a dress that was a real eye popper, and I with a suit that actually fit. I still hadn't exchanged my money in for francs so I gave him fifteen dollars in the usual stealthy and underhanded way. This netted us nearly the best table in the house. The waiter appeared after dinner and we ordered a bottle of champagne; then the show began.

It was a typical show with bare breasts, posh costumes and filler acts for background changes. After the show it was directly to our room, a quick glance out the patio, and then straight to bed.

Having had one of the most restful nights of our lives, we awoke after ten hours to an unbelievable morning. With just a breath of wind to enhance the already sweet aromatic air, we gazed out at our surroundings in wordless awe. The azure blue of the water was the most breathtaking sight of all. We were speechless for twenty minutes just absorbing the heady vista of the area.

The Monte Carlo marina, which was just to our right, was full of the fanciest boats that we had ever seen. The bigger ones, belonging to the filthy rich, had to be anchored outside the marina due to their enormity, and the personnel had to be shuttled in with the use of smaller crafts. Just above the marina was the palace of Monte Carlo, offering a vantage point for viewing in any direction. Behind us the mountains rose abruptly from the sea featuring roads that are engineering marvels.

The morning air had awakened our appetites, and we proceeded to the room service menu. We ordered an ample breakfast with more fruit to replenish those which we had eaten.

The familiar tapping on the door is heard fifteen minutes later, and I instructed the busboy to set up the outside table so we can further enjoy the refreshing air with its inspiring scenery. There was a fresh flower adorning the middle of the table and the set up was meticulous. My gal inspected it and a wide grin emerged from her face, indicating her approval. We have to almost pinch ourselves to make sure that this is all real. Because I still haven't any francs I have to tip the busboy in American money. After breakfast the first order of business was to rectify that little problem.

Having slept, eaten and showered, I went down stairs to engage myself in a little blackjack and coffee while Carla was getting ready. When I reached the casino, I found it was closed. At the hotel desk they informed me that the casino opens at noon, but the table games generally start at 4:00 pm, yet these wouldn't open till 6:00 pm due to a dealers strike. Although the slots were available at noon I wasn't going to wrestle with the one armed bandit, because it would probably win. Basically we just had to hang out at the hotel till the casino opened to get my hands on some French francs.

Arriving back at the room I told Carla the bad news, but instead of being negative she was very upbeat and suggested that we grab our bathing suits and relax at the pool for a couple of hours. Actually that was a great idea, we could catch some rays while knocking back some drinks at poolside, and enjoy the spectacular view from the rooftop swimming area.

Like most Hungarians, I turn brown just walking past a window on a sunny day. So, after fifteen minutes of sun, I felt that I could flip over and get some rays on my back. I happened to open my eyes to get my drink and saw a pretty brunette without a top. She was streaking past my field of vision and dove into the pool. As calmly as I could, I said to Carla, "You're not going to believe what I just saw," and motioned towards the lady who, a few seconds ago, plunged into the water. She in turn said, "If you think that is interesting take a look to your left." I guess in the time that I had my eyes closed a lot more people had shown up. Perhaps Carla didn't want to rouse me earlier, or maybe arouse would have been a more accurate choice of words. There was a gaggle of girls, all topless, chatting up the great formula-one driver, Mario Andretti. Smiling, I related to her a story about a client of mine who wanted to buy a house in Mount Royal, an upscale area in Calgary. The home was around the million-dollar figure but was rather plain looking. To garner up some interest in the property I walked over to the window and opened the curtain, "Hey, check the view" I said, to which he replied, "For a million bucks, when I open the curtains for a view, I want to see a pair of tits." And there was Mario, with not just one set to look at but six and all this at full comp. Now that's truly a million dollar view.

After that episode I was unable to totally relax as I eagerly awaited the next half nude streaker. Sitting up I chatted with Carla. She told me that she also was tempted to remove her top. I wasn't too sure if this sentiment derived from the seventies "burn your bra movement," or more realistically from a desire to conform to our immediate environment. As the pool area became more and more crowded we were rapidly eclipsed into the minority. Like parking diagonally in a parallel zone, we were now the ones getting the looks.

Although I would have liked to stay there all afternoon Carla, who has red hair and blue eyes, was predisposed to burn after long periods of exposure to the sun. So we departed for our suite to freshen up, although it was I that was leaving with some reluctance, glancing over my shoulder all the way out.

We were going to walk along the beach, check out the sights, and kill some time until the table games at the casino opened. On the way we came across a girl lying topless on the shore wall, sun bathing. It seemed that the entire area was topless and moreover no one seemed surprised, except the new arrivals like us.

We walked along the coast road to the public beach and there too, the same conditions prevailed. I noticed one gorgeous red head in particular, who was extremely well endowed returning from a concession stand carrying some drinks. Unfortunately, she was wearing a top. Nodding toward the lady in question I said to Carla, "It's always the really good ones that are the most modest." We resumed our conversation about the beauty of the general surroundings. She interrupted me in mid sentence and said, "You know that modest lady you made reference to earlier, well you ought to see her now." The entire beach, including myself, had their eyes glued on that lady's assets.

The layout of the town was well thought out. The mixture of medieval and modern gives a sense of historical continuity. That we are linked somehow to the past with an unbreakable bond is undeniable, but I'm apprehensive about the encroachment of modern, sterile mass produced building designs. To flood this Eden with tasteless structures housing mediocre people would cause a leveling effect, robbing this centuries old pristine city of its unique character. There are fewer grand buildings being built, because there are fewer grand people around with the vision to build them it seems.

Back at our hotel, as we enjoyed the scenery from our balcony our next-door neighbors came out to greet us. We introduced ourselves to Darryl and Angie P., from Somers Point, New Jersey. He manufactured car parts for the Dodge Chrysler Corporation. They said that they get away to Monte Carlo once every two years on a junket, not only to gamble, but also to enjoy the ambiance; I must say they couldn't have picked a nicer spot.

They mentioned that they lived very close to Atlantic City, a town which also offers gambling. I had never been there; he assured me that compared to Monte Carlo, it was just another run down Eastern American city.

We socialized for a while over drinks, and they suggested we dine together. I thought that was a great idea because Carla and Angie hit it off right away. Darryl and I, on the other hand, could talk about the upcoming session in the casino.

Meeting in the lobby we picked out a quaint little restaurant. Darryl, like me, didn't look at the wine list, only the corresponding price. After all, weren't we fully comped, and anyway how could you go wrong with the most expensive wine on the list? By the way, all casinos have even more expensive wines, which they offer to their "better healed" customers, but you have to be persistent; they don't offer unless pressed. Usually "peons" like us are only offered the run of the mill vintages.

The wine came, and like most French wines it was delightful. We ordered our meal, then another bottle of the same, and things started to get mellow. Darryl started to opening up and asked if I employed a system when playing blackjack. I readily said, "Yes, basic strategy." "Boy that's pretty ballsy, playing for large sums of money and not using real strategy," he added. I asked him what exactly he meant by that, and he casually said that he would never go on a junket unless he could achieve an edge on the game." And how does one do that," I asked? "By counting cards." There's that term again, the one that I had had heard years before. He proceeded to explain that it was tens and aces that were the real secret in playing a successful round of blackjack. In a nut shell, all one had to do was to count the little cards with the big cards and if there were more small cards spent than big cards, then the deck would be a positive. Conversely, if there were more big cards spent than little cards, it would be deemed a negative deck. On a positive deck, you would raise your bet because chances were better for making double downs, i.e. getting a ten. Also, dealers would break more often when stiffed, because the deck was face card rich. There would also be a lot more blackjacks in a deck rife with aces and faces, which pays one and a half times your bet. Conversely again, if the deck was anemic in face cards you would, in all likely hood, not make your double downs, and the dealer would make more of his stiffs.

I can't tell you how unarmed I felt after talking to my first card counter. He seemed to know so much about the game; and I knew so little. Everything that he talked about made so much sense. "These guys are going to spank me," I thought to myself as the food arrived. The waiter's entrance was a Godsend because all four of us started talking, relieving much of the inner gloom I was feeling.

We ate our meal and savored every bite. We had built up an enormous appetite, she from walking and I from gawking. Finally, I had ordered a steak from a casino that I could actually eat. I did have a taste of Carla's fish and between the two meals hers, certainly, was the better choice. For desert, the two of us shared a soufflé that was out of this world. Now we were ready to do battle with the casino.

Arm in arm, Carla and I entered the room. There we encountered a remarkable international assemblage. Along with fancy dresses and tuxedos, there was traditional attire from around the world; turbans, saris, togas, fezzes and every language imaginable filled the grand room. James Bond would have felt at home in such a setting.

I got a marker for 5000 French francs, at that time worth just under $1000 US. I noticed the casino was using a four-deck shoe, with about a deck cut off. They were also playing what is known as English rules, which meant that the dealer got one card, an up card only, playing everyone at the table first, dealing a second card to himself last. The obvious advantage to the casino would have been the elimination of the "peek," a procedure that might relay information to the player about the dealer's hole card. The disadvantage to the house is that they would spend far too many cards, plus consume time, only to realize, when it came the dealer's turn to hit, that they occasionally ended with a blackjack.

I placed my minimum bet, 300 francs, into the square and the deal is begun. Though dealt a lousy hand I got lucky, and the dealer broke. It is the same for yet another shoe, and I was up about 1500 francs, I raised my bet to 500 on the first hand of the new shoe, and was dealt an eight and a three facing a ten. I doubled and got a ten; the dealer pulled an ace giving him a blackjack. The dealer picked up everyone's bet, including my original one, along with my double. Well, this was very unusual to say the least. I protested, and he informed me that under English rules, the dealer retains all bets except for ties with the blackjack. That was the last time I would double against the ten or the ace. In North America, if you double or split, or double down after a split, with the dealer getting a two card twenty-one you would only lose your original bet.

As the play went on I was learning the ropes as they say. The German sitting next to me asked for a card in his native tongue, "Ein cart bitte," (one card please) and the dealer told him in English that he needs a hand signal, otherwise he couldn't give him a card. He had quite a loud voice, and I think that in Germany, where he is used to playing, there must be an endless litany of "ein carts;" it must be deafening.

After playing for about an hour I made a minimum bet and got quite startled. Before the deal started I saw a hand dart by my left shoulder, and place a bet on a smaller box behind my large one. So that's what those boxes were for. Anyone can place a bet behind your square and, if it's larger than yours, he makes the decision whether or not to take cards, not you. The person behind me had placed a 5000 franc bet. I was dealt a twelve facing a dealer's three; the dealer asked him if he wanted to hit or stand. The chap was nice enough to motion to me to cast the verdict. I hit drawing an eight. Good thing I took that card, because no one else hit, and the next two cards were face cards, breaking the dealer. An enterprising individual, not knowing too much about the game, could walk up behind a player who is doing well, make his bets and eliminate the inexperience factor.

Carla had been my stalwart supporter for well over an hour and having a grand time talking to people who were standing around taking in the action, but who were not participants. I asked her if she wanted to do something else then I'd be more than happy to oblige. She was enjoying herself too much, conversing with the various people that sporadically showed up at the table, so the play resumed.

After another hour and a half I lost five hands in a row and called it quits. I bought back my marker at the table and we walked away with approximately 3000 francs.

Going to Darryl's table, he too was showing signs of wanting to leave. He asked Carla to locate Angie, who was playing at some slot machine, and ask her to cash out. Then he suggested that we should all go to the hotel's in-house disco.

Darryl told me that he was up a bit, but he had taken a "bath" in the last fifteen minutes. When push came to shove, he was up 2000 francs and I, the unarmed one, beat him by 1000 francs playing a lot less money. "Hmm," I thought to myself, maybe the "real strategy" that he was talking about earlier was not entirely what it was cracked up to be.

On the way to the disco, Darryl apologized for not telling me about the double down rule against the blackjack. He said that he too fell victim to that rule, not only once, but on several occasions. Old habits are hard to break, but a good way of avoiding those surprises was to keep a side count of aces. According to him, if the count was high and the deck was anemic in aces, not only were your chances of getting twenty-one greatly enhanced on a double down situation with an eleven, but at the same time the dealers chances of getting a black-jack with a ten showing, have been dramatically reduced.

Well, all that made perfectly good sense, but that would have to wait because there was no time to start honing a new skill just yet. Perhaps after this trip I would look into it.

In the disco we ordered some cocktails and started to unwind. I told him that I had been to Europe before on several occasions, and had been to Hungary as well. He was wondering how I got along in Hungary, because the language was totally different from any other European tongue. I explained that I spoke the language fluently and had no communication problems. Politically I was naturally opposed to the Russian occupation. Then he really surprised me by mention-ing that he too was part Hungarian. The only words in that language he ever learned were from his grandparents. I told him that at our house if you spoke any language other than Hungarian, you immedi-ately got a swift kick in the ass. This method was great in preserving the mother tongue, but was sheer folly in maintaining retention in any other language. I used to speak fluent German when we were there after the war. Of course I couldn't speak German in the parental house, but would play with others who spoke the language. As a child your mind easily absorbs matters pertaining to speech, but alas, just as easily forgets them when not used. Upon arriving in Canada at the age of four, I wasn't allowed to speak German in the house, and with-out those kids around to play with, and talk with, I quickly lost facility of that language. The old saying, "use it or you'll lose it" applies lethally in linguistic matters.

The next morning looking over the blue sea, and breathing the dawning air was like a massage for the soul. I heard Carla stirring, and asked if she was ready to eat. She answered in the affirmative. I asked her, "What is your pleasure?" "Eggs Benedict," she replied, with an early morning raspy voice. I called room service, instructing them to add lots of fruit, plenty of coffee, juice, and of course, cham-pagne. Well I have to reiterate that they sure treat you well if you risk your money.

The waiter arrived with the food and we had him set it up outside. After he left we scurried out to see what surprises he had brought in the form of fruits. They would never bring the same fruit, unless you specifically asked for it.

Just as we sat down our friendly neighbors came out on to the balcony and bid us a pleasant morning. Carla got up and brought out two more glasses and poured them a little champagne. We toast to the fabulous view, and fortunes aplenty for the evening session.

The phone rang and Carla answered. She yelled, "Hey Al, it's for you." Picking it up, I am elated to hear that it's Howard H. calling from the ferry making his way to Nice from Corsica. He informed me that he and his comrades in arms are to be on parade in Paris, and that he can see me briefly at the train station in Nice at about 5:00 pm.

What wonderful news, I hadn't seen Howard in about two years; he must have a lot to tell me about his newfound adventurous life. This would, however, abruptly change the plans that we had made with our new friends. I told them of the phone call, and they agreed to rendezvous after Carla and I returned from Nice.

We rented a car, had breakfast and clean up. It was about 12:00 noon so we had the entire afternoon to ourselves. Carla suggested that we drive around the area and check out the breathtaking vista from the top of the steep cliffs that protect the Rivera from Europe's harsh weather.

We made our way out of the city getting on the road that took us up the side of the mountain overlooking the city. The view was absolutely stunning. We were looking down a precipice of perhaps 2000 feet. Laid out before us was the Palace and the Marina, planned in such a meticulous fashion that it looked like a fantasy. Continuing on our way to Nice, using the serpentine road leading to Monte Carlo, we hooked up with the main four-lane highway, which led to our destination. It was about a twenty-minute drive into the city. There we found the train station where we were to meet Howard. This done we parked our car near one of the beaches and went on a stroll.

The beaches in Nice are like none that I had had seen before. They were full of huge boulders that in turn were full of people laying on them in the quest for a tan. Of course, here too, topless babes were stretched out on top of those rocks; unabashed thank God. They were taking up positions matching the curvatures of those stones, arching their backs to maximize, for connoisseurs like myself, the view of their upper torsos. They looked as if they were swollen with pride.

They say it takes three days for the novelty of the naked breast to wear off; so in the mean time I was going to enjoy the sights.

In downtown Nice, all the women dress like models. Carla and I looked like paupers amongst the office crowd in our slightly faded blue jeans. Although I am sure they also wear jeans, they don't make a habit of putting them on for the work place.

At 4:00 pm we got the bright idea of meeting Howard's boat at the pier. When we arrived it had already docked, the troops had disembarked and had left for the station. Learning this, we immediately rushed over there so as not to miss him.

At the station we finally spotted the Legionnaires. Howard, being one of the few Europeans in the modern day version of the legion, stood out like a sore thumb. He couldn't be missed, with his six foot four inch stature, his good looks and his good-looking Nordic features. The Legionnaires were preparing to board when he finally saw us. He walked over with the biggest smile I have ever seen, and immediately offered an apology for giving us the wrong arrival time. Doffing his hat, he revealed a shaved head, which was a Legionnaire tradition. We talked for ten minutes and then he was gone. What a bloody shame that we couldn't at least sit down over a beer; letting him in on the all the news from back home. Oh well, at least we got to see each other, have a good laugh and share a few stories. The train slowly pulled away, and we turned and walked out.

There is nothing like meeting an old friend in a strange land, especially when you see eye to eye politically. Howard didn't have a disciplined up bringing, and in true Nietzschian fashion he was determined to carve a man out of himself by joining the Foreign Legion.

As we drove along the winding road back to Monte Carlo, we came out of a hairpin turn and saw a hot dog stand in a scenic park area. This gave us a chance to feast on the food, and the panorama from up high.

The French prepare a hot dog a little differently than we do in North America. I can't be absolutely certain but I think the style of the wurst was what is called a Parisianer. For those of you not familiar with the European tradition of sausage making, here is a quick lesson. Each city name or region that is given to a particular sausage has certain spices and fillings that give it a unique flavor. For example, a frankfurter is in the tradition of the city of Frankfurt, a wiener is in the tradition of Wien, or as we say in North America Vienna, a Bavarian is in the tradition of Bavaria, Debreceni for Debrecen and so on. What makes the Parisianer unique is that they incorporate the use of goat meat as well as pork. The bread was a short French loaf, cut into two separate buns giving each of us an end piece. A hole is then put into the unsplit buns, French mustard added, and then the sausage was slid into the hole making it the best hot dog ever. And if you think things go better with coke, you ought to try to spoil yourself with a good German beer. You'll be in heaven.

We arrived back at the hotel at about 7:00 pm and got ready for the evening session at the casino. Upon entering the gaming hall we noticed that Darryl was already playing alone at one of the 500-franc tables. I stopped to say hi and watched him play for a while. I noticed that the floor man was observing him intently and was on the phone when he put in a 3000-franc bet. They really got nervous when he was dealt a blackjack. Bidding him adieu and continued good fortune, I moved to a lower limit table.

I requisitioned a 5000-franc marker at a 100 minimum table, and began to play. The cards were ho hum to say the least, in fact so much so, that Carla requested a few hundred francs from me and promptly vanished to the slot machines for the rest of the evening. My flat betting of 300 francs cost me about 3000 for the night.

The price of my non-descript play was my previous night's gain. I couldn't really raise my bet because it was pretty much a win, then a loss session. Darryl did say that the best time to raise your bet was when the count was high, but he wasn't there so I didn't have a model around which to structure my betting. I would make it a point to sit at his table the next time to see if I could gain some valuable knowledge, and of course some valuable currency.

I walked away licking my wounds, and went to see how Carla was faring. She and Angie were playing slot machines in a quieter part of the casino. They were both in good cheer, so I ordered a drink and got up to speed. While downing my cocktail the credits were piling up on their machines, unfortunately for Carla a lot more was being amassed on Angie's "one armed bandit." She was up a few thousand; Carla only a couple of hundred.

They were having a good time and being tired from the hectic day, I bid everyone a good night and went to bed for a decent night's rest.

Opening the door to our room, I noticed an envelope just inside. It was an invitation to the La Truffe restaurant for the following evening. Our reservation pre-set for 6:00 pm, and a RSVP request no later than 1:00 pm the following day. I couldn't wait to tell Carla that a first rate meal was awaiting us the following evening. Then went to bed sleeping so soundly that I didn't even hear my gal come home a short while later.

The next morning I opened my eyes just as the busboy was finishing up the set-up for breakfast on our veranda. Now, that was a first, Carla waking up before me and making the call to get the morning meal.

I went out to greet the morning. Oh but it feels so grand to be all slept out; sleep is like honey for the tired mind, body, and soul. I told Carla how impressed I was with the breakfast arrangements, and how glorious it felt to have things looked after in such a fashion. I suggested that perhaps taking turns getting up early might just be the best thing since sliced bread. She missed the humor and just scowled at me.

Squirming out of a bad situation, I mentioned the invitation to the La Truffe restaurant. She was delighted and we confirmed the reservation; then we poured into our breakfast.

Darryl and Angie also ordered breakfast brought up so they too could enjoy the fabulous air that morning brings to paradise, but this time, it is they who treated us to champagne. They coaxed us into mixing it with orange juice, and indeed the concoction was a natural; a pleasant tang from the orange and the mellowing effect from the spirits. I think they called it a "shanty."

After breakfast Darryl told me he won 12,000 francs the night before. Due to the casinos' staff shortage he wasn't being watched too closely. "Man, that's about $2500 US," I said. I told him that I lost all that I had won the night before. I said, "Perhaps we should sit together one evening so that I could pick up a few pointers?" He stated that would be fine, and the sooner the better.

We finished our leisurely breakfast while we took in the wonderful vista that our surroundings offered. I asked them if they were aware that the Jacques Cousteau Oceanographic Research Center was in Monte Carlo. We spotted it on our way home yesterday afternoon but did not see his ship, the "Calypso," in port. I had a lot of respect for the man, as a pioneer in under water exploration, and as the inventor of the aqualung. His National Geographic specials were first rate, and were a must watch for my children as they were growing up. It would have been a pleasure to sit and chat with him, harvesting some of his deep insight in the nature of things before he passed away.

The girls suggested that we go to the pool and just lounge around till two or three o'clock and take in the beautiful weather. As it turned out, we spent most of the time in the shade because both girls were red heads.

We met at the pool just before noon with only a hand full of people present, but from experience we knew that situation would be short lived. We sauntered over to a nice sunny spot with a great view of the mountains, ordered some cocktails and started talking blackjack.

Darryl explained, that knowing the deck or shoe in this case, was to the player's advantage, but didn't guarantee a win. At best, it only gave a few percentage points of an edge to the player, more or less eliminating the gamble from the game. After all, if 50/50 is a gamble, then a one or two point edge that the house enjoys, and indeed prospers on, over a person using basic strategy should be considered an edge. The same must also hold true if the player achieves the same edge over the house, the sole difference being that the house has a seemingly endless reserve or "bankroll," compared to the player. The casino, although retaining the edge over the basic player, will occasionally suffer a loss, sometimes sizable, due to a factor called luck. Luck, however, is sporadic and mathematics is a constant. When the luck has ended, the math will take over and grind or nibble away at the bankroll of the "basic" user. The edge for the house is small allowing the player to win on occasion. Let's face it, if nobody ever won, would anyone ever engage in a game of chance. Hope, no matter how slim, is the last thing you lose.

The same dynamics apply when the player achieves the advantage by counting. He has to bet his maximum, which should only be about 3% of his entire bankroll, and by making a lot of bets when the edge has shifted to the player, he can grind a win out of the casino.

On high counts, the player should win most of the bets, except for the fact that luck is a two edged sword; the house too can get lucky against the player. Take for example the dealer who is constantly stiffed on a high count, meaning of course an abundance of face cards, and still manages to somehow make a hand. When he does this, more often than he breaks on a high count, he is then considered lucky. This usually occurs when the card counter has his highest bet. On the other hand, when the count is low, indicating an abundance of small cards, and the dealer makes a hand, it is then considered the norm; this when the card counter has the table minimum as a bet. This situation is not luck, it's a mathematical certainty. To the basic player on the other hand, this is considered luck on the dealer's part, and usually evokes the most over used word in the casino, complete with spicy adjectives sprinkled in to show extreme displeasure. "UN------BELIEVABLE," he mutters, usually audible only to the dealer and the nearby players at his table. This he does looking away from the table avoiding eye contact with the dealer, as if in some strange and mysterious way, he had conspired to take the player's money. The basic player, in his naivety, failed to realize that the shoe was anemic in face cards. At this point if a break were to occur it would be unlucky for the dealer, and lucky for the player. The dealer will occasionally break on a low count, but will make his hand more often than on a high count.

For the player, the "big" advantage in twenty-one is that he doesn't have to hit sixteen, or for that matter any stiff. In a low count this edge is detrimental if a stiff is not hit. You must sacrifice this benefit in the low count because now it's a matter of who will get the highest hand; basically, you have lost the "advantage of no hit," thus the need for a smaller bet.

Darryl said that if he were at a table where a dealer is making most of his stiffs on a high count he would generally leave the table because, to quote him, "It's a lot easier to beat an unlucky dealer than a lucky one,"

This "counting cards" seemed to make more and more sense as we talked. The intimidation that I had felt years ago seemed to be returning. Realizing that I knew virtually zero about the game made me feel uncertain. I was now convinced that basic strategy only scratched the surface of the game, and that the science of blackjack was the way to go.

I felt like a Christian in the coliseum, about to do battle with a pride of lions, armed with nothing, not even my wit. Darryl would be gorging himself at La Truffe while the Emperor was giving me the thumbs down. That didn't exactly put a smile on my, by now, long face.

Darryl seemed to detect my concern, so he offered some last minute advice: "When you see a lot of little cards coming out, raise your bet; when you see a lot of big cards come out, lower your bet. The bet is the most important part of the game. If you have a double down after the bet, don't miss any opportunity to use it, because the dealer has the same chance as you to get stiffed; if he gets stiffed on a high count, his chances of breaking are a lot greater." "This was all well and good," I said, "but where was the precision? What if the little cards that were coming out were just evening out a smattering of big cards that came out the hand before?" "Exactly the point," he said, you can only achieve that by counting cards, but that will take practice."

3:00 pm came rapidly. I excused myself and rushed down to the gift shop to grab a deck of cards in order to improve my proficiency at the tables. Darryl had given me a simple count to practice. Cards from two to six were a plus one, the seven, eight and nine were zero, and the ten to the ace were a minus one. The simple rule was: bet more money the higher the count.

Back at the room, I sat down and diligently went through the deck starting at zero yet never ending at zero, in other words screwing up. I could accomplish this feat in about three minutes but that was woefully slow for casino play. Every time I tried to pick up speed I would come to the end of the deck with a minus or a plus two or three; this could be disastrous for determining the bet.

Carla finally showed up and I tried to relax with her a bit before supper, but found it impossible. My mind was racing wildly with the expectation of impending doom. After talking with her a while, the heebie-jeebies finally left, and I again slipped into a resolute calm. "Hell if I find the count can't be followed," I thought to myself, "then I will do exactly as my mentor suggested, and raise my bet when I see a bunch of small cards; barring that, I can always revert to basic strategy."

It was nearly 5:00 pm so we got ready for the big supper. We heard our friends on the balcony, and stuck out our heads to say we were leaving. Darryl stood up and pretended to be a priest, making the sign of the cross, as a priest would bless soldiers going off to a war. Well that nearly cracked us up. "Wasn't your advice sound enough, now you have to invoke the power of the Almighty to be on my side too." With that, we exited for our rendezvous.

Shaky First Steps

At La Truffe we were escorted immediately to our table. We were given the wine list and right off ordered their version of Cabernet Sauvignon. It proved to be a great choice surpassing the one we had the previous night with Darryl and Angie. Slowly savoring our wine, we leisurely grazed through the menu. Carla put a cigarette into her mouth and in a wink of an eye our waiter was there to light it for her. So we had our very own server, just waiting to grant our slightest wish. But, I'm not sure whether we liked that very much, since it stole our intimacy. Always no more than a few steps away, he could have been privy to our most secret conversations.

Ready to order, we beckoned the waiter. I wanted to know what the "la maison spéciale" was, and to impress Carla with the only three French words that I knew. He pointed out the two specials of the house, thankfully in English, and the one that caught our imagination was fish stuffed with truffles and a sour cream sauce. We had heard about truffles before; that they were very good and very expensive. So that was for us, with garlic sautéed frog legs in butter sauce as an appetizer.

After another bottle of the Cabernet, we were well on our way to enjoying all that the establishment had to offer. The frog's legs arrived and at first Carla was a bit squeamish; but with just one taste her reluctance disappeared. A half an hour later our dinner arrived with much pomp and ceremony. A porter came from the kitchen area and set up the serving stand near our table. Our server then took our plates individually meting out equal portions of our order. I eagerly waded into my meal in search of the much-touted truffles. But maybe I was given the wrong order, because they were nowhere to be found. Summoning the waiter, I asked if he could point out the whereabouts of those gastronomical gems. Without even a blush he singled out what appeared to be a small black dot in the middle of the sour cream stuffing. "That sir is your truffle." I suggested that the meal was slightly misrepresented. He countered by saying that the truffles, valued at a whopping $700 US per pound, had to be used sparingly in order to make the dish affordable. I searched the fish for that precious morsel and managed to salvage a piece about the size of a pea.

Indeed it was quite tasty, but pound for pound, I would sooner have had the lobster or crab. After the main course we ordered another great tasting soufflé to top off an otherwise iffy meal.

It was close to 7:30, and Darryl and Angie could be seen entering the restaurant. They came over and asked how everything was, so I told them about the wee little truffle that was advertised so boldly. Laughing they promised to order something else. Leaving a 300-franc tip we got up and left.

In the casino, the only table with a vacant seat was at the 100-franc minimum, so I sat down at the empty first base spot. Asking for a 5000 francs marker, the deal resumed. (Although a person on a junket is sitting at a lower limit table, he must still bet the minimum obligatory bet, which in my case was 300 francs).

I was alternately winning and losing for the entire shoe until the reshuffle. With about one deck dealt, I noticed a lot of little cards appear. I promptly raised my bet to 1000 francs and was dealt a twenty, winning the hand, with the dealer drawing a seventeen. That was good news. With my previous strategy after a win I would press up the bet a little, but not seeing any more small cards I correctly lowered the bet to 500. The dealer and I were stiffed, so I refused a card. When it was his turn, he hit his card several times making a hand. Noticing that he used several small cards on that deal, I again raised my bet to 1000 and got a two card twenty-one for my efforts. That was quite gratifying indeed. This strategy went on for a couple of hours till Darryl arrived and asked if I wanted to join him at the 500-franc table. I declined his offer, stating that the table was running very smoothly, and that his tip about raising one's bet at the appearance of small cards was paying off. He leaned over and quietly whispered into my ear that the information that we talked about earlier was to be held in the strictest secrecy, as the casino will bar anyone who counts cards and wins from the use of counting techniques.

So that's what the lady was talking about years before at the Silver Slipper. In retrospect, her ears weren't that long after all.

After playing a while longer, just putting in my required time, I bought back my marker and noticed about a 5000 win. Quite pleased with myself, and thankful to Darryl for the much-needed help, I walked over to see how Carla was doing at the slot machines. She was talking with Angie. Because she had lost a few hundred, and was tired, she suggested that we retire for the evening. I wholeheartedly agreed, I bid Angie a good night. Before leaving the casino we stopped at Darryl's table, and planned to have breakfast together the next morning.

The next day I told Darryl that I managed to pull off a 5000-franc win that was largely as a result of his advice. He unfortunately, had lost 2000 and considering that in three hours of play if you only lose four bets when the cards are not falling in your favor; that can't be totally unnerving.

During breakfast Angie ran to her room and brought back a guide-book on France. It had a small piece on Monte Carlo, and all the great places to dine. She suggested that the four of us go to "Le Bec Rouge" (The Red Beak), one of the ten best restaurants in town, and the most reasonably priced of the lot. We thought that was a great idea, so we set the reservation for 6:00 pm the same evening. Maybe I could get a few more pointers from Darryl before we were to lock horns with our adversaries in the casino.

Carla and I begged off doing anything till later on so we could spend some time together. We told them that if they cared to we would meet them at the pool at about 3:00 that afternoon. They said, "That's a plan," and bid us a good morning.

That afternoon Carla and I visited the town square. We viewed the magnificent buildings and the hardy people that inhabit that wonder-ful city. The older folks here are a lot more active than our seniors back home. The 80 and 90 year olds are walking around, shopping, sweeping the sidewalks in front of their apartments and enjoying the many convenient benches throughout the city.

Monte Carlo rises sharply from the coast; much of it is built on a steep rise, making walking quite difficult. Like most cities in Europe, some streets are built too narrow to allow anything but pedestrian traffic; and of this there was plenty. People opted to walk five or ten blocks to run errands rather than using their cars as we do back home.

Maybe they are just born tough due to a millennium of diseases like the "Black Plague" that ran rampant throughout Europe. These ill-nesses would mercilessly take the weak and infirm, robbing them of the opportunity to procreate, thereby ensuring a stronger future generation of hardy people. In short, if the plague couldn't kill them nothing could.

Later on, back at our hotel, a bit tired from our outing, we went poolside to catch some shuteye in the warm sun. We met our neigh-bors, engaged in small talk, had a few cocktails and left for our respective rooms to get ready to leave by 5:30.

That evening, we all met in the lobby and grabbed a cab to our destination. On a dark wooden sign, hung from two weathered chains, dangled the image of a bird with a bright red beak. My guess was that we were only ten blocks away from our hotel so we vowed to walk back after the meal; this would burn off some calories and we could also see more of that fine city.

The interior of the Red Beak was handsomely decorated with dark walnut paneling and portrayals of scenery from around France. The restaurant could seat up to forty people. When we arrived there were only two tables available so, I suppose we could consider ourselves lucky to have gotten a reservation with such short notice. We were seated right away and given our menus. The first thing that was apparent was the wine. The same ones that we had at the hotel were offered at a more reasonable price. Maybe the wines at the hotel were of a better vintage, or more obviously the hotel could fetch a higher amount for theirs because they cater to a more sedentary group, or a group that can't be bothered to shop around to save ten bucks on a bottle. Don't forget, we were at a five star hotel with some of the richest cliental in Europe who didn't care about the freebees offered on a junket.

We chose a Pinot Noir and our friends selected a Cabernet; then we got down to ordering our food.

The menus were in French and we couldn't make head or tail out of them. Fortunately, one of the waiters knew a little English, and rather than go through the entire menu Carla suggested that we go with the special of the day. After all, the main idea was to get out and sample some regional food, rather than the hotel fare. The old saying is that "If you cook for everyone you cook for no one." As a result, Darryl and I ordered the veal hocks in a baby pea sauce, the girls chosing the halibut in an almandine sauce with lemon and butter. The French, by the way, are famous for their saucy dishes giving them a unique flavor that many say is unsurpassed in the world. Well, it happens that it was the guys that got the tastiest dishes that night. It is truly amazing how delicious a simple veal hock can be, roasted to perfection, lavishly soaked in Cognac, with a butter and pea sauce.

Over dinner we discussed the need to hit a player's stiff card when the dealer also displaying a stiff. This went against everything that I had previously learned about the game. The premise being, that if it is true that card counters and mathematicians devised the basic strategy system, based on a count of zero, which it was, then it also must be true that when the count changes to a low minus, then the hitting strategy must also be readjusted. For instance, if the deck is sitting at a minus seven, and the player has a twelve looking at a dealer's six, the need to hit is vital because the dealer will probably make a contending hand due to the preponderance of small cards. To drive the point home more solidly, if there were no ten valued cards in the deck in the above situation, you would severely handicap yourself by not hitting. It would be almost as if you didn't hit an ace five; if you can't break then take the hit. Now, if there is only one ten left in the deck, the situation is virtually the same except the risk factor of breaking has increased marginally. In short, you the player are hitting to try to improve a very bad hand when the dealer has a hitting advantage. You are accepting the perils of breaking over the more immediate danger of the dealer making his hand. Now assuming, in the above situation, that you hit and got an ace, the count will then drop to minus eight. This robs the dealer of a great card, but puts you on a borderline decision to hit the hard thirteen; the deck now having an undetermined number of nines, and a set number of anemic tens in the deck, to cause you to break.

If one were at the casino on a junket, as we were, then naturally we would be placing a minimum bet when the count is at our disadvantage. Unfortunately the minimum is quite high, so play strategy is also paramount. A person just cruising the casino would be wise to avoid playing at tables with such low counts. The golden rule when playing at tables that do have these low counts is to play aggressively, and to hit your stiffs, (assuming that the hit doesn't exceed the parameters recommended on the hit and stand charts located in the back of this book). Remember this rhyme to keep you on the right track. "Don't be a sap, close the advantage gap." Don't be like the guy that we talked about earlier, the one that turns his head in disbelief with that 100-yard stare, uttering those immortal words, just barely audible; the words that I call "The Loser's Lament." If you let the dealer outdraw you constantly, you will end up being just another disrespected casualty on "Blackjack's Boot Hill;" knocked out of the running at an early stage of your blackjack career. An epitaph to mark your famous last words complete with adjectives; "UN F**KEN BELIEVABLE."

After dinner we went for our scenic walk back to the hotel. What a good feeling it was paying half of what one would normally pay at the hotel, including tip. If not on a junket, why would anyone waste their time going to a hotel? The food is much better and the atmosphere friendlier at a local establishment like the "Le Bec Rouge."

We arrived back at Loews just before 8:00 and went straight to the casino. I had intended to sit with Darryl, but the place was packed so we had to postpone that scheme. I found a spot at a 100-franc table, sat down, ordered a marker and commenced play.

The game was going my way for the first two shoes and then took a dramatic turn for the worse. Using all the tips that I had gained from my new and highly respected friend, I still registered a loss of 6000. "I guess I will just have to be at his table next time," I said to myself. I just couldn't get the count straight, and was always losing it. Maybe I was doing the unthinkable; raising the bet on a low count. That would be a sure way of losing a lot of hands, maybe even losing one's mind at the same time. Looking away from the dealer and muttering the word "unbelievable" was just not "me," but I found myself doing just that. Oh well, I was only down about 1000 and if I could just stay at that mark for only a couple of more days I would be very pleased with myself.

With these thoughts on my mind Carla and I wished everyone a good night, and after making plans to have a patio breakfast together, we retired for the evening.

In the morning I made the usual eating arrangements as before, and just lounged around waiting." I am just 1000 francs down," I thought to myself, but in reality I could consider myself up due to the airfares, food and accommodations. After all, was I not using the junket system as a vehicle to travel and see the world at the expense of those more readily able to afford such things, namely the casinos?

I was actually falling into the vortex of the "Loser's Lament." The idea had crossed my mind that "I was holding my own" or "holding up my end." Isn't that more or less just dancing around the periphery of mental masturbation? It's always nice to visit different places, meet new people, and make new friends, but when you go through a shirt every session, don't be fooled into thinking that you are in some way not working. Indeed you are working and damn hard to get compensated monetarily for your time and expertise. Remember you could be at home earning a living but instead you are here "holding up your end" or worse, someone else's; and then what does that make you?

The sweat of work will have its rewards, but if it doesn't, you have been wasting your time.

Consider for a moment the Capitalistic business trip. Would you or anyone you know leave to work somewhere, anywhere, without the benefit of a wage? Consider the junket to be a business trip that has profit as its prime motivation. You are a self-employed business-man out to make a profit for your time and talent. Imagine me thinking that I was pulling a fast one over a casino that had worked out all the variables. Breaking out even, or slightly down is no sub-stitute for a resounding win. I was stroking myself into believing my own propaganda. Believing that breaking out even or losing a little is okay because I was having a good time, or seeing some place that I had not been to before. These days if I break out even I feel like crap. Although I have comps coming out of my ying yang, I still have no monetary gain to show for my efforts.

Breakfast arrived and I woke Carla after the set up was complete. We sat down and our conversation brought out Darryl and Angie, who were just getting up. I told Darryl about the bad turn of events, and the 6000 loss. He said that could happen just as easily as I had won the 5000 the night before. He himself had been down that amount, but managed to nail one particular shoe, and register a 5000 win for the night.

Darryl said that the pit crew was watching him intently, especially when he was "on the come back trail." I unfortunately, didn't merit that kind of respect due to my dismal performance; but I did notice them looking closely the previous evening when I won the 5000. "Yeah," he said, "it wasn't too bad now because they were short staffed, but when they are fully manned they can be brutal." I guess they are prone to sweating bullets because, like most endeavors, the casino is a business as well, and if they show a sizable loss, that too has to be accounted for. He mentioned in passing that occasionally, when in a fully staffed casino, he would stray from his disciplined rou-tine and raise his bet on a low count to give him more playing time. Well, at the time I didn't know what the heck he was talking about.

The girls had evidently planned the rest of the day for us; they would go shopping, and we would wait at the pool for a couple of hours till they returned. That was fine by us as long as we didn't have to tag along.

They got ready and left about noon, leaving us on our own. Shortly afterward we were up by the pool and oddly enough, the bare tits were no longer a distraction. The strange part was that one could discern who were the new guests, and who were the longer-term tenants by how far their eyes popped out of their heads. There was even one guy shamelessly taking pictures with a telephoto lens. I thought I noticed some drool emanating form his mouth, but then again maybe not. I suppose we are all somewhat distracted when thrust into new surroundings but hopefully my condition wasn't as extreme as the chap with the camera.

Slowly our conversation strayed back to 21. I felt as if Darryl was a "well of wine, and I an empty bucket." My curiosity about the game was insatiable; the questions to him were endless.

I asked him about splitting cards during high and low counts; his answer surprised me. For instance, the classic eight split is not always a split; it is up to the dealer's eight, but after that the count plays a primary role. For example, they are not to be split against the nine at plus seventeen, a rare number, and against the ten when the count exceeds plus six. Under English rules, the problem arises of the player losing all bets if the dealer turns up the blackjack. "What is to be done if the count does exceed plus six," I asked? "If you can surrender, do it; if you can't you're better off staying put because you will probably end up with two eighteens, against a dealers nineteen. It's always better to lose one bet rather than two."

He said that the aces posed a somewhat different problem against the ten, especially with the English rules, because again in the event of a blackjack, they take all bets. If one were playing in North America, the eight split would be used down to a count of minus two. Because the ace is such a powerful card, the dealer gets two tries at making a hand; first the soft try then if they miss there they get a shot at the hard try. If the count is more than three, you would have bought insurance in any case and probably end up with two eighteens. If the dealer gets a two card twenty-one, all is even, but if he misses twenty-one, then there is only an eight and a nine that is an immediate threat on a one card pull. If he misses that you will either tie, or just as likely win.

When one strays from basic strategy new opportunities appear. Take for example the nines against the ace. Although this is not a split in Monte Carlo under English rules, it certainly is the case in America; assuming the count is plus three or more. The reason is that even if you don't buy insurance, only your original bet is lost if the dealer happens to draw a ten valued card; and you can't do anything about that. The assumption can be made, however, that the likely hood of the dealer having another nine has been somewhat diminished by the fact of you possessing two. Therefore, assuming that you draw two hands, each totaling nineteen, the dealer probably won't have an immediate twenty; which isn't to say that he won't draw twenty taking more than one hit; making a hand after getting stiffed is more difficult on a higher count. If the eight is drawn then of course it is a tie, and you would break out even, rather than losing with your paltry eighteen. The other scenario might be that the dealer gets lucky and draws the nine. But we are trying to remove luck as much as possible from the game. If the nines were to be split in a minus situation, you can see by previous example that the dealer has the advantage because he has a card that can be used in two tries to beat you, and worse yet, you are first to hit and hit you will, if you have some how managed to get a sixteen on one, or both of your splits. The ace should, at this point, be considered as a danger not because of the potential two card twenty-one, but because it is the lowest card in the deck. Bear in mind that the nines are not a split against a three for instance, due to a preponderance of small cards at a count of minus four. So don't split nines against an even more dangerous "low card" on a low count.

There was much more to this game than I had originally thought. I had mastered only a small aspect of twenty-one, that is, all the strategy used as a basis for what is officially termed "basic strategy" in the blackjack player's lexicon. Knowing now that this was based on the count of zero, it offered just a rudimentary aspect of the game, and adjustments had to be made constantly after viewing each and every card. But in saying this, the "kindergarten" strategy should be regarded as a very important first step in the learning of the game (In the back of the book a basic strategy table has been included, complements of Michael Shackleford, The Wizard of Odds). After all, one has to stand on his own two feet eventually and what better position to start than neutral zero. But a warning is issued here: unless you progress to a higher sophistication of play, i.e. the use of a count, you will be doomed to failure, missing out on the monetary rewards of a successful player.

I had a lot to think about, and felt a bit nervous about the upcoming bout at the casino. I excused myself apologetically, stating that I was going to my room to practice the deck count. Darryl said that he understood, and that the four of us would meet later for supper

I must have worked that deck for two hours and just couldn't get the time down to a respectable length. If I picked up speed the deck still wouldn't end with the number zero, slowing down I would get the numbers right, but the time was in the range of about two minutes. "I'm not going to be able to do this," I thought to myself. Doing battle in a state of unready-ness is a mortal sin and should not be attempted, but this is exactly what I was about to do.

Carla arrived back with a couple of shopping bags full of goodies from her foray into Monte Carlo. She was as pleased as punch with herself as could readily be seen by the smile on her pretty face. I told her that the four of us were all going out for supper again, before we put in our time at the casino. We relaxed for a while, and then with everything set we slowly began to get ready.

In the lobby we decided to try out one of their bistros and just have something quick to eat so we wouldn't be jostling for a seat when we entered the casino.

After our wonderful meal we found the casino was so packed, there was no way for Darryl and I to sit at the same table yet again. We parted company to find the odd table that had one seat available. Darryl got one almost immediately because he could allow himself to play the higher limits. I on the other hand couldn't afford such luxuries, and had to wait for a seat at one of the 300 minimum tables.

An important thing to bear in mind is that people who are winning usually stay at their seats; and people who are losing, relinquish theirs. I had evidently taken the seat of a loser, because I had a string of losses till the end of the shoe. The cards were so bad in fact, that it was almost physically painful to endure, but only at my square. The other positions didn't fare too badly, but mine was in a state of "stiffsville," a state that is experienced occasionally by those of us that play a lot of cards; when every hand you are dealt is a stiff, and every hit you take is a break.

The following shoe was much better for me in the sense that I had managed to break even. Sometimes, after a string of defeats even a tying hand feels like a victory. It took a couple of shoes and a new dealer to change the course of events. After an hour of play, I was back to even and threatening to make a "profit," a word that makes a casino's blood run cold when it benefits a player. I was starting to notice more and more the posturing of the floor staff stationed behind the dealer; when they were winning, they were a jovial lot, but as soon as the casino was losing I would often wonder whether or not the anguish they felt was greater than mine, when I was losing. "Let the bastards suffer." I didn't care much for their jovial attitude because it usually meant that the player was being taken to the proverbial cleaners.

On went the fun for some time until I was again hit by another "reversal of fortune." This rapidly eroded my winnings until I eventually registered a loss of 2000 francs, ending my session and prescribed time for the evening. To consol myself, I reasoned that I was only down 3000 in total and that was only half of one airfare, a $600 US hit, which was just a "piss in the bucket" for what it could have been. Naturally this kind of logic is laughable now, but back then I was using it as a sort of moral massage to ease the "agony of defeat."

Gathering Carla from the slots was no easy task because she was winning; at least one of us was making money. Eventually, convincing her to take the money and run, we retired for the evening. She was understandably pleased with her good showing, but the real "thrill of victory" would have to wait till our final night at this resort of resorts.

The gentle sound of the waves lazily nudging at the shore, and the sea birds struggling for their morning meal awoke me to the reality that a new day had begun. The streams of sunlight accompanied by the occasional wisp of wind made the curtains dance; natures very own concert using our suite as a stage. The rays of light offered a ballet of images, and the drawstrings offered the rhythm, as they gently bounced off the wall.

I got up quickly and phoned for breakfast to be brought to our room. The rap on the door awoke Carla and she was fully aware of things just as the busboy left. We made our way to the patio, greeted the morning sun, although it is already 9:00 am; we considered it a courtesy to this giver of life to our planet. We watched as a yacht gently slipped by beneath our vantage point revealing two lovely maidens giving themselves the "full tan" treatment. Even this novelty got little fanfare from us; by now we were seasoned veterans in an overseas campaign.

The conversation turned to gambling and Carla insisted that she would try her hand at blackjack that evening, if a spot were available at the 25-franc minimum table. I of course told her that if she knew nothing about the game she would be taking too great a risk, and that it was sheer lunacy to even entertain that idea. I told her of my first experiences with the game, about how badly I had fared, and the silly mistakes I had made as a novice. She wasn't convinced, feeling that it was basically a game of luck and stated that she was determined to play. Well, "she is gong to have to learn by her own mistakes," I thought to myself. My dad used to relate an old parable from either ancient Persia or Greece, it went something like this: "A wise man learns through the mistakes of others, a stupid man through the mistakes of his own." This I thought would apply to Carla's foray that night.

After breakfast, we woke Darryl and Angie. He told me that he too had fared badly at the tables the night before, dropping about 4000. I told him that it was imperative that we sit together on our last night so that I could learn first hand how the count was implemented to our advantage. So again we were going to try to drain some funds from this well healed casino by putting them at our mercy. This is called the "Robin Hood Syndrome," take from the rich, and give to the poor. So a plan was fomented that I would not speak about the count, or anything at all pertaining to the system that he was using. I was to follow his bet quietly, only asking him about a hit, if he forgot to offer any suggestions. Also I wasn't to engage him in any small talk during the deal, only during the shuffle.

At noon we all decided to head to the pool for some R and R. We talked a lot getting to know each other a whole lot better. It never ceases to amaze me that no matter where I travel, whenever I meet a Hungarian, he or she is at least a small c conservative. Darryl was no exception, he came fully equipped with the standard package. He didn't take any crap, he didn't throw his money around, he had manners, he served his country loyally, truly enjoyed meeting challenges; in short the entire gambit of conservatism times ten. I wonder if this was a learned response, or perhaps more interestingly an inherited trait. Well one can only wonder, with the new study of twins it turns out that something that is inherited carries more weight than that which is acquired from the environment. In other words, genetics is more important than your surroundings in determining your behavior.

Well I couldn't ponder these innovative ideas any further, as I had the evening's play on my mind. I excused myself and went to our room to run through the cards in order to gain speed as well as accuracy for the count.

Try as I may, I couldn't gain any speed without sacrificing precision. I found that if I increased the speed the deck would not end up even. However, I did manage to bring down the time with some exactitude. After practicing for a couple of hours, I got it down to just under two minutes; still not fast enough for casino play. According to Darryl it should be 30 seconds or less." Man, I'm never going to get this counting down so why even bother."

About 2:00 o'clock Carla came back to the room and announced that we were all going back to the bistro that we had been to the night before. That was just fine by me but first I was going to rest my mind from the tedium of counting cards. The drone of going through the deck over and over again was mind numbing and some sleewould surely remove some of the cobwebs. So we set the timer for 5:00 pm and lay down for the afternoon.

After dreaming about cards for what seemed to be the entire length of my nap, I woke up truly more tired than when I went to bed. It was like an "Alice in Wonderland" dream, with talking cards, also biblical in a sense, with big cards eating the little cards. I was hoping that this wasn't some kind of awful omen forecasting my doom. This was our last night in Monte Carlo and I didn't want to be chasing any "white rabbits" on this, our final session.

After a great dinner, I looked at Darryl, cracked my knuckles and said, "Let's ride." So off we "galloped" to meet the "bad guys" in good old Calgary cowboy fashion.

In we went, and to our amazement not a single spot was to be had at the blackjack area. So the plan was foiled once more with Darryl and I going our separate ways.

After fifteen minutes I finally noticed someone stand up to get ready and leave; I took his spot pronto. After starting the play I realized why the chap had left. It was the worst spot on the entire table.

Sometimes I guess it's better to test the water before jumping in. That move had just cost me 3000 francs. After a few more shoes, the blood letting abated and I managed to recoup about 1000 of my previous loss. I guess I should have left, but there were no other seats available. I kept losing for about an hour and a half, and was now down 10,000 for the night, a very depressing situation to say the least. I decided to take a break to walk over to the 500 table to tell Darryl the bad news, and to see if there was a vacant seat beside him.

I saw him "pulling" on a huge Cuban cigar with chips galore in front of him. He told me that he would hold the first available seat for me. Since the dealer at his table could not make a single hand, this would be an excellent learning opportunity. Just then a player spoke up mentioning that he had to leave for supper with his wife, so I took his spot. What a welcome relief, I was finally to sit at someone's table that really knew what the hell they were doing.

The first shoe, I basically just bet the minimum 500-francs, and would only raise the bet slightly, as Darryl raised his. But now I was winning, and the next shoe I would double my bet when my buddy pressed his. I must have played close to an hour and was almost even; thanks to the table move and Darryl's kind help.

Carla came over with the announcement that she had lost all her money at the slot machines, and wanted to try her hand at blackjack. She asked for 1000 and said that she was going to be at the table that I had vacated a while before. I just rolled my eyes thinking she would be back for more money in a few minutes. So Darryl and I kept playing; and we kept winning. Life was good again, as I was once more in the plus side of the ledger.

30 minutes after Carla had left me, I could hear clapping and cheering coming from the table where she was seated. In general someone making large bets, and as a result making loads of money generating a lot of excitement. Well I couldn't let all that enthusiasm deter me from the job of hand; we had the dealer on the ropes and we were pounding him with a series of damaging blows.

In another half an hour we were betting up to 3000 per hand, and still nailing most of our large bets. I was up 20,000 francs and was in possession of the broadest smile in the whole casino. Just then Carla showed up at our table, and like a cat with it's freshly killed prey, she plopped down two racks of chips on the table, totaling 10,000 francs. She told us later, that she started betting the minimum, slowly progressing up. She was being coaxed on by the crowd gathering at her table and by the people making huge bets behind her square. She said that she made all the decisions, although she had bet the lowest amount. Every move she made turned out to be the right one. She told them that it was her first time gambling. I guess they must have been piggy backing on her "beginners luck." In any event she sure endeared herself to the crowd. Such events leave a person with fond memories; just thinking about that moment put a smile on her face for years afterwards.

Back at our play, we were still "beating the dealer" until he was relieved by a floor man. The new guy rolled up his sleeves, buried a card, and said, "bets please." Now it was near closing time and because previously we were beating him, I decided to raise the bet. Not a very bright thing to do, without testing the new card arrangement. My thinking at the time was that I had a $10,000 second mortgage on my home in Calgary. Wouldn't it be nice to get rid of that nagging bill that tormented me every month? Like a complete novice I went 10,000, two hands of 5000 apiece, and I lost. Not learning from my lesson I repeated the bet with the exact same result; then it was all over. Managing to lose 20,000 in just a few minutes filled me with disgust and self-loathing. A gross over bet, but I wasn't about to risk any more of my money. I could have had a $4000 US profit to show for my trip, but greed had got the better of me. I could have taken a lesson from Carla; as soon as she started losing she rapidly cashed in and left. This was truly a costly lesson that I would never want to repeat.

We all went to the cage, got reimbursed for our flights, refunded our deposits and thus we ended our commitments. A wonderful vacation and a good time were had by all. We met some great people and had the time of our lives.

Our plane was to leave at 10:00 am from Nice airport. We took our leave early, getting our new friend's phone number and address, promising to keep in touch. With that we retired for the night.

Having some after thoughts about the trip, I observed that Carla was the only one between the two of us to make any hard cash, Darryl was up about 30,000 francs for the trip because he didn't stray from his initial game strategy. I too could have been up 20,000 had I not displayed the greed of a novice. In retrospect I should have gone back to a minimum bet at the sight of a new dealer, just as Darryl had done; because it indicated a low count. I was up and I should have made the casino sweat for that money. Even Carla, who had never played the game before, knew that her time to quit had come when she suffered a string of losses.

This was an expensive lesson, a lesson that I vowed never to repeat in the future. We had a great time at the casino's expense, but the next time it would be even more so. We were not only going to loot their coffers of hospitality; we were also going to ruthlessly break into their vault, and actually get paid for the job.

I learned a lot about blackjack, and the way events would unfold, this game was to make a huge impact on my life; probably more than any other single thing. Blackjack was to be, more or less, pivotal in determining the course of my whole future.

Chapter Five: Doing it Solo

It was the summer of 1981, and the real estate market in Calgary was in serious trouble. I had acquired a lot of property through the years as a normal process in doing business. I had always assumed that the purchase of property was the best form of investment; as they used to say in real estate lingo, "buy land, they stopped making it years ago."

I was terribly over levered on most of my holdings, and unfortunately at record high interest rates. This situation was maintained for about six months because the rental income was covering the payments. Now, I had a feeling that due to the high lending rates all was not well with the economy; still I kept making optimistic excuses.

Back then downtown Calgary was a huge construction site with billions of dollars being marshaled for the construction of gigantic office buildings to house phantom clientele that wouldn't occupy the structures for another fifteen years. I suppose that I could exempt myself from blame by saying that the people, who were used to dealing with massive amounts of money, must have known what they were doing investing in these projects. But I now understand that these "pros," in their "ivory towers," were totally out of touch with reality. In those days, I was in awe of so-called financial giants, and assumed that they knew what the hell they were doing. As a result I mistakenly hooked my star to theirs. After all what was I compared to them with my puny investment? Surely they knew more about the economy than I, a mere beggar in comparison.

The most disappointing revelation was that they were bigger dopes than me, because they had a more plentiful pool of money to fool around with; and fool around they did. Once the economy was wrestled to the ground by none other than our own government, under the guise of fighting inflation, the jobs in Calgary began to evaporate. With the job base gone, the people started leaving town, causing the vacancy rate to soar. All those buildings that were constructed, due to

Calgary's rosy economy, were now empty. No tenants translated into no rent, and you can only live in one house at a time, so as a result my "empire" was lost to the banks.

A huge propaganda campaign was launched by our government, to hoodwink the population at large, by saying that we were "merely" in a recession. What a bad joke, we were in a full-blown depression, but to use those words would be much too pessimistic in our "just" society, as it turned out it was just for the filthy rich.

Discovering that the financial gurus knew little more than I did, my urgent concern was to get some liquid assets while I still could. Accordingly, I mortgaged all my properties to the maximum, knowing that the bankers would be wringing their hands at the prospect of an 18% return on their money. I also knew that I wouldn't have the tenant base to service the loans, and that I would eventually lose the properties financed in this manner. I was fed up, running around putting out financial fires for months; this was not my idea of having fun. The banks were, after all, in a better position to handle a foreclosure. As a result of my desperate efforts, and the limitless greed of the banks, I was fortunate enough to liquefy a small amount of my assets. In some cases, the mortgages on the properties were only 50 to 65% of the value of the homes. Who knew that in a period of only one year the banks would be inundated with a flood of foreclosures; I just escaped under the wire. The same places that I had mortgaged I could have bought back for much less, in some instances half of what I received for the loan.

So the banks finally got caught with their hands in the till and I felt great. All the usury they employed against the people had come back to haunt them. But our government orchestrated a massive bailout of the banks, although many trust companies failed regardless of this assistance. In my mind, this was a little like throwing the devil a rope to avert his demise from a fatal plunge. So we, the taxpayers, were left "holding the bag" again. I guess this is the true definition of a "free society;" the rulers are free to plunder the society that they govern.

After mortgaging out of my properties, I had some money but I didn't know what to do with it, after all, the business that I was comfortable in had just become highly unprofitable. Poking my nose around some venture opportunities, I came across a guy by the name of Lou P. who, as it turned out, not only knew about counting cards, but also actually had a book on the subject. The book was entitled "The World's Greatest Blackjack Book" dealing with matters on the GRV counting system, and written by a chap known as Lance Humble.

The book used a similar system that Darryl had shown me (2-6 was plus one, 10-ace was minus one and 7-9 was zero), except in the book the 2s and the aces were also not counted. But more important, it told the reader what to do with their hands at the various counts. Lou and I would spend countless hours playing round after round of blackjack between us, and most of the time he would wind up being the winner. He had once mentioned that he would be more than happy to split the profits with me, if I were to bankroll him on a trip to Vegas. Can you imagine giving a guy your hard earned money to gamble with, make bets with, and at the same time leaving him with no incentive to walk away from an obvious losing table just because the count was strong?

Many times on a hot count you may be the only one losing at the table, or perhaps the dealer is the only one winning. So of what use is a "strong count" then? Why in the world would you stay at a table like that? That's what makes a professional a "pro," knowing when to pick up and leave. Lou was like a loose cannon rolling about aimlessly on the deck of a creaky old scow. He would make one bet after another, increasing them constantly, sometimes losing his entire bankroll. By increasing his bets to absurd proportions, far exceeding the three percent maximum rule, he would be wiped out when I, as the dealer, got lucky.

One night, we went to a local casino in Calgary to apply our new knowledge in a more practical way. We were sitting at a full table of Orientals, the deck had just turned to a plus six, so we each put out a maximum bet. Lou was dealt an eighteen, and I a twenty; with an ace and a nine. The dealer had his usual face card. I was sitting at third base (sometimes called the anchor), and he insisted that I double my bet because a ten was a double against a dealer's, ten. I argued that the play might be a correct one if you have a hard ten, but how is it possible to be correct on a soft twenty? It was almost like splitting tens when the dealer was showing a ten. The Asians at the table stopped calling us names in their own language and now were regarding us as lucky buffoons because that ace that I received on the double, would have been the dealer's next card giving him a blackjack; instead he got a stiff, and proceeded to break.

After that episode, we annulled our partnership gradually and went our separate ways as far as 21 was concerned. We did remain friends however, and he let me know were to order the book, a book, which I was skimming through within two weeks.

As Darryl had mentioned earlier, the betting strategy was the most important part to a successful twenty-one session. If you learn nothing else about the game of blackjack remember this little rhyme, "Raise your bets the hotter it gets." Often people will come out with a larger bet just because they have a notion, or are exhibiting so called ESP (gut feeling) about what would happen on the following hand. The funny thing is, they might fluke a correct call, but if you look at the deck, more often than not, you will notice that their use of "voodoo" coincided with a higher count. I reject this clairvoyant nonsense and prefer the certainty of science instead. "Primal urge" is best left to the realm of the beast.

Look what you can do with a system of counting: Consider for a moment that you are analyzing a deck of cards in play, and the dealer is forever making his hand on a plus count and losing on the negative count. First of all, you have got to ask yourself; "Well, what am I doing here," and if there isn't an opportunity to leave you might consider a modest bet on a low count situation. The point is that you, like a doctor, put your stethoscope on the deck and figure out the problem. If there are no good answers just get up and move to a different table.

The fallout from the crumbling real estate situation didn't afford me an opportunity to fully study the book for about a year. Losing one property after another was truly a gut-wrenching ordeal and had kept me very busy. However, some of my fellow agents and friends did try to hang on by subsidizing their mortgages from the money they had amply earned in the "years of plenty." To me that was like trying to get a better grip on one of the hand rails of the Titanic. I believed if the economic situation was hopeless I should abandon ship and try something new. As it was, I had fared better than many people I knew. I suffered a loss of about a half a million dollars on the big gamble, but now I was truly free of real estate in a high vacancy market. After facing those enormous losses, gambling at a blackjack table would be a cakewalk.

Doing It Solo

It was now 1983, and with all my financial fences mended, I decided to call Dennis B. and make arrangements for Carla and I to go for a quick trip to Lake Tahoe.

Dennis dropped off the material and told me we would have to purchase our own tickets and get reimbursed from Harrah's hotel on our return leg, when we left Tahoe. He also mentioned there would be a private limo waiting at the airport so "just look out for a sign with your name on it." With a little fun in mind I neglected to tell Carla about this last little "VIP" perk.

It was mid January, and the weather had become nasty in the Calgary; the outlook for Tahoe was also gloomy. When we arrived in Reno and going to the baggage pick-up area, I noticed the chauffer displaying my name on a sign. I waited till we got our luggage and asked Carla to see it there were any cabs in front of the airport arrivals. Meanwhile I secretly introduced myself to the driver. I told him that I wanted to surprise my gal with the limo. He said that he was parked across from the taxi lane and he would wait there for us. Carla then returned and said there was no shortage of cabs, and we made our way outside the terminal. She proceeded to one of the taxis. Breezing by her I headed for the limo, opened the back door and motioned to her and said, "Hey this looks like a nice ride, let's take it." Red in the face, she told me to stop embarrassing her and get into the cab. I finally had to persuade our driver to come over and convince her to get into the long black Lincoln with the darkened windows. Once in, we rolled up the privacy glass between the chauffeur and ourselves, made a drink from the bar, and laughed ourselves silly.

The long, winding road took us to Lake Tahoe in about 45 minutes, although it seemed a lot faster with two or three cocktails. First we rode through Carson City, the state capital of Nevada, past some casinos, up a curvy mountainous road and at last we saw the expanse of the lake; it shimmering in the sun like a lost trove of gems that somehow no one dared to stash away.

On arriving I gave our driver a handsome tip for a great ride, and for going along with my little surprise.

We checked into our room to find a Heavenly view (Heavenly is a ski resort located almost directly behind Harrah's). The room had two baths with a TV in each one, also in the main room there was a computerized mini bar. If you were running short on a particular drink, a restock message would appear at the service desk, and a bus-boy would promptly show up to fill it. This is not huge technology today, but in 1983 it was well in advance of any hotel that I had ever stayed at.

Mack Davis was the headliner at the show with Hamada supplying the magical interludes; an unknown psychic was to entertain during backdrop changes that night. We made reservations and got ready for an evening of fun.

We made our way passed the clanking slot machines and the gaming tables till we at last arrived at the show room. We proceeded to the "INVITED GUESTS LINE" where the maitre de greeted us and in his nonchalant way, put his hand out for a gratuity. I rolled up a ten and five ones, the ten appearing on the outside, into his hand. He quickly glanced at it and told one of his underlings to "show Mr. and Mrs. Simon to a booth."

Davis opened the show, and later when he took his intermission the psychic came on. He got on stage with his microphone, put his thumb and index finger on top of his nose, squeezed, as if in deep thought, and asked if there was anyone in the audience with the initials CJM. Carla looked at me quizzically and I told her to stand up. The psychic was truly amazed to find that there were two ladies present who responded to his query. He tried to eliminate one by saying, "Will the lady from Canada remain standing." Again both ladies remained as they were. You could see that the guy was starting to lose it, not only his credibility but also his composure. It was plain to see that this "pretender" was also losing his patience with Carla. He then asked the lady residing on the sixth floor to remain standing. Well, we nearly burst out laughing, I mean how desperate can you get. Sure, we were staying on a higher level, and so Carla sat down, but it would have been interesting to hear his next elimination question. The psychic then zeroed in on his real mark; guessing her favorite color, not too hard to do, provided you know the color of her car. Girls, once they have decided on the make of a vehicle will undoubtedly choose their favorite color from the chart the salesman shows her. Many other things were disclosed by this "pooh bah," like the lady's street, town and province. This was very easy magic, especially if you're in cahoots with the front desk and hotel registration.

Doing It Solo

After his act this guy actually got a thunderous applause from the audience. For us, the real hilarity was in how the audience could be so easily hoodwinked by amateurish nonsense. Oh well, so much for the opinions of the crowd, and what the crowd calls good. For much too long has, "what the crowd calls good been held up as something truly worthy of praise." I like to distance myself from the compassion of "mercy applause." If the performance is lousy, don't give the person bogus encouragement, which implies some talent. Hell, you might be doing him a favor by not applauding; perhaps that way he might excel at a different career. And that might well be the start of a process to make an asset of himself rather an ass.

Well, we were "bagged out," as some people say, and went straight to our room; too tired for a quick snack, which we are sure to make up for in the morning.

Getting up at ten we were ready to face the new day. Surprisingly neither of us was hungry, so we decided to go for a walk and check out the surroundings.

Lake Tahoe is a pristine body of water shared by both Nevada and California. As it is Nevada casino strategy to build hotels on or near bordering states so it is in this beautiful area. Basically the lake stretches north to south, and it is on the south shore that the casinos are located abutting on the California border, at a place called Stateline. The view from the casinos are unmatched, especially from the better restaurants built on the higher levels, which capture the breathtaking panorama.

We strolled a few blocks and we were in California. There we got our mandatory bottle of liquor for the trip back to Canada. On the way back to the hotel we saw some snow, over six feet high, piled up in one of the supermarket parking lots. I suppose that could be considered proof as to the amount of snowfall that is received in this skier's Mecca. Back at the hotel at last, we went to the Forest buffet for a light lunch and prepared for my first shift at the tables.

When we checked in at the VIP registration they gave us a special tie clip made of pewter. It displaying a royal flush that we were supposed to wear whenever we were at the tables, this would identify us as junketeers. They also encouraged us to wear it to ensure that we complied with the minimum bet guidelines. That way they could tell at a glance that we were on a junket and could make sure that the $25 bare minimum bet was in place.

I got a marker for $1000 and began my play. The table I was sitting at offered single deck; although shoe games were also available, they were virtually devoid of players. Right after the first hand was dealt, I noticed the pit crew watching the play intensely, just as Darryl had predicted they would months earlier. I was more aware now that I had experienced some valuable play with a real card counter. Although, they were short staffed in Monte Carlo, this was not the case in Tahoe; the all-seeing "Orwellian" eye was omni-present. When I raised my bet on one occasion, the floor man even walked up to the discard tray, removed the spent cards and counted back the deck. Well, this wasn't going to be as easy as it initially seemed. In the nervousness of the house, I sensed that they were afraid of something, and that something may have been my newly acquired skill; their scrutiny of me was actually quite flattering. So I just varied my bets to about four units, and that seemed to be just fine with them. After about two hours of play I was up over $1000, so I redeemed my marker, quiting for the afternoon.

Up at the room I was practicing the count with a deck that I acquired at the gift shop; it was like buying 52 rounds of ammo from the enemy. I had the time down to about forty seconds with fairly consistent accuracy. Now my major worry was strategy (what to do with the cards you are dealt, as opposed to the dealer's up card). Now that I was more comfortable with my speed, I planned to do one more session; this time I would bet a little more on the high count, after all, the bet was the most important thing, right?

Entering the casino, I spotted a table where I could sit at all by myself. Not the greatest idea, because you become the center of the floor man's world. I was the only one there that he had to worry about, and who's every move he could monitor. Had there been other players present he would have been distracted by their activities. Needless to say I just put in my time for the day, and left the table thankfully richer for the experience.

That evening Carla and I went to the Summit restaurant. It was renown for it's excellent food. It had a menu, which included wild meat such as deer and boar. Thanks to our VIP status our appointment was met right on time and we were immediately seated. The wine list was presented, and we didn't have to look further than the price. A bottle of Robert Mondovi Special Reserve caught our eye at a mind-boggling price of $175. Of course that's what we ordered and it was absolutely out of this world. For dinner, Carla had a lobster tail and I had the roast duck in orange and brandy sauce. The waiter suggested that if we wanted a soufflé for desert, we should place our order early because it takes a while to prepare. We did just that; but only one serving with two spoons.

The bill came to over $300, and after leaving a $40 tip, we left for our room and locked ourselves in for the night.

The next morning after breakfast, I thought that I would go downstairs to test the water at the blackjack table. It was about 11:00 am and quite busy, although not all the pits were open. There were three other players at the table and I sat down, at what, in 21 lingo, is referred to as second base (second person at the table). I had a fairly even run of cards; getting a lot of ties with the dealer, occasionally winning. The others didn't fare as well; the dealer got two blackjacks in a row and my tablemates couldn't run away fast enough.

I held my post for several more decks when the haunting event that originally sparked the writing of this book confronted me. The count was running four, with half the deck gone; the people in the pit were not scrutinizing me closely at all, when the two $300 bets were cast. I guess my hitting that fifteen must have reassured everyone that I wasn't a card counter, at least not a very good one, because they were all in good humor when I returned later that day. They fully expected to win back any money I had won in the previous session; management loves a confident sucker (a sucker is a person who hasn't figured himself out yet).

In the mean time, I had been up in our room poring over the hitting strategy from Stanford Wong's excellent book, "Professional Blackjack." Knowing what I know today I would have a negative turn around of $1200 in my total winnings, probably $1500 because I would have bought insurance. To this day, when I have a large bet out, I don't rant or rave when some "Jolly Jackass" hits a stiff against a dealer's six; because sometimes they take the dealer's make card. When they take the dealer's break card, and the dealer makes his hand, you would swear that they are on the casino's payroll. Like a gambler once said, "It's hard to believe that he beat out a million other sperm."

So it is the bet that is of the utmost importance; the play is secondary. However, in order to become a potent force at the table, I had to become truly efficient, and marry the bet to the play. Memorizing the hitting chart as the count changed, was crucial for this union to be fruitful, and memorize it I would.

Back at the tables, to finish off my time in the afternoon, I noticed that the floor man was very friendly indeed. He thought that I had gone from two $25 bets to two, $300 on a mere whim; no wonder he was smiling like a snake. Let's face it, if the count was high why would I hit the fifteen, and more important why was insurance not purchased? That is what must have happened, because they didn't casually go to the discard tray and count down the cards. Casinos hate to lose but love gamblers because they know the profits that can be reaped from them. When all the reaping and raping is over, the gambler is cast aside like a guest that has overstayed his welcome. As a guest I was determined to raid the fridge and their piggy bank at every opportunity. But for the remainder of the afternoon, the focus was on putting in my time, and rarely going more than three times my minimum bet.

My obligatory playing over, I was up about $2000. Carla and I decided to celebrate and just hang out at the lounge and maybe, with the right tune, we could do some "twisting and twirling" on the dance floor. We went down stairs at about 9:00 pm to a place that was "rocking." It had a cowboy atmosphere so we got to do the two-step until midnight, when we went back up to our room.

In the morning we got up early, had breakfast and took a shuttle to the Heavenly ski lift.

Carla and I weren't the best skiers in the world, and we were used to ski slopes in Canada, not those of Nevada. At home there are far fewer trees because of the altitude. Basically one could ski the upper extremities of our mountains without ever encountering a single tree. It seemed that you had the entire hill to roam about freely, not worrying about hitting someone or something due to the unobstructed slope. In Canada the tree line was only encountered at much lower levels of the mountains, where trees can grow more readily. On Heavenly, the entire area seemed to be a maze of ski-outs or narrow trails coursing through forests; only the occasional clearing brought relief to a couple of beginners like us. The narrow, heavily wooded trails created a fearful claustrophobic feeling. Who needed the impending danger of hitting a tree anyway? Fortunately after an hour our apprehension ceased, and we began to thoroughly enjoy ourselves. Many years later, Sonny Bono met his doom on a hill very much like the one we were on. Legend has it that a plaque was placed on the tree which read, "I GOT YOU BABE."

About 3:00 pm we went back to the hotel, cleaned up, got in some play, and then went for something to eat. We were scheduled to leave the following day, so I had to get in the required play that night in order to redeem our airfare before the departure.

After a quick shower I hurried down, got a marker and started playing; I couldn't do anything wrong. I just flat bet, varying my wager very little for about two hours, and managed to win another $1500; my only mistake was not betting more money. Had I been a gambler, and not the "enlightened" person that I am today, I could have paid off my mortgage in that one sitting. Come to think of it, if I weren't the guy that I am today I would have had to re-mortgage my home several times over the years. I quit playing at around 6:00 pm to see if my gal wanted to go for something to eat, and to take a well-deserved rest.

After a workout, a swim and a snack, I went back to play another two hours to complete my time, and could now relax for the rest of the evening. Unfortunately, I lost $500 and had to be satisfied with a $3500 profit for the trip. Topping off our trip, we went back to the summit restaurant for another great meal.

Before leaving the hotel in the morning, I redeemed my airfare from the casino cage. We hopped into the limo, which took us to the Reno airport and ultimately we arrived back in Calgary.

The trip was a real confidence builder for me. First, because I had taken my "first steps" in determining my own destiny with a more or less educated approach to game of blackjack. Second I had lost all fear of going against an opponent who had a built in edge in the odds department.

The saying "all this and money too," rang true for us on that trip. Sure, there would be losing sessions, but slowly I put myself in the same frame of mind as the casinos themselves, which was to retain the edge in the game. If the customer wins, (I consider the casino as a customer because I make money off them) it is good fortune at work. This of course was a liberating feeling. Everybody goes to a gambling haven at some point in their lives and the question you must ask yourself is, "Do I want to go as a lion or a lamb?" Don't be a patsy, go with a feeling of confidence; know well the ins and outs of the game and arm yourself with the knowledge that will make you the master. If you take the time to learn the simple steps of counting cards, and what to do with that count, you can go to virtually any casino in the world and have an excellent shot at making some money, and at the same time earning a free trip. There is a motto out there, "See the world before you leave it," and this is one of the most cost-effective ways to accomplish this at a minimum expense to you.

Chapter Six: The Big Event

After returning to Calgary, I spent the next year, 1983 digging myself out of the rubble of the collapsed real estate market. An old buddy of mine, whom I loved dearly, was a cookware salesman, and a damn good one at that. He wanted to get his own line of cookware in order to be more profitable in the business. In helping him, I inadvertently embroiled myself in the business end of the company. Before I knew it, I was in the cookware "game." We were doing sales calls all over Alberta, and the company that my friend, Doug W. and I set up, was doing quite well.

In December of 1983, I was at the office tending to some last minute business and emptying my car to get ready to meet Doug in Vancouver to do some skiing. It was Boxing Day (December 26) and one of the biggest snowstorms on record was dumped on us. Attempting to park my car, I unintentionaly drove up on a small snow bank and got stuck. I tried rocking the car, but it was just not going to be moved. So I did what any red-blooded Northern boy would do in a similar circumstance: I rolled down the window, put the car in reverse, went to the front of the car and manually started rocking the vehicle. Just as it was about to come loose from the snow, I gave it one more mighty heave and the car rolled free, but the bicep at my right elbow ruptured; it curled up to my shoulder, like a snapped guitar string and hurt like hell. I drove home and had a neighbor take me to the hospital; and that's where I stayed until my release, a few days after surgery.

I couldn't do anything with my arm for about eight weeks so I had to let Doug do the lion's share of the work. Unfortunately, he wasn't up to the task and opted instead to take ten sets of cookware and who knows what else and go out on his own.

There I was, stuck with the lease on the building for another six months and again unemployed. I couldn't work for about three months; when I finally could, I had to go back to surgery to remove the surgical screw. This screw, used to reattach the tendon back on to the radius bone, had backed out causing some muscle group to get snagged on this misaligned piece of metal. When I extended my arm the muscles twanged like a strummed guitar. After surgery, I was instructed not to work for another twelve weeks. About mid 1984, rather than go stir crazy, I decided to go to one of the local casinos to hone my skills at card counting. It was a small game, but one dollar to 25 was perfect for regaining my skills. In about ten days I could keep up with the count at a speed I considered satisfactory. I would go to this small time casino faithfully every single day before it opened, and remained there till closing.

In those days the casinos sure had it easy; the places were jam packed from noon till midnight. As soon as a place at the table was vacated like sharks at a feeding frenzy, there would be someone right behind him to take his spot. In reality they were like turkeys hoping for an early Thanksgiving.

But playing there for several months did take its toll. My relationship with Carla, already strained from my financial problems and also from my accident, finally blew up in my face. She packed her things and left for greener pastures. I couldn't blame her but it was still a severe blow.

Guys are always the last to know. Perhaps it's because we are late maturing. I, for instance, didn't really know what was going on till I was forty. Hell I'm well into my fifties and I still don't think I'm totally clued in as far as the psychology of the fairer sex is concerned. Anyway she was out of my life and there was nothing I could do about it but move on.

The crowd that hung out at our local casino was an interesting bunch, a mixture of people looking for instant gratification, hookers, pimps, drug dealers and degenerates of every race and mixture known to man. There were also the odd misfits like myself. If not for that handful of people that I have grown to appreciate, I'm sure that I would have gone off the deep end.

Just as in a business whose only product is the removal of money from your pocket, the lure of the occasional "lucky person" immerging as a winner is all-powerful. This "winning process" has the effect of creating the illusion that allows people to think that they too can ultimately end up in the "winner's circle." These "something for nothing" people, littered the slot machines and gaming tables at the Calgary casinos; and I am sure they overpopulate every casino around the world. At times one felt that they were in a "Twilight Zone" surrounded by snarling beasts, blaming everybody but themselves for the bad outcome of a hand. The same person craves recognition for some self-perceived brilliantly executed play that had caused the dealer to break. When this happened one would subconsciously hear that eerie theme that was the hallmark of that famous series. The voice of Rod Serling would echo in my brain saying, "Imagine for a moment that you are in a world where gambling is the sole industry, and where every skid in the city ends up, at one time or another, at your table;" pretty scary stuff.

The guys that I hung with were all there for the same reasons as myself. Either they were out of work as a result of the poor economy or some other unhappy circumstance in their lives that ensured them a lot of free time.

Due to the low maximum bets at the table, no one could ever gain any real wealth. But if you didn't watch your backside, you could dig yourself into a hole in a relatively short time.

We were all at the casino with a commitment to a system that would in some way occupy the spare time at our disposal, and to subsidize our meager income.

The ladies too were a totally different breed of people. As is the rule of life, you socialized with people in your immediate venue; I started dating the gals in the casino scene. From pit bosses to aspiring card counters, I ran the entire gambit. I am sure there were and are a lot of wonderful ladies in the gaming profession on either side of the table, because I talked to them on a daily basis. I found many of them to be intelligent and witty. Some even claimed to be following a system, when in reality they were hooked on the poison of gambling; a poison with no known antidote. These were the very people that I vowed to steer clear of, and yet found them in my most intimate surroundings.

Soon things began to change. One day a gent by the name of Fred V. walked into the casino were I was playing and introduced himself. He was representing the Marina Hotel and Casino, one of the casinos located on the Las Vegas strip. He said that he would offer flight, hotel and food for a three-day junket, and all that was required of us was a minimum bet of ten dollars. This I thought was truly amazing, and had to ask again about the player's minimum requirements in case I heard him wrong. He repeated his pitch and went on to tell me of the qualifications. I was to open a $5000 US line of credit at the casino and play three to four hours a day while I was there. I rapidly figured out the possibilities; even flat betting at a two percent disadvantage, one could lose perhaps a couple of hundred dollars, incredibly cheap compared to the previous junkets I had taken. I gave him the okay to open the credit line and we were set to leave on the following Friday night.

The week went by swiftly, I packed my bags and went to the airport on the designated night and found about fifteen others who also were flying down on the same junket. Amongst all the people present, there was a chap by the name of Hilton S. who seemed to have his head screwed on the tightest; so tight in fact, that I eventually called him the COMMANDER. He evidently had a Ph.D. in mathematics and was quite comfortable at the blackjack table. He would come out betting his maximum at a true plus one. "Why not" he said. With his count on a plus one, the casino's advantage has been eroded. That made sense, but to this day I don't come out till I have reached a plus three.

The flight took the usual two and a half hours and we arrived at about 10:00 pm. A quick survey of the place uncovered the fact that they were using five decks for their shoe game, and as a bonus also had one single deck and two double deck games. We made haste registering, dropped off our luggage and returning to the tables pronto.

I sat down and got a $500 marker at the single deck game; it was a five-dollar game to a maximum of $1000. I stayed there for about three hours, varying my bets from ten dollars to about a hundred. The problem was that if you varied your bet too much, the dealers were instructed to just automatically shuffle up. This suited me just fine as long as the dealer was fairly green, because on a low count you would just put in a black chip and get a shuffle bringing the count back up to zero. The problem with this approach was encountering a dealer who could not only deal, but also was able to track the deck fairly accurately. So when you came out with your black chip, on a low count, to initiate a shuffle, he would ignore the shuffle up rule of thumb, and go right ahead dealing out the hand when the deck was clearly at a miserable disadvantage to you. Man, don't you just hate it when people can't follow orders, and take it upon themselves to determine when to deal and when not to. Needless to say he got few tips from me, and I avoided him like the plague.

Time whizzed by quickly, and a new dealer came on shift; his name was Jeno. Right away I said to him, "Hey that's not an Italian name, the way it's spelt it sounds Hungarian." This comment seemed to gain his favor, he warmed up after that; the way Hungarians do as soon as you identify yourself as one of Attila's tribe.

I started losing, and he told me to go to bed and start fresh in the morning." I want to break out even before I go," I said. The tribal magic must have kicked in because I started winning. Several times he would have an ace up, and he would callout, "Insurance," and when I pretended to ignore him he would call out again, this time in somewhat of a louder voice, "INSURANCE." Then I would know that somehow he got a peek at his hole card, and I would slip in my insurance before he turned over his blackjack. Nobody at the table ever caught the play, just Jeno and I. Once I got even, I stayed true to my word and went to bed.

In the morning, I went down to "terrorize" the casino at 9:00 am. I say this because if you are suspected of counting cards they treat you like a criminal and eventually throw you out. Certainly the Marina suspected Hilton and I, but they didn't quite know for sure. So on we played.

Hilton had an interesting strategy. He noticed that he would often get a winning hand on the first deal after the shuffle, so he started with a black chip right off the top. A ballsy move, but one that not only got him more time at the tables before expulsion, but also more money. He also used luck to his advantage. After making the initial bet and winning, he would keep the black chip in his square even though the count had dropped. So he could successfully play, not only as a card counter, but as a gambler as well. I was totally surprised at how aggressively he played without getting removed from the premises of the casinos where he employed these tactics. Being a relative novice, compared to him, I tried to incorporate some of his tactics but to no avail; he would get the blackjack and I would get the "black eye." This usually drew a high-pitched epithet from me, "Luckeeee skunk" I would say. This would put a smirk on my scientific friend's usually stoic face.

Without a doubt he was not only one of the "winningest" players that I had ever known, but he also proved to be one of the luckiest. That night, we were playing on the double deck game and he had two huge stacks of chips in front of him. He was just flat betting black and getting some incredible hands. I was getting creamed and down about $500 even though I was flat betting only ten; the count went up and I went to a "quarter." He raised his to $150, got a twenty and I got a stiff; the dealer drew and got a seventeen. He then said if you want to win you have to bet a lot more. Being the man of science, he offered to switch seats with me, and being the kind of man that I was, I accepted. I raised my bet at his old position and got a 21 right off the bat; he in turn got my hand and broke. He just looked at me with his all-knowing smile and watched as I not only regained my loses but added to my bankroll. Then it all changed again after about three decks. He again was getting the lion's share of blackjacks and resumed his winning ways. Again he looked at me and said in his self assured tone," See, if you would have stayed here, the same thing would have happened to you." Of course he was right, but I wanted him to acknowledge that he was just plain lucky. So instead of him eating crow it was I that had to digest that nasty bird.

The trip was most enjoyable and when all the winning and losing was over, I was up $1200. Not bad for a weekend foray. I thanked Fred for bringing me along, and told him to keep me in mind for the next junket. I told him to put me down for two on the upcoming New Year's junket, just in case I found a companion.

The month went by quickly, and Fred phoned to ask if I still wanted two reservations for the New Year get away. Sadly, I told him it was to be for only one. A week later we were making our way for Las Vegas to again lock horns with the Marina Hotel and Casino for a three-day junket.

After arriving at the hotel I went right to work. My card playing expertise had improved greatly as did my play strategy, and the first night went without a hitch. On the eve of the New Year however, things went haywire. The playing conditions weren't the best, because it was hard to switch tables in the jam-packed casino. Unfortunately, I lost all the money that I had earned on the previous night.

That evening, the casino threw a heck of a party for the so-called "VIPs" that had answered the invitation to the New Year's bash. Even though I had only played there once, they must have regarded me as a member of this select group. They had a band that played the big band stuff like In the Mood and other Oldie Goldie's. I had a great time carousing around the dance floor; regrettably there were no single women around with whom to socialize. There were only three other guys that were single, and they sat us all at the same table. To make matters worse two of them were the "strong silent type." Getting a conversation going with them was like pulling teeth.

At least there was one older gent there that was talkative. His name was Art R., and he loved to let loose. The junket, it seemed, was the perfect vehicle to help him do just that. He wasn't much of a gambler and more or less followed the bets of the others. He rarely won, but did manage to keep his loses to a minimum. He and I were room-mates because there were no comps for single occupants at New Year unless you were a big player.

The two top places to be in North America on New Year's eve is either New York, where you can watch the ball drop in Times Square, or Las Vegas, where you could observe the drop box magically pull a disappearing act with your money at a blackjack table or any other game that you chose to play. Myself, I preferred the latter city, although I didn't relish the thought of my cash going down the proverbial drain. As a consequence of this New Year's demand, there was overcrowding, the rates in Las Vegas are the highest during this annual event.

I went down to the tables after midnight and noticed that the place was a lot quieter as I pulled up a chair at Jeno's table. We played and at the same time carried on a pleasant conversation, exchanging stories about our lives. He was an aspiring actor, getting the odd part in movie shoots around the city. He was fifty years old at the time, and full of charm and wit; I wasn't at all surprised to find out that he had a girlfriend half his age. So I often teased him about the age difference, deep down I was very envious. Imagine being fifty with a twenty five year old at your side. Isn't that every guy's dream? Is it a dream or a nightmare when a guy is ninety years old, in a wheel chair being chased by a jealous teenage husband? Anyway, I made no bones about the fact that he was one lucky dude.

Time was moving on, and I was getting tired. Luckily I was also up a few hundred so I gladly cashed in my chips and left the table. He said that one night we should get together and go out for a couple of drinks so we could chat at greater length. I said that was a terrific idea. We bid one another a very happy New Year, in our mother tongue, and retired for the night.

In the morning I got up to the loud snores of my roommate. It's real hard to get used to a guy in the same room when one is accustomed to being with ladies. If a girl snores its usually low intensity, when a guy snores on the other hand it seems like a deliberate and obnoxious act. No doubt Art's wife was happy to have him out of the house.

Slowly we awoke, got ready, and went down stairs to have a bite to eat. While eating he told me that Fred had arranged for the singles in our group go on a flight to the second most "notorious" brothel in North America, the famous "Chicken Ranch," located in Pahrump, Nevada. We weren't obligated to carry through with a carnal transaction, but if we did the price was $100.

The flight to the ranch left at 1:00 pm, so with little time remaining we grabbed a cab from the hotel and left for the airport. In those days there was a lot less traffic, and fewer hotels, so you could get away with leaving much later. The air taxi flying us out was, more or less, just down the street from our hotel at a hanger at the Hughes Air Terminal. There we met the three other chaps that we would share our flight with, and of course the pilot, poor chap, who was in a miserable state from the night before.

As we made our way out on to the tarmac the pilot asked if any one of us had piloted a plane before and I said that I had. I did have a private license in the seventies, but hadn't flown for about ten years. Naturally I didn't tell him that, as I welcomed the opportunity to fly the Cessna 206, an aircraft that I had not flown before. It was a single engine six passenger aircraft and I didn't need any special instructions to fly it. He said," Then you will sit up front." Still not too nervous, the others clamored on board, then the pilot, then me.

The engine was brought to life, and he went through his checklist, a routine matter for all pilots. He then radioed for clearance to an acceptable runway and we were taxiing for takeoff. He wasn't about to let me take off or land the craft, but once we were airborne and up a few thousand feet he trimmed the Cessna for a steady climb and pointed to a saddle in the mountains; that was my heading. I wasn't about to tell anyone that even a child could fly an aircraft after it was in the air, I just let them "stew in their own juices." The pilot then slumped down in his seat after assuring himself that I was competent enough to fly the craft. After that I was on my own.

The ride went smoothly until we reached the mountains. Then the bumpiness associated with rising air from the west started, gently at first, then becoming more violent as we proceeded directly over the steep rise. Again this was not new for me because I had taken my training at Springbank, a remote airport west of Calgary, nestled in the foothills near the Rocky Mountain range. At times we would be exposed to updrafts in that area so severe that I thought we would shed our wings. In comparison, the winds that we were now encountering outside Vegas were relatively mild. Unfortunately, for those people that haven't been in a small aircraft before, it was rather unnerving. Watching their faces in the mirror you could tell quite clearly that they weren't having as much fun as I was.

Once over the mountain I could see the airstrip at the "Ranch" come into view and the flight again smoothed out. The Pilot, who must have made this same trip hundreds of times, sat up in his seat when I throttled back in preparation for landing. I was just in the process of trimming down the nose when he said," I got it." This came as a welcome relief to the other passengers, including Art, who had no idea that I could fly and perhaps thought that I was going to land as well.

Finally on the ground the three passengers, the pilot and I made our way to the brothel. We were greeted by the "chief of security." He was a guy that looked like a "Mr. Clean" double, with a thick well-waxed handle bar moustache, and totting a pair of pearl handled pistols. He indeed posed as a menacing obstacle to any would be troublemaker.

Since the girls were all busy, he entertained us by giving us the "royal tour." This place, like the Mustang Ranch, had many trailers in a configuration, which made it look huge from the inside. We never had "the tour" at the Mustang, so I can't be sure if they featured any rooms for sexual "connoisseurs;" but I can vouch for the "special treatment" rooms at the Chicken Ranch. Mr. Clean showed us rooms with unique swings, the seat of which had a titillating opening, which one can only leave to the imagination. Another room had stirrups, two way mirrors, a room to make a video. Just about anything that you could possibly imagine pertaining to sex, or a sexual adventure, could be found at the ranch. Our guide also mentioned that the establishment catered to all sorts of people; from senators to street sweepers. They had peep holes all around the special rooms to make sure that the girls were in no danger and to ensure that everything was on the up and up. What if they were to place a politician, a sick group of people overall, in a compromising position for instance, on a video? These individuals might then be black mailed by the "Ranch" or any other party that got their hand on the film.

About a dozen girls were now ready and we made our choices. I tried to negotiate as usual, but because the airfare was some how weaved into the package, I had no success. Damn those middlemen. The girl that I chose was the prettiest, and we went to her room without any further delay.

Later, when we all met in the lobby, Art, an old hand at this sort of thing, immerged with a gorgeous brunette. On the way back to the plane he told me that he had caught a glimpse of her as she escorted another client to the back, so he decided to wait for her particular services. That's what a guy gets when he is still wet behind the ears. Fortunately I have never been back to one of those houses where I could have applied the techniques of a master such as Art.

On the flight back to Las Vegas the pilot confided in me that although the pay for flying this "special taxi service" was not great, the fringe benefits were excellent. He didn't elaborate as to how or when these benefits were enjoyed, but he left me with the impression that both parties found it mutually agreeable.

So another happy flight returned from the "Ranch," and we all piled into a cab to make our way back to the Marina.

At the room Art and I were pleasantly surprised. On our respective beds there was a gift that the hotel gave to all its players on the New Year junket. It is a silver plate used for nuts, condiments or something of a similar nature. It seemed very expensive as well as a grand gesture, especially for a guy like myself, whose only concern is to "bite the hand that feeds it." I had no urge to say, "Oh how nice, lets exchange gifts then shall we," knowing full well that the only gift that interested the casino was my money. Remember the casino is only one bet away from recovering the value of their gift. Of the thousands of bets that you will make throughout the year or have made, especially if you don't use a counting system, that gift is considered a tawdry pay back for being a loser.

I almost felt "biblical," as in the Old Testament, when Abraham's god appeared to him and instructed the children of Israel to borrow a silver plate from their neighbor along with many other assets just before their expulsion from Egypt. The bible uses code words, which of course have two meanings. To "know" someone means to have sex with them and to "borrow" something could only mean theft, because you have no intention of paying it back, particularly if your plan is "leaving town" next day. Isn't religion wonderful, a god can council thieves? So I too am going to show my gratitude to the casino for its perks and comps; I will take all that was "loaned" or given to me before I, like the Jews, got the boot.

Some may think that this is an extremely callous attitude, but keep in mind that I had the same objective as the casino. PROFIT. They were to be generators of money for me. They were my valued customers, the very thing that they expected from me.

When a customer takes me out for lunch it is not for an altruistic purpose; it is ultimately for commercial reasons. It is a classic application of corporation, client interaction. My customer hasn't necessarily benefited financially but they have high hopes and expectations. Unless I employ some low down, malicious, and sleazy tactic like card counting. They are showing their courteous thanks to me for sampling their product and perhaps sometime in the future, my support will manifest itself in a cash outlay.

Keep in mind that no casino is so lucky as to win all the time; just as no player is so unlucky as to lose all the time; if a casino did all the winning, who then would fill the those same casinos. Therefore a kind of a gray area is built around the relationship between the casino and the card counter. Who is the hunted and who is the prey?

Going into a casino where I am known often reminds me of that cartoon which depicts a coyote and a sheep dog punching the clock. It's all very polite; one says' "Good morning Harry" while the other replies "Good morning Ralph." But when they reach their respective stations, suddenly, their rolls become serious. The coyote ends up being the "whipping boy," and always gets clobbered by the alert sheep dog, loyally at his post defending the helpless flock. The coyote even tries slipping into a sheep skin suit and manages to scoot off with a lamb, unfortunately for him it turns out to be the sheep dog dressed in sheep skin, and the antagonist again gets a beating. The whistle sounds signaling the end of the workday and again the politeness returns as they meet at the punch clock.

We all know that if a casino is viewed as a "money tree" and virtually every visit turns into a financial red entry for the house, right beside your name, your days as a VIP at that casino are numbered. You will be considered a "Freddy the freeloader" type and as such are "persona non grata." Take while you can, because there is a signpost that glares at every winning blackjack player, ROUGH ROAD AHEAD. A corporation doesn't lay out a billion dollars so a nation of cherry pickers can pluck the fruits of their labor.

As a card counter, because the casino is viewed as a potential client, the gray area previously mentioned, confuses the normal company client relationship. This confusion causes a tremendous amount of stress applied on the shoulders of individuals hired to look after the casino's interests. The "sheep dogs" get overworked.

Assume for a moment that you hire a law firm to defend you in some court action, they do a good job and you pay them accordingly. You do business with this firm for some time and occasionally they make a pro bono phone call or type the occasional letter. This could be classified as a normal company-client relationship; with the sporadic perk thrown in as a PR gesture. Now consider for a moment a situation where this same law firm does real work for you and they only occasionally get a perk from you in the form of real money. Do you think they would be pleased with this inconsistent arrangement? Of course not, but neither was Pavlov's dog. That's why at all times you must be courteous and always show an upbeat attitude because there is not a single client out there that enjoys watching your play when you are rude, inconsiderate, and win in a consistent, obvious way. You must engage everyone in pleasant conversation especially when plucking the juiciest of fruit from their "tree of plenty." Like the lyric from a Beatles' tune," lying with your eyes while your hands are busy working overtime." There will be times that you will feel yourself mistreated. Then you should ask in a courteous and friendly way, for an explanation. Although you have created a "gray area" you are still considered by definition a customer.

The Big Event

When I enter a casino and take my seat, mutual respect is assured. When the money goes into the drop box it's like punching the clock. You are on the job, and if you have to change into a sheepskin to extend your time then so it must be. Many times I have seen Hilton coming out like a battle cruiser with his maximum bet; he is disguising his play. Due to his consistent wins, the casino has their suspicions of him; but rather than lose a potential client, (anticipating a future loser) they opt instead to do nothing. So the game goes on between two combatants. Just like the coyote and the sheep dog, we all have our work cut out for us. Although the card counter alone knows his job description, and knows where he draws his paycheck from.

After a sumptuous supper with Art at the Port of Call restaurant, I finally went back to the table and resumed playing. The casino was full to the rafters; a great day to be an owner. Many people had been over indulging in spirits and as a result were over indulging in betting. This does not subside till past midnight and I still can only sit down at a shoe game. The minimum bet at the table was five dollars but my minimum is ten so I did what came naturally, I bet five when the floor man was not looking on a negative count, and ten as a minimum when he was. This way I maintained the illusion of betting the lowest amount, as per contract. They were so busy that night that I don't think they even gave a second glance to a small time player like me. Anyway, at least I put in my allotted time and decided to cash out with about a $300 edge.

Breakfast in bed had lost it's allure, being single again had made me crave contact with other people, particularly ladies. So it was breakfast at the Galley coffee shop for Art and I, then shop talk with the other "believers" in this new craft.

As soon as we finished "jawing," it was time for "clawing" at the tables. Our flight was to leave that evening, so I wanted to get in some more play, not so much due to the obligatory three or four hours, but to win some money.

The sitting started out slowly, but after an hour and a half I started to make some headway. Soon I was up $1500, shortly after that I dropped a quick $500 and decided to call it quits.

For the rest of the day, I just hung out and chatted with other clientele. The flight was scheduled to depart in a couple of hours, and I just didn't want to risk losing any of my hard earned dough. I was up $1500 for the trip and considered that to be an adequate amount for effort.

The flight back went off without a hitch, arriving back in Calgary just before midnight.

Chapter Seven: The Traveling Man

In the later part of January 1985, my arm was not a major problem, as I used it more and more it became apparent that my shoulder had also sustained some injury. Like a nagging toothache the pain caused me sleepless nights without end. I was diagnosed as having a rotator cuff tear, and again my plans for retuning to work were delayed. My surgery was four months away so I had a lot of time on my hands.

Out of boredom I phoned Fred and inquired about junkets; to my surprise he said that he was just about to call me about a trip to Colombia; on a little island called San Andres. For up front money of only $2800, (that is to say, if you lost all that money, you wouldn't have to gamble any further and all the expenses would be taken care of) I could go for a fabulous one-week holiday.

What a great deal I thought; where does he come up with these bargain junkets. The airfare and the all inclusive would come close to that price by itself, and all we had to do was to gamble three hours a day. I gave my hearty assent right on the spot. The only difference was that I had to bring the money with me, but I had already did that once when I went to Monte Carlo, so that was not to be a huge step for me.

With all the arrangements made I was set to leave. The weather was getting colder and on the day we left it got so cold, rumor had it that the politicians had their hands in their own pockets.

At the airport I met the rest of the entourage. They included Hilton, his wife and a few more couples. Art, my brother, and then a new chap called Volker D., who was a huge Berlin type German that I took a liking to immediately. I could never get an answer from him as to what he did for a living, but I assumed that it was the stock market, because he used to tell me that he was doing well in that game. As for his other business ventures, he just said that he was in the import and export racket.

We boarded the redeye special from Calgary to Toronto, landing at about 6:00 am. From there another flight took us to Miami. After waiting a couple of hours, we boarded an Avianca flight, Columbia's national air carrier, bound for San Andres. On board I met Gordon C., the casino owner. He seemed like a nice enough chap, with a thick Texas drawl and an aggressive demeanor.

Upon landing at the little island airport he whisked us through immigration without the authorities even looking at our passports. It almost seemed that he was the "el padrino" of the island. I assumed that he didn't want the stamp in place due to the rather poor reputation that Columbia had with its second most profitable export. In fact, the immigration seemed to be bowing and scraping to him through the entire process; at one point even pointing out to him that his passport had expired. Most likely Gordon slipped the official some money and the entire matter was resolved. Not a bad way of doing business it gives the little guy an equal opportunity to make a bribe. All you need is money. In our so-called "democracy," you have to be a president or a powerful senator to get away with a felony. Ask yourself how you would fare lying under oath in an impeachment hearing, like Clinton's for example, and getting away with it. Not very well I am sure. Rumor had it that there was a tape with Monica telling the president, "Let me make one thing straight."

Well that got me thinking. "What kind of a casino does this guy run anyway?" Hell, maybe he doesn't even have a license. And if he does, how much did he pay and to whom did he pay it?

No matter. A van picked us up and we were driven to a fabulous motel. I ended up getting my own room for a change, and as a bonus at our hotel they had a terrific restaurant complete with a palapa style roof (a roof made from reeds). The eatery was built on stilts, positioned out on the coral reef, and was accessed by the use of a short pier. Volker, Kevin and I went to the restaurant and took advantage of the million-dollar view. We talked till sunset and then, surprisingly, the owner turned on the under water lights which illuminated the waters, hi-lighting the turquoise colored sea around us. We dined with this incredible backdrop positioned in such a way that we could watch the struggle for life in the water below our very feet. The temperature during the day was about 95 degrees and at night dipped to a very comfortable 80.

The Traveling Man

San Andres is closer to Nicaragua than it is to Colombia, and is located deep in the Caribbean Sea. Its location creates problems, territorially, between the two countries, and is constantly monitored by the Columbian armed forces. Twice a day, the one and only jet fighter, an antique Saber, lumbers over the various cays located near San Andres in a twenty-minute circuit.

We were not required to play on the first night, so we just relaxed and shot the breeze until 10:00 pm. The accommodations were quite adequate, but like most Latin American countries the windows did not have screens. Oh, did I say windows? I really meant window openings with shutters and louvers in them that could be closed for privacy. There was also a scent of petroleum in the air as they had just sprayed the room, to either kill the mosquitoes or make their environment so miserable that they wouldn't want to come in. If they used fuel I was hoping they used unleaded for obvious reasons. I had to open the shutters to air out my "casa" a bit to make it more habitable for both "me and the insects." As they say in Spanish, "Mia casa es su casa," (my house is your house).

The night gave way to a gorgeous morning, and the three of us made our way for breakfast at the motel bistro and learned about the day's upcoming activities; these included a trip to a cay within view of our island. The boat was scheduled to leave about 1:00 pm, so we had several hours to kill.

We decided to spend the idle hours at a public beach located two blocks from our motel, and from where we could board the boat that was to take us directly to the cay. Unfortunately, we got there about 11:00 am, so we had two hours under the blazing Caribbean sun, that was hovering virtually overhead. Keep in mind that the next country south of Columbia is Ecuador; this was not the "Sun for a Hun." It was so intense, that it could have ripped the hide off a rhino. The burn only manifested itself in the late afternoon causing me great discomfort and also kept me from enjoying some of the more interesting "perks" arranged for us by Gord.

At 1:00 o'clock we loaded into the boat, and I noted that there were three single women also on the craft. With my limited knowledge of Spanish, I tried to engage them in conversation and somehow got the impression that they were students vacationing on the island. Being totally naive of the set up, I asked them, what they were studying; their answer was, "anatomy." Gordon had obviously arranged the three girls on the boat, for us single men.

After arriving on the cay, our boatman jumped out to pull us in a little closer, and in the process, almost drowned. I had no idea that so many blacks could not swim. They have a higher bone density requiring greater effort to maintain buoyancy; thus their poor showing in Olympic events where water is the medium. Finally on shore we were greeted with the typical island fare, a "coco loco," which I translated to mean crazy coconut. This drink comprised of a coconut with the top lopped off, the "milk" saved, to be used as a mix, and then filled with rum. I suppose, after a few of those one would go a bit "loco" as they say on the islands. I for one didn't like them, and instead drank water to reverse the severe dehydration that I had endured.

The water surrounding the cay was as warm as a bathtub, and quite inviting. I spent about an hour snorkeling and watching the fish going about their business. At about 2:30 lunch was served which included a lot of the grouper and parrotfish, the same species that I had just observing in their own environment. There was nothing like the taste of fresh fish right out of the ocean, and into the pan. I had worked up a voracious appetite, and put a huge dent in the bounty from the sea. After lunch it was back to the water, this time with the girls along, for further exploration of the rocky atoll.

On the way back, one of the girls was getting very friendly with me, although I still hadn't the slightest notion as to her motive; some swinger I was, eh? Reaching the shore of our island I started making my way back to the motel and realized that the girl was tagging along. The time was just after 5:00 pm, and all I wanted to do was to have a shower, take a nap to be fresh for play at 8:00 pm. Quite aggressively, she followed me into my room, and failed to understand my disinterest in her. She caught me totally off guard when she followed me into the shower without a stitch of clothing. Though She was young and healthy, I was in so much pain with my sunburn that having sex was the last thing on my mind. I guess that's why the Latins called it "sol invictus" (the unconquerable sun). After the shower she told me a bit about her personal circumstances and her cultural environment.

In South America there is no such thing as divorce as such, because once you split up there is really only one profession that will accept you, and that is prostitution. It is a male dominated and highly Catholic society. If you are not a virgin your options are rather limited; you are looked at as if you are damaged goods.

The Castilian girls from Columbia, that is the ones that display light-skinned Spanish traits, are truly racially conscious, and refuse to have anything to do with the local blacks on the island. In so doing their clientele is composed of the Hispanic minority and the "gringos" like us, who occasionally come to the island to gamble. This also gives them a shot at "hooking" up with someone that is better off financially, and is able to afford to take them to restaurants, and away from their miserable surroundings. The one that I showered with said that she stays at one of the local houses (bordellos), called the "La Casa del Elafante," which I took to mean the Elephant House. This place was ineptly named from our perspective, because none of the girls there were over weight. If they weren't carousing with one of us, they would be fed twice a day with a meal consisting of rice and beans.

After hearing her story, we fell asleep and woke up about seven. I got dressed took her for supper, handed her ten dollars and bid her "adios." By then it was 8:00 o'clock, and I made my way to the casino to put in my time.

Once there I noticed that our entire group was present. I took a seat at one of the tables at the third base or last position and started to play. Our table spanked them pretty good that night, I think everyone at the table made some money; as for me I made just over $1000.

We played till midnight and I went home to nurse my nagging sunburn. When morning arrived the worst of the pain had left me, only my shoulders were still a bit painful. This was understandable as they endured the most direct overhead rays.

The previous night I was informed of a plan to go fishing on Gordon's boat. This I agreed to eagerly, as I thought I would feel a lot better the next day. I didn't feel the best, but yielded to group pressure and went regardless of pain and lightheadedness. The first mate, also a likable black guy, gave me some kind of sulfur based anti seasickness medication about an hour before we were set to launch. This livened me up a bit and all seemed to be fine after that.

We cast off at the arranged, time and were headed for the open sea, which I must say was quite rough. Although all seemed to be okay as far as seasickness went for the first hour, I went on top to get a captain's view of the panorama, and watched the people fishing off the back of the boat. Hilton came up, and we were carrying on a conversation when one of the other passengers cramming the area, let go of the foulest smelling wind that had ever passed by my nose. Hilton must have also caught a whiff of "the fragrant fudgie," because as hard as he tried to get out of the area it was too late. He started vomiting behind the captain, luckily missing all the instruments, but spraying all over the back of the boat. We were probably doing ten to fifteen mph so the breeze suspended a lot of the spray, and sent it to the back of the boat where Fred and his girlfriend were fishing. There wasn't a cloud in the sky, but Fred looked up, with one hand firmly grasping the fishing rod and the other hand outstretched, palm up, and said to his gal, "You know, I think it's raining." Well I laughed so hard I think I made myself sick. It was either from that, the vomit spraying all over the place, or from the sulfur tainted odor emanating from someone's bowels. As the witches in Shakespeare's Mac Beth said, "Round about the cauldron go, in the poisoned entrails throw."

I rushed down stairs to get sick, out of eyeshot from everyone. I succeeded, but just barely. Going back up to the main deck I saw poor Hilton, who is a big guy anyway, getting washed down with buckets of seawater. Vomit was all over the deck, all over him and there he laid, "the Commander," moaning and groaning. Like a Green Peace volunteer, one of the crewmembers was throwing water on him like they would on a huge beached whale. After getting an eyeball full of that I got sick again but this time for good.

The kindly first mate took me to the very bottom of the boat, into the crew's quarter's bathroom. There I could hug the toilet bowl without the prying eyes of my peers gazing at me in my violent throws of seasickness. But that wasn't to be for long, as everyone that had a weak stomach was heading to the lowest part of the boat to avoid the violent rocking motions. I stayed there for hours till we returned back to shore.

It was 3:00 pm when we returned to the marina, and a more welcome sight couldn't be imagined. I can't remember who got off the boat first, the "Commander" or me. The poor bastard looked sorrier than a "coonskin coat in a Georgia rainstorm." We both made a beeline to our rooms to get cleaned up, gaining strength with every step we took on the dry land. I made it to my room and showered away the stench of hour's worth of accumulated sweat from that afternoon. Then I collapsed in the bed, drained of all my vigor.

I woke up about 6:00 pm, showered once more, and then went to our quaint restaurant. There I met the rest of the gang and they all had a little something to eat, except for me, I had a lot.

We all arrived at the casino about 8:00 pm and took our positions. The dealers had that lean and hungry look. The play started, and I immediately detected that something was terribly wrong; a lot of us were miscuing on our double downs and the dealer was making far too many of his hands. Also, on double down situations the dealer would inadvertently, but often, bring out more that one card. That night I lost about eight hundred dollars, and was not too pleased about a lot of the double downs. I also noticed that the Texas "Godfather" had federal police, drinking, fully comped, at his bar, certainly not a very comforting sign, from a complainant's perspective.

The following day our host, Mr. C. as he is known on the island, was full of mirth and unusual gayety, having won big the night before. We had nothing planned for the day so convinced that they had done something to the shoe, we concocted a plan to thwart whatever they where doing with the cards. My brother was to sit at first base, with his eyes glued to the shoe making sure that the dealer was aware of his glare. I would take care of the count, and perhaps the multi cards wouldn't come out of the shoe like they did the night before, just at the crucial moment of a high bet double down.

The day was spent in a very happy laid back way with nothing to do but plan our revenge, just as our host had probably planned his revenge against us. After supper that night we went down to the casino arriving at the usual time and took our positions, with my bro at first base, to eyeball the cards and the shoe.

The play started, and within fifteen minutes we knew what they were doing. When one of us had a double down situation for big money, the first card in the shoe would be lifted by the dealer's middle finger, and then with the right hand, the second card would be extracted. They were using "Bee" brand name cards, which had the small diamond design on their backs, and were without borders; as a result, this tricky maneuver was difficult to detect. What we didn't know was how they knew when to lift the card, and when not to. Perhaps, more disturbing was the fact that they would continue to draw "seconds" even after our tactic of intimidation; refusing to remove our stare from that shoe. I guess having a cop eating and drinking free with an ugly machine pistol at his side, kept the sheep at bay. After the smoke had cleared there were no winners, and I personally had lost another $500.

We completed our minimum time, and vacated the premises, a little dizzy from what we had just witnessed. We had a late snack and a few drinks, it seemed that the only way we could get our money back was to eat our way to our host's bankruptcy. After that we all went to our rooms to mull over what had happened that evening.

The next morning the bistro was full, and somehow I was the last one to get there. Fred informed us that our "gracious" host had offered to take us to one of the outlying cays for a little picnic on his boat. It was approximately a one-hour sail so I agreed to go; a longer time would have risked further exposure to the malady of seasickness.

We were on the dock before 11:00 am, our departure time. No sulfur pills this time for the commander and I because I had suspected that those pills were the cause of our violent sickness. We went straight on board, to be greeted by our host, who was yet again in an extremely jovial mood. So he should be, I guess since his ulterior motive is the blatant theft of our money; an endeavor at which he was so far successful.

Arriving at the little cay, the real reason for the trip became apparent; it was to supply the tiny garrison stationed there with little extras in the form of food, beer, ammunition and women. These concessions must have been most welcome to these "marooned" soldiers who would repay their benefactor in some way or another. Little wonder that the dealers so blatantly cheated us under our vigilant shift, because they knew we had no recourse. Who could we complain to, perhaps the "Commadente" drinking his free beer at the "Godfather's" casino? The situation was now even bleaker than we had originally thought. Our host was owed favors from all sectors of law enforcement and the military. One must always adapt to new situations. If there was nothing to be done then just relax and try to enjoy your surroundings. Thus I decided to enjoy the warm ocean and went snorkeling.

I noticed that the fish were extremely plentiful on this small cay. Away from a heavily populated area, the underwater life could flourish and develop in a more natural way. This little isle was built on the shells and the residue of the wildlife that lived there before; the well that had been drilled on the island, had evidence of conch shells all the way down to the water source. The salt in the seawater must have slowly filtered out as it made its way down to the well, giving the soldiers a terrific fresh water source.

At lunch fresh fish was served, speared by the first mate. Lopping the top off some coconuts, he would boil off their liquid until only the oil remained; the fish were fried in this oil.

The first mate told me that he was born in San Andres, but in search of fortune he had gone to Miami. There he became totally disenchanted with the constant need for work to attain wealth. The ever-present taxman whirling around your pockets like an unwelcome fly was especially irksome. So after five years he decided to return to his native island. He said that he had left to seek a paradise that was in reality right under his very nose. Sometimes a person has to step back and analyze things from a different perspective to come to the realization that a far off "paradise" can also be a hell. I gained a lot of respect for out first mate that day. Applying his wisdom, I was determined not to make my stay on his paradise my purgatory.

On the way back we encountered a dozen dolphins playfully leaping across our bow. It was somehow gratifying to see fellow mammals in their aquatic world as they hitch hiked in our wake. Not a single person aboard was left unmoved by the company of these intelligent creatures.

We arrived back without the slightest hint of seasickness. It was mid afternoon, and a bunch of us went to the lounge next to "our" bistro to plan the strategy for the upcoming evening's play.

We were all convinced that something had to be done about the cheating; but not knowing how it was accomplished posed a huge problem. We decided to arrive early, and I would confront the floor person with a demand to inspect the cards that were about to be used. This, we hoped, would yield some idea of how they knew the values of the cards that were to be dealt.

Getting to the casino early like an unwanted "posse" we just sat at the blackjack tables waiting for the place to open. When the staff showed up, the floor lady brought out the cards that were to be used that night, and place four decks on each table. I noticed that the various packs of cards were without their familiar cellophane wrapper, and the seal on each deck was broken. Very casually I asked her to let me inspect the decks that were in front of us before we started play because they had been opened. I saw her swallow deeply, and since most of the junket players were present she complied with my request and handed me all four decks. I opened the first deck and going through the cards noticed that although the cards were exactly the same color, the texture was different. The ace to the nine, were smooth, and the ten to the king had a sandy feel to them. This was my first successful try at unmasking a cheat.

Now it finally dawned on me how it was done. Even to a person that doesn't deal, the difference between the feel of a smooth card and one that is gritty is obvious. During play, assuming that one of us had a large double down, the dealer already knows the value of the card, small for smooth large for rough. Thus he could discern whether to lift his middle finger, as in the case of a gritty textured card, and deal us the second card. Incidentally, this may have been a large card as well; over the second one he had no control.

By taking hits himself he too had the advantage in knowing what card would follow. If he had a stiff showing, and then if a face was to follow, he would simply lift the ten valued card and deal himself a second; that too could have been a face, but as you can see the randomness had been removed giving the house a huge advantage.

I demanded and got new decks from the red-faced floor person, and the game proceeded as normal. As a result, everyone seemed to fare a lot better. I got back my previous night's loses, and was ahead on the tally sheet once again. But unfortuately our host was not present that night, and now we had to await his revenge. What form that would take was anyone's guess.

After putting in our time we made our way back to the lounge to pull back a few drinks and revel in our improved circumstances. The cloak of doom that had enveloped us had vanished; we now knew that he knew that we knew. Most important was the fact that everyone on that junket realized that Gordon was nothing but a snake.

As I lay in bed a smile appeared on my face. Maybe in some small way the tactics, like those employed by our "gracious" host, were utilized to invent the game of "Spanish blackjack." This is a game that has all the tens removed from the deck. The difference between the Columbian and North American style is that they have many more advantageous rules. Most important than anything else; they make you aware that the deck has been compromised.

In the morning, I made my way to the eatery, and the gang was all there. Much backslapping was taking place throughout breakfast. Fred informed us that the activities that our host had planned for that day had been cancelled, undoubtedly because we had caught him cheating. Everyone already knew what a worm he was, and with this little trick, the people were introduced to his pettiness. I wondered how we would face off that evening. With not much to do for the remainder of the day we decided to rent some mopeds and explore our little island.

By Canadian or North American standards this little land mass was nothing more than a dot in the ocean. With its two-mile width, and ten mile length, it was hardly more than a big cay; one that would support many people from birth to death. Some people would even live their entire lives on San Andres, dying without having ever set foot on any other land mass.

The small island got its electricity from two diesel engines hooked up to two generators; these were alternated for maintenance purposes. While we were there, power blackouts were frequent, but for short periods of time.

The circumference of San Andres was about twenty-four miles, and except for stopping to look around, it would take no more than one hour to circumnavigate the place.

After we rented the motorbikes, five of us started on our way. All of us had single bikes except for the Commander; using the seat behind him, he took his wife on board. She was a pretty little lass who looked to be about half his age, and a third his weight. I often pestered him about robbing the cradle. It was quite comical watching the little bike, challenged so to speak, as it labored up the smallest of inclines under the ample girth of Hilton, with his petit wife Evelynn holding on for dear life.

We made a stop at one of the ocean geysers, so named because when the ocean rolled in, a gigantic spout would be created through a hole in one of the rocks. Further down the island there was a cave, touted to be a treasure depot of none other than the great pirate,

"Capt. Morgan." There were no historical studies taken to verify such a claim; it was just a tourist magnet. We were back were we had started in under two hours, and we spent the rest of the time getting some sun on the beautiful beach.

At six o'clock, we went back to our motel and got ready for supper and gambling. After a great meal, and a few cocktails we were ready once again to do battle at Gordon's infamous casino.

Entering the gaming hall I noticed Gord just scowling at my bro and I. We took our table positions; Kevin on first, and myself on third, at one of the available tables. The new decks were delivered to the tables, and the shuffle commenced. About three or four shoes into the session, our host took it upon himself to sit right in front of me and next to the dealer. He would be chatting to the dealer, whose name was Pedro, and all the while playing with the discard tray, and the cards it contained. While he was doing this he would pointedly greet the police as they came and left the casino. I noticed that he was placing and arranging the cards in two clumps in the shoe; one containing the small cards, and the other containing the large. In his Texas drawl he would say to the dealer, "Aw, y'all put them theah ones righ'cheer Paadro." Then he would lift the cards to the little card clump on the bottom; of course, the big cards would end up on the top. When it was time to reshuffle, he would take the big valued cards and shuffle them thoroughly; then he would do the same to the little card stack. But he wouldn't shuffle these two stacks together; instead, he would just place one stack on top of the other, and call for a cut.

As we sat there and watched, he was actually teaching Pedro how to cheat us. He was using the classic, "stacked deck shuffle." If you were an every day, garden variety, card counter it wouldn't matter where you cut the deck; either way you would be a loser. If you cut rich up to the front, the next hand would be a minimum bet because of the count drop, and you would win most of the minimums. If you were unfortunate enough to cut the little ones to the front, the worst scenario would occur. A high count would be created in a way that is not random, and if for instance, you double a ten against a six and get a small card you will in all probability lose; because of all the small cards left in the deck to make the dealer's hand. The dealer's aces would all require insurance due to the high count, but no face cards would appear; in reality that bet would be a give away for the house. A person would have to play virtually like a dealer, (try to make a hand) and if that's the case, then just where is the advantage?

So I suffered a loss of $500, basically flat betting the shoe for fear of making a bet due to the artificial count. Everyone else fared no better.

Had I been a more sophisticated player, I would have cut the rich cards up front, made my high bets then, and lowered the bet to minimum when the big cards were spent. As a blackjack player, I was still wet behind the ears, and it never occurred to me then to use that ploy. Who knows, Gordon hated me so much that he might well have had me arrested, and even roughed up by his "police force." In fact, I might still be rotting in one of their stinking jails, or worse. That man had enormous power; he had the island wrapped around his little finger with bribes and favors. It would have been extremely difficult, even dangerous to lodge a complaint.

Imagine confronting the cop at the bar, who is just wiping his greasy moustache after enjoying a taco with a few beers, and demanding an investigation into the nefarious dealings of his benefactor. How totally naive that would have been? As a visitor, and a "gringo," who would never return to the island, your influence would be nil. You couldn't expect justice from a man who is attracting tourism to the island, bolstering it's economy and subsidizing, not only it's inhabitants but also the local constabulary and the federal police. The best thing to do is to tell everyone, for their own protection not to go there. Most important: steer clear of any establishment that is not monitored by a "neutral" third party, like a gaming board or commission.

Keep in mind, that if the random shuffle process is interfered with, it can be deemed cheating. That is to say, I too am cheating if I am using the same process. In other words, if I front load a deck, make all my big bets in advance, leave the table, and then let the house maul the remaining victims because the count is low, I not only took unfair advantage of the house, I also threw the remaining people under the bus.

These are further gray areas in the game that perhaps in this particular venue, may well have led to my arrest. It may have been reasonably argued that putting in the different textured decks into the same shoe was a means of foiling the unfair advantage gained as a result of card counting. And once discovered, the other way to exact revenge for the house was to employ a method of corporal punishment which, let's face it, is not entirely unheard of in Columbia.

Always remember, that a casino is a venture built and geared for one thing, and one thing only; PROFIT. The best thing to do would have been to go on a vacation yourself, take a small profit and not interfere with the losses of your peers. I heard someone say once, "All the people that gamble can't win, someone has to pay the freight." Keep that in mind the next time you travel. If with a friend, don't sit at the same table, if you see a betting situation bet it, without alerting anyone of the possible advantages. If you see a "damsel in distress," try not to council her, if you feel that much pity buy her lunch or a drink but don't trip up your win process.

You can very well imagine, that after such a scenario of blatant cheating by overt card manipulation, once more we were in a gloomy mood. The consumption of food and drink was the only way to get even with the house. Volker went as far as picking up a lady at the "La Casa del Elefante," wining and dining her on our host's expense, and afterward merely driving her back.

The next day after breakfast, we went sun bathing at the beach. The top of my scalp was unbearably itchy. I thought that somehow I had contacted lice or was a host for some other parasite. I asked my bro if he would be so kind as to inspect for that possibility. He looked at it and burst into laughter saying that my malady was not due to lice but rather the sun, adding that the little bald spot had the worst burn that he had ever seen. So added to my problems, I was now confronted with this little sunburned bald spot scenario.

Because of the hatred that the host felt for us, the fishing trip that was scheduled had been cancelled. So the gloves were off, and he was paring back his expenses in the realization that his profits hadn't met his expectations. Now we had to worry about our money that he had on deposit. Think about it for a moment. He cheats us blatantly, has the legal representatives of the government drinking in his establishment, delivers military hardware, food and women to outlying garrisons and has our money in his private lockup. I asked Fred if he had some signed papers, concerning reimbursements of our deposits, he assured me that there would be no problems in that department, because we had the receipts for our money; the markers that we had signed would be removed and the remainder returned to us. So the rest of the trip, we had to restrict our losses.

The Traveling Man

The day seemed to rush by, and three of us decided to step out for supper and go to a restaurant that served turtle. This was meat that tasted much like veal, and due to the turtle's protected species status I would have preferred to eat veal. The meal was quite reasonable and came to about eight dollars including the tip. This meager price was certainly worth this once in a lifetime opportunity to taste the meat of this armored reptile for the last time. This was also the only meal that we paid for during our entire stay.

At meals end, it was 8:00 pm and the casino awaited our presence. We arrived in ten minutes and the "bastard" was again at my table, and right next to me. I did what any red blooded Canadian would have done, I went and played craps. On the way over, I was hoping that the dice, like the cards were not in some way compromised; or that the "host" would not play with them and put in a quick switch. I spent the rest of the evening at the craps table, losing only $300, far less than I would have lost, playing blackjack.

The way it turned out, Gordon never came to the crap table because of course the game has a built in edge for the house of slightly more than a half of a percent, even if you played a perfect game. I yearned to retrieve my deposit and then I could tell him what I thought of him.

It would have to wait till after the next day's session, because you can't get a refund until you have put in all your time at the table. I will have to bite my lip until "manana."

Upon leaving the casino all of us were antsy to just get all the crap over with and be done with the island and our petty host with his cheating ways. We together then went straight to our little bar, and proceeded to get loaded.

I awoke to a gentle drizzle that seemed as mild as the water in our shower. I walked over to the cafe and met the usual suspects. During breakfast they informed me that the evening session would commence at 6:00 pm so that we may complete our play, redeem our markers and get our deposit returned, if we had any coming. So maybe we would see the remainder of our deposits after all.

What the heck is there to do on a rainy day in paradise? "Hey" said Volker, "let's go to the Casa Elefante and chat up some ladies." This guy just loved to be in the company of women. About noon we acted on his suggestion, and went to the whorehouse.

What squalid conditions, there was a bar with women hanging around trying to snag a "date" with stray guys as they walked into the cantina. The more normal looking girls zeroed in on the three of us as we came through the entrance. Volker started rapping with a pretty Columbian senorita, and they went to the bar for a drink. In this bar, the only people that drink were the customers; the girls get a concoction that looks like a drink but is in reality a non-alcoholic beverage. This costs the patron one dollar fifty cents, of which one dollar goes to the bar and the fifty cents to the lady. A pretty blonde approached me and I agreed to buy her a drink but abstained from having one myself. I was always suspicious of the hygiene conditions in these places, and as a result rarely drink or eat unless I could see some effort being made at cleanliness by food servers or bartenders.

After a while, to get out of the smoke, the lady and I left the bar to sit out on the veranda. There she propositioned me to take her out, and at no charge. Inquiring as to how that was possible, she told me that her rent at the casa was one dollar a day for living expenses. Any money that she earned above that was hers to keep. She could cover her living expenses with a couple of drinks and after that she would prefer to "date" men of her own choosing. Guys like me can afford to take them to restaurants and feed them something other than beans and rice. The Casa must be a government subsidized institution to provide a minimum existence for girls who for some reason have fell through the cracks of the religiously dominated social grid. Some of these girls apparently have children of their own, and the reason that they are at the casa is because they left their husbands due to spousal abuse. The "Casa" must second as a women's shelter, albeit one that is bizarre by our standards. All I can say is that if you are a girl in a Latin American country, "choose your husband very carefully."

I made a suggestion to my cohorts that we go for lunch with the girls, after all isn't our host paying the tab? I wanted him to squirm a little when he got my meal and beverage receipts. We piled into a dinky little cab and scooted off to our motel bistro. We told the ladies to order anything that they desired, as money was no object. We laughed and joked throughout the afternoon, and soon it was time to get ready for the casino. We made our way back to our rooms and the lady that I was with insisted on coming in and showing me her gratitude for the "time off." With little persuasion we entered the privacy of the room to enjoy some "rest and relax" until it was time to go to the casino for our final day.

The gal that I was with wanted to stay until I returned from the tables. But since it was to be our final night I told her that would be impossible because we had to get up early to catch our flight to Miami. I slipped her a few dollars and paid for her cab back to the casa. Later I was told that instead of hiring a cab she opted to walk home and pocketed the money. These poor girls certainly deserve a better lot in life. But for one bad choice, they are now condemned to a purgatory, catering to the peculiar lusts of a multitude of men that come to their island "paradise."

I joined everyone at the casino just after it opened and began to play twenty-one. The host saw me and dashed over to my table like a long lost friend. He sat right by the shoe. I decided he was going to jump through hoops that I set up, not the other way around. When that shoe was done, I went to the next table and left the stacked deck for someone else to worry about.

I went to a nearby table and sat down. The dealer shuffled the cards in that same peculiar way and it didn't take long to realize that he knew how to stack them all by himself. I guess the other night Gordon was giving personal, "on the job training" in the art of the stack to a novice like Pedro. Due to those devious obstacles I played for only two-hours, then I went to the wicket cash out and redeemed my deposit prematurely; further play was pointless. Our host's wife was there and penalized me $200 for quitting early. I think many others did the same as me now that the owner was exposed as a cheat and a charlatan. Why play any further, knowing that he is literally trying to squeeze every last penny from our unprotected pockets.

I wasn't totally downcast however, because I met some interesting people with whom I have maintained contact. Even though I was down a total of $800, I was really pleased that the "bastard" who tried to cheat us took a bath on the trip. In addition to the cost of the flight from Canada to Columbia, all the other extras had to come out of his pocket, too. I also got some valuable experience in about how easy it was to get cheated if you are not "manning the gate" at all times.

Later on all of us went to a fiesta. The strains of the trip began to fade as we let down our guard, and let loose with laughter; and there was plenty of that. We partied well into the night, and why not, we could always sleep on the plane.

I woke up at 7:00 am, had a shower, packed and met the gang for breakfast at the bistro. Unfortunately, I ate so much the night before that I couldn't find the room. So, it would seem that our Mr. C. saved the cost of at least one meal.

A van picked us up a short while later at the congregation area and soon we were on our way back to Miami; without even a "bon voyage" from Gordon. On board Fred told me that he was really pissed with my bro and I for exposing his operation as a swindle. As a result, Kevin and I were 86ed (not welcome) at his casino. How silly, as if the others would be busting down the doors to go back.

Once we arrived in Miami I talked Kevin into taking a side trip to the Bahamas, so I could recoup my $800 loss. I had seen an introductory offer advertising for $69, a return ticket to the Cable Beach Casino and Resort, including a two night stay; this was to celebrate it's grand opening. Without too much persuasion he agreed to go. After making all the arrangements at a local travel agent we set off on this new leg of our original journey.

What a difference. No looking over your shoulder for the cops at the bar, or watching for cheating, just old fashion rest and relaxation. Kevin wasn't under the gun as much as I was because he had broke out even in Columbia; it was I who had to play catch up.

I lost a couple of hundred before my fortunes turned. By the end of the first night I was even, and hungry to show a profit for the week. Unfortunately, after many sessions of up and down reversals the following day, I remained at that level. My bro fared a lot better, and was up $1200.

We took off for Miami the next morning, making a connection to Toronto. An old friend of ours, Peter R., worked for Air Canada at the time, and fixed it so we could stay over night without any extra charges. Ed K., a dear old friend of mine, originally from Calgary, met us later. The four of us went to his place and had a howling great time; the four comrades in one room, plotting, scheming, roaring with laughter and great humor; looking at the lighter side of a world, seemingly gone mad. It is always a pleasure to meet with these two interesting and intelligent characters. Like plugging into a battery charger, I get reinvigorated and am lighter of step than I was when I arrived. We all agreed, that some how the street sweepers of the world have gained control of the reins of government through a system called "democracy," definable also as "fashionable anarchy." The mob's bad taste and bad judgment has swept the rogues into power with the connivance of the "elitist" media. Any attempt to thwart this trend is immediately nipped in the bud like some weed by the managers of correct thinking. These managers are totally out of touch with events at street level, and are preoccupied with money, power, and the new world order.

Thus we roar at the socially accepted stupidity of thinking that a vote cast is actually serving the greater social good. Like sheep in a flock we are steered by an "all too common" desire to be accepted by the communal warmth of the herd. A true leader stands apart from the whole, and is able to apply cold calculated reason, without the fetters that bind him to that which is generally referred to as "the common man." We, the unrepresented middle class, have been effectively robbed of a say in international, national and local events to a point that is almost criminal insanity.

We closed our "summit meeting" formulating a slogan for future battle. "Middle classes of the world unite and throw the bums out of office," and replace them with…? Blackjack players and Nihilists?

The next day we "uncommon gamblers" were on our way home to regroup, and start plans for our next foray.

Chapter Eight: Getting Involved

Fred had set up another junket going to the Marina, slated to leave in mid February 1985. Las Vegas was getting to be one of the favorite places for my brother and I to hang out, so we happily agreed.

We were required to put in seven hours of play for the full comp; so I decided to get right on it. Picking a table with two other players, I ask for a marker, and was playing a few hands later.

After my experience in San Andres, I become extremely sensitive to irregularities in dealer's antics. A fellow by the name of Chuck was dealing to us, and was constantly looking at his watch. He wore his watch on his left hand, which also happens to be the same hand in which he holds the deck. When he looked at his watch he turned his hand from the palm up position, to the palm down position. This is a natural move in order to extend the thumb, as the ulna and the radius bones in the forearm are re-positioned from palm up to palm down. A move like that makes me very nervous, because as the thumb is extended, it can be mechanically maneuvered to push out the top card to see its value. I'm not saying that I will be cheated by virtue of the fact that the value of the card is now known, but if there is a personality glitch between us, the temptation might be too great to resist. If for instance, I am doubling down on an eleven, the dealer pretending to look at his watch notices a ten, he can then quite easily pull back the ten all the way, exposing the second card and giving me that one instead of the sure winner. This is known in the trade as dealing "seconds."

A fluid dealer can make this move virtually undetectable; this is why it is so dangerous. If you happen to be at a table where this is taking place, first, as nicely as you can, notify the guilty party that his antics make you nervous and would he please refrain from those tactics in the future. Most of the time they are just antsy to take a break, and are looking at their watch to see how much longer they have before they can "take a load off." Work with them. Remember, their job is a lot more boring than yours.

119

Getting Involved

In reality, it doesn't matter from where in the deck the dealer pulls the card; if he hasn't looked at it so as to maintain its randomness. Would it change the outcome? It may but I wouldn't care if I were dealt the second, third or even the bottom card, just as long as there haven't been any "sneak peeks." The next card could be a five or a ten I have no idea. If it's a ten, that's great, if not I would then hope for the dealer to break, or hope that I end up with a higher valued hand. The advantage is this: IF I GET STIFFED, I DON'T HAVE TO HIT, IF HE GETS STIFFED HE MUST, especially on a high count. If there is a small card coming in the next two cards, your chances of getting stuck with it are exactly the same as his, it's not the end of the world, even if you lose.

Remember, a lot of times you will be stiffed on a double down, at least have the common courtesy not to whine about your misfortune until the dealer makes his hand. How many times have you doubled on the eleven, ending up with the ace and bemoaned your bad luck; only to win in the end regardless of being stiffed. If no one knows the next card, it even makes the game more exciting. Adding the element of risk to playing twenty-one is not uncommon.

As you can see, I'm not at all high on single or double deck play with dealers who know the "ropes." They have the option to shuffle up at any time during the play, taking away any positive tendencies that the deck might garner. So, if they don't "cheat" you blatantly, they can do so in a more "legal" fashion, by taking away the high count.

Imagine some poor scamp, who is a confirmed flat better, entering a casino to test his luck at a 21 table. He flat bets through a negative run of cards, losing most of his bets. Then just as the deck turns positive, a situation where he now can win most of the hands, the dealer shuffles up, robbing him of the chance to recoup his losses. In this exercise, our player better have a lot of exceptional luck or he will again go home a loser. Playing mostly negative situations ensures that the house is playing mostly with a positive edge. Like stacking the deck, I consider this to be another form of cheating. The only real way of dealing with this situation is to befriend the dealer or leave the table.

After about an hour at the single deck, I called it quits and moved to the Marina's five-deck shoe game. At least in a shoe game they insert a cut card to indicate when a shuffle is to occur; or so I thought in my naivety. I played there for another hour to an even draw and called it a night.

The following morning Kevin and I went straight to the shoe game after breakfast. A lady was dealing to us and the floor man was a gent by the name of John T., who was to become an associate of mine at a later time. We started playing to an extremely low count and I got a pair of fives, which I proceeded to split against a seven. I knew that it was a very unorthodox play but I had the minimum bet out and wanted to see some cards. I split and re-split to the maximum and the dealer told me that what I was doing was not advisable play. I told her that when your learning a game you can expect it to cost you some money. That clump of low cards kept resurfacing, until another dealer relieved her. Chuck, the guy that was dealing to me the night before was on a strange schedule, and was back after eight hours off. He shuffled the cards and began the deal. The count was on a steady ascent, and so were our bets. We kept winning every hand and would press half of the previous bet for the next hand. Chuck would yell out "checks play" every time, and finally, on our last bet of $600 a piece, John came running over and told Chuck to "pull" the shoe with two decks left. As if he didn't hear him correctly he asked him again what he wanted. John raised his voice a bit more and said, "You heard me, I said pull the damn shoe;" and he did just that. He apologized, telling us that he had never seen that happen previously and then he reshuffled.

Kevin and I were totally taken aback; because we had never encountered a dealer who removes cards from a shoe in mid play. We were so dumbfounded we went to the lounge to appraise what had just happened. We were really over betting, but were winning every hand so why not "ride a streak" of luck while it was in our favor. It must have dawned on John that we didn't know what we were doing when we split the fives, not once, but to the max. Or perhaps it had the opposite effect, suspecting us of perhaps knowing too much. In any book that I have ever read about the game you are instructed to either hit or double a pair of fives, never to split them.

Now when I go to a Nevada casino, I never do outlandish things like splitting tens or fives, or doubling on a hard twelve unless, the floor man is vacant from his post. If these antics work they think you are some kind of a card "guru," or too lucky to be playing in their casino. If it doesn't work, you are out a lot of money; it's a lose lose situation. You could either be barred, or they can make your stay miserable.

Getting Involved

There we were, at the casino afraid of the single deck; and they were afraid of our shoe play. From now on they would watch us like hawks. I asked Fred V. if they would call a truce and let us eat their food, drink their wine, and rest when we got tired and then, when it's all over, fly us home. He just laughed and told me to do the "right thing" and all will be taken care of." You mean use your head instead of your brawn," I iterated. "Not exactly," he said laughing, "The only creatures that make good use of their heads are woodpeckers and c**k suckers."

We had to put in four hours apiece before the entire tab was forgiven; so on we went to the double deck.

For the most part, playing the double deck can become an art form. It is somewhat like a shoe because it is multi deck, and a lot like the single deck, because it plays out rapidly. The problem is that you can't get the dealer on the ropes like you can on a shoe, because often they deal just more than a deck and then shuffle up, often in the middle of a good situation. We played at the double deck for about two hours, each of us losing about $100 before we realized that our place should have been back at the shoe.

John's shift ended, and a new floor man took over. We raced over to the "shoe pit" to capitalize on the situation. We told them that we were on the junket from Calgary, and then started to play. Losing $100 right off the bat, I asked for another $500 and the new floor man, named Fred, brought the marker over in a snit. I asked him what the hell was picking his ass. His only reply was, "You know Goddamn well," then turned and left. This really bugged me, so I told the dealer to leave me out of the next hand while I had a little chat with Fred.

Cornering him by the crap table, I told him in no uncertain terms that I thought his attitude was not only rude and disrespectful, not only to me but also to the other people at the table. I felt his unprofessionalism warranted an immediate apology. He said basically that I was counting cards, and that he wouldn't apologize. "Look Freddy my boy," I said, "if you don't, I'm going to tell your shift boss that you swore in front of a bunch of sweet little old ladies, so if you value your chicken shit job, get your ass over there right now or I'll blow the whistle on you."

I went back to the table and gave Kevin a wink. He knew that I had attacked the sickness; but wasn't aware of what I prescribed for the cure. A few minutes later the bungling old fart came over to our table, face red as a beet and blurted out an apology to everyone there. I didn't want any more trouble from this guy so I said, "At times we all bring the problems that we face at home to our work place. Some of us, luckily, don't have to deal with the public like you do, but it's refreshing to see that you have the fortitude to acknowledge your mistake." That's the last time that guy ever gave us any problems. He even tried to be nice to me after that by giving me comps and other perks. The moral of the story is if somebody is presenting himself as an obstacle, find out their weak spot and nail them. Don't let yourself be bullied, if you do, you will have earned their disrespect, and will forever be back-pedaling in their presence.

Now, we had them exactly where we wanted them: in a game with a cut card buried to a point where we had just under four decks to play with. As a bonus we also had a floor man who would sweat bullets, but would also hesitate to "pull a shoe" on us. Now all we needed was some cards and a good count to smash open their "piggy bank."

To fantasize about recreating the earlier events and actually having them happen were two different things. We just couldn't replay the events as they had occurred that very morning. It turned out that we had only won a couple of hundred at the shoe, but having put in all our time at the Marina, we made plans to go down town.

We heard that the El Cortez had the best rules in town for its single deck game. They had a feature that no other casino had at the time, double down after a split. The casino was located about three blocks east of the Horseshoe and the Mint, in case we felt a need to go.

The El Cortez seemed to be an old casino, and to add a little known trivia, was even owned at one time by "Bugsy" Segal and the boys; this was before his famous Flamingo venture. They had evidently bought it for about a quarter of a million and then flipped it a year later for about a $100,000 profit.

Upon entering the place you could detect a foul odor emanating from the carpets that seemed to be there from day one. We walked through the dreary slot area that reeked of cigar stench, then on to the even drearier blackjack pit where we each bought $100 worth of chips. Play started and the floor man walked right up to our table and watched our every bet. On a good count I would go from five to ten without a reaction from his sad, horse like face, getting a good run of cards regardless of the count. The floor man seemed to get truly perturbed at the "break-in" dealer who had a hard time winning a hand. Once I raised the bet to twenty-five, and she dealt us two terrific hands. On seeing this he came over and gave her a kick as if to say that a five times rise in the bet is grounds for a reshuffle. When he left I asked her why she allowed the guy to kick her. She said that all the casinos in the downtown area are break-in casinos, that is to say, places where novice dealers get trained in actual playing conditions. She said that after a couple of weeks in a dive like the El Cortez, she would go on to the Horseshoe. After about six months time she would then go to work on the strip. All the dealers complain about the inhumane conditions there, but it's a job; a real enlightenment for me. Welcome to the employee's world of gambling.

Another dealer relieved the girl and we carried on with our winning ways until the pit boss pushed our bets out of the squares, and said that we could no longer play twenty-one at that casino again.

This should be a test for some budding card counters or maybe we could inaugurate a "21" Olympics aptly called, "How long can you last at the El Cortez?" Remember that anyone can get barred from virtually any casino, but it takes cunning and guile to stay undetected. Check out the El Cortez, and see how long you can spar with the pit crew. If you last an hour, you get a gold medal, 45 minutes will earn you silver, and half an hour will get you the bronze. Anything less than that, and you don't qualify.

One caveat however, girls last a lot longer than guys as card counters because Vegas is still a macho town, in other words the gentler sex is not expected to burst into that male dominated field of blackjack. Therefore if she is found to be attractive in some way to the floor man, or indeed a dealer, they will be flirted with, perhaps propositioned to. But for sure the last thing to enter the mind of a male employed by a casino is that "this chick knows what the hell she is doing." If she at first wins, well, she got lucky. If she again wins, she got extremely lucky. So for the girl blackjack players out there vying for the gold in our private little contest, go for it, because it's there for the taking.

Due to their chauvinistic attitudes, the pit crews are setting themselves up for a fall. When I first starting out I would get the eyes that were snide and the lady got the free ride, and to make matters worse she was, admittedly a lot better than I.

After getting the "bums rush" from the El Cortez we walked down to the Mint, to try our luck there. The Mint and the Horseshoe were made into one casino in the later 80's by knocking out a wall that was shared between the two buildings. However in 1985, they were considered two of the liveliest casinos in "single deck country."

We sat down at a table with a lady who had some very interesting features. She wasn't what I would call exceptionally beautiful, but she carried herself with a sort of "elitist" air that was almost captivating. She was tall, with dark hair, dark eyes, full lips and very sexy in her own way. She flirted with every one, but not the players. These are the very people she should have talked to, because that is where she earns her tips; and those tips as a rule net her far more than her wages. On New Year's eve for example, it isn't unusual to hear dealers, at Caesars Palace for instance, getting $1000 for the night. So obviously, courtesy should be in the forefront of every dealer's mind. I can't stress politeness and courtesy strongly enough, whether a player or a dealer, keep a civil tongue in your head. Because our snobbish dealer didn't understand these hard fast rules of the dealing game, I am sure she couldn't find her way to "the toke box."

Making bets in a single deck is a little more difficult than in a standard shoe game; because of the paranoia due to card counters on one hand, and the shortness of the deal on the other. I usually start out with twice the minimum bet; in most cases a minimum of ten dollars. At the count of zero, the advantage to the casino is about one percent but when the count goes up, you can easily get away with quadrupling your bet to forty dollars. This can be accomplished without too much anxiety on the part of the pit. If they are busy with other things, raise your bet even higher. The nice part of this strategy is that if you lose and the count drops, you can also lower your bet, which is a typical gambler's tactic, "this isn't my deck" mentality. When the count stabilizes, usually on the re-shuffle, double the minimum bet again. Using this method you will find that you will be kicked out less frequently.

While playing at the Horseshoe, I did however find that this method doesn't always work. Employing the same tactics that I had previously used at the Mint, after an hour of play, the floor man approached me from behind, tapped me on the shoulder and informed me in a low voice that I couldn't lower my bet. The guy next to me was betting all over, from five to a hundred dollars, so I asked the floor man in a loud voice, "How about that guy there, he has been betting $50, then $10, then $100. Why don't you tell him that he can't lower his bet?" He said that this restriction applied only to me. If I didn't like it I should then leave the casino. I replied that if he gave me a comp for food and beverages for two, that I would leave, putting an end to the commotion. To my surprise he readily complied. Kevin and I then ate, discussing a plan at the same time to target the Union Plaza, at the end of Freemont.

We entered the casino and plopped down $100 a piece at a single deck game resuming play. An hour into the game I noticed a commotion at the crap table, located right behind us. The paramedics were there and a guy was on the floor with a bewildered look on his face. An oxygen mask was being applied around his nose and mouth. As if in a surreal world, while this man's life was hanging in the balance, the crap dice continued to roll until the number was made. The box man even stepped over him once to retrieve the dice that jumped the table rolling onto the floor. The man evidently suffered a heart attack mid game, and the roll had to be finished before the table could be shut down. It all seemed very callous, but as they say in football and Las Vegas, "The game must go on."

After that little display of wanton materialism, we decided to leave the place for the more "civilized" haunts of the strip. But first I wanted to see if the conditions at the El Cortez were any different on the night shift.

Once there, we noticed a couple of spots open at a five-dollar single deck table. We started playing and were getting nowhere fast. There was one chap at the table doing quite well, and I appraised his play as that of a card counter. He was a pleasant guy and told me that he works at a restaurant in the Four Queens, called Hugo's. He invited us to have supper there sometime and he would get a 20% discount on the bill. It took me a couple of years to "call in that marker," but when I showed up with a lady friend, not only did he recognize me but knew my name as well.

He was the only one at the table making any "dough." Although the conditions seemed to be much better in the evening than they were during the day, we decided to leave and let our man from Hugo's continue his winning streak.

At the Marina once more, I sat down with the only dealer that I could trust, Jeno. It was late at night as we played and talked about cooking. Playing for about an hour, I told him that I was going to call it a night and he reiterated that we should get together for an evening out on the town. I told him that would be great, but as I was leaving the next day it would have to be at another date. He suggested going to the Elephant Bar, a little bistro on Eastern, the next time I was down.

In the morning, at breakfast, I heard that a few months earlier, the Marina along with other casinos were the object of a scam and were hit for a lot of money by some people with highly sophisticated equipment. Jeno evidently, although not having a starring role, did get honorable mention. Here's how it worked. A miniature TV camera was worn on the belt buckle of the person who entered the casino as a player. He would go to the blackjack table, and stand at the first base position. In the old days they didn't have a built in peeping device as they do now. The dealer would have to actually physically look under face cards and aces to determine whether or not they had a blackjack under their up card. The man standing at the first position with the TV camera had an excellent view at table height. As if you put your face down flat on the table as the dealer lifted his hole card high enough so he could have a look. The resulting picture would then be transmitted to a receiver located in a van just outside the casino. An accomplice inside the van would be monitoring the dealer's down card, and would signal back to the person with the camera the value of his hole card. This was done by giving him a coded series of mild shocks via electrodes hooked up to his body.

They were discovered one day after a phony bomb scare was called in by a disgruntled loser, and security was scouring the place looking for possible leads. A security guard challenged the occupant in the van and caught him in the act. Carefully searching the van, they found a diary on various casinos around town on how much they made, and notes on various dealers. Above the Marina they had an interesting note about a big guy who wore a lot of gold chains. It said that with that dealer you didn't really have to use the camera, because he was so sloppy that he would flash his hole card all the time. Naturally, they were referring to my new buddy, Jeno. Well the next time I see him I'm certainly going to make sport of that entry.

We finished breakfast and sat down to a losing session at the double deck game; this kind of sitting I like to call, the "$300 free-drink." You just want to have a nice low-keyed game prior to leaving Las Vegas, the count goes up, unfortunately, so does your bet, and the dealer gets lucky. Oh well, it wouldn't as much fun if there was no risk involved in the game.

After we prepared our things, we got a ride to the airport in their limo. The flight home is always an interesting time as you reach into your pocket and count the profits of the trip. This weekend it was $1700.

My immediate thought was that I should open a US bank account to minimize the exchange losses that can occur when you occasionally suffer a setback at the casino. These are further proofs of professionalism done on a corporate level. You can always cut costs to make the company run smoother. Thus, I gave myself, as sole shareholder a higher dividend and higher profits.

Playing in Calgary at one of our casinos, I heard of another junketeer who took a flight to Nevada on a weekly basis rotating from Reno to Vegas weekly. One week he would go to the MGM Grande, in Reno, the next week it would be the Golden Nugget in Las Vegas. His name was Ike H. The arrangements on his trips were quite liberal. The requirements were $1200 up front to cover flight, food and accommodations, and the minimum bet was to be five dollars. Using basic strategy on playing through the $1200 would net you a loss of about 25 bucks. You can't live that cheap at home.

Ike's next scheduled trip was to be at the MGM Grand, in Reno. Reno was usually a single deck town offering the odd shoe game. At the MGM it was to be all shoe, but with excellent rules, including double down after split plus late surrender; not the best rule, but on a super high count it has saved me a bundle.

The plane arrived at 10:00 pm, and even before checking in we were at the tables checking out the game. We put in our mandatory three hours of play, cashed in, got our rooms and went to bed.

At the cashier cage I noticed a sign that Canadian currency would be honored at ninety cents for one of our dollars. Well that was damn good because the prevailing exchange rate was eighty-five per US dollar. As luck would have it, I had no "Canuck" currency at all on this trip. That was the last time that I went to that town without our "faltering dollar" in tow. They did have a limit of $1000 per person, but that was easily circumvented however, by opening a line of credit for $10,000, then maxing it out, and paying off the entire amount in Canadian dollars at the posted rate of 90%.

Our money at one time exceeded the US by as much as ten cents. But that was a time when the men running our government chose to produce things of quality. You can protect your economy in two ways, firstly by producing things that are high in demand and of good quality, or secondly by devaluing our dollar, making our lower quality products available at a lower price on the export market. The latter method is usually chosen by third rate or to put it in a more politically correct fashion, "third world" countries. Most European countries picked the quality method. One country in particular stands as a beacon in Asia pointing to a better way, and that country is Japan. Canada has thrown in her lot with countries such as Malaysia, India, Philippines and countless others who export lower quality products at bargain prices due to low valued currency. It really doesn't take an economist to figure out that even the USA is lagging behind Europe qualitatively. I had always thought that, in the not too distant future, the German mark would be at a par with the US dollar. As things turned out Europe chose to go to a common currency called the Euro. It has since pared the US dollar, and indeed has exceeded it, and is valued at $1.30 at the time of this writing. Till wiser heads ruled I was determined to take full advantage of the disparity between our two currencies.

The following day we went to the downtown area to get in some good old single deck play. There were a lot of casinos offering premium exchange on Canadian currency. Little did they know, or better put, they found out pretty late in the game that the Canadians love to gamble just like anyone else. Currency inducements were an added bonus for "scammers" like me. The Cal Neva was the best. If you played, they would give you ninety-five US for one Canadian dollar. Some casinos would even negotiate rates. Next trip I will be in my glory.

The nicest hotel in the downtown was the Mapes. Its late forties, "Art Deco" architecture displayed a time when style and craftsmanship really meant something. It was the first casino in the world to combine rooms, dining, entertainment and gambling under one roof. It stood out defiantly, amongst the plastic and the glitz, like a stately oak surrounded by weeds. The only problem with the Mapes was that it had been closed since December 1982. There were few people with the insight that were willing to make a go of it, and to the eternal shame of the city fathers, it was imploded, January 30/00. A city that can't preserve its history will compromise its future. F. H. Slocombe, the architect of the Mapes, must be rolling in his grave. The excuse for its destruction was that the land couldn't be utilized for its "highest and best use." What a bunch of crap. That was real estate talk for "let's rip it down and build some condos." The Palace of Versailles could also be ripped down to promote a "project" that could house a thousand people. The population of France would string up the leaders that would even propose such lunacy, let alone implement it. All for materialistic gain, the soul of the city was removed, and the place were it once stood proud is now an empty parking lot, more than three and a half years later. My cup indeed runs over with venom when I think of some of the things perpetrated in the name of progress. Where were all the voices for the educated opposition, or did they earn instead their "Bachelor of Silence Degree?"

Finally back at the MGM we went to the gourmet restaurant and really had a feast fit for a king. We then took in a great show called "Hallelujah Hollywood," after which we went out to the casino floor to do some gambling.

In total, all the play in the Reno area netted me about $1200. I almost felt guilty, but that feeling soon dissipated as we were landing in Calgary early Sunday afternoon facing another week of cold weather.

The next five days dragged by ever so slowly due to a daily snow fall, but eventually we were lining up at the wicket at the Calgary airport, two and a half hours later we were landing at Las Vegas for a weekend, complements of Ike and the Golden Nugget, in the down town area.

It was always exciting going to a new casino with a junket. Although I've played at the Nugget before I hadn't played as a comped player and consequently didn't get to sample the things that they had to offer, this I would try to rectify amply.

We got our markers and started to play the six-deck shoe. I hadn't played a six-deck shoe since the Dunes junket with Dennis B., so it seemed a little odd. We did eventually get acclimatized, and all went smoothly.

We were only supposed to dine at certain eateries mainly due to Steve Wynn, the owner and the darling of the gaming commission in Las Vegas. He was very frugal with his comps to be sure. However, Ike did manage to get comps for our immediate group to wine and dine in "high roller" dinning areas. After we put in some time at the tables we retired for the evening.

The next morning after breakfast we went across the street to the Las Vegas Club, which touted the "most liberal rules in the world." And really they were. You could double down after a split, double down after three or four cards, surrender, re-split aces, automatic pay on a five card non-breaking hand (five card Charlie), in short it had it all. The only problem was that they would take the six-deck shoe and cut it in half. However, this hindrance was overcome by the liberal rules. Whenever I was nearby, I would always pop in for a while and play, get a comp for lunch or supper, then leave; usually with a plus mark on my ledger. We had a blast playing there for several hours, and only got back to the Nugget in the late afternoon.

Again I showed a $1200 profit when the flight left for Calgary that Sunday morning. It seemed that the figure of $1200 was typical for my style of play.

As we were landing we could see that the weather was much nicer, and so was my disposition. What I was really lacking in was sleep. A wise old sage had once said, "In order to sleep all night, you have to be up all day." This was particularly true because I had stayed up Saturday night as well. Sleep would be a welcome release for all the sweat and toil that I had put myself through the last few nights.

Getting Involved

All week I had been trying to marshal enough money for the up coming trip to Reno. I was determined to take enough Canadian money to make it worth my time and effort. By the time Friday night came I had thirty thousand dollars. I convinced Volker to accompany me. He had never been to Reno, and I was sure that we would thoroughly enjoy ourselves.

We landed just before ten, checked in at the MGM, jumped into a cab and were on our way downtown to our first stop, the Cal Neva. We went straight to the crap table, where we each plopped down $1000 Canadian, which in turn was converted into $950 US. I put mine on the "Pass Line," Volker putting his on the, "Don't Pass." We would have bet more, but unfortunately that was the maximum allowable at that casino. Finally after a few rolls Volker had won, taking my $950 US, a gain of $200 in just one roll. "You lucky skunk," I said and put down another $1000 Canadian, awaiting a conversion again to $950 US. The box man looked at me and said, "I know what the hell you are doing and I'm not going to cash any more of your money." The gig of course was over because they must have been "burned" before by people using the same tactics. They wanted us to play with the American currency that Volker had just won. We weren't prepared to do that because let's face it, craps in unbeatable. So out we went, much to the disgust of the box man sitting at the crap table. $200 bucks in a few minutes, "not bad" we said to ourselves as we went to the next casino.

No one else would take our bet at the crap game at ninety-five cents on the dollar. We could have done it for ninety cents on the dollar, but didn't want to risk rolling box cars (two sixes), which would have meant a push on the "Don't" and a loss on the "Pass." So the game had to be blackjack. I guess too many Northerners had been through this area before, making the casinos just a little bit wary.

We offered to play the $100 dollar minimum table for a minimum of one hour, if they would cash $3000 of our Canadian currency. The first to accept our terms was the Eldorado. We both peeled off three grand, each of us receiving $2850 US. Play resumed, and we both lost about a $1000. The pit crew was indeed jovial, until it turned around. In the second half hour of our commitment we recovered it all plus a bunch. Each of us had a $3000 profit when we walked out. My, what long faces appeared on the pit crew then.

Now keep in mind that this was supposed to be strictly a money converting operation. We were trying to get the best exchange for our money, but unless you could strike a deal for more, the normal exchange was only ninety cents on the dollar, leaving me with a potential profit of only $1500 US, all winnings aside. No wonder that "Canucks" found this place to be inexpensive. They would play a bit and even if they lost a small amount they would break out even. In the mean time, they enjoyed free drinks, and of course fully comped meals.

If I were a "snowbird," I would always carry a sizable amount of traveler checks, let's say $10,000 Canadian, all in one thousand dollar denominations. I would then make the rounds applying the money for the best deals that I could get, obtaining the things that go with risking your money like free hotels, food and beverage. Once I had used up the $10,000, I would go to an American Express office and again buy Canadian dollars with the US cash and start the process all over again.

Another option that I had not explored as yet was going to the management and buying back the Canadian currency for two percent less than the posted rate at the New York central exchange. Hypothetically, the casinos should welcome an eighty-three cent buy back of their Canadian currency. In some instances it takes as much as six weeks to get a credit back to your account when dealing with international monies. The currency is deposited into the casino's bank and from there it is moved physically to one of the bank's clearing houses' in New York; from there it is sent to Toronto. Only then does the casino get the credit for their Canadian money. As you know the banks don't do this for free, and charge their customers for the service. The advantage to the casino would be that the money could be applied as a credit without the usual long waiting period. The obvious advantage to you is the opportunity to use the money again at an even better rate than before.

We went over to the Comstock hotel and Casino where, after vigorous negotiations, they allowed each of us to cash in $1000 Canadian, in order to play twenty-one. We didn't set any time limit, however we were required to play at the twenty-five dollar table. There we met a dealer by the name of Willy. He was a black guy who could deal with flair. His biggest trick was giving you a card that stood on its edge balancing for a second, and then fell over exposing it's value. He also had an antic that made me quite nervous. He would take the deck in two hands, and stiffly lift it up to about eye level pitching you a card. We stayed at his table for about a half an hour, playing to a draw. We then went back to the Cal Neva to try some blackjack there. Unfortunately they too would only allow us to cash in $1000 Can. with the stipulation of play at the twenty-five dollar table. Here we were a bit luckier and managed a $500 dollar win.

It sure was fun playing with an edge. We had the best of both worlds; we had the edge on the exchange and also the play. I am still baffled as to why they promoted the exchange rate so aggressively.

It was in the wee hours of the morning before we got back to the MGM and went to our rooms for some well-earned sleep.

The morning came, and we served our penance at the MGM black-jack pit, for a loss of $500. We then went downtown to do some more "money laundering." I still had about $20,000 to convert to US dollars, so I had my work cut out for me. Try as I may, I couldn't get more than 90 cents on the dollar. Even the Eldorado wasn't interested, because my play was "too tough." So I guess I had bitten off more than I could chew for a short weekend excursion. When we got back to the MGM, I had only cashed $15,000 of my original thirty. I guess that was okay, because I had no idea how much a guy could convert on one of Ike's short weekend junkets. Now that we knew the routine, it would be sheer folly to bring more than $15,000 on any future short trip. It is also better to bring more instead of less; so you won't catch yourself short.

Ike cornered me, saying that he had made arrangements to have me as the signing authority for the gourmet restaurant if we wanted to go that evening. He gave a nudge and asked that we take it easy on the hotel. I nudged him back and said that they would only get what they deserved.

There were six of us that kicked around together. As comrades, we all shared the 'thrill of victory and the agony of defeat'. "So what the hell," I thought, "we deserve whatever we desire." That night we had plenty of wine and all the courses suggested to us by the eagar waiters. We even had the photo lady sitting on our laps, sipping on a drink while the waiter took our pictures.

After supper we all went our separate ways and I headed for the venue that suited me most, the 21 pit. Playing there for about fifteen minutes, I was joined at the table by a lady who was very friendly indeed. We chatted for a while as we played, and somehow got on to the subject of the extravaganza that was playing in the show room. I told her that I had seen it before, but it was so good that I wouldn't mind seeing it again. "Would you like to be my guest," I asked. She said that she would be delighted. Calling the floor person over, I asked him to make the necessary arrangements and then proceeded to the invited guests' line.

Being in that line sure is interesting, especially if you have never been there before. The maitre de talks to you as if he was your intimate long time friend. The people accompanying you, who are "first timers," look at you as if you had a lot of money and influence; little did it matter that I had neither. The questions that my lady friend asked revealed her biases. "What do you do for a living?" Well, I was convalescing from an injury, gambling and exchanging money. I didn't want any biblical overtones as to the money changing, or for that matter, convalescence. I simply opted to tell her that I was engaged in gambling at the present time.

After a couple of bottles of champagne, the questions stopped and we watched the show. When it was over, I escorted her to her room and was invited in for a nightcap.

In the morning, without breakfast, I bid her a gracious good bye, rushed to pack my things, checked out and met the bus for the airport.

On the flight back, I calculated that I was up just under $4000, including exchange profits and twenty-one play; not bad for a dude aspiring to be a "professional."

The following week I went down with Fred on his junket to the Marina. It was the beginning of April and the weather was extremely pleasant in Vegas. I went straight to Jeno's table to let him know that I was in town. Maybe we could get together for some drinks and a chat session the next day. Unfortunately, he was tied up and so it would have to wait for another visit. I played there for a couple of hours on a few hundred dollars and went to bed.

Getting Involved

The following morning I went to try the shoe game at the same table where my brother and I had a great run several weeks earlier. Sadly I ended up with a $1000 loss. That was the biggest loss that I ever had since starting the counting system in a serious way. And it wasn't the last one either, because I would have my big bet out when the count rose to a reasonably high level, win lose or draw. I would have to grow a "few more whiskers" before it dawned on me that it was futile in some instances to make a big bet if the big cards were all trapped behind the cut card.

I went downtown to try some single deck with the same result. By this time, like every fresh card counter, I was questioning the value of counting. Was I just plain lucky in the past while I was winning, and now it was payback time? I just wasn't experienced enough to know that luck is a "two way street." If the count isn't working for you, keep your bets lower till lady luck sits beside you once more. If in every round that's dealt, you are left staring at a dealer's face card, then what the hell are you doing there? Move on to a different table where the dealer gets his fair share of bad cards, just as the player does.

Of course there is the dealer who will make his or her hand no matter what they have showing, in that case the same logic must be used, move to a different venue. Why get beat up with an unbeatable deck?

At times you will end up playing "Russian Roulette" at a six square table; your seat programmed to blow up in your face every time. No matter what you do, you cannot win, you hit, double down against a stiff, you get stiffed. While everyone has eighteen or better, the dealer pulls seventeen. Buy insurance with your nineteen and the dealer turns up a nine.

Do what the casino did to me when they were confronted with a similar situation. "Pull the shoe." In the player's case, this translates into just pulling yourself off the chair and leaving. You see a casino knows when it is confronted with an untenable situation, and takes action. You too, must take evasive action, abandoning your post amidst a string of unanswered losses. You just can't win all the time. It goes back to the previous point on customer relations, you being the corporation and the casino being the client. Sure you will incur losses on occasion, but keep in mind that if you always registered a win your presence at the establishment would no longer be tolerated. What you owe your self is a restriction of your losses. So either move spots, move tables, move casinos, or move your butt to a lounge; just attempt to relax and try playing again later.

I kept on my losing ways, and was in a state of disbelief at what was happening. Finally Sunday arrived and I was whisked back to Canada, $3000 down. I had "morphed" from a winner to a loser, in the span of one short week. Now I could get a taste of what it must be like being a casino and taking a hit. I wish that I could have shown some self-restraint, but my long ears, and short sightedness gave way to my sense of invincibility.

So that week I paid my dues, chosing to call it "investing in black-jack futures," in hopes that someday I would get a dividend for the high cost of doing business. After that weekend I would never again be cocky, when it came to the game of twenty-one.

I read that when Ken Uston, also known as the "Wandering Jew," set up three teams of card counters; two were very successful, while the other one kept losing money. He suspected the latter of cheating, so he had to let them go. He later realized that they weren't, because he too fell into a losing streak that lasted several sessions, losing scads of money as a result. So you see, even a super counter like Kenny can have his bad days, so don't get discouraged.

The following Friday it was back to Reno with Ike. I was a little nervous now that I had taken my first real hit. We landed at the airport in Reno at the usual time, and I put in my stint at the MGM. I then high tailed it to my room about 2:00 am. I went to bed a winner, relieving that feeling of impending doom.

The next day I went down town to pluck a few bucks off the money tree and convert some Canadian moola into "real" currency.

First stop was at the CalNeva club. I started to play about 11:00 am at a table that featured a pretty "femme fatale" pitching the cards. We started flirting, and before you knew it we had a budding verbal relationship. She was going for a break in a few minutes and asked to meet with me. I readily complied.

The CalNeva was different than all the other casinos as the dealers had to go to the regular coffee shops to eat instead of a separate "break room" provided by the casino; this to avoid contact with the clientele. We agreed to meet in one of the little eateries on the second floor. There I noticed her sitting, munching on her sandwich. I walked over to her and started up a conversation. Since her break was ending soon, I managed to get her phone number. She asked me to call her later for a rendezvous, perhaps for supper. I stuffed the number into my shirt pocket and headed to Haralds Club with a smile on my face.

By now it was afternoon, and the place was getting packed except for one five-dollar, table slightly out of the "loop." There stood a dealer with his arms crossed, looking rather bored, at his bleak surroundings. I sat down all by myself, directly in front of him for some one on one. He quickly shuffled up and I opened with ten dollars; promptly losing it, along with the next four hands. He reshuffled, and then it became my deck. For the next five shuffles, that deck became "my sweetheart." Whatever I wanted to do with it, I did, and was always rewarded. Every time the count went up I put out a black chip, every time there were extra aces in a plus situation, I went to two squares with one usually getting a blackjack. It was all going very smoothly with no one paying me a second glance. Then, I was dealt a twenty with two face cards which I split against a dealer's six. I received a two on my first face card to which the dealer said, "It doesn't seem to have been a good idea to split a sure winner." "Daddy always said, split till you don't have a hand," I replied. The second card was a ten and I re-split getting two zero cards. The dealer then proceeded to break. Then "stuff" started happening. With the next shuffle, a pit boss came over to scrutinize my play. I realized that my time at that particular casino was running out. I decided to take my $1100 profit, and leave before the inevitable arrival of security.

By now, I had been barred from play by about four or five casinos. Each time I noticed their hesitation at banning me because they didn't really know how some people might respond to such treatment. I would often say to the players beside me at the table, "Make damn sure that you don't win any money, or the same thing will happen to you." I didn't want anyone thinking that I was some kind of thief, stealing from the casino. If I didn't mention that I was being kicked out for winning, (which was presumably their reason for playing), they might give me a dirty look as I was escorted out. Oh the injustice of it all, "To play like a master and be treated like a thief."

There was no one at my table this time, and I figured that they wouldn't hesitate to give me "the bum's rush," even on the thinnest evidence of card counting. If I had been using my head, I wouldn't have had to deal with this problem. Instead of splitting, I should have just carried on my "merry" way, emptying the dealer's tray; that's what I came to do after all. I interfered with this process by doing a "classic" counter move of splitting tens and winning. By the way, it is a classic move only if you win. If you lose, you are considered an idiot, not only by the players, but also the floor staff alike. So, it is basically a lose, lose situation. Try to avoid it. That's one of the surest ways to get the boot. I was up $1100 and it could have been a lot more had I not screwed up. Now I had to collect my things and "high tail it out of Dodge," cause this here casino was too small for the likes of me.

It was always nice to get the extra value for your dollar, but Vegas was still my destination of choice between Nevada's two casino saturated cities. I bummed around town till about 6:00 pm then I made a call to the gal that I had met earlier. She picked me up in front of the Sands hotel about an hour later. We went for cocktails and then for a steak dinner, compliments of the MGM. Later we took in the show, which I still enjoyed, even tough seeing it three times now.

Later we went up to my room for some R and R. The conversation somehow turned to what we did for a living. In a stunning moment of honesty she informed me that she used to be a hooker in L.A. That came as a serious let down, but being in the company of a prostitute, even though she was on a sabbatical from the profession, didn't deter me in the least. I was very pragmatic about the situation. I, after all, had no intentions of marrying her.

As we chatted on, she told me that her mother had gotten her a dealer's job and she too worked at the Cal Neva. As the conversation widened, she informed me that her mom had cheated on behalf of players, for half of the take. Well, this was a new one on me, a veiled proposition to cheat the casino out of money.

The caper worked like this: In the early eighties, the peeping window had not yet been invented. Dealers would have to peek at their hole card by manually lifting, and looking under it. Information would be transferred to the player by various moves in her tray; this would indicate to the player whether she had a card with value of between two and six, as well as any card between seven and ten. Of course a blackjack would be immediately flipped up without a chance to hit. She asked me if I would be a willing partner, as her mother needed the money. I told her that I had my reservations about this kind of cheating, but at the same time I was willing to experiment with all the facets of the industry, from the honorable to the not so honorable, all the way to the unmentionable.

This was certainly a new twist on twenty-one from the perspective of a scammer; I had never been a party to cheating before. I wondered how it would all play out. Well, that was to be the next new experience in the game of twenty-one.

She left in the wee hours of the morning, and now happily I could get caught up on my sleep.

Back in Calgary, I had pressing business to attend to, so I had to cancel the trip to Vegas for the following week; but Reno was definitely a go.

The following Thursday I called the gal in Reno and told her that I would be in town the following night. She offered to pick me up at the airport; I accepted.

When we arrived, there she was, complete with her rabbit fur coat, tight jeans, high heels and heavy makeup. Maybe she thought that she was still doing the "stroll," or picking up a "John." Man, did she ever stand out; she looked like Sharon Stone in the movie "Casino." I realized I had made a serious mistake, and was up to my neck with a lady whose fashion statement started and ended at street level. I just wanted to get the hell out of there. I grabbed her hand and fast walked out to her car.

She drove me to see her mother, and we set up the rendezvous for next day. The signals were quickly rehearsed and we were set to go. I asked the gal for a ride back to the hotel so I could play my required time. After we arrived she couldn't take a hint that I wanted to get to the tables; I was stuck with her for the night.

Mercifully, about 3:00 am she left me in my slumber. In the morning after breakfast, I went to the CalNeva for twelve o'clock, as we had arranged. I saw the mother's table and grabbed a seat at third base. That way I wouldn't be under the gun when the decision to hit came, I could more readily figure out what she had for a hole card. We played her entire shift and after a half an hour I was up a whopping $1500. She quickly looked at the stack of chips before she went for her break.

Upon her return, I showed her that I still had the $1500, and we resumed our "cheating ways." The second session was totally different from the first, because I had too much information as pertaining to her hole card. Had I played my usual game, I would have been up another $500. I lost because I handicapped myself by not hitting against her ten, knowing full well that she was stiffed. She made virtually everyone of her hands, resulting in a $1600 loss.

I phoned her later and told her that I had lost the original profit, and was in fact $100 in the hole. I did this to adhere to a code that I had heard or read about somewhere, that there was honor among thieves; that may be the case at some morally higher level, but certainly not at street level where I now felt that I belonged. At that level it is basically a dog eat dog existence. She said that she was aware of the heavy losses I had incurred on her second shift and offered a weak apology. I left it at that, with no hard feelings. I gained a lot of education from the bottom of the gambling barrel.

Reflecting on the experience, I felt that it was a sleazy way of making money. In the first session, I would have probably made in the range of $1000 and in the second session, I would have at least broke out even by hitting in a normal manner. Besides, this kind of chicanery left the bad taste in my mouth. I would have had to split the $1500 netting me a total of $750, a total out of pocket loss of $250 from the estimated $1000 that I could have earned on my own. My advice is never to go into this kind of arrangement. Although the odds of winning are greatly enhanced, you could still stand to lose a lot of money with little risk for the other party.

I repeated this cheat tactic only on one other occasion, years later, as a favor to my wife, who had a friend that needed money in a hurry. I told her friend that victory is not at all certain and that I didn't like cheating. She begged me until I finally relented and agreed to a session the following evening.

When I arrived that night, and sat down at her table, the friend blatantly paid me on my losses, pushes, a few times even when I had broke, much to the disbelief of the other players that were at the table. The floor man, standing behind her was a "coke" head, and was totally unaware of the action; in fact it looked like he was on another planet. On that occasion, the take was $2000, split two ways.

I didn't have the guilt pangs that were present on the first episode, because I somehow felt that I was on a good deed mission; besides, I was the only reliable person that she knew.

The main problem at this casino was that the management didn't do their homework in hiring people to fill sensitive positions like floor man. The dealers obviously knew that the guy was a "junkie" and took advantage of him. She told me that many dealers set up "shills" to dump money on because of this guy's drug habit.

Anyway, I was glad to be rid of the "unhappy hooker" and dishonest mother combo. Associating with people of dubious morals can corrupt one's character. I was happy to have had the experience of dealing with cheats so I could relate these things in writing and apply the lessons learnt to my lexicon of life. A cheat is like a thief, and being one, no matter how briefly, has left a bad taste in my mouth. Bear in mind that the employment of these tactics is a mindless attempt to rob the casino's coffers. The more intelligent and legal approach of card counting will open that vault just as easily. Cheating in blackjack is like kicking in an unlocked door. As this little rhyme states, you should learn the intelligent way to win at cards because, "If you don't get your education at Yale, one slip up, and you go directly to jail."

By learning how to count cards we are arming ourselves with a skill that is presently viewed as cheating by the casinos, but can't be prosecuted as such in criminal court. Although, prosecution of thought crimes is going ahead as forecast in Orwell's book "1984," it's still pretty hard for a jury of your peers to find you guilty of card counting without first being "re-educated" into thinking that the individual has somehow gained an unfair advantage over the "corporation." Perhaps, somewhere in the future this thought process would be deemed criminally incorrect.

Remember what "political correctness" is. All individual thought is looked at by the forces of "good" to be "bad." The "corporation" is deemed as "good" in the international capitalistic sense because it signifies "herd." A person outside the herd is viewed as a potentially dangerous element. These outsiders in turn, find the tenets of the herd's thinking to be the outcome of state propaganda, or more nicely put, "over education." To question "that which is good" is deemed as "that which is bad," and puts you on the outside of the herd, looking in. This "herd" or slavish attitude can be used by a surprisingly small number of people, to stampede the herd in the direction of their choosing. Take for example the sheep dog and his flock. What a monumental task he has if each member of the flock was in possession of individual thought? In this "land of the spree and home of the slave," to escape the yoke, "you must first prove that you have the right to escape the yoke." Perhaps Ezra Pound put it most eloquently, "A slave is one who waits for someone to come and set him free."

Freedom of thought isn't for everyone. In fact, freedom isn't for everyone. Some people just swallow what is fed to them without qualification; that's what I call a "sheeple" attitude. Men of freedom enjoy flaring their nostrils, posing questions about the small problems of proof and truth. On the other side of the spectrum, the slave nods his head in complete agreement with whatever view is enjoying the most popularity at the time. By questioning current values one is walking across the face of popular opinion; suddenly you are "politically incorrect," and there is no limit to the epithets that can be hurled at you. In fact if you become a "zealot," you could easily end up dead. Just ask the survivors of Waco. Is this the kind of attitude that deserves the "high throne" touted by a "free country;" or is this just "sugar coated totalitarianism."

Some of our ancestors stood on the gallows, refusing to renounce their revolutionary ways. Now, some people will turn a blind eye to reality and nod their heads because to think otherwise may condemn them to the punishment of "unpopularity." Imagine someone who has never had an original thought in his entire life, condemning you for standing out. Thus speaks the flock.

Card counting is much like this; it puts you on the very fringe of the system, unpopular to the casino because of winning, and unpopular with most players because of stealthful strategy.

I act in an absolute prejudicial fashion, that is to say, I prejudge the cards that are to come by the placement of a large or small bet, depending on the existing "prejudice." I am also guilty of blatant "discrimination." I discriminate as to what table I sit at. I prefer a non-smoking table away from drunks and rude people. In fact many places where I play have a non-smoking sign at my table without my having to ask for one.

Getting Involved

I pride myself on my biases as well. I am partial about the casinos I attend, like individual people, each has a personality all it's own; comprised of the unique personalities in attendance. I am proud to say that I am the epitome of "political incorrectness." Thus speaks the ego.

The people where I do business, all have their distinct personalities, unique to each individual. They have either acquired these personalities either as a direct result of their marginalized environment or have an organic predisposition. We fringe people, have divorced ourselves from the herd and the "great leveler" of personalities. There will always be those that think that 21 is unbeatable, these are the "egalitarians" who say everyone eventually loses; this is true for them. Right there we can place a line of demarcation, because we are the polar opposites of this train of thought. This leveling urge or "equality," is a bane to us who are only equal in our unequal ness. "Equality for those who are equal, inequality for those of 'us' who are not." Thus speaks the philosopher.

With these thoughts ringing in my head and my conscience literally extinguishing my "guilt receptors," I returned to the MGM put in my hours, and ultimately won only $300 or $400 in that fruitless adventure. I felt that I had wasted the entire weekend in petty thievery.

As every cloud has a silver lining, so it is with fate. A car that I had been "horny" for came up for sale in Vancouver, so I went there to consolidate the deal. The car was a 1936 Auburn Boat Tail Speedster, a remake of the original owned by movie stars like Clark Gable back in that era. There were a few parts missing, but I knew of a dealership in Pasadena, Ca. that handled the car. I could use my free trips to Vegas to pick up parts.

✳   ✳   ✳   ✳   ✳

Early in May, Calgarians experience their first real spring, the spring that most Easterners enjoy at the beginning of April. I suppose it's our proximity to the mountains that keeps the frost on our windshields for an extra couple of weeks. It sure feels good when you can leave the window wide open at night, only to shut it during the many rains that breath life into the soil. This weather is quite agreeable with me, but I find myself craving the warmer temperatures inherent in Southern Nevada.

I made arrangements to go to Vegas with Ike the following Friday. I noticed on the weather channel that it would be very pleasant there. The thermometer was hovering between 90 and 100 degrees Fahrenheit, perfect for my physical well being; too much warmer, and I become extremely uncomfortable.

Upon arriving at the Golden Nugget, I parked my butt at a five-dollar minimum table and went through the "drill;" raising the bet when the count is high, and lowering it when it was low. I noticed the floor man was watching intently my every move. His face was wrinkled as if in deep concentration, counting the shoe down in parallel with me. He too must have noticed the shoe soaring in strength as did I, but I just waited. I kept my bet at ten dollars until there was a flurry of large cards, creating for me a win. Only then did I raise my bet to fifty. The count was still there, but the $50 bet wasn't warranted according to the floor man, because he just walked away.

This is what I like to call "flying under the radar." The "high flying" antics of the typical card counter, betting high when the count is high, will get you barred from a downtown casino in less than an hour. If you predictably raise and lower your bets when the count changes you are going to encounter a lot of headaches in your career.

By deliberately holding off on a couple of big bets while being watched, assured for me the mark of a typical gambler; from the casino's standpoint, I was a "sucker." This is the self-created persona that I want to instill into the casino. By not "flying in formation" for a couple of hands, I earned a respite of a few weeks before they checked up on me again. In essence, my tactics were to pretend that I didn't have an overall strategy. If I couldn't get the bet out when he was watching I would get it out the next time that he wasn't. Since I was playing the game for the long haul, and playing it professionally I didn't have to take unnecessary risks. I was "imbedded" and wouldn't blow my cover on easy targets. For me it was a never ending round.

To throw off the "sentinel" even further, you could raise the bet on an obvious low count. I can't tell you the number of times that I "nickeled" up the bet, although the count was dropping; only to be rewarded by having a $100 bet out at the end of a dismally low counted shoe; winning every bet. This is the "luck factor," to which I alluded earlier. No matter what anybody did at the table, it played right into my hand all the time. It often happens in reverse, and then you must leave the table, and go look for "greener felts."

Another advantageous act is to engage the pit boss in conversation. This not only throws him off on his count, but also reduces his scrutiny of your play. In other words, you shouldn't behave like a guy that "lights up the pit bosses world when he leaves." If you are a gregarious person like me, you may wish to learn the tactic of talking, and at the same time carrying an on-going, accurate count.

One thing that I did learn from Humble's book was how to remember the count with your hand. Let's say that the count is ten when you engage some one in small talk. You have a thumb and four fingers. On the four fingers you have three digits on each, giving you a total of twelve positions. When interrupted, merely press your thumb on the corresponding digit and you have registered the count. If the pit crew carries on chatting with you, the only option you have is estimating the count, or moving your thumb up or down, keeping a fairly accurate accounting about the value, making the appropriate bets. If the count is dismally low, you may wish to opt out of the hand, and refrain from "protecting" a twelve against a six by hitting it. Plays like that, tend to raise a floor man's suspicions, especially when you are displaying the minimum bet.

Always keep in mind that courtesy and a good wit are highly prized when dealing with the casino. A sales motivator once told me, "You always get more flies with honey than you do with shit." It's hard to get angry with a person that is amiable. I've engaged a lot of "pit" personnel in conversations, exchanging jokes and laughter even while they were in the process of removing another "evil card counter" from a different table. The very same people that kicked out card counters came over to my table, welcoming me back to their casinos when I was in town. This certainly isn't the kind of reception that awaits me all the time, but "flying under the radar" certainly has its advantages. Enjoy the perks as if there are no tomorrows.

A card counter is typically quiet and in deep thought as he concentrates on the card values as they are revealed. An experienced counter can just glance at the table, giving a fairly accurate rendering of the cards, and their values to within a running point; all this taking place during a normal conversation with the pit staff.

Engaging dealers in conversation shouldn't be taken lightly either. If he is keeping a count, the chatter will throw his calculations off considerably. The best topics of course are those that focus on them. People love talking about them selves, and will go to great lengths in explaining their own particular philosophy on life. If the dealer is a proven counter, his superiors rely on them to inform on a player's card counting prowess. If the two of you hit it off, and he didn't get an accurate count, the likely hood of him "throwing you under the bus" is pretty remote.

The Golden Nugget was a couple of thousand poorer as a result of that weekend's session.

The more often I went down to Vegas, the more experience I amassed, and the more experience that I amassed the more money I made. It was just that simple.

Finally the summer came. Calgary braced for the world famous Calgary Stampede with all the cowboy competitions, such as chuck wagon races, bronco busting, bull riding and western nostalgia. These events were played out competitively in an arena, in something that the cowboys call a rodeo. It is a time when the city kicks up its heels a bit and turns a blind eye to the rowdier elements in our town. People drink and dance on the streets. They give blood-curdling yells and in general have the time of their lives. It is also probably the only time that you can see a cowboy cited for being "drunk while in the saddle."

The Stampede is the kind of festivity that attracts a lot of tourists to our city on the first Friday of every July. For the odd card counter there is another attraction, called the Frontier Casino. It is a huge hall with countless blackjack tables, roulette wheels, crap tables and poker rooms to entertain the minions that wish to try their luck in the "halls of chance."

1985 brought a special breed of player to our "yahoo, extravaganza." This was a small group of card counters from Atlantic City, N. J. They were introducing a "new way," new to some of us anyway, of dealing with a shoe. They introduced me to a system commonly known as "tracking." This entailed watching for strong and weak clumps of cards, trying to get them segregated into the shoe. The result was, that you could be relatively certain where in the shoe the big valued cards were located. In short, one could come out with a black chip right off the get go, and lowering it to a minimum as soon as the strong cards were used up. This was done instead of waiting to get in the big bet, and discovering that the cut card had just made its exit. This system had the huge advantage of knowing what was in the cut off portion. One would like to ensure that a bunch of small cards were stuck in there. That way you would have a tendency to increase the count immediately. The conventional way would occasionally leave some large cards in the back, giving the card counter a false reading.

Let me give you an example. Assuming that you have a plus ten behind the cut card and nearing the end of a shoe, you have a double down situation, with a large bet against the dealer's ten. Your count is a plus three and you eagerly put in the money for the double down. Please note the reality of the situation. Although you have what amounts to a running plus three, you really only have a minus seven, because of those ten "pictures" stuck behind the cut card, that "will never see the light of play." The double down chart has you doing a double down up to minus five, after which the deck becomes too anemic to attempt the maneuver. You are more likely to get a small card because of the true minus seven, and worse, the dealer may out draw you with more than one hit, because the count is so low.

To avoid this situation, you may choose to stuff some small cards behind the cut card; thus eliminating a false count. To put the small cards in the front would of course be defeating the purpose, unless you know for sure that what remains in the back will be at least a zero or a neutral deck. Then, once those small cards in the front have been spent, you can come out with a larger bet. The advantage can be readily seen when you can hit a sixteen even though the deck is showing itself to be positive because you have the knowledge that you are in the midst of the small card clump. Once you are out of the clump, it's business as usual; except you have a larger bet.

The best situation is the burying of a small card clump, putting another one on the top. This has a tendency to "turbo charge" your count after the front "garbage" has been eliminated. In a four-deck game, this gives you a chance of biting into an incredibly "meaty" two decks of black chip play. If you are lucky enough to be playing on a table by yourself, you are going to have an enjoyable time. The knowledge that there are small cards in the back, should give you confidence with your double downs against the ten, and eliminate a lot of the surprises that come with a "false count."

It was a sober awakening when I first sat down at the table with one of these people from Atlantic City, a.k.a. "AC." They would "front load" the shoe, unbeknownst to me, make their large bets, then leave when the large cards were spent. This was rather frustrating because I wasn't privy to the play. I made the small bets when I shouldn't have; and made the large bets when they should have been small.

I cornered one of them to get some direction about what they were doing. Only then all was revealed to me. The way the shuffle was prescribed for the dealers was the same throughout the entire casino. As a result, one could determine exactly which stack of cards contained mainly large cards and which stack had the small ones; an educated cut followed. It took a day or two for the process to sink in, but when it did, I noticed an increase in my earnings. The frontier casino had given me $9000 in the ten days that it was open. Not a huge earning by any stretch of the imagination, but certainly an eye-opening venture. I had explored yet another avenue in my quest for cash. Due to the obvious condition that the cards were left in after "plundering the deck" of its value, I did a lot more walking between tables than usual. It would have been counter productive staying at a shoe, remaining a viable player, after the good cards had been siphoned off. Walking was the only prudent thing to do.

This new method was potentially so lethal, that I went to the fair up in Edmonton, 180 miles north of Calgary to play at their version of the Stampede called "Klondike Days." The Klondike Day's celebration was a ten-day shindig using the theme of the "gold rush" as an excuse to compete with Calgary for their "fair" share of the tourist dollar.

I took the entire $9000 that I made in Calgary, rented a motel room and started to play. The place was jam packed, smoky and very hard to find a seat unless you went very early; not my kind of "atmosphere" to say the least. The next day I arrived early to get a seat close to a ventilator because the smoke was unbearable. In this business you can be driven to an early grave by smokers, so jostling for the best seats becomes a high priority. Asians love to gamble but it's a rare thing to find one that doesn't smoke, at least back in the mid 80s. Even if one smokes it is a good thing to sit at non-smoking tables because one can always excuse them selves from play by stepping back and having a smoke so as not to interfere with the rest of the tables wishes, this of course should only be done on a low count.

Getting Involved

Because the Klondike venue was packed, one could only get the cut card one out of seven times because there were seven positions at each table. We would all get our respective turns at cutting the cards, but you couldn't rely on getting an obvious clump located all the time. As a result, when it came to your turn, it didn't necessarily mean that you could make a bet. When someone else cut and you could predetermine where the clump was, often the rich cards would make their appearance mid way in a particular deal, somewhere down from the start of the shoe, destroying the clump. It was definitely more profitable to put the power right up front. Then you could determine exactly when it was to be dealt. You could then have a large bet out, precisely when the big cards arrived. I can't tell you how many times I've had a minimum bet out only to be surprised by a flurry of big cards coming out near the end of that particular round.

When the "smoke" cleared, the Edmonton trip had cost me a total of $6000 and was a waste of time. After a week and a half I limped back to Calgary, a poorer man but wiser for the experience.

Still convinced that tracking was an important tool in my arsenal, I refined the process whenever the right conditions prevailed.

Once the Fairs in Alberta were over, my brother and I went on a two-week trip to Reno, then on to Las Vegas. The Reno part of the outing was wrought with failure as I lost $8000 working the single deck. The trip to Vegas on the other hand, was a shinning success, registering a win of $6000.

The fact that I had lost so much in Reno couldn't be blamed on much more that bad luck; just a string of losses, no matter which casino that I had the misfortune of attending, ended with the same woefully outcome.

The complete opposite occurred in Vegas. Unfortunately, the experience in Reno had "castrated" me somewhat, as a consequence the bets were slightly lower and as a result so were the earnings.

One can only conclude that if the cards aren't running in your favor, get up and find another table, or go change the venue. What I prefer doing now is going to the lounge, engaging a pretty girl in some conversation. You have to be prepared for diversionary tactics if the cards are falling wrong. Hell, that's why they invented lounges, to go drown your sorrow, or in my case just to wind down a bit.

If you are on a junket and have to put in your required hours, do it for a short while. If the deck is "keyed" against you go and relax some more; eventually you will get over your bad streak. You see, that's another advantage that we have over the casinos; they have to stay there, catering to the customer, win, lose, or draw. We aren't burdened with that responsibility. If for whatever reason you don't want to play, don't. They might be reluctant to re-invite you but you don't have to lose a whack of money when your luck is in dire need of resuscitation. Just go for a swim or a massage, or just get out of there; you can make up the time at a later date. The casino can't stay lucky forever. You have got three or four days to make up the necessary time anyway. On at least one of those days your prospects are bound to improve. When the count is there it will be your hand getting the blackjacks and not the dealer's. The dealer will seem as if he is the one that's "snake bit" and can't make a hand; a complete reversal of roles from the time before. That's when to put in your time. Remember it's your job to either win as much money as you can, or to keep your losses to a minimum. It's their job to get as much of your money as they can, and also to restrict their losses. One more thing, it is also your job to make their job next to impossible.

Winning has a tendency of smoothing out your temperament, making you jovial and talkative. Isn't that the way the game should be played? So cheer up. A wise old sage once related to me, "The higher you soar the bigger you appear to the eye of envy, but be assured that the casinos hate all those who fly." Maintaining a high, even during heavy losses is a prerequisite for a card counter because even he has his losing days. You might just as well "roll with the punch" as they say. And when "evil" things are happening, the only "good" you may do is to leave.

I took an afternoon off to get some parts in California for my project car that was slowly getting off the ground. I noticed that the parts were astronomically priced in some cases and that I would have to manufacture some of them myself. The tailpiece for the Auburn's boat tail was $250, and it looked as if it was easy to reproduce.

I picked up those parts that were reasonably priced, and made my way back to Vegas, and from there back again to Calgary.

Chapter Nine: Flams, Scams and Automobiles

The car project occupied my time for the next couple of months, and temporarily took me out of the gambling loop. But by December I was ready to get back to my "gambling" ways.

The first trip took me to Vegas with Fred's Marina junket. There I learned that my favorite dealer Jeno, had died. Evidently he was the victim of a heart attack, a disease that claims a lot of Hungarians as a result of rich food. He was sadly missed, not only by me but also by many of the staff at the Marina. We celebrated his life by reminiscing about his antics and jovial nature.

The next evening, while I was playing at one of the tables, a lady dealer asked me if my brother and I would care to join herself and a friend for a drink. I said that we would be delighted and made arrangements to meet them at the Tropicana, the casino directly across the street from the Marina.

When we arrived, the girls were sitting in the lounge and chatting at one of the tables. I was introduced to a lady called Cindy. She was pretty enough, but no sparks could be detected during our initial conversation. Then she mentioned Jeno, my favorite dealer; it dawned on me that she was his girlfriend. Also, I realized that he must have had a premonition of his impending doom, because he dearly wanted to introduce us a few months before his demise. Well now, wasn't that a coincidence? She told me that he went to get something in the kitchen, and she heard a thud, then silence. She rushed in to see what was wrong, but it was all over; he didn't know what hit him. He was the victim of a massive coronary attack.

It was still relatively soon after his death, and I knew that she was still hurting from her loss, so I steered the conversation into another direction. We talked for some time while my brother and the other lady went to do some gambling. Cindy and I agreed to go out the next time I was in town; which was probably in two weeks time. Leaving me her phone number, Cindy left after an hour to tend to her daughter. We bid each other a pleasant evening and went our separate ways. I for my part went back to the Marina to extract some more funds from their coffers.

I had no idea how much that meeting would determine the events that were to shortly unfold. I went about my business oblivious to what had just occurred.

In Calgary I would bum around for a week and a half until Ike called to see if I was available to go with them to the Nugget that Friday. Of course I readily agreed, and phoned Cindy to made arrangements to see her on the day after we arrived. Ike was nice enough to use his influence to arrange for an unlimited comp at their Italian restaurant.

When she showed up Cindy was wearing a cute little pink jump suit that really complimented her figure. We went straight away to the lounge, had a few cocktails and got to know each other a little better. After we got a little "loose" we made our way to the eatery and enjoyed a great meal complete with the most expensive wines and Champagnes that the restaurant had to offer. We enjoyed ourselves immensely, laughing and joking right through to desert. She exhibited a great sense of humor, which is really a prerequisite to any lasting relationships, judging from my past experiences.

Later on, we went down to try our luck at the tables; surprisingly, she knew a lot about the game. We played for a couple of hours and then retired to my room with a modest profit. She left about 5:00 am, which suited me fine, as my return flight left at about 8:30 am, giving me only one and a half hours sleep.

I would alternate between Fred and Ike on my trips to Vegas. But it was Fred's junket to the Marina that took priority around the New Year. When he called it didn't take much prodding to accept his invitation. Remembering the great gift that I had received last year, I gladly consented. I decided not to call Cindy ahead of time. I could meet her at her work place, which coincidently was at the Marina.

On the 29th of December we were on our way to Vegas courtesy of the Marina Hotel and Casino to try our luck in the land of "milk and money." A lot of people think that the Vegas area is warm year round, that is definitely not the case. Now for the second time, I saw snowfall at this oasis in the desert.

The place was fairly quiet at the time, but for sure it was going to be busy next day and go totally nuts the day after, which was New Year's Eve. I "strapped on my helmet" and prepared myself for battle as soon as I checked in. The conditions were ripe for table-hopping, but as things turned out I was quite happy where I was. Many of you that play 21, will know what I mean when I say that I was blessed with a "shoe from heaven." Whatever one did it was the right thing to do, just the opposite from "the shoe from hell." After playing for about two hours, I called it quits and went to the bar to chat with the gang on the junket. Shortly after that, I went to my room with a big smile and a big two thousand dollar wad in my pocket.

In the morning I went down to see if Cindy would like to go out on the town. She told me that she was busy, and that the following night would be better for her. That was okay with me, but I did have the New Year's Eve party to attend at the Marina's ballroom. That event was held every year, along with the "silver give away," to show player appreciation. In other words the casino would thank all the "loyal suckers" for the year's donations. There were four of us from Calgary that didn't fit that description, so I wondered how long we would last before we heard those dreaded words, "You can play craps, or roulette, but you can't play 21 at this casino." Oh well, it was the New Year, so we didn't dwell on those negative thoughts.

I put in my time on the eve of the eve and did quite well, nailing the casino for another thousand. It was unbelievable that the casino could withstand those losses for too much longer, especially from the same four people. Could it be that they didn't know that we were card counters, or even stranger, that they didn't know how to count cards themselves? That possibility seemed inconceivable to me, but indeed stranger things had occurred. Maybe that was one of the reasons that the hotel had to declare chapter eleven, a process in the US that would protect it from creditors and therefore immediate bankruptcy.

The management at the Marina was corrupt as well. One of them, during the casino's journey through chapter eleven, even had a lady dealer stationed in a room, exchanging sex for an easier shift, or worse. This was done much to the displeasure of many of the other dealers. With a group like that running the show, little wonder that the Marina was failing. When you compare this management to some of the people that were on the "corporate" scene at the time, pioneering the city's transformation from small town to big town status, the Marina's "movers and shakers" were nothing short of pathetic.

One of the "big players" in Vegas was Kirk Kerkorian. He had just sold his MGM Grand hotel chain in Reno and Vegas, but retained the lion emblem for future use. In 1986, Kerkorian bought the Sands and the Desert Inn from Howard Hughes' Summa Corporation, for $110 million. A year later he sold the Sands, keeping the Desert Inn with the golf course as a freebie for the same amount. Now that's called thinking several moves in advance. In those days, poorly managed hotels were bought, put under competent management, and turned over quite rapidly, realizing an immediate profit.

Another entrepreneur of the first order was Steve Wynn of Mirage Hotel fame. He bought the Dunes Hotel and golf course for $75 million, and immediately started selling golf memberships for an alleged quarter of a million a piece. This guy was a real go-getter. First getting his mitts on the Golden Nugget downtown, then expanding on to the strip, building the Mirage Hotel and Casino with the help of Michael Milken of junk bond fame. He became the "darling" of Las Vegas in a very short time. Mr. Wynn was a good friend of Ike's, and I was surprised to find out that Mr. Wynn was half blind. Even so he was always seen cruising around his casino "seeing" to it that all was in good order.

Ralph Engelstad of the Imperial Palace was another businessman with his head screwed on real tight. He had a degree in commerce from the University of North Dakota, and some electrical know how when he landed in Vegas in 1959, just as the town was awakening. He somehow got control of the Flamingo Capri Motel in 1971, which was on the lot where the Imperial Hotel now stands. In 1972 after putting up a couple of buildings, gambling became an established fact at the Flamingo Capri. In 1974, he phased in the Imperial Palace's Asian theme and the famous hotel was well on its way, to making a legend of itself.

In 1981, he opened his automobile collection with just 200 autos. He collected cars owned by presidents, movie stars and other famous and infamous people. The car that ultimately got him into hot water was Hitler's personal Mercedes 770K, called the "Lorch," for which he paid well over a million dollars. He had it rebuilt from top to bottom, a project that took several years and cost many millions more. Evidently the mechanics did such a great job on the car, that he threw a big party to celebrate the event. The car was absolutely original, with Swastika flags on either fender, an emblem that some people found offensive. As a result the "free" city of Las Vegas gave him a fine. I kind of scratched my head on that one, because he offered to give his entire Nazi collection to the holocaust memorial that was just being built in Washington D.C. Finally the matter was closed with the imposition of a fine of $1.5 million for besmirching the "good" name of Nevada by incorrectly displaying a flag that some people found offensive.

You know, I find a lot of things offensive, but I was under the impression that in the "land of the free and the home of the brave," they could at least cut Englestad a little slack and permit a chauffer manikin to be dressed in an appropriate Nazi uniform rather than a "politically correct" suit. After all "Der Fuhrer" was in the back seat. Isn't originality the main idea in a restoration? Hell, you can't put the stars and stripes on the car or have Adolph wearing an American armband. Like a vampire that has seen a cross, some people have been so conditioned that even observing a Swastika makes them sick. Hmmm, I wonder if that is a response to well orchestrated propaganda.

Another household name in Vegas was Bob Stupak. He was a hardcore gambler from Pittsburgh who saw an opportunity and seized it with the purchase of one and a half acres, just north of Sahara Avenue on the strip, a place known as the naked city. It got that name because years before a lot of the showgirls would live there and endeavor to achieve the perfect tan by lying out in the sun, nude. As Vegas grew, the girls moved to the "nicer" areas of suburbia and the once classy naked city reverted to a high crime zone. Although his property's address was 2000 Las Vegas Blvd., technically Stupak was not on the strip. The strip in reality, started at Sahara Avenue then south. That was before Stupak's purchase. He opened up a place called "The Million Dollar Historic Gambling Museum" on March 31, 1974. In May of that year, after a dismal showing, the place caught fire and he eventually got three hundred thousand in damages from the insurance company.

In 1978 groundbreaking ceremonies took place on the new casino that was to be known as "Vegas World." On the 13th of July 1979 it was open for business. Within hours after he opened, his table's maximum bets shot up from $50 to $2000, making Vegas World one of the highest stake casinos on "the strip." After a huge profit in 1980 he again expanded the hotel to almost 1000 rooms. By 1985 the hotel was bringing in $100 million a year. By 1991, he laid out plans for a 1000-foot tower ultimately known as the Stratosphere Tower. Vegas World shut its doors in 1995 making way for the Stratosphere, which was ready for it's grand opening on April 30, 1996.

This colorful character, who had a fleet of Rolls-Royce autos available for use by VIPs, seemed to prefer driving his little Messerschmidt automobile or sport around on his motorcycle. Maybe one day the Imperial Palace can get hold of that sweet little gem of a car and add it to Engelstad's collection.

The car was very unique since it was originally designed to be a fighter aircraft. After the Second World War Willy Messerschmidt, the designer of the famous German fighter, the Me109, had thousands of fuselages sitting around. Forbidden to make any more aircraft, he converted the cockpit into the driver's area with a gull wing entry on the clear glass portion. The car's front wheels protruded from stubs where the wing was normally attached, and the steering mechanism was one single wheel in the back. What absence of waste; we could all take a few lessons from Willy.

These were just some of the personalities involved in the Las Vegas scene of the 70s and 80s', and somehow I felt myself drawn to them. They all had a free wheeling attitude and maverick personality, which suited my temperament. These were the guys transforming Vegas, and I wanted to be there to partake in the action.

Being an absolute realist, I also knew that if I were caught plying my craft at any one of their respective casinos, I would be treated as some sort of "pariah," and refused future entry. These actions were in no way to be taken personally, as it was their job to make as much money as they could. On the other hand it was my job to deprive them of that right when it came to me at least. I could care less if the other guy lost his ass, after all someone has to pay to keep the doors of my "client" casinos open, for without them I too would be out of work. P. T. Barnum once said that "there was a sucker born every minute," that is not to say that I look down on them but it is just a fact that can't be disputed. Besides didn't some of these so called "cherished" guests regard me as "bad" for winning, while they were losing their shirts. Perhaps they regarded themselves as "good" for doing so. However they wish to regard themselves, I regard them as "necessary." In the gaming business as indeed, in life nothing is equal, only equal to the task or a loser.

I often wondered why these "good" people thought me "bad," I certainly could see the casinos side, but had a hard time figuring out the patron's attitude towards me. There is a logo at Caesar's Hotel and Casino, "Come, and loot the Empire." I took these kinds of advertising gimmicks, not as cute little phrases worked out by a bunch of ad men on Madison Avenue, but as an invitation to grab the riches that are plentiful enough, not only at Caesar's, but all the other "empires" or theme casinos based on the strip. Maybe some of these "good people" thought that I was robbing the joint, or making off with what wasn't mine. Perhaps in some grotesque way they hated me for breaking out of the prison we were in. After all weren't we all under house arrest with our mandatory playtime.

These are the very same people who without a whimper or a protest think the government has a right to put its hand in their pocket; as if it was the government's god given right to do so. To earn without work is a travesty, and these people failed to see that fact. So, why should I be surprised to find that they fully expected to lose a certain amount every trip, the same as on their taxes every year? Their failure to see how much they could save in either venture, brands them as "suckers." How much personal tax do you think Stupak paid on his casino's $100 million profit in 1985? Not much, because he figured out how to beat the system "legally."

By now the hotels were starting to fill up with gamblers, revelers, drunks and misfits, myself included. The New Year's celebration promised to be the biggest event yet for the area. I played around town, getting a feel for the liveliest hotels and came to the decision that Caesars Palace was a good place to hang out. The problem was that the "cheap" seats, were all taken by cheap players, a group to which I too belonged. The $100 tables were largely vacant, except for the odd person who had too much money. By this I mean people who would vary their bets from $100, which was the minimum, to maybe

$300. The casinos love those flat bet types, because they know they can grind them down with enough exposure to the game.

To work this over crowded situation to your advantage you may want to employ a strategy called "Wonging" it. Stanford Wong, a noted blackjack expert, would observe a table till the deck became rich in face cards. He would then jump in and flat bet his maximum, until the count dropped, and then leave. What a beautiful way of playing; never wagering a negative bet. The casino would think that you are "one of those flat betters" to be ground down, eventually losing to the house. When this didn't happen the casino's sonar kicked in to find out why. Up to that point you work in tune with their expectation by being involved in lucrative betting situations, and also getting valuable RFBs, (rooms, food and beverages) from the establishment.

Gamblers get a high from wagering money. The guy that works for Taco Bell may get a high betting two dollars. Bill Gates, if he gambled, might get a high betting ten thousand; it's all relative on how much you have, or how much you earn. With the Wong method you can be a Taco Bell employee with a $5000 bankroll and walk around a casino with black chips in your hand, circulating among "middle class" clientele (Here I use the word class in the capitalistic sense only, because having "class" involves a lot more than just how much money you have or make). In other words, if you are a low wage earner you can bet two days wages on a single "turn of the cards;" you can leave the impression that you are an affluent player. This of course opens the doors of "privilege," that is comps, earned by people who have a high risk profile, and believe me when you flat bet on a basic system you are at high risk of losing your money.

The Champagne flows free on New Years Eve like no other place in North America. Sin City is my favorite place in the world during the turning of the calendar year. However despite the great festive mood I had a problem. Due to the huge volume of people; you couldn't get a cheap table. The casinos also realize that it is the time of year to capitalize on the influx of patrons. As a result, the table's minimums, are bumped up. The five dollar tables get raised to twenty-five, and the twenty-fives are raised to one hundred. As you can see, it can become very costly if you are a card counter trying to get a maximum spread up to your maximum bet of $100. If you're like me, the "Wong walk about" is probably the only solution.

Recently, however, the casinos in Vegas have implemented a policy of "no mid shoe entry." This basically means that you can't step into a game once it is in progress. This rule was introduced quite effectively in Atlantic City, as a counter measure against "back counters." They would stand behind a table, place a bet when the deck got rich, and then take their bets off, and leave as soon as the table became negative. The casinos offer the rather lame excuse that the rule is "player friendly," because many players don't like people jumping in and out of games. They say that it ruins the natural flow of the cards. I don't like people jumping in and out either, but for totally different reasons. They take some high valued cards out of play when the deck is rich; these cards would otherwise have been spent on me. On the other hand I welcome people to sit down when the count is low for the same reason, they take some low valued cards destined for me. Also the cards are spent a lot sooner, saving me a few low waiting bets at the table minimum. The real reason for this practice is to deter card counters. Rather than reveal that there might be something to this card counting stuff, the casino will not give the real reason for this practice to a player who is getting pulverized on the low count.

In 1985 however, the casinos had not yet implemented this new rule. I stalked the tables all day looking for a high count, and then put in my black chip. This can take a lot more work than simply sitting down and putting in your time fluctuating your bet from minimum to your maximum because you rarely get a chance to sit down to rest. As soon as the count is over, you must seek a new table looking for another positive opportunity. Like a shark cruising the sea, you must forever be on the move or die choking from asphyxia.

In the evening I called Cindy to see if she would like to kick up her heels that night and her answer was no. She did say, however, that she would like to see me, and invited me over to spend the evening with her, a great sounding plan. So I jumped into a cab and made my way over with a couple of bottles of Champagne. We "watched the ball drop" as the New Year was heralded in at various locations around the country.

The next day, I drove her to work in her car and she told me when to pick her up after work. Once the car was parked I went to work myself, in the same casino. I ran up to my room and got ready. Then proceeded to put in some time before the crowd descended onto the casino floor with the inevitable result of the minimum bets getting raised. The time was put in for the day, and I was now at liberty to visit other casinos and to do the "Wong Walk."

The holiday season is a time of great joy, especially for dealers in Vegas and perhaps other gaming towns like Reno and Atlantic City. This is the time that dealers get their highest "tokes" (tips) for the year. Although I played often at Christmas, and indeed tipped the same as I do at any other time, it is New Years that people crowd the casinos and for some reason alter their tipping behavior.

This "alms race" contributed to the investigation of the casino industry workers by the IRS. They were bound and determined to nail the dealers regarding these undeclared tips, on their tax returns. It was learned that some casino dealers were making $800 a night in tips, but only declaring ten percent of their wages on their returns. In most cases the casino industry pays minimum wages so tips are really vitally important for employees. Ten percent of something small, turns out to be something really small.

The government saw a chance to put the squeeze on the employees over the issue of tips; and they took full advantage of it. From now on, the dealer's tips would be scrutinized as never before. But how about previous years, when the croupiers declared the standard 10%; were they now going to have to pay? Most people involved, worked out a deal with the government but some were audited and ended up owing a whopping $250,000. Imagine a dealer owing that much. Basically he was indebted for the remainder of his days. The criminal actions of the government against its own citizens, was a real eye opener to me. Instead of the "from now on" rule, they went back several years to redeem their "pound of flesh." All this seemed to do was foster great mistrust, and in some cases even hatred against a government that was seen as a vulture tearing at the workingman's carcass. Ronald Reagan correctly said once that "Government doesn't tax to get money it needs; government always finds a need for the tax revenue it gets."

Many people wonder about tipping, some even feel duty bound to offer some sort of reward to the dealer for giving them a great hand.

To tip or not to tip, that is the question. I remember reading in some newspaper column that proper etiquette dictates a 5% tip for the dealer when betting. Who writes this stuff? Imagine for a minute that if you have a two percent advantage in certain situations that you are going to relieve yourself of that by slipping in a self imposed 3% disadvantage at an opportune time. I generally tip a modest amount if I am winning, or if the dealer gives me a deep cut, or if they help me in some manner. I appreciate the assistance and I show my appreciation the only way that a dealer understands, in the form of a tip. The dealers for the most part, pool their tips, which are distributed the next day.

It is rare for dealers to retain their own tips. For one thing some dealers are so rude that they couldn't find their way to the "toke box," or are so inept verbally that they inadvertently alienate the people that they are dealing to. Another reason is that a dealer, who is extremely lucky, rarely gets tipped and the one that is "dumping" his or her tray is awash with tips, this has a tendency to level out the strong days with the weak days.

This brings us to the most important reason to pool the tips. GREED. If a person is winning, the tips generally flow, when losing; the spigot is shut tight. Here is a personal example. I went out with a group of friends who knew very little about gambling in general, and nothing about blackjack in particularly. At that time in the Aladdin Hotel, the dealers retained all their own tips. Our plan was simple; we pooled our money, $200 a piece, and agreed to split the profits if there were any after the session. I didn't tell them of the tipping procedure implemented at the hotel but told them to follow meticulously the value of my bet.

The hotel was in chapter eleven at the time, so loyalties to the hotel seemed to be on the wane. At that time the hotels still had not been introduced to the mirror system of looking at the hole card, and as a result the dealer had to "peek" at the card to determine if it was a face or an ace, which would in turn indicate a blackjack. When the count went up, we all came out with a $50 bet. There were five of us, so that meant a total of $250 in play. I would slip in a fiver for the dealer, if she won it would net her $10. If she had a face card or an ace I would ask her, naively, after she peeked of course, whether or not to hit the hand. If she was stiffed, she would indicate that I should not hit the hand, when she said that I should hit I would then surrender and give the necessary instructions to the rest of my cohorts. Once I was dealt a pair of eights with a dealer having a ten up. I asked a typical question. Would you split the eights at this time? She responded by telling me without question that I should. I proceeded to put in another five for her on the split and after the win she netted $20.

Peter W., a friend of mine, always trying to be a perfectionist at whatever he tried, decided to emulate me by putting in a five in front of his bet. I could see that at this rate the dealer was going to be the only one making any money in the long run and there was no way to tell him politely that I was finessing information via a bribe. In short I told him to stop "putting the dealer up" because I had that angle covered. Indeed the others were also showing signs that they too were going to put the dealer up for a five-dollar tip. We called a hasty end to the session so that I could enlighten him about what I had been doing. He later told me that he thought it unusual that I would be asking a dealer what to do against a dealer's face card when I had a pair of eights. As a professional you must retain every possible edge that the game has to offer, and that was one huge advantage that could be used when the opportunity presented itself.

So as a rule, it is dangerous for a casino to allow dealers to retain their own tips. It is the most experienced ones that will always make the most money. Whether they do it by "the gift of the gab" or "the gift of the grab," as was demonstrated by our sinister but friendly dealer from the Aladdin.

Many casinos dislike patrons who tip the dealer for one important reason; less money for the casino. If a player, has a $10,000 line of credit and is a guest for three or four days, he could easily tip the dealers $1000. Let's assume that the player loses his total limit of $10,000; the casino only wins $9000. The other $1000 is a sum that went into someone else's pocket. When extrapolated to 200 gamblers, this could certainly mean a lot of revenues lost for the casino.

At some casinos the management would in effect tell the players that the dealers were sufficiently paid and that tipping was not necessary. Steve Wynn, of the Mirage, addressed this problem and went on record to say that the hotels should pay more money to the dealers as a wage and ban tipping altogether. To air these problems only meant one thing, the corporation's stockholders wanted more "bang for their buck." As is the norm, when people are seeking higher profits, it's usually at the cost of labor.

When it comes to tipping, you have to be your own guide. Don't over do it, because it cuts into your profits. If I won a thousand, and was ready to leave, I would ask the dealer if he wanted the twenty-five dollar chip as a toke, or would he like it wagered. Almost always their answer would be to bet it, usually with a caveat, "Bet it when you think the time is right."

Once a friend of mine was watching my brother play and on a particular instance a dealer screwed up and paid him $75, on a tie. He flipped the lady a five-dollar chip, to which he said to Kevin, "Who do you think you are Donald Trump?" We all had a good laugh over that one, but I am personally not averse to tossing an obliging dealer a gratuity just as long as they are somehow benefiting me. Not all the benefits are as blatant as the $75 pay off, but an unwarranted payoff certainly deserves some attention.

If someone at the table asks why you don't tip often, just tell them quite frankly that's none of their business. Some have even said "Let's take care of the dealer" in a feeble attempt to get the person pitching us the cards to be more or less on our side; as if they had anything to do with the arrangement of the deck. As for the dealers, let it be known that you do a lot of gambling, and that although you don't do a lot of heavy tipping, you will always be around to tip; unlike the next guy who tips like crazy and will never be seen again.

A lot of strange things happen during play, and a lot of mistakes are made on both sides of the table that should be mentioned at this time, in the event that similar circumstances occur to you. Once at Caesar's Palace, sitting at first base, I made a black chip bet because of a rather high count. I was not surprised one bit when I received a blackjack. As the dealer was finishing off his deal to the other players I was doodling with another black chip trying to put a backspin on it, when it got away from me. The dealer was busy changing some money for some another player at the opposite end of the table. The chip, in the mean time, rolled quietly around my bet, caught the edge of the chip, and fell near perfectly on top of my previous bet. I'm sure everyone saw it, except the dealer and the chap at the end. I felt pretty silly so I didn't say a word, and he paid out an extra $150. Did the guy get a tip for that error? You bet he did. I didn't feel bad or guilty at all, in fact I felt pretty good about the whole thing, because the night before I got whizzed for a black chip in the very same casino. Instead of pushing on a bet, he took it. The guy next to me made me aware of the fact, but the new deal had already commenced, and I foolishly chose to say nothing. It was payback time with a $50 bonus. You might say, "What goes around has just come around."

Another common error that dealers make is the insurance call. Playing at Caesar's, again in Las Vegas, at a quarter table the dealer was showing an ace, and I was sitting on a blackjack. He asked, "Insurance anyone?" And because the numbers were not there or for some other reason, I decided not to take even money. He turned over the B J and proceeded to take everyone's bet, even mine. This is usually done because the dealer is negligent, bored, high on drugs or all three. I quietly asked him, "Isn't it this casino's policy to push on a blackjack?" As he wiped the excess powder from his nose, he replied, "Why didn't you say so?" "I am saying so," I said. As he backed up the cards he saw that I did have a B J, and asked, "How much was your bet?" Shrugging my shoulders I said "twenty-five, fifty, maybe more." He gave me a dirty look and plopped down a fifty. After that he sure wasn't as complacent, and he paid a lot more attention to the game. Whatever they end up giving you, that amount should be re-bet on the following hand; to go back down to a minimum bet again would be fairly brazen.

Remember, even if chips are incorrectly placed into your square as a payoff, it is yours, if not noticed. Think about it for a moment, he could just as easily have made the mistake the other way, and taken your bet if not noticed by you. It has already happened to you many times, and you have been unaware of it. Mistakes are made on both sides of the table, and the more you play, the fewer mistakes you will make; this is the sure sign of a professional. Consider it pay back for previous errors intentional and otherwise made against you by the various casinos that you have patronized. If the dealer pays you and notices that he paid you in error, put him at ease with some humor. I like saying, "Come on, quit teasing me, I already had that money spent." This usually evokes a smile, and erases any animosity that might arise from the incident. I have noticed that dealers as a rule make two or three mistakes every time I go on a junket. Again, I can only comment on the mistakes I have personally noticed.

The time flew by on the first day of the year, and soon it was time to pick up Cindy at work. I made it to the parking lot and it wasn't long before she showed up. She asked if I would like to come over to her house again, and I agreed, but said that first I should pick up some toiletries. While upstairs I messed up my bed to make it look like I had stayed there. Then we departed.

We arrived at her place and she started making supper, which came as a complete surprise. I told her that I had comps from virtually any casino, and not to bother, but she insisted, saying that it was too crowded for her on the busiest day of the year. Instead, I went out and got some wine and some more Champagne.

She succeeded in making a fabulous supper consisting of Cornish hen, in orange and Pernot sauce with all the fixings. Later we sat around, getting into one another's mind. She struck me as quite a lady, with her head screwed on tight. She seemed to know what she wanted, and a general idea of how to get there. She had a great sense of humor and displayed an intelligence that was very refreshing.

She also had another talent; card counting. She could keep track of a deck with an accuracy that astounded me. I told her that we would have to go out one day and "ply" our luck at the tables as they say. She agreed fully, but the date had to be postponed because I was returning to Calgary the very next day.

The following morning we both arrived at work and we said our goodbyes early, since she would be on the job when my plane was leaving. It was rather unusual dating a girl working at the same casino from where I too draw my income. Our two occupations are brought into conflict, and of course the management frowns on the arrangement for obvious reasons; the potential favoritism that she may show me in monetary benefits. Therefore, our budding relationship was to flourish on a more clandestine level.

This suited me just fine because I was now planning to go on more than just one casino junket per trip. Here's how it would work. I would book two hotels for a one-week stay, using each one for a three-day period and like in the bible, I would rest on the seventh day. After each stay I would earn comps, which naturally included the much-coveted RFBs. Being a "qualifying" guest of the casino I would also submit a coupon and get reimbursed for my flight. In this fashion, I would get refunded twice for a single ticket. Naturally, I couldn't do that all the time due to schedule restraints, but would incorporate the tactic whenever the opportunity presented itself. This would also insure that we did a lot of dining out at the fanciest restaurants in the various casinos that I frequented.

One could also purchase an open ended Calgary to Vegas return ticket, come down with Ike on one of his junkets for free and fly back two weeks later, again for free when he came back again to Las Vegas. In this way you would have a full fare flight, the price of which would be refunded by a casino, if your play warranted. You could either use these tickets on future flights, or just return them to the airline for a "no questions asked" refund. This, in essence, meant that you would get paid for a flight that you received for free.

Back in those days the airlines operated in a more or less laid-back way, especially the charters that flew in and out of the old Hugh's Air terminal. I often had to go back early, and back then, to nail down a cheap flight, if I was returning on a Thursday or a Sunday night, you just had to show up early at the Canadian Airlines wicket. Those were the folks who ran some of the charters from Calgary. They would put you on board for $50, if there was room on the flight of course. The money most likely went to a Christmas bonus for the employees, a bonus which I wholeheartedly supported.

There were a lot of ways to work the fare reimbursement as added income. I would buy an open-ended ticket from Calgary to Reno return, and one from Calgary to Vegas return, with a separate one-way flight, Vegas from Reno. I would then go down to Reno on a junket and say goodbye to Ike after putting in my time. Then I would phone Harrah's to pick me up at the MGM in Reno. There they would meet me in a limo and drive me up to Lake Tahoe, and host me there for a three-day visit. When the junket was over, they would refund my Calgary to Reno flight. They would then drive me to the international airport back in Reno in their fancy limo, and I would be whisked away to Vegas to do the same thing at the Dunes. After my three days there, I would transfer to Caesar's Palace and again get reimbursed for the Calgary Vegas flight. As you can see there were several combinations that would pay off, almost like hitting three cherries on a slot machine.

Meanwhile, Cindy and I were talking and calling each other on a regular basis, during my absence from Vegas. You might even say we really liked one another. Once in Vegas I would get the use of her car with the only condition that I had to make sure that she was picked up on time. That seemed to be a fair trade off although I didn't like the car, which was a 1979 Camero in poor condition. This prompted me to look for a car of my own.

I settled on a 1981, 928 Porsche which was valued at $30,000 in Canada but only $15,000 in the US. It seemed like a good move at the time because the real cost was under $18,000 CAN. The car was what is referred to as a "gray market" vehicle, which meant that the speedometer was in kilometers and the gauges had German script. Now who couldn't put up with that for $12,000? I decided to register it with Alberta plates because the insurance was cheaper in Canada. I knew I couldn't take it to Canada because at that time they weren't allowing any imports of vehicles that were less than eleven years old. I could park it at Cindy's, and then use it when I was in town. This too was advantageous, as I could zip around in a reliable automobile with ease, and speed.

This arrangement worked well for a few weeks until Cindy's car broke down and she came to me almost in tears, saying that she couldn't afford a new car at the time and was wondering if I would let her use my Porsche when I was out of town. What could I say? It was parked at her place anyway, and we were dating, so I told her to go right ahead and use the car. That is the way it stood for a few weeks until I found it totally inconvenient so I volunteered to get hers repaired.

After driving a Porsche how could I expect her not to drive it while I was out of town? I too would have opted for similar arrangements if the situation were reversed. How was I to know that situations change? It just never occurred to me that two people could get into disagreements over trivial matters.

One day, as one of my trips was winding down, she and I got into a row over something. I packed my bag and took off, not even considering the consequences of what I had just done. Where was I going to park my "cherished Porsche?" It wasn't allowed into Canada due to its age, so that was out of the question. Or was it? After sitting down for lunch at the Cafe Roma in Caesar's Palace I decided to drive back and forgo my flight that was to leave later that afternoon. It was a risky ploy, but it was only temporary until I could find a place to park it, sometime in the future. I would then drive it back.

The drive up was fast and pleasant. I made it home with only one speeding ticket. Even that wasn't "technically" a speeding ticket because I had been caught In Montana, where they cited me for using too much fuel. Back then the speed limit was 55 mph and the state of Montana opted not to enforce the federal limit, and only issued a fifteen-dollar fine for that "misdemeanor." Not bad for a 90 mph infraction.

At the Canadian border they didn't ask me about my car, and of course I never volunteered any information. The usual questions were asked: How long was I gone? What was the reason for my trip? Did I have any liquor and how much? Not one question about my car. Without further ado, I was on my way to Calgary. "Boy that was sure easy," I thought to myself, I wondered why more people don't do that? Or maybe they do, in just that way.

Well at least the car was in a place where I could keep track of it, but I wanted to return it to the desert as soon as possible, because of the rust problems caused due to the salt used to de-ice the streets of Calgary.

Soon after arriving home I got a hold of Volker. He suggested that we go to the Executive Club for a workout, and a couple of games of squash. After, we went back to his Mount Royal condo, drank tea and chatted about many things. He mentioned that he was in the "import export" business, and said that I should consider going to work for him. He showed me some of his products. One was a Breathalyzer, to be used by an individual to detect whether or not he or she was over the legal limit of intoxication, prior to getting behind the wheel. In Alberta this was .08. The other was a fake US dollar detector. This latter item, now defunct because of the new bills, would detect the existence of a magnetic strip, integral to the old money. The strip was extremely difficult for an aspiring forger to install; a red light would start flashing along with a series of sharp beeps, indicating a counterfeit bill.

Unbeknownst to me at the time was his more lucrative import, marijuana. Also unknown to me was the fact that he had been the focus of an intense investigation, including wiretapping by a suspicious police force. This unfortunate turn of events dragged me into a situation that I had not anticipated. When the bust came down, I too was brought into the investigation.

Associating with Volker had implicated me too. The Calgary police issued a statement that it was the biggest crime bust of its kind in the city and they managed to take tons of the illegal substance off the streets. He later confided in me and said that the conspiracy was even more vast than what the cops had uncovered. The coordinating RCMP screwed up in Vancouver, when an unexpected call came in from Montreal to a location the authorities were staking out. The callers name from Montreal was the same as the investigating constable's commanding officer, and when he said to the undercover policeman, "Hi, this is John, how is everything going?" The officer gave the sting away updating the felon, all the while thinking him to be his boss.

What seemed to be a "Keystone Cops" episode when it came to Volker became brutally efficient when it came to me. They couldn't find any trace whatsoever of the cannabis on me, but the investigation turned up the illegal auto, and a fine was levied against me for smuggling. I had to get the vehicle out of the country, and they only gave me three weeks to do this, after a $2500 fine. All this because I didn't know that Volker's "import export" business included huge amounts of pot.

I wish I would have known; I could have avoided a lot of heartache.

He later told me that the stuff came from Afghanistan, and at a time when the Mujahadeen were considered "freedom fighters," not "terrorists." My how things change, perhaps they were neither. Maybe they were always entrepreneurial types, and just wanted "freedom" from the Russians, to grow their pot and other "lucrative exports." Once they were "free," with an about face from America, they were suddenly terrorists, who refused to change their "evil ways." But isn't that how gangs operate? They make temporary alliances with people that can further their ends. Hey, without even realizing it, I just defined American foreign policy. Didn't they do the same thing in Columbia, Panama and Chile? And what about Pakistan, wasn't the leader an evil dictator when he deposed the duly elected leader of that country. Evidently he became forward thinking again when he allowed US forces into Pakistan to fight the Taliban, next door in Afghanistan. It is truly a shame when we in North America, are led around by the rings in our slavish noses because our governments are determined to cloud our reasoning and take away our rights. The Russians and the Chinese jettisoned communism, which employed such deceit, and what did we do, we tolerate that same vile form of tyranny.

Facing the ultimatum from customs to remove my car a.s.a.p. or have it confiscated in "The Name of The Queen," I was forced to reconcile with the only person that I knew in Las Vegas, and that was Cindy. I phoned her up a couple of weeks after the incident, and to my surprise she was very receptive. I told her that I would be down soon and she insisted that I stay at her place.

After a few days, I drove down Interstate 15. What a marvelous drive. Idaho's roads from Dubois down showed evidence of "recent" volcano activity; in geological time, less than 5000 years ago. There in the middle of the magma field, about 15 miles past Idaho Falls, is erected the nicest rest area along the entire road. In Utah's southern regions there are things of beauty too; the red rocks around Hurricane were awe-inspiring. Then the St. George area, the last large town before arriving at the final destination, is rife with dormant volcanoes. From there, driving down the winding road through the Virgin River Gorge, offered some of the most breathtaking vistas of the entire trip. Like a mini Grand Canyon, the towering walls of rock, shoot straight up, blocking out any hint of direct sunlight. After dazzling the senses with a menu of geological wonderment, the last 90 miles of desert landscape seemed to be etched into the brain, as if to acclimatize the traveler to their ultimate objective, Las Vegas.

There I got a warm reception from Cindy. Apologies flowed like water from the both of us and the feud was over. Soon I was back working the casinos.

One thing that didn't sit right with me was her reliance on me for a ride. I told her that I would go half and half with her on buying a cheap second hand vehicle, so we could each come and go as we pleased. She loved the idea so we sold her car for $500 and purchased a VW rabbit for $3000, freedom at last with a two-car household.

The arrangement was simple enough, she would pay the rent, and I would purchase all the groceries, do the necessary cooking, and supply the ample comps to maintain our high life style. The cooking was cool. It was like mental therapy to taper off the anxieties of the day.

The moderate weather in Vegas was therapeutic and suited my sparse wardrobe. No need to wear anything other than a tee shirt and sweat pants. The town had gone ultra casual. Now, you were allowed into fancy restaurants and nightclubs with literally the shirt on your back, and a pair of shorts; shoes however, were compulsory. Everything seemed to be open 24 hrs. a day; movies, dry cleaners, fast food joints, super markets and, naturally, the liquor store. These were just some of the services that I remember because I often used them.

As the attraction of the city seemed to grow on me with every passing day, so did the magnetism that Cindy and I had for one another. In between our love making, I would do early morning "forays" into the down town, late evening "search and destroy" missions on the strip, and occasionally come home to "clean house," a short distance from the action.

Chapter Ten: European Delight

It was the spring of 1987. The money from 21 kept on coming in. I eventually went into savings mode, squirreling away $50,000 US, into a bank account. Credit cards started to roll in, and I was well on my way to making a small financial inroad, using the casinos. Even my gal had run into a little bit of money, and the thought of taking off for a European vacation to escape the oppressive heat of July and August could now become a reality.

A plan was worked out for her to fly from Phoenix with her mom, and spend two weeks with relatives in England. I would then meet with her on the last day of the trip, show her some of London's sites, and fly together to see some of continental Europe. She would drive my car up from Vegas to Phoenix, because it was fast and could handle the tight two lane curves with ease. I on the other, hand was to fly from Calgary, direct to London's Heathrow airport.

I wish I could say that the trip over was uneventful, but that was not the case. On the flight to England, I broke a toothpick after gnawing on one of Air Canada's steaks. A piece of the wood got imbedded between my tooth and my gums. By the time I landed in England it was throbbing.

I quickly went to Victoria Station, the main rail center in London, to get a lead on some cheap accommodations. I managed to nail one down for $25 per night at the Hotel Europa. A bargain I thought, as others were asking anywhere from $100 to $200 a night US. As luck would have it I was only five blocks from the hotel where Cindy and her mom would be staying, but they wouldn't be there till next day.

I scoured the neighborhood for a dental clinic, and finally located one in the center of a hospital courtyard. I thought to myself, "What a curious place to put a clinic?" As I got nearer I had an eerie feeling, like walking to the center of a football field, a field with no players, no crowd, no seats, just the dim glow of several lights illuminating the Atco structure. Finally at the front door, I peered in and noticed some movement inside. I knocked on the door, and a pretty black assistant answered and asked me what I wanted. I related to her my problem, and she informed me that the clinic was set aside, for HIV infected patients mainly from Nigeria. I couldn't believe my ears. She said that aids is in epidemic proportions in that country and that is why she was surprised to see me as they catered to mainly Nigerians.

Why the United Kingdom accepted aids ridden people into the country is absolutely beyond my understanding. If you disregard the cost of treatment you are still exposing the population to an unnecessary and unwarranted risk. To my way of thinking that was not a very responsible way of dealing with immigration at best, and at worst, was criminally negligent. In Canada to treat a person infected with the HIV virus would cost the taxpayers $90,000 per year, and if the disease progresses to "full blown aids," the cost then escalates to $250,000 yearly. If you hang a heavy chain like that around the taxpayer's neck I wondered, whether or not, THAT would deem them as slaves? A movie was made years ago titled, "No sex please, we're British." When it comes to this sort of thing, the word "sex" could and should be substituted for "sanity." I couldn't get out of there fast enough, and decided that I would wait till I got to Hungary, a communist country, to arrive at a vestige of common sense when it came to these matters.

After suffering all night with the pain I woke up and went to look up Cindy and her mom at their hotel. They had arrived late the previous evening, which was perfect because I was in no condition to socialize with the constant nagging pain and jet lag.

I entered the posh foyer of their hotel, and strode past a doorman dressed up in the classic uniform of a "Beefeater." Making my way to the front desk, I got their unit number and made my way quickly to their room.

Cindy looked great. A few pounds thinner from the English diet but that would all change once we arrived in Hungary. I was taken aback when I noticed that their room. Like mine, it was extremely small as are most rooms in London hotels. They were paying $200 per night, not for the room, but only for the lobby décor and the door man's fancy uniform.

Cindy and her mom had visited the North of England, around Bedford, from where the hardier Anglos hailed from. They enjoyed themselves greatly, and wished that they could have spent more time with their relatives. But then I came on the scene intent to show Cindy the "real" Europe, continental Europe that is, from where "real history" stems.

Cindy and I later escorted her mom to Heathrow, for her return to Phoenix. We said our goodbyes, and went to my hotel. When we arrived we spent much of the time writhing in one another's arms. In the afternoon, we too went to Heathrow on London's excellent subway system, and took off for the mainland.

We landed at Schiphol airport in Amsterdam at about 10:00 pm the following day, but we were in no condition to drive. The tooth was aching terribly and driving me crazy. We got a terrific deal on a hotel room right there at the airport, and in the morning rented a car to start our trek across Europe.

After a short drive we reached the German frontier, and from there drove right through to Austria. There were many casinos on the way, but I was in no condition to concentrate, so we just decided to go right through to Hungary where I was certain to receive good medical attention because many of my relatives there were doctors.

Arriving in Budapest we went to a place called the "Ibusz" where you could rent an accommodation at a private home quite cheaply. We got lucky, and managed to secure a place on the Buda part of the city, which was on the western side of the Danube River. We rented a room from a sweet lady for ten dollars a night. Once we settled in, we just fell asleep until the morning.

The lady's husband woke us up with a gentle tapping on the door, informing us that breakfast was ready. We went out on to the veranda to a beautiful horticultural treat. The yard was full of fruit trees of all kinds, billowing their various bouquets of sweet scents under our nostrils. Unfortunately, I couldn't truly enjoy these blessed aromas due to my lingering tooth pain.

I engaged the gentleman of the house in conversation, and told him of my malady, asking him if there was a dental clinic nearby so I could have my problem attended to.

His name was Peterdy Pal, (Hungarians always use last names first) and as luck would have it he was a famous sports caster, known throughout Hungary for his spicy language in broadcasting the soccer matches. He personally made a phone call and told me where to go and who to see, that way I could queue jump to the front of a long column. The dentistry at these clinics are free, if you could put up with the line-ups. Leaving the dentist a ten or twenty dollar tip as he suggested, would be more than worth the hours one would otherwise have to wait in the long queue.

At the clinic I was immediately struck by the fact that there was no privacy. Entering the facilities on the second floor, you were greeted with a battery of about fifteen dentist chairs set up much like a barber shop school, and every one could witness the procedure that was taking place at all the stations. My dentist even asked one of his colleagues how he should cut my gum open. The other dentist casually dropped what he was doing, and came over to offer his advice; an in house second opinion. A very "democratic" approach to dentistry I thought. With the removal of the toothpick, (gourmet's shrapnel) he sewed up my gum, gave me some opium to deaden the pain and sent me on my way. Naturally I was very appreciative and tipped him $20.

Now that I felt much better we walked to the center of the capital, along the famous Vaci Utsza. This famous road, designed like a ten block mall, attracted not only us, but also many of the tourists that ventured into the heart of Budapest. How perfect, they had built casinos right smack dab in the center of the city.

The first casino we visited was Caesar's; perhaps called so after its namesake in Las Vegas, or even harkening back to the Romans, who had occupied the Buda region centuries ago.

Upon entering the gambling premises we were asked for our passports, and had to pay a five dollar entrance fee. We were given a five dollar chip which could only be negotiated at the tables. We sat down and started to play.

At first we lost about a $100, then the cards started turning to our favor. Within one shoe we recouped our losses and managed to get $200 ahead. We made several 21s with fairly small bets and even managed to get a twenty-one with three of a kind. They offered a cute little incentive for "nailing" three sevens. The lucky person received a bottle of champagne. We made a couple of friends immediately by ordering the bottle opened and asked them to supply three extra stems so the other three people at the table could also enjoy a sip of the "bubbly."

We swaggered out and went back out to the mall. Two blocks later, we were at a casino called the Tropicana. As you are probably aware this casino too had a namesake in Las Vegas. My Hungarian countrymen were either not too inventive with names, or they wanted to capitalize on those more famous casinos in the state of Nevada.

Entering the premises, we were again asked for our passports and charged a five-dollar entry fee, which they replaced with a chip to ensure some play. The casino was on the main floor and nicely appointed with chandeliers, posh carpets and hard wood throughout, as one would expect to see in a similar gaming club in Vegas. The big difference was that when you order a drink, you just didn't get away with merely paying a tip, you were charged, or more correctly, "supercharged" for your beverage. Normally, a bottle of "hooch" might cost two bucks so paying five dollars US for a "high ball" was a little outrageous. This was prevalent all over Europe, with the exception of Monte Carlo. All this was hard to get used to, especially if you did most of your gaming in the USA, where drinks could be had for a gratuity.

We sat down at a table that had "Las Vegas style blackjack" written on a sign dangling over it. We were pleasantly surprised to find that the game offered a two-deck style of play, with double down on any two cards. We were the only ones at the table for about half an hour and interestingly enough never got any of the heat that is common in any casino in Nevada. We were left alone with the pit boss sitting on his elevated chair, over seeing the dealer's moves with little concern over our bets, or betting patterns; needless to say, we fully capitalized on this situation. We managed to siphon off a further $400 from the table before some bigger betters joined us. We played another half an hour and then broke off the engagement to check out the sights.

Budapest is one of the most beautiful cities in Europe. It actually consists of two cities; Buda on the west side of the Danube, and Pest

The parliament house (Rat House).

St. Stephens Cathedral, Vienna.

1936 Auburn boat tail speedster, top up.

The Toronto "Mob." Ed, Peter and
myself on a recent visit.

The "Blue Goose" in the Desert.

Sarah and I with the Swedes in Prague.

My two boys, Dylan and Beau.

Top down.

Fluke meeting with Dennis in Mexico.

Carla and I in better times.

Getting a "snapper" on a cruise.

Kathy getting a blackjack.

Tito, Kevin, Kathy and I.

A typical voucher for a comp to a buffet for a single party, received prior to play.

Key West character.

Key West, Start of Dixie hwy.

Kathy and I (after one too many
meals) on a cruise.

The Grande Casino,
Monte Carlo.

Towel art, Ocean Breeze.

Depiction of a rabbit.

Inside the Hotel Phoenix, Baia de Cris.

on the east side. Several well-located bridges that keep the traffic humming in an efficient manner, even in the 21st century, connect these two cities. The wide streets and thoroughfares are indicative of a planning scheme done on a world-class level, with streetcars and autos sharing the roads. Under the ground there is a subway system that is the second oldest in Europe and runs with typical European efficiency.

On the Buda side you get a commanding view of the grand Danube river. This older part of Budapest is festooned with fortresses and castles that fended off enemies such as the Turks and the Mongols, invading from the East.

The architecture is typically Baroque, seemingly that way to acclimatize the traveler coming from the Byzantine east, to the Gothic west. Perhaps many years from now, people will walk among the ruins debating how those cultures were related due to the similarity of building plans; just as today comparisons are made relating the pyramid plans of Mayans and Egyptians.

Also on top of the hill overlooking the Danube, is the Budapest Hilton. This hotel is located in an area called the "Var," meaning castle. The Hilton had a casino in its lofty peaks, with a charge of three dollars just to gain entry. The gaming areas were much smaller than either Caesar's or the Tropicana, and seemed to be frequented exclusively by the guests at the hotel. The only thing missing at this casino was personality. It was truly "hum drum" and seemed to lack the professionalism that was evident at the other two establishments. The staff wouldn't engage you in conversation; only abrupt answers were given. The place was permeated in an aura of coolness or stiffness that almost smacked of unmerited elitism. Cindy and I played only a single shoe in one of the tightest games we had ever played, because to lose even a dollar at that casino would have put a kibosh on the entire evening. The way it turned out, we won about twenty bucks, and left the place totally disillusioned.

Later on we went up to the "Citadel," a kind of fortress, which still shows the scars of the brave Hungarian defense against the communist invasion in the later stages of the Second World War; and also the wounds inflicted during Hungarian uprising in 1956. The view from the Citadel was heady. Gone were the dark days of communist rule when the lights were turned off all along the river at night, and were only illuminated during a visit by some "Commie" dignitary, or for propaganda "photo ops." These alien rulers, like Rakosi, failed to realize the intense pride that Hungarians felt for their city, their history and their culture. The Hungarians are neither Slavs nor slaves. The negativity to display these things in a festival of lights was just one of the many things that robbed the people's spirit of the gaiety and the drive necessary for a country like Hungary to prosper. The Communist system sucked the life out of Hungary and of course the Hungarians lost their happiness along with their hope. Thank God that era is over; now the lights are back on again, displaying the city at night. A smile was returning to the faces of a people pushed down by Orwellian drudgery and fear. No matter what system a country chooses to adopt, or in Hungary's case, was forced to adopt, the grayness has to be eliminated, and the fun put back in life and the life put back into living and earning an existence.

My uncle once related a story to me about a meeting organized by the "party" higher ups, to get the workers to cough up 10% of their wages to the government for the next year, thereby showing their loyalty and solidarity. This was a time when low wages kept both spouses in a family working six days a week. Such was the "Communist Paradise."

To show how "earnest" he was, my uncle got up in front of the designated group and told them that the proposed 10% was far too low, and should be raised to 50%. The workers roared with laughter, and later in a private meeting the party boss was going to make an example of him, with "enlightenment" in jail, but couldn't prove that there was mockery behind my uncle's statement. The party later dropped this new form of "tax" realizing that it might lead to another revolution.

Yes, the country was coming back to life. It would take a few more years before the Russian troops would vacate Hungary, but you could see that the writing was on the wall. The fraud perpetrated on the Europeans, that the Russians were there to protect them from an invasion by the Americans, and the fraud that the Americans were there to protect the West against an invasion from the Soviets from the east, was finally removed. Now Europe could rid itself of both the occupiers.

But sadly, only the Soviets vacated Eastern Europe, leaving the west part of the continent under "de facto" occupation since 1945; fourteen years after "The Evil Empire" beat a hasty retreat from their assigned sector in the East. Hmmm, I wonder what excuse they have to still be there.

European Delight

I remember President Reagan say, "Mr. Gorbechev tear down this wall," referring to the Berlin wall, and I saluted him when he said it because shortly after that, the wall was dismantled by the people in both the east and the west sector of that city. I wonder if Western Europe too can jettison its puppet governments in the same way. "Mr. Bush, allow the rest of Europe to prosper, pursue their own destiny, stop the 'Bush' whacking, and remove the yoke of your "New World Order." Your weight is too great for even Europeans to bear. Friendships aren't imposed or bought; they are gained by allowing countries their own breathing space and to become sovereign in their own right. So Mr. Bush, tear down this facade."

To put one nation in the role of a slave, and the other in the role of a tyrant, ensures future hostilities. A tyrant and a slave cannot be friends. Someone once said that, "For too long has a tyrant and a slave been hidden in America, she cannot know friendship therefore she must love." Perhaps more to the point, idle talk of love or the kind that inspired the building of women's shelters all over North America, is the only form of affection practiced by the rulers of the "land of the free." Korea, Vietnam, Nicaragua, Granada, Chile, Panama, Libya, Yugoslavia, Afghanistan and Iraq; these are just some of the conflicts in the last 50 years that come to mind. Like an abusive husband, "The Commander and Thief" says, "If you don't do it my way, I'll kick the shit out of you."

Isn't it a strange kind of love that makes an enemy out of a nation whose only sin is the pursuit of its own national interests? To be true friends of Europe and the rest of the world, America must abandon it's occupation and "world policing" policies, and allow Western Europe, and indeed the world to suckle on the teat of freedom. In this way, other nations may look forward to a future with self-confidence without the interference and intimidation of a third party.

I read the other day that some kid killed his parents because God had told him to do so. He was sent to a lunatic asylum to be evaluated, and rightfully so. Yet when a President states publicly that god told him to attack Iraq at the cost of perhaps as many as 500,000 civilians and well over 3,300 of America's finest, we do nothing. Like many sensetive jobs, a prerequisite to swearing in a leader of a nation should be the manditory request, "Would you please proceed to the bathroom and pee into this little bottle?"

A country that "bullies" smaller nations eventually ends up bullying their own citizens. This was evident in the last 30 years. Spectacles like Waco and Ruby Ridge are just the "tip of the ice berg," and the corresponding responses like Oklahoma City, may well become the norm. The ruling "elite" is out of touch with their citizens and will eventually look in the mirror for their next victim. "Look," writes the sage, "they eat each other and yet cannot digest themselves."

We spent about a week looking around Hungary, occasionally popping into the Trop or Caesars, for a round of 21; this we found to be an excellent way of subsidizing the trip. If you go to Budapest, do remember that English rules prevail. If you double against a face card, and the dealer happens to turn up a blackjack, you lose both bets.

On the way back to Amsterdam, we stopped in Vienna to see the sites of that beautiful city. In the inner part of Vienna (in Europe known as Wien), lay the oldest area, and coincidently, block for block, the most architecturally gifted center in all of Europe. A road appropriately called the "Ring Strasse" circles that sector. The circular road is renamed at various points of its circumference, by assuming the name of the most prominent building that touched its perimeter. For instance, the road would be named the Museumring, since that is the main building on that stretch of road. If you were traveling on the Operaring, you were certain to be near the Opera house. The Burgring, would put you in front of the elegant palace of the former dynasty ruling Austria, the Hapsburgs.

There is one beautiful building called the Rat Haus on the "Ring." This architectural masterpiece houses none other than the city administration. In North America we call it "City Hall." Using the street naming logic of the Viennese, most Calgarians would demand the frontage street in front of our city administration be appropriately named "Rat Street," judging from the unwarrented property tax hikes that our "city fathers" have tied around our necks.

In the very center of the "old town" is the magnificent St. Stephens Cathedral. This was the centerpiece of the city. The structure's tall steeple seemed to reach out and command dominion over all its architectural peers; stabbing at the heavens, piercing open some imaginary portal to a perceived life hereafter. The interior was designed with such grandeur as to humble the most skeptical non-believer, or the most powerful king, as they crossed the thresh hold.

We spent hours gazing at its immensity along with the tourists that thronged to its lure. At noon the bell would peal out a sound so deep that it was audible in all neighborhoods of the "ringed" city. The eerie staccato, reverberating its "mea culpas" had the entire mall standing at attention looking skyward searching for the source of the sound.

I have since learned that the bells in Europe ring at noon to commemorate the battle of Nandorfehervar, where commander Hunyady, a Hungarian, defeated the Turks thus ending their incursions into Europe, "saving" the continent for Christianity.

Walking out from the cathedral, and nearing the Kartnerring on the right, there stands the Casino Wien, (Vienna Casino). You entered the building and ascended to the second floor to an incredibly packed area; standing room only at the 21 tables. The conditions were not advantageous for Cindy and I; after "Wonging" it for about 30 minutes we made our exit.

We went to our not too fancy accommodations that I commandeered at a university being used as a "hostel" for the summer break. The rate there was twenty dollars as compared to $300 at "nicer" hotels. The room was designed to sleep four, but when we retired there were just the two of us. The room had no air conditioning, and as a result we slept in the nude all night to gain some relief from the heat. We awoke to the sounds of bags being zipped, and upon opening our eyes, to our embarrassment, we found another couple in the room; they had both come and were going while we were asleep. We must have been so tired the night before that we never heard them come in. Nervous good morning greetings were exchanged and half smiling, they left.

We resumed our trip back to Holland, sleeping at rest areas along the "Auto Bahns" until we arrived in Amsterdam; from there we flew back to London.

We then spent another night at the Hotel Europa, after which we then departed London. Cindy headed for Phoenix and I went to Calgary via Toronto.

Chapter Eleven: Working the Town

On the way back to Calgary I stopped in Toronto to visit my "comrades in arms," Ed and Peter. And again with Peter's help, I managed to get a two-day stop over for free. This worked out well as the three of us again could enjoy each other's company. Peter is the more serious of the two; Ed keeps us in stitches, always seeing the humorous side of things no matter how serious the situation. Again I felt a surge of life return to my soul. Connecting with two good friends, "who held down the Eastern front," has revitalized me. Very well for me, but I often queried as to where these two lovable scamps went to recharge their own spirits.

Immediately on my return to Calgary, I got the bad news that my beloved Porsche had broken down in Kingman, a small town in Arizona, half way between Vegas and Phoenix. Cindy had the car towed to a Porsche dealership in Vegas, and took it upon herself to have the engine dismantled and analyzed. When I got back to Vegas they showed me a basket of parts, proving that the engine was burnt out.

What evidently happened, was that due to the brutally hot weather, the radiator hose had burst causing the loss of coolant from the engine. Instead of stopping, Cindy kept driving till the engine finally seized. The rebuild cost would have been about $12,000 so I decided to part out the car for $6000.

It was back to square one again with no vehicle. Thinking that desert transportation should involve an air-cooled engine rather than water-cooled, I was now kicking myself in the ass for not springing for the extra cash to buy an air-cooled Porsche. To say that I was upset with Cindy would have been an under statement because I told her before that, the only two gauges that mattered were the oil pressure, and the water temperature. The rest were there just for show, and if either one "red lined" she should pull over and shut off the engine.

I was now out about $10,000 and on the hunt for an air-cooled vehicle. After seeing that beautiful Thunderbird "keyed" from bumper to tail light at the Silver Slipper years ago, I had second thoughts about owning another Porsche. So it was decided to now go on the hunt for a VW beetle convertible.

I scoured the papers every day for weeks till finally one came available at Falconi's Honda, on West Tropicana Avenue. It was a 1978 convertible, priced at $2500. Even back then they were asking $5000 for a similar car in Canada. Unfortunately, my worse fears were confirmed. The vehicle was in appalling condition, but on the plus side it was a desert car and was rust free. After a long session of bargaining, where I was made to jump through "hoops" between the manager and the salesman, I finally ended up getting the car for $2000.

My philosophy in car buying is to fall in love with the vehicle after you own it, that way you are assured of getting it for "market value" (the lowest price the owner will sell for and the highest price that a buyer will pay). As I drove it home, the love affair was kindled.

The repairs needed were basically cosmetic; seats, door panels, carpet and roof were all showing signs of dry rot from the merciless desert sun. But most important, I was mobile again, in a mini Porsche; just as the great man had intended, with the bonus of air conditioning. Now I could go around town on my forays to various casinos, and deprive them of the very thing that they held most dear to their hearts, their money. True, I couldn't go "casino hopping" with the speed that I had been able to in the past with my Porsche, but I would do it with more frugality. The big difference between a 1978 Porsche and the 1978 "bug" was the speed and the handling, but fuel efficiency was in the Bug's favor.

I opened an account with one of the after market VW suppliers under the aptly chosen name of "Mirage Autos." This was a name that had popped up years before in a conversation with Ed K., during one of our "idea sessions." The silent motto was, "We're here, but really we're not." For a couple of hundred dollars I got all the parts required to redo the interior of my new acquisition. Now I could devote my time to a meaningful hobby between trips to the casinos.

I was cutting a wide swath through the assets of my chosen "victims" for about a month. Then, quite unexpectedly, I received the news that I was to go into surgery for that nagging shoulder problem that just wouldn't go away. So hopefully after the rotator cuff operation the pain would vanish. Even if I could just get a good night's sleep, post surgery, it would be worth it. Arrangements were made through my friend Ike, who assured me that there would be enough room for me on the flight back on the upcoming Sunday, from Vegas to Calgary. He said, "I leased the damn plane off Canadian for $30,000, I should know how many extra seats are available." This was gratifying news as the surgery was set for Tuesday of that week.

For the next six weeks after surgery, my mobility was seriously compromised. I decided to stay in Calgary until the immediate health matters were resolved; after removal of the stitches, I would take the next flight with Ike to the Nugget.

Even with the post surgery pains, the shoulder felt much better and sleep came a lot easier. Six weeks after the removal of the sling I would be sleeping like a baby. In the mean time I might just as well hang out in Vegas as anywhere else. Why not? There was work for the disabled, kind of, and a chick that I was growing very fond of to keep me company.

That month was spent pursuing the various gimmicks that the smaller casinos around Las Vegas would come up with to gain your business.

One of the hangouts that catered to locals was the Continental Hotel and Casino. They were offering multiple pay offs on consecutive blackjacks. Here is how it worked. The first BJ would net you the usual one and a half times your bet, if you got one back to back you would receive three times your bet, and if you got one after that you would receive five times your bet. Man, they took a bath on that one. The program had to be discontinued after two weeks. People like me were queuing up to get a seat. The guy that thought up that program must have been cooling his heels at the unemployment line shortly after.

If I bet $25 on a two card 21, I would get paid $37.50. Naturally, if you have a plus count with extra aces, you would make damn sure that a higher bet was now placed because you were now vying for a three to one payout. This huge advantage on the blackjack game makes it very beatable, even if you don't count cards. With 300% on blackjack payouts, the game at the Continental was the best game in town. Everyone could now beat the game; at the very least counters and basic players. If you got 21 with two cards again you now had a chance to get a five to one pay out on your next bet. That seemed to me a "no brainer" as far as counting is concerned.

Even a person that notices a blackjack-friendly square could capitalize on a fortunate set of rules that puts a casino at a disadvantage. How many times have we sat down and noticed that one person seemed to get the lion's share of the two card 21s. Even if you don't count cards, and are a minimum bet player, if you are on a twenty-one friendly spot, you will certainly raise your bets after the first BJ.

I can only guess as to what motivated the casino to implement this rule. Because the casino has just lost a hand on which they have paid out one and a half times, they probably expected that the average player would press their bet by half. Considering that the count had just dropped, the casino was now in a position to win back the loss. Unfortunately, they failed to take into consideration the "repeater" spots, and more importantly, the 300% payout variable, which was a huge advantage especially on the high count.

I get back-to-back BJs a lot, especially on a high count and if any casino is silly enough to offer the "triple" for consecutive 21s they're going to interfere with their "keep rate" which is around 14% (for every dollar bet they make a profit of fourteen cents). If this drops below, let's say ten percent they are in serious trouble. With the formula adopted by the Continental, this ensured the keep rate to be in that serious category.

The Horseshoe also had gimmicks such as the two for one blackjack, but, and I stress the word but, to a maximum of five dollars, and this to lure players for the slow Christmas season.

Some of these gimmicks weren't thought out properly at all. Let me give you a classic one, of which I took full advantage. I used to have about $20,000 Canadian kicking around the apartment at all times, in the event that some hare brain casino gimmick would fall like a plum into my "scheming lap."

One day I was driving on the strip just south of the Tropicana Hotel, and on the marquee of the Hacienda Hotel I noticed a sign that stated, "Canadian money honored at par." Upon seeing that, I slammed on the brakes turned into the parking lot and headed straight to the casino's main cage. I asked about the sign, if in fact the information on it held any merit. They told me that I wouldn't really get par for my Canadian money, but that I would get the going rate, which was 85%, and then 15% in coupons that were to be played with a matching chip. These were called "match play coupons." In other words I would have to make a five-dollar wager and if I also had a coupon with that wager I would end up with fifteen dollars left in the square, if I won. They would then take the coupon, and put it down the drop box. I quickly worked out the possibilities if I flat bet a five-dollar chip with a coupon, every win would be like getting a "turbo" blackjack. In other words one with a payout of two to one, and this translates into a scenario where losing is virtually impossible.

You can imagine how fast I made it home in my "cute" little bug to pick up $5000 Canadian cash for play that afternoon. On returning, their eyes nearly bulged out of their heads when I laid the money down at the cage and instructed them to honor their ad. They begrudgingly counted out $4245 in chips, which was the going exchange rate at the time, and 151 five-dollar match play coupons. I quickly went to the double deck table and took out about twenty of them and started to play. It was like being in blackjack heaven, every win was basically the usual two card 21. The pit boss was hovering around my table asking where I had gotten so many match play certificates. I told him that I had five thousand to spend, and if they gave me such a good rate of exchange on my "dough" I would honor them with my play. I don't know if that remark vindicated any skepticism that the staff may have harbored about the Canadian money "campaign," or whether they thought that I was mocking them; quite frankly I didn't care. They had kicked me out about a year before for "aggressive" play and either didn't recognize me or because of my flat betting thought that I would pose no danger. It took about two hours to play all of the coupons and as soon as the last one was played I proceeded to color up all my winnings and left.

I had basically flat bet the entire amount only raising the bet occasionally to twenty, plus the coupon of course, so they must have felt that I wasn't much of a card counter.

I walked out of the casino with over $500 in profit. Not bad for two hours of relaxing play. I call this kind of play "easy money" because it is a mathematical certainty that you will win. I wondered who thought up that ploy to get Canadians into the Hacienda. Wouldn't it have been better to offer them let us say 87%, instead of the going rate of 85%. They would then have avoided the obvious give away of fifteen dollars in match play money.

Whoever floated this "gimmick" was a "bone head" and I knew that it wouldn't take long before they would cut down that money tree, so I planned to make a "return engagement," for the night shift. After arriving home I "reloaded" with another $5000 Canadian, and waited for the shift change.

I returned at about eleven o'clock with my daughter Alana that night and plopped down the five grand. They dutifully cashed it and we went on to play the two hour session but this time we would vary our bets a little more as the count went up, but not too much, as I didn't want to screw up a good thing. The new pit boss again asked from where we had gotten so many coupons. I gave him the same reply that I gave the day shift boss. After the certificates were spent we walked out to our car and counted about $800 in profit.

The next afternoon I went back with another $5000 and was notified that $3000 was the maximum that they were allowed to convert. "So," I thought to myself, "after only one day they're already feeling the pinch." Not good news from two perspectives. The first being they were such a "chicken shit outfit" that they "sweat" the thought of someone winning off their gimmick. Secondly, and most important was that somebody who knew something about percentages actually did the math, and realized that it was unworkable.

With 90 "match play" coupons I played just over an hour with some fairly bad luck and barely made $100. In the evening I took down $5000 again, but word had been passed down and it became policy. $3000 was to be the maximum that they would convert. Playing a little more aggressively, and using the certificates I managed to pull out a $700 profit.

Upon returning the next day, the rules had again been changed to allow a maximum of only $300 converted per day; that is for a twenty-four hour period. So I now knew for sure that it was me that had caused the policy changes. I could now only get nine coupons per 24-hour period, making that play unprofitable for the effort.

Boy, if I had a casino I would hire a guy like myself to go over gimmicks or play features before incorporating them into policy, let alone advertising them on the marquee. In fact I drove by there a few days later and the "heralded" sign that had been exhibited boldly for the town to see, had been hastily removed.

Some inducements are ill-conceived flops while other have some merit like the one that was touted by the Maxim Hotel.

It was 1988 around February, when Cindy and I strolled into the Maxim, she to play poker while I, on the other hand, would try my luck at 21. My attention was drawn to a single deck table that was played till they would physically run out of cards, then shuffle up the discards, and resume the deal. The only time the deck was shuffled in its entirety was either when a new dealer came to the table, or when a new deck was introduced to it.

Well this certainly seemed like a huge improvement over the Horseshoe game, or for that matter over any single deck game that I had ever played at before. Usually, by yourself at one of those down-town casinos they would give you about three or four deals, and then reshuffle, rarely giving you more than a half deck of penetration or twice around on a full five seat table as at the Horseshoe. This seemed like an interesting change, probably introduced to generate a little business for the club, as it was about two blocks east off the strip, on Flamingo Avenue, and classed as "out of the loop."

It took about ten minutes before a spot became available for me to sit down. I eagerly took my position, got some chips and placed down the minimum bet of five-dollars. For about fifteen minutes the deck was either in the minus range or hovering around zero. Then it happened, the moment that I had been anticipating. The count soared up to a plus five, with more than half the deck spent; the true count must have been a bit more than plus ten. My eyes glanced around making sure that only the dealer would be aware of my bet when I put it in, so as not to attract too much attention. "It must be my lucky day," I thought to myself as I noticed that the pit person was busy fetching a marker for the neighboring table. Agonizingly, I watched as the dealer made change for one of the players at my table at what seemed to be a snail's pace. I didn't want to draw attention to myself prematurely, so I waited till the last second to put in the bet. To my surprise, he didn't even call out "CHECKS PLAY" when I put in the black $100 chip.

After what seemed to be an infinity the deal began again as anticipated. My first card was a face card, and the dealer had a seven up. I was just visualizing what my second one was to be when to my shock he ran out of cards just before getting to me. As advertised it was to be a continuously played deck so as a result, he took the cards out of the discard tray, shuffled them up, got a cut, put the cut card on the bottom of the deck, and resumed play.

Now, because the deck was running at about a plus five when the deal began, it was now running at a minus five because we were missing those five face cards that had been turned up as player cards, the ones for which I had made my original bet. So now I had made a hundred dollar bet on a minus five count. As a result of the reshuffle, I would probably have to hit my stiff against the dealer's seven. On the positive side, because the count was now low, I would probably not break. On the negative side the dealer would in all probability get a better hand than a seventeen. As it turned out I didn't have to worry about the dealer's hand at all because I was dealt a five, and hit it later with an eight, breaking my hand.

Not knowing the full implications of the continuous play had cost me dearly. It wouldn't have been too silly if I had just made that mistake once, but I repeated it again many times, almost always with the same results. I reached in my pocket so many times that I was affected by a condition that I call "the loser's lean." In retrospect, the big bet would have been better utilized had it been made on the low count because the dealer would have presumably been stiffed like me but then I wouldn't have been facing a must hit position and he would have to hit a stiff, with a deck now in a plus condition.

To play this "gimmick" successfully, one would have to employ a side count of the total amount of cards spent in play to determine when to come out with "the bet." This would insure that there were sufficient cards left to have the occasional double down, and of course enough cards left to break the dealer. If the count is high you must have the knowledge that the cards won't be shuffled up mid way in the hand; and if the count is low you also must have the knowledge that the cards WILL be shuffled up mid way into the hand. Unfortunately, in order to do that, the scenario becomes extremely difficult to follow. I am sure some people could do it but it is beyond my limited capabilities. I would need the connivance of another player, counting the total number of cards in play.

It seems to me that someone did just that, because by the time I was ready to act on the new game, the game had been cancelled. Too bad that I wasn't adroit enough to act on it a lot quicker than I did, because "manna" doesn't fall from the sky on an every day basis.

This screw up happened as a result of my inability to adapt rapidly enough to the new conditions thrown at the player by the casino. Remember that it is infinitely better, financially speaking of course, for the casino to change its rules because of your triumphs than maintain them due to your losses. He who figures out the system first reaps the largest dividends.

The Lady Luck Casino, in the downtown area had and interesting "incentive." In their show room they would pass out a coupon with the drinks; one per order. It had emblazoned on it an ace of spades with a caption that read, "You may use this coupon as your first card with a bet to a maximum of $25." You could put this coupon down on a square, with your bet on top. They would deal everyone but you a first card, and then deal everybody, including you a second card in the usual manner. Often times I would get the "snapper" or another ace. In the eighties it was common practice downtown to allow the re-split of aces, making that a powerful hand.

Naturally with only one of these coupons in a person's possession the "special" trip to the Lady Luck wouldn't be worth it. After all wasn't it the casino's way of getting you interested in risking money following the show? What they didn't take into account was that you could take all the "aces" that most people just left behind on the table as you were walking out. Now 25 or 30 coupons at $25 per play were indeed worth the $20 admission fee. Add to this the power of the count and as you can see it would net you a lot of BJs.

Don't ever pass up an opportunity to "stick" it to the casino, even if the game is not blackjack. One day Bill, my father in law to be, told me about a bingo game at the Holiday Inn on the strip, the one that used to have the riverboat facade. Bill and his wife played a lot of bingo and one day they went to, what the casino called, the "early session." It started at 8:00 am, and ended at 10:00 am. The problem for the hotel was that they couldn't get the place filled, bad for them, good for us when it comes to a game like bingo.

Working the Town

There were computers for lazy people (or smart ones, depending on perspective) who would just enter the number called, then sit back, and watch how close they were to getting a bingo. The machine would even alert you as to which cards were only one number out. Bill told me that he went into the place and bought the maximum number that the machine would hold, I think it was around 80, for twenty-five cents per card. His out lay in cash was around $20 and the jackpot was $100. The beauty of it was that there were only ten other people playing and none were using the computers, therefore he had the majority of the cards.

I went down with him once and he showed me how it all worked. We went 50/50 on the wins, and the losses should there be any. There were a total of eight games played, and if you won a game the money lady would turn the key on your computer and give you a free bevy of cards; the same amount with which you had won with. We played the first game, won and also got the "free ride" for the second. In total they paid us $400; we had won half the games with less than half the cards. With the number of cards we had, I guessed we should-n't have won that much, so in effect we were lucky in the extra wins department. Luck has its merits but believe me in most games of chance, it's volume and not luck that will determine your win rate most of the time.

So here it was, yet another money tree that could be had at 8:00 am if you were an early riser, or one at 12:00 midnight if you were "night hawk." I found there were fewer people playing the morning game than the midnight one, so I decided to concentrate all my efforts on the morning shift. I also opened a separate "bingo" account to buy things like cars and accessories. Unfortunately, the game was discontinued after two more weeks with only $2000 in that special fund.

I thought, "What a wonderful way for some adroit thinking pensioner to augment his meager income." That is exactly what Bill was doing when he was in town. The problem was that when he wasn't in town, I was siphoning off the "fat of the land." That is what probably extinguished that source of revenue.

Later that month, in Calgary, I went to consult the doctor about my shoulder. He told me that with mild exercise, gradually increasing in intensity, I could be back to work in just a few months.

That was all very good if I would have wanted to return to my previous employment, but the way things were shaping up I thought that I would keep plugging away at the 21 game. I found the game to be totally relaxing and the beauty of it was that I didn't have any deadlines to meet, or cater to some one else's wishes. The irresponsibility of it all was almost intoxicating.

Taking up the game of blackjack truly makes you an "independent contractor." You can probably end up making more money in less time than at your regular job. The government in most cases is so greedy that they want to get into your pockets at every opportunity. They would be the first to "terrorize" winning patrons if they knew what we were doing.

They hate winners. Assume that you make $40,000 a year. In Canada the tax is about 50%. Now when I say that, I am talking about all taxes, hidden or those that are all to obvious, so in effect you have made only $20,000. Now, let's take another situation. Let's say that you make $20,000 gambling, or more correctly, playing 21 because only losers gamble. You have in fact made $40,000 because had you had a job to put $20,000 into your pocket, you would have had to earn the $40,000. Now what part time job would you rather be involved with, one that penalizes you for making more money, or one that puts every blessed dollar you earn straight into your wallet?

Every North American should, dutifully promote anything that reduces the instances of looting by the government via their income tax levies. The more money you put into their greasy little hands, the more money they want. Like a spoiled brat, "Uncle Scam" has driven good people into bankruptcy with their endless and increasing demands. When I have a hundred-bucks in my pocket, I know that the poor bastard that punches the clock had to earn two hundred for the same buying potential. The beautiful thing is that the "higher ups" feel that the game is unbeatable and push the gambling bug like a pusher with his narcotics. They know that some people will find the urge to gamble irresistible, and as a result will destroy their lives. The only thing the government desires is to corner more revenue for their own selfish ends. This can take the form of dictatorial raises and fat pensions. If they could save a billion here or there I could see a reward of a raise, but when you see the country going further and further into debt, rewarding them for their incompetence invites more than a polite response. Any parent that can balance their family budget successfully is far more competent to be running the affairs of nations than those mindless finks in power. And guess what? The parents would do it a lot cheaper.

Years ago when sanity reined, an elected representative would sit down with his peers for a month or two, and hash out laws that they felt would help navigate the "ship of state" on a smooth journey. Then they would go out and do their "real" job to see how smoothly the new laws were working. If the laws weren't functioning as intended, then they were either tweaked or just downright dropped, or replaced with new ones that would work. The whole idea behind it was not to lose sight of the common man, the guy on the street who would be most affected by the laws newly imposed. This is accomplished by going down to street level. How on earth can you delegate authority from an "ivory tower?" You lose touch with the very people that you are in the business of governing.

Davy Crockett was just this kind of man. I doubt very much if he would have been in favor of any foreign war, but when it came to aggrandizing America he put his life on the line to wrestle Texas from the Mexicans. What present day politician would have the balls to do that? As a congressman he packed his duffle bag, a musket, some ammunition, and rode to the Alamo to increase the size of his beloved country. The shiftless bunch of bastards that run the county today, have the youngest and the brightest, go off to some far distant shore, to visit strange lands, and meet all kinds of people (terrorists) that eventually do a lot of them them in. They say that they want to prevent border incursions in other lands, yet we have the most porous borders on the entire globe. Hmmm, I wonder if they are just feeding us yet more propaganda?

That settled that question. I was going to do my patriotic duty and stand aside to let someone else do my work for me. That way I would in effect be creating employment for other souls who weren't working. This kind of thought is no doubt construed by the higher ups as "free loading," but how could they be so hypocritical. When I work I sweat for every dollar that I earn, and am careful not to spend it foolishly. When they reach into our pockets, we only get a receipt for what we could have earned on our paychecks had they not taken their "slab" of the pie. They then spend our hard earned money on $500 hammers and $1500 pillows. Then with a straight face ask you to be patriotic and pay your "rightful" share. They all have free medical plans, paid for by us through our tax dollars, yet some of us who pay the tax can't afford medical insurance. That is parasitical and evil. The entire matter reeks of scandal. If we were really patriotic, we would all withhold our taxes entirely and let the spoiled brats throw their tantrums and try locking us in jail as a group. They couldn't do it. They would have to yield to saner ideas and pare back on a lot of things that are deemed essential by the powers that be.

Thus I went back to doing what I increasingly did better and better.

A lot of things in twenty-one, using basic strategy, are pretty much straight forward. But even to the most closed minded basic player, the one mistake that they make over and over again, is their play once they have been dealt their hands. One of the biggest mistakes they make is the "no hit" when they have an ace-seven. It is clearly stated in any table on strategy that I have ever read, that the ace-seven is hit when the dealer is showing a nine, ten or an ace. These same people that use the system as their "bible," totally disregard the recommendation, and stay put on that feeble hand. If the average hand that the dealer has is over eighteen then why not hit the soft 18?

If the dealer is showing a nine, you have a total of 27 cards that will either better your hand, or keep it the same value. There are three aces, sixteen faces, four threes and four deuces that give you 27 cards. That is 27/52, better than a fifty percent chance, and if it is better than a fifty percent chance you should be doing it because it is no longer a gamble. If you, as a 21 player, are going into a blackjack game armed with the knowledge that you are going to reverse the tables in the odds department, then a two percent advantage isn't a bad place to start. So hit that soft eighteen. There is only one circumstance that I can think of in which I wouldn't hit a soft eighteen against a ten, and that is close to the end of a shoe, where the count just started to soar, and taking a hit may create a situation where the cut card is in danger of coming out. Thus the high count would merely be shuffled up rather than played. But in retrospect if I had the minimum bet in play with the above situation, I wouldn't hit anything whether it was a hard five, an ace-three or a stiff. I would just take my "lumps" on the minimum bet and come back with a maximum bet next hand, with more squares if that was at all possible. In that way, you will be able to take full advantage of the positive count if the cut card doesn't appear.

Another huge mistake made by basic players occurs when they don't double the ace-seven against the dealer's stiff. The ace-seven is a double against all stiffs if the count is in the plus range. In fact it is such a good play that it is even a double against the six up to a minus thirteen. Many people just don't know when to do the double down. Had they learned to count cards, they could do the double down with confidence. Knowing the number for the double is achieved through the skill of counting. If you have a big bet, again due to the count, you know that if you get a small card on the double, it gives the dealer an even better chance of breaking his hand. That is the kind of confidence that you can only achieve by learning the fundamentals of the system.

Some people that just start experimenting with the count fall into that common delusion, if the count is there then you should be able to bet your entire bankroll on one or two big bets; nothing could be further from the truth. The only reason that you have an advantage is due to the regularity with which you make your maximum bet. This shouldn't exceed three percent of your bankroll. If you bet your entire gambling allowance when you only have a two percent advantage; what will your next bet be if you lose? To paraphrase one of the smartest men to have lived, "What good doth it do a man if he gaineth all the knowledge of the game, yet suffers the loss of his own bankroll."

To clarify this a bit, assume that there are 100 little balls in a barrel, 51 white ones, and 49 black ones. The barrel gets rolled around until the balls are well mixed. Then somebody offers you a one time chance to bet your house against $200,000, assuming of course that your house was clear titled and worth that much, and all you had to do is to put you hand in the barrel and pick out a white ball, blindfolded. There are two more white balls than black balls, so you definitely have the advantage of about one percent. This is a scenario that is definably a gamble.

Now, let's assume that you could have 200 tries picking out the white ball for let's say $1000 a pick which still adds up to $200,000. You will, in all likely hood win a couple of thousand dollars because it is not a gamble when you have that slight advantage, and are allowed to ply that advantage many times over. This is what the casinos do and so should you. They hate it when a person goes to the table and makes one large bet. That's why on a junket they make you play for three hours a day, at a medium limit table, because they know that they are eventually going to win all your money, unless you count cards. Then of course the "shoe is on the other side." If there was one black ball in the barrel, and ninety-nine white ones you could lose "your house" by picking the black one, although that situation would be very unlikely. But now, if you could have the advantage of picking five times, you couldn't lose or the chances would be so remote as to not warrant mention. I hope you see the point.

Most aspects of the game require that you learn a rudimentary counting system. How do you buy insurance for instance, unless you have a gauge to measure how many face cards are left in the deck. Some of you must have played with counters before. Usually when they have a big bet, and a dealer turns up an ace, they make an insurance bet. If you observe carefully, you will notice that they are right more often than they are wrong. The person that doesn't count goes with "gut feeling," in other words emotion over science. The same guy that "gets a hunch and bets a bunch."

Making correct insurance bets takes a little bit of brainwork, but will come more naturally with time. The rule of thumb is that if there is more than a third of the deck consisting of ten valued cards then an insurance bet is warranted. But unless you count face cards separately, how do you really know? If the count is a true three, wouldn't that make the purchase of insurance warranted? Not necessarily so. Let us assume for instance that we are nearing the end of a four deck shoe, the count is a plus six and the dealer turns up an ace, with about a deck left to play. You have only seen six aces, and there are another ten that are yet to be played. The bare fact of the matter is that with one deck left, there should only be four aces unseen, and not ten. Because most counts include the ace along with the face cards as equal values, you cannot with any degree of accuracy, determine the number of face cards left in the deck. Remember that it is the face card that will deliver the dealer a blackjack, and not the ace. This is because you don't insure against the dealer's ten-value card. Also, remember that because there are six more aces than there should be, they have in fact replaced the faces, effectively bringing the real count down to zero; which nullifies an insurance bet. This is an unusual circumstance and can only be picked up if you maintain a side count of aces, thereby effectively saving you more money in the long run.

As card counters we take advantage of "unusual" events that occur in a deck, like the occurrence of extra aces. This is what I call "the ace dominant syndrome," in other words, a false count. It's always great to have a lot of aces, but without faces the ace is just another card that is apt to cause you trouble. Oddly enough, the ace at this point should be considered to be the smallest card in the deck. To split aces on a miserably low count may net you two small cards. Remember that it takes at least three cards for the dealer to break, with you having two non-contending hands (a contending hand is a seventeen, eighteen, nineteen, twenty and twenty-one). Ask yourself how likely that event would be in the above situation.

Odd or "unusual" occurrences are exactly what a card counter trains for. If the deck didn't have a tendency to meander, the game would truly be a game of "shit house luck." When the deck strays "off course," either on the plus or the minus side of power, this can be titled as "an odd occurrence." Tension mounts, the further the deck meanders off the median. The count starts at zero, and must end up the same unless the deck was tampered with. The observance of this meandering phenomenon can be quite profitable indeed. If the tension is built up negatively, the deck demands small cards to free it of the built up stress. If I have an eleven against a ten, I just hit on an extreme minus, expecting either a zero card or two or more small cards to ease the tension built up in the deck on the negative side. If the tension is built up on the positive side, the deck is yearning to release some face cards to ease the pressure imposed on it from that side. When the deck is "positively charged," I make a larger bet just in case I get that same opportunity, doubling down eleven against the face and fully expecting to get a face card to successfully culminate the transaction. On the other hand, if the dealer has a ten and I get dealt a stiff, I can usually surrender half the bet and "come back swinging," hopefully before the cut card comes out on the next deal.

Even surrender requires that you count cards. There is a lovable chap that plays in one of the local casinos who people refer to as "Mr. Surrender." His real name is Jake, and basically he surrenders everything. Twelve against a two, six against a ten, ace-four against a nine and well, you get the picture. The surrenders at face value wouldn't be counterproductive, but he doesn't understand that those surrenders should only be done on extreme high counts if at all. To surrender those hands on a low minus count, which he often does, actually takes money out of his pocket.

To his credit he has been hitting more, and surrendering less, in the past few months. He seems to understand that when I have the minimum bet, what remains in the deck is generally quite soft, therefore quite hittable.

The low count means that there are a lot of little cards in the deck. To surrender a twelve against a deuce would be silly, but not as silly as waving it off at a time when there is a scarcity of face cards remaining, the only cards that can break you. Let's assume that the count is minus eight and you hit the twelve with a deuce. Fourteen is still a hit against the deuce because it is now a race to see who can get the better hand or highest value in one of the five "contending" positions of blackjack, 17-21. The dealer is unlikely to break, so a hit is essential; unfortunately it is you, the player who must hit first.

"To surrender or not to surrender that is the other question." I know it seems silly to give up half your bet without a fight, but sometimes that is precisely the thing to do. If you have sixteen staring at a face card on a plus count, and are probably going to break by taking a hit, then the prudent thing to do is surrender. If you have a plus count, take the 50% loss and get them back next deal if the count is still there. Alternatively, stay and sweat out the probable loser with your stiff, thus sparing a face card for next round.

At a place that offers early surrender, there is a lot of surrendering, especially by card counters because often a person can avoid the automatic loss when the dealer turns up a blackjack. If your count is at zero, a fourteen is a surrender against the ten. In a late surrender situation it is not a profitable surrender, because you have already crossed one hurdle; the dealer doesn't have the BJ. Early surrender is a great rule that can be turned to favor the "calculating" player more so than the late surrender rule, which is just about an even proposition. Remember, that surrender is merely a recommendation and if you are on a hit-friendly spot, consistently getting the cards that you need, then by all means carry on hitting.

I threatened Jake once that I was going to teach him how to play 21 one day after seeing him surrender an ace-five against a ten in a minus situation. He just laughed shyly and watched as I hit my hand with four small cards ending up at twenty. Some people are just plain stubborn but I guess I like a challenge. I enjoy having him play at my table as I often buy his surrender and usually profit thereby.

In some instances hitting a stiff on a high count may net you a good hand, in most cases however by hitting, you will break. The question should be, do I want to lose $100 or $50? It's that simple. I cut my losses and come back with a maximum bet next hand, and if I get stiffed again I do the same thing all over again. If the cut card comes out I will try to get "cutting privileges," and cut back the rich clump so I can do it yet again.

Some casinos offer a side game, which includes the acquisition of sevens. By putting out one dollar you have a chance of winning $5000. In order to do this, you must get three sevens of the same suit. Three sevens of unmatched suits will get you $500, two sevens matching get you $100, and two unmatched sevens earn you $50. If you get one, you get rewarded with three dollars. This is a real moneymaker for the casino because as you can see there is only one seven per thirteen cards. If you get that seven you get three bucks. The odds on nailing three sevens is about 1 in 2500, and for three sevens of the same suit the odds are about 50,000 to 1. So if you have a lot of money burning a hole in your pocket, then by all means flat bet the sevens.

Another way you can approach the "game within the game" is to count the number of sevens in the deck, and come out with a bet when they become four rich. For example if two decks have been played with only four sevens noticed, then bet the seven spot. Again, when you choose a card to count and it becomes rich, that's the time that pairs appear. How many times have you been in a pair of eights situation and making the split you then notice another eight falling on the one just split. We don't notice the eights that much because they are irrelevant as pertaining to an extra bet. But the sevens, now that's a different story. If the casino offers the game, then a "side track" is warranted. When they come out they usually come out in a flurry, so be prepared and have your dollar bet.

There is a chap at one of the local casinos in Calgary. His name is Rick B. He has been dealt the $500 bonus 62 times, and has even zapped the three sevens of one suit once for $5000. That is a total of $36,000. With a little know how he even manages to do reasonably well on the 21 game, all this because he counts cards. Counting cards is a bit more difficult than just looking around the casino in your own little world, so why not set the brain in motion.

"If there is some easy money lying around, no one is going to force it into your pocket," (Jesse Livermore). Using Jesse's reasoning it could also be implied that no one can force a person into keeping their money in their pockets by not betting a futile bet. Often times I have been playing at tables where all the sevens have been spent, and there are still some people that instinctively put in their extra bet. This can be attributed to nothing else but laziness.

A lady by the name of Bea has amassed a total of $13,500 playing blackjack in 2004, and this mostly from the "old seven" game. She merely risked a dollar, either when the sevens were rich, or were put into a clump via an educated cut. She has also informed me recently that she has had the three suited sevens in all four suits. So, as you can see, it pays to count the sevens.

The mindless people that sit down to play 21 are surrealistically predicable. They will invariably turn their heads and stare when they lose a hand, looking for some imaginary person to offer them condolences as the dealer rakes in their bet. "Yeah man, what a swine, he took your money." The failure to constantly affirm that you are in a "gambling hall," a place where one puts his money at risk, should never be forgotten. How about the equally predictable guy that gives nods of approval when he makes a hand and actually wins? It's reminiscent of the jaunty steed about to get a bucket of oats. In saying this, even they get lucky at times. A great man once said, "Even a blind chicken can peck the occasional kernel of corn."

Is it just me that sees these things or are people programmed to act a certain way? How about that guy we just mentioned, the one that cocks his head like a chicken that is eyeing up a speck of grain, as he looks at his cards to discern the value after taking a hit? These little anecdotal gestures are part and parcel of the "losers lament." I can barely keep a straight face when I observe some chap doing the above. I have also noticed that it is the guys that are usually guilty of this kind of conduct. It seems to be a "male thing." If I take a liking to somebody, I will try to point these things out to them. If these antics look funny to me imagine what they look like to a person who has to deal with it every day, day in and day out. Observing the monotonous head movements of people who seemed to have gone to the same school of "physical quirkery." Hmmm, isn't conformity that which North America is all about?

These same people are mindless robots that cast blame on other people when they lose, and pat themselves on the back when the dealer somehow manages to break. They could never challenge themselves with the mental exercise of counting cards. Victory to them is based on luck. One would think that these same people, who watch card counters on a daily bases, as they accumulate huge stacks of money, would stop scratching their heads and saying "lucky skunk," and finally admit that there is considerable skill involved in playing winning BJ.

In August, Cindy notified me that she was pregnant. So it would seem that our relationship would now be on a more permanent level. Perhaps even marriage should be contemplated. One thing was for sure; I would be spending a lot more time in what some people refer to as "Sin City."

Chapter Twelve: Taking the Plunge

Since I was moving to Vegas, the first order of business was to buy a house that had a double garage and a pool. It was just too hot for a northern boy to wallow in the heat without recourse to a refreshing dip after a hard day's work. I had to have a double garage in the event that I would be working on some unique automobile.

We looked at a house that was a "for sale by owner." It was a gorgeous 3000 sq. ft. bungalow on one acre of land, with a triple garage and a pool for $145,000. After carefully weighing our options, we gave a verbal offer of $135,000 over the phone. To my surprise the owner asked us to come over to write up the offer. After I arrived she started talking about the $145,000 figure again so we just left.

Next day, she called me to come over. I made it perfectly clear that the price was to be not a penny more than $135,000 or I wasn't even prepared to drop by. She said that would be fine, so off we went again to write up the offer. Upon arriving, she again started talking about that $145,000 figure so Cindy and I, with jaws agape, just stared at one another in disbelief. Was she high on drugs, or did she not know the English language? I ended up giving her a piece of my mind for wasting our time and left in a huff.

I knew that it was time to hire a realtor who could steer clear of these "freaks" that you run into on occasion. He came over and introduced himself as Mike J. My gal reminded me about racial problems in various parts of town, so I told the realtor that under no circumstances was he to take us to any "ethnically diverse" areas. He said that was against the law, and that he couldn't target any "lily-white" areas for the benefit of his clients. "Then I'll just have to look for another agent," I told him.

These are options that everyone would have to consider, but in my case I had to be extra vigilant because I would now have a wife and child to protect. To place them into a dangerous environment, or some hellhole that would endanger their well being would have been unconscionable.

I just wanted to lay it on the line to the guy so we wouldn't waste each other's time as we did with the previous vendor. I heard all the horror stories of some low life family moving next door, and the gangs would start showing up selling their crack. Before you knew it you could hear gunshots in the middle of the night. I didn't want an exclusive neighborhood by any means, just a decent one with other people in the same boat as us. I didn't mind paying more for the place as long as it was in an area aesthetically pleasing to us. With the prospect of losing a sale our enterprising realtor relented.

He showed us a couple of "turkeys," then after about a week he phoned me in a panic. He said that he might have found something that we would like. I now knew how a buyer felt, when you taxi them around to various houses that just don't fill the requirements that were laid out before hand.

How difficult could it be to follow a simple formula of area, double garage, pool and assumable mortgage? When I was in the real estate business, I would never have phoned a client unless I had the prerequisites that were agreed upon. Anyway he drove us to a completely different area than we had wanted him to target, and I had to set him straight. "Don't phone us again until you have the house in Paradise Valley that meets our needs or we'll hire a realtor that can." I thought that he finally got the picture. With some people you have to be plain rude, or they won't do what they were asked.

About a week and a half later he showed us a place that fit the bill. The price was $100,000 with a $90,000 mortgage. It was kind of a fixer upper. It needed new carpets, roof and floors. A pretty good deal all and all we thought. We put in an offer and ended up buying it for $97,000. It was about six blocks from "Mr. Las Vegas's" house (Wayne Newton) so I knew it was in a solid part of town, "Danke shane" to Mr. Newton.

Possession dates are fast in Vegas, and we agreed to a three-week take over.

We "tied the knot" in August 1988, adding normality to our lives but more importantly to offer some stability for our future off spring. A wife, house and family all in one month, kind of a big jump for a

44 year old bachelor who vowed never to get married until the "right one came along." I was from the school of thought that clearly wanted to get "hitched" only once, no looking over the fence at other women, assuming the role of responsible husband and parent.

I didn't feel a need to proclaim my vows to my wife before family and friends, feeling that my promise to her and myself, to remain by her side and that of the children resulting from our union was sufficient. As a result it was a typical Las Vegas wedding.

After obtaining a license, we went down to a justice of the peace and validated our pledge to one another in shorts, sneakers and polo shirt. The immediate honeymoon was spent at Caesar's Palace because I was in the middle of a junket at that hotel, and we both loved the atmosphere. The suite had the Caesar's signature raised tub, and a smoked mirrored ceiling over the bed. We enjoyed a fabulous dinner at the Spanish Steps restaurant, did some dancing on Cleopatra's Barge, and then we went to play some 21 at one of Caesar's more than convenient tables. "Only in Amerika."

Our table was soon filled with some world ranked figure skaters that were doing a show at the Circus Maximus. I never did see that show, but from their 21 play it was obvious that they shouldn't hang up their skates anytime soon and enter the profession of blackjack.

After our last glass of champagne, we retired to our suite and before consummating our marriage I told Cindy that I had fallen in love with her in the last few months and vowed to be a faithful husband, a considerate father, a lover and a friend.

We had agreed to have a more in depth honeymoon after our child was born. Hawaii was to be the destination, but for now it was to be work as usual for the both of us.

I played blackjack around the town on "my route;" a string of casinos that tolerated my play. After about two weeks of pounding "the beat," I was down thousands. What a bad time to run a losing streak, a child on the way and covering all the hidden costs involved with buying a house in the USA. "Oh well," I thought to myself, "I'll get it back next week, and then some." But the losses kept piling up. Every time the count was hot, I'd come out blazing with both barrels, ending up with the same results; I got "cut down" mercilessly. There seemed to be no end in sight to this depressing turn of events. Then one day I met Joey L.

I had been playing at the Maxim one afternoon when I spotted a guy that I had seen around town at various casinos. He was a card counter without a doubt, but he seemed to be low keyed with his betting. When the count was high, he would have a twenty-dollar bet, and I would have my customary hundred. We would all get "whacked," but the big difference was that he would lose his paltry twenty and I my black chip. The "chasm of what was, and that which ought to be" was growing wider and wider.

I started talking to Joey at the table, and told him that I had been getting "spanked" all over town and that I just couldn't shake that big black cloud hovering above my head for the last month. I asked for a comp for a few of rounds of drinks and then broke off the session temporarily to "shoot the shit" with him in the lounge.

After ordering a glass of orange juice he told me that he lives in New York, in Manhattan, where he maintains an apartment, which he subleases for six months out of the year. He can then come to Las Vegas unfettered of any responsibility. He was a jazz and blues saxophone, and trumpet player who used to play at various clubs around the New York area and the Midwest, in cities like Chicago and Indianapolis. When in New York he used to drive cab to raise instant cash, and to keep his financial equilibrium between gigs. He was a highly intelligent individual who was well read and knowledgeable, not only in blackjack but also current events and history; the very things that interested me. We in fact were almost "painted with the same brush" as they say. We later went out to his car to get some reading material, and I couldn't believe that he too had a VW convertible just like mine.

These coincidences were truly amazing and we took an instant liking to one another. We exchanged phone numbers to get together at a later date when we could swap strategies pertaining to 21. It was indeed odd how one meets the people that one meets. Here he was a comrade in arms whose thought processes were in sync with mine, "working the tables" eking out an existence amidst the sharks that inhabit the sea of sand in and around Las Vegas.

I called him a few days later to buy him breakfast at the Cafe Roma at Caesar's. I met him there about 11 am and we enjoyed a sumptuous meal, compliments of Caesar's, but technically comped by me due to yet another loss.

I went on to tell him about my "one month in hell." He listened intently and just said, "Lower your bet." If you are getting mauled at a table, other than leaving that table altogether just make sure that your bet is lowered. Like getting into a tub full of hot water one usually tests the water with his toes before making the final commitment to enter with both feet, and then, only later with the entire body. "Besides," he said, "what's the rush, you're here for a long time, not a good time." The regular tourist variety, come to "our" little oasis in the desert usually for the opposite reasons. That was certainly true, because my whole operation was in the midst of being transferred to Vegas as we spoke.

I told him that I had lowered the bet from $100 to just over $50, depending on the count. Of course sometimes I just couldn't resist a "sizzler" and would come out regardless of losses, in the vain hope that the high count would somehow overcome my bad luck. Joey stating that reducing the bet was good, since otherwise the $6000 loss that I had incurred would be much higher. Also he explained that my bet should be even lower to minimize "the struggle" on the counter attack, when the tide finally changed to my benefit.

He was talking about a "defensive posture," and it sure made a lot of sense. Why was I wasting my heavy weaponry "shooting at phantoms" when "light arms fire" should have been the order of the day? When the tide changes, only then should I unfurl the camouflage covering on the "Howitzers," and only then bring them on to the field to lay a merciless barrage on the enemy. Using a low bet could also deflect suspicion from me, as it is a typical card counter who raises and lowers bets methodically as he observes the power remaining in the deck.

He mentioned that he too had noticed me around town getting my "ass kicked," but unlike me he would pick up and leave a table that wasn't "gleanable" and move on to "greener pastures." His bet too was structured around the $100 maximum, but if he were getting "whacked" he would quickly lower that to $10; it made the recovery that much faster.

Many aspiring card counters who have the extreme "bad luck" of sitting at a table that posed a lot of high count opportunities, favorable to only a select few squares, have fallen into a "black hole" that seems to gobble up most of the assets of those unfortunates who happened to be "passing by." But the "counter's creed" dictates that if there is a high count, then a correspondingly high bet must also be made. Thus they fall to the bottom of a void, in a place that houses the financial carcasses of countless players devoted to a system that may have worked if not for an anomaly, or a glitch that appeared so early in their short careers. Only experience can nullify this trend, or the heeding of wise counsel from those that have "passed" near the pitfalls that have doomed so many. Those that have skirted danger-ously close to that precipice, often say, that the danger in itself was the attraction, enticing them to returning again and again. As a philosopher once said, "Better a void for a purpose than no purpose at all."

Joey was the kind of player who had "seen it all." He had been on the edge, but had avoided falling over the "brink." He has been on those winning streaks that went on for weeks, as well as enduring prolonged losing streaks. Where there was a high, there also must somewhere be a low. After all, aren't all things subject to "the level-ing effect," or the yin and the yang, as it is known in Asia? The professional knows when to "pull in his horns" and lower his bet when the yang makes her presence felt.

Sometimes a force that is unseen can be more powerful than one that is visible. Observe the wind, as it bends the tree in the direction of "its" will. This invisible power makes a "mockery" out of the myth of "the mighty oak." It twists, creaks and groans under her hidden power, occasionally breaking off its weakest boughs. Luck is just such a force, invisible yet emotionally draining, breaking off that which is too weak, plunging those of us that rely too much on her charms into their own chasms, their own purgatory's, to be used as fodder for giant corporations, or Gambler's Anonymous functions in their tomorrows. For them, all their tomorrows hold nothing but sorrows.

Strap on your helmet, and strap it on tight because to keep a bet low on a high count is an act worthy of only the most disciplined card counter. A lot of tables have an inordinate number of high-count sit-uations on which a player just can't seem to capitalize on, and if you can't, then you should stop trying. Luck is a "fickle" maiden, granti-ng her affection sporadically to each individual around the table. To take the "fickle" out of twenty-one and bring back the science, we have to remove the "maiden" or just plainly move venues.

If that which is, varies somehow from that which ought to be, then the bet "ought" to be lower. In other words if you're observing a steady decline in your assets, all is not right. If you are getting "nailed" only on the high count, all is not right.

Like a dare devil trying to jump an obstacle with a motorcycle, finding himself in trouble due to an unforeseen gust of wind, so too can the 21 player encounter difficulties; especially he who has yet to experience the power of that which is called perpetual luck. If luck is on the player's side, then that is quite easy to bear. On the other hand, if it happens in reverse, the inexperienced player is taken off guard. Train as you may, work out all the possibilities, make the adventure as risk free as you can, it is that unforeseen "gust of wind" that may cause your undoing. Prepare for it, because if you play long enough it will happen. Then you will be somewhat aware and can "hunker down" into your foxhole. Being safer with a lower bet, you may then wait out the maelstrom that unleashes her fury.

We who are not "corporate" have limited funds, more pointedly we have a bankroll that limits us to a certain bet and we are also limited to a certain loss level. If this loss level is breached we can no longer pursue the bet; therefore we cannot be in a position to register a win.

The corporation or casino isn't fettered by these restraints. Consequently it will go on to dominate, bypassing the luck factor of various players with sheer volume of cash. He who has the most, will generally outlast those who have less. If we are to be "the corporation" we must be able to take "the hit" (with a lower bet) and counter attack (with a bigger bet) once the storm has passed over.

So then, Joey had convinced me to make smaller bets until I regained my confidence in the game, and the only way you can do that is by registering a string of wins. That is exactly what I proposed to do.

I went out that night and played. The heavy chains that held me tightly to my losses were still securely fastened. I was dealt a loss of only $100. This sum could easily have been $500 or more had I bet higher. It seems to me, that if one really is "snake bit," then it doesn't matter where you sit; the one constant that remains is that you are always sitting in the wrong position. Whether you hit a stiff and break all the time, double down and get stiffed consistently, the word best describing your circumstance is "LOSER."

The only high point, if there is to be one, is that you are losing a lot less "dough" than you would have following the "credo" of the typical card counter, "If it's there, go with it and make the bet." This is a sure way to get infected by the "loser's lean." Please don't misunderstand me, the count is the way to approach the 21 game, but if it isn't working for you, then you must extricate yourself from that immediate environment and move tables or lower your bet.

After four nights of combat fatigue the "jinx," that was my intimate companion, had finally ceased to use me as its host. It all happened very suddenly at Caesar's Palace. Just as I was imagining the police cordoning off the table with their yellow "crime scene tape," indicating yet another felonious act perpetrated against me, things started to change. Sitting at a five-dollar table the count started to soar and as usual I was getting slapped around for about five hands. Then like the ending of a perpetual rain, the sun broke through the black clouds. I won three hands in a row with the count still rising. I doubled the bet to ten, and I got a great hand again. I spread to two squares and again beat the dealer with a double on one of the hands. Now the bet was $25 each on the two spots. I surrendered one, and beat the dealer with the other. The count dropped slightly so I refrained from increasing the bet and kept them at $25 a piece. The next two hands had to be hit up again, raising the count to where I could again justify raising the wager to $40 a piece. Surrendering one, with blackjack on the other, I now raised the bets to $50 per square. After winning these with respectable hands, the count was lowered slightly. I decided to keep the bets as they were, and again won them both. Luck indeed had turned her back on the casino, and was flirting with me once more, smiling broadly at me as I again basked in victories.

That night I registered a $1000 gain. Why I didn't think about betting the minimum when I was being inundated with losses, I will never know. I guess we all need a tune up occasionally, a chat with a fellow player who understands the particular situation and emotional "roller coasters" that are encountered playing the game. The ups, the downs, the streaks of winning and of losing that can blur the vision and instill self doubt and fear. When I now see a drop in my assets, my bet is immediately lowered till I see an improvement in the cards.

By lowering the bet in times of "lean," one loses a lot less. In my case I saved perhaps thousands of dollars. To win that money back would have taken days. Remember that a dollar saved is one that doesn't have to be "re-earned."

Evaluating a shoe was something that Joey said he often did. He sits down at an empty table and petty much flat bets it through to see how it reacts under stress, that is, the "power of the count." To describe it better, I would have to say that he subjects the deck similar to a procedure done by motor analysts, when they hook up an engine to a "dynamometer." He, in effect, subjects the shoe to a load test, betting the shoe moderately to determine performance on low and high counts. He puts in $30 or $40 instead of the usual $100. If a loss occurs it could be deemed that it wasn't as bad as if it happened with the black chip on the square. If he wins, on the other hand, well, how can you argue with profit?

How many times have you been at a $25 minimum table just flat betting, unable to justify a raise in the bet only to keep winning. You can say to yourself, "Great shoe, the only thing negative that I can say about it is that I didn't bet more." Well if you have won the first three hands, what is stopping you from testing the shoe or "probing" your luck by adding a nickel chip? Remember you are only risking one nickel. If your winning streak is still with you after five hands, you are already up to a fifty-dollar bet, not including all the added revenue earned, and that was all accomplished on a low count. Imagine what can be done on a high count.

I used to do a lot of walking, looking for counts. I noticed a smattering of little cards on a $100 table at Caesar's again, while I was strolling through the main casino pit. I estimated a running count of plus ten, so I quietly strolled over to the table and pulled out $500 and the dealer promptly gave me five black chips. I placed one of them on the square and won, the dealer breaking his hand. This happened three hands in a row then the count went down to zero and I started to cash out. The rest of the players protested my leaving and told me that the shoe had been "crappy" until my arrival. Well, I told them that I would play till I lost a hand, but then I would surely have to go. They all agreed, and the play resumed. The only reason I agreed to play was because I didn't know the value of the previously dealt cards, and just maybe the count was still up, without my knowing it. I played five more hands before the dealer made one that bested mine. That was a $400 gift that I wouldn't have had if I had "walked" on the zero count. The way it was, the deck was probably charged with rich cards when I arrived, and the game, which I estimated to be plus ten, may in reality have been plus twenty, with "that which I didn't see."

At the same casino a few weeks later I thought that I would apply my new friend's "dyno" technique on a shoe that I was playing by myself. On the high count the dealer was making the lion's share of the hands, on the low count it was anyone's game. On the moderate high count however, at about a true count of plus three-quarters, running count at plus four, the shoe was mine. I experimented first by putting in $50 then finally raising it to $100 with great results. If any one had been watching the play, they would have been convinced that I was just another customer about to be relieved of his money. And little wonder, lowering the bet moderately as the high went higher, raising it as the high went lower. It seemed backwards to me also, but it worked. Again, it's tough to argue with a successful strategy.

Joey had all kinds of little tricks up his sleeves, and the beauty of it was that he would actually put his theories into practice. He once told me that he was mulling over a scenario where he would land in Vegas without a penny in his pocket, and through 21 would slowly build up a bankroll to play the game on a regular basis.

As it turned out, one day a friend of his came to town, and he thought that it would be a good opportunity to try out his new theory. His friend was a "nay-sayer" from the New York area who, like most people, thought that the game was unbeatable. If he could convince this guy, he could convince anybody.

They left his apartment without a penny and made the rounds, checking slot machines for "unredeemed" credits; in about an hour they had thirty bucks. Back then there was a casino in Vegas called the Silver dollar, which had 25-cent blackjack. It was also a non-smoking casino, which ultimately brought on its untimely demise.

Off went Joey and his buddy to play two-bit BJ at the Silver dollar. Within a couple of hours they had $200. Now I'm not going to tell you that this was a normal occurrence, but the fact remains that with the use of his imagination he got a small bankroll, and got lucky, increasing his stake seven times over. His pal was very impressed to say the least. With that $200 bankroll they could now go to the Horseshoe to play at a one-dollar table and also receive comps for food and drink. By the end of the afternoon they had amassed $500. They went home with full bellies feeling tipsy from drinking.

This must have been an eye opener for Joey's friend, because it sure was for me. This was quite a unique approach to starting a BR by cruising around casinos snagging loose change and ultimately using that to win at blackjack. He was certainly not the "Freddie the Free Loader" type, but just had to prove to himself that his method worked. It is the lucky man who can get tutored by a guy as versatile as Joey. Why would one strive for mediocrity, continuing to do things his own way, when one can emulate genius, by following the ways of a "maestro?"

There are many ways to amass a BR but usually it is a result of a lot of self-denial. "He who deprives himself of all things will be the 'freest of spirits.' He who owns little is in turn owned that much less. He who deprives himself of nothing will end up with nothing." So it would seem that saving up is the key to ending up with a sizable stake, and it is a hard thing to do, especially if you are not used to sacrificing some of the small luxuries of life. Yet sacrifice builds character, and truly great people throughout history have forsaken small and large things to achieve a greater end.

A friend of mine used to borrow $400 from me in the middle of the month, paying me back at the end of the same month. He once confided, that he would socialize in a bar one day out of the week, and it would set him back about $100 for that pleasure. I couldn't resist telling him that if he didn't go out for an entire month he would no longer have to borrow any money from me; as a result borrowing money would be unnecessary. Staying out of the bars for two months would set him up to face the odd emergency that may crop up in everyday life.

If you smoke a pack of cigarettes every day, in Canada that translates into a cost of about ten dollars a pack, or a three hundred dollar a month habit. Liquor is about $25 a quart, and if you go through one of those every week, that is another $100 a month. You can see that in rapid order with a little discipline you can swiftly gain for yourself a small BR to start the ball rolling. And if you are a serious player you may well be taking that important first step into a more or less lucrative profession, or at the very least a part time diversion.

Not everyone that reads this book will profit from it. Some may take every last penny of their rent and try to double it. For that person

Taking the Plunge

I can only say that this system is not for you. You are the very person that I referred to when I talked about a gambler. You need the self-control not to bet beyond your means. First you need to amass a bankroll, which is untouched and untouchable, used exclusively for playing the game of 21. Your bankroll should only be considered a tool to make more money. If you think it is money to be spent, you have already lost, and perhaps the nine to five route is better suited for you. You need to be "cold blooded" in your reasoning and calculations to be a master of the craft. After applying the knowledge that you have gained here, you will no longer be fit to be a slave. If you fail to apply these principles you will likely end up in one of those "Gamblers Anonymous" meetings, spilling your guts to people in the same pathetic circumstances as yourself.

If you have noticed, only losers attend those whining sessions. I think Gamblers Anonymous should be changed to "Losers Anonymous." Imagine a winner attending one of those meetings. He would probably say "Ladies and gentlemen my name is John and I'm a hopeless gambler. Last year I made $50,000, and the way it looks I will achieve my earning goal of $100,000 for the year ending at 2006. Projections for the year 2007 look even rosier. Somebody stop me! Please, I need help urgently! Gambling is starting to dominate my life! It may cause me to lose my day job! For Christ's sake shut the gaming houses down! I feel guilty earning all this untaxed money."

Yes, it's a fact that winners avoid GA (gamblers anonymous) like the plague, because it's a place that caters to "losers." Winners and losers don't get along because it is a different mindset, or perhaps because they have a different aggression level. Like the hunter and the hunted, they each have a useful role in the nature of things. One is meticulous in the planning and the execution of that plan, the other is mindlessly ruminating on that over used cliché "luck," and is the object of the casino's undivided interest.

So you do have a choice. You can either be "the cock of the block" and make luck work for you, or just another "skid on the grid" looking for "that lucky break."

After that long losing streak I was back in business and on the road to recovery, to recoup the losses that I had incurred during "the bad times." As if wielding the "fiery sword of retribution," my stocks in the 21 game were again on the rise. It took about three weeks to win back the losses inflicted on me during this depressing episode, but it happened and I continued to win a further $4000. Thus as quickly as it was lost, it was also regained. The meteoric "good luck" was a result of an adjustment of fortune mentioned earlier. The "leveling effect" had worked it's magic. What goes down, it seems, must also rise. Or so the good book says.

Chapter Thirteen: Volker's China

Just as things were getting settled down, my old friend Volker phoned, and asked me if I would be interested in taking a small Asian adventure. I told him that if it didn't include drugs or murder that he could count me in. I was still rather leery because of his previous encounter with the law. But as far as I knew he had kept his nose clean since his arrest. Besides, the matter was yet to be heard in a court of law.

The trip was slated for the middle of October/1988; I had about two weeks to arrange for a ticket.

I made sure that the solo trip was all right with Cindy, and the next day I bought the tickets and relayed the necessary data to Volker. We planned to stay in Taiwan for one-week since he had to complete some business with his Breathalyzer product and bogus dollar detector.

On the return flight we would board a plane from Taipei to Hong Kong and after a one week stay there, we would fly directly back to LA. While in Hong Kong, I planned a side trip to Macao, an island off the coast of Hong Kong to check out the action in their "world class" casino.

I boarded the aircraft from Las Vegas for the short flight to "The City of Angels," and shortly after, alit on the tarmac of LA's international airport, LAX. There to greet me was Volker with his broad smile and his booming voice.

He confided in me that he wanted to button up some loose ends before he went on trial. Because, if found guilty, he then would ultimately be out of circulation for a while. The so-called loose ends consisted of money in various bank accounts in the LA area, and a boat that he had commissioned for construction. He truly had a lot of bank accounts. I guess the drug business was kind to him monetarily, but physically and emotionally you could see that it had taken its toll. The wrinkles on his forehead, that were barely noticeable when we first met, were now deep ruts caused by many sleepless nights, rife with worry about his impending fate.

His boat was half finished and he wanted somehow to get out of his contract with the builder. He had put $35,000 into the vessel but was willing to "bite the bullet," and sell it for $10,000 cash. Ultimately he learned that some things are a lot easier to buy than they are to sell.

After making the necessary withdraws from three banks, we went in search for a friend of his that might have been interested in buying the half finished boat. This was the very same guy that was caught with him in Vancouver ferrying the pot from some off shore craft. The chap wasn't at home, or was on vacation, and we ended up renting a motel for the night, close to a nearby highway.

In the morning we returned and left him a note, to get in touch with Volker in two weeks regarding the boat issue. Then we went and stood in line at the Taiwan consulate to obtain our visas at a fee of $35. We were now ready for the flight to Taiwan on board Korean Airlines.

KAL, as the airline company is known, has a fleet of Boeing 747s, the elongated type, in typical Asian form. With the multitude of people on their continent, they ordered their aircraft to carry about an extra hundred people. You could tell that it was the stretched type by the elongated hump on its dolphin like front.

The ride over wouldn't have been complete without the new army of South Koreans, the businessman. They complimented the armies of their Northern brethren well. The South had blue suits, and each of their soldiers were armed with a brief case and a tie. The North had snappy khaki colored uniforms, and were armed with AK 47's. The North was adept at throwing "Molotov cocktails." The South was skilled in the throwing of "cocktails" of a different sort. These cocktail parties were incorporated to lure people to their venues to buy their products. Which of these two ideologies would prevail, was anyone's guess? The Japanese considered the South to be a greater threat to world stability due to their ability to fight as "guerrillas," after all many Japanese also wore blue suits in their battle for Western currency. Like Sparta and Athens of old, these two states, North and South Korea, were destined, it seemed to be re-united to one another. Proving again that "blood is indeed thicker than water."

The flight was extremely long, and the jet lag was difficult to overcome due to jumping the International dateline, and losing a whole day. The long journey started out from LA at about 9:00 am, arriving in San Francisco about an hour later. At about 12:00 noon we boarded our Korean airlines flight to Seoul, arriving about 12 hrs later. Volker had obviously been this way many times, as he knew all the ins and outs of Oriental travel.

We changed planes in Seoul, and continued on to Taipei. After clearing customs and making our way out to the main airport lobby, a "welcoming committee" greeted us. Each passenger's name was broadcast over the intercom as we immerged from customs and immigration. In turn each of us was given a round of applause from either a paid contingent of greeters, or the crowd was applauding as a regular courtesy shown to potential traders with the ROC (Republic Of China).

We exited the airport, hailed a cab and proceeded to a hotel in the central part of the city. The hotel was rather full, and only had one room available with a double bed. We booked it because we were too tired and unable to plod another step. Leaving SF at noon on Friday and arriving at our hotel in Taipei early Sunday morning, had taken its toll.

Once inside we heard a rapping on the door. I answered it and it turned out to be a "mama san" (madam) asking if we would like to have a girl for the evening. I thought that I was being courteous by politely saying no, using as an excuse that we were very tired. After relating the conversation to my buddy he said that now everyone in the hotel would think we were gay; sleeping in a double bed and refusing female company was a sure giveaway. Maybe he was right, because next evening we were given a room with twin beds and no one "came-a-calling."

In the morning he got in touch with his broker who was handling his Breathalyzer and Detector to get a reimbursement on his prepaid order. I wasn't sure how much it was, but I am sure that it was a hefty amount. It was evident that he was not going to get all his money back, but did make a deal to get back one third.

We then went out for something to eat at a sidewalk eatery, complete with portable kitchen which would vanish without a trace after the lunch meal. For fifty cents we were served a huge bowl of noodles with broth, meat and veggies that sustained us till dinner.

He then treated me to a massage at a parlor that he frequented during his many previous stays. The odd thing about these parlors was that unless you knew what to look for, you would never locate one. The "secret" symbol was that of our very own barber shops; the "spiraled peppermint stick." Only later did I notice that these signs were liberally located all over town. I am sure that they offered the seedier spin offs of a sexual nature, but we were never approached. We then went to an English pub and there, for the first time since we checked into our hotel, we encountered our first "white skinned foreigners."

The bar was quite straight laced and presented the Anglo pub theme; small, cozy and easy to meet people. I told the bartender that I had thought that Taiwan was a democratic country because of all the hype I was hearing about "the friends of the United States and our democratically elected allies." I told him that I had seen army trucks deploying troops all over town, and that I hadn't seen that kind of activity even in Communist countries. He motioned me to stop talking too loud as the walls had ears.

Later we went to have a look at a military sale were a person could buy all kinds of equipment like rocket launchers, grenades, machine guns and other military hardware. On the way out we hailed a cab, and before we got to the street a "Gestapo" type individual complete with the long leather trench coat and an automatic side arm hanging loosely over his shoulders stopped us. It was like having a flash back to the forties except for the fact that they had yellow skin and couldn't pronounce their Ls very well. He asked what hotel we were at, took down some notes and told us to proceed.

We made our way back to our room to get some much-needed rest because we were still hampered with "jet lag." In the morning Volker was going to show me Taiwan's very own "Convention and Trade Center," but first we opted to get something to eat.

Close to our hotel there was something akin to an all you can eat buffet except for one small twist. You were given a Styrofoam multi compartment tray, and for 75 cents you could fill it but once. I had a real problem eating it all, not because I couldn't wolf it all down, but I just couldn't get used to the chopsticks. Back home I would always ask for a fork at Chinese restaurants because I didn't have the patience to observe the food as it slipped off the sticks just before it entered my mouth. In China they have no forks so you have to get used to chopsticks. The way it turned out I became quite proficient in their use just prior to our return trip. After supper we retired for the evening, and slept like logs.

"Hey Volker turn the music down, I didn't know that you liked Chinese music." I looked over at his bed and Volker was still asleep. We were awakened by a loud tape recorder blaring out some Oriental music. Looking out the window we noticed the lot beside our hotel was full of elderly inhabitants doing Tai Chi, a form of exercise combined with a martial arts regimen. Maybe that's one of the reasons they have an elongated life span.

We had a fifty-cent brunch at the "collapsible" sidewalk eatery, and then set out to visit Taiwan's Convention and Trade Center.

The building was huge, five stories high and packed full of new and innovative items ready to be marketed in Europe and North America. One item that caught my eye was a physiotherapy device that passed mild electric impulses to various targeted muscle groups. A sample of this item would set you back about $50, a lot less if you bought it bulk of course. This was interesting because a therapist about a year later used the very same item on me. When queried as to how much the device cost, she told me that they had four of them at $950 a unit.

There was a lot of money to be made in franchising these items, why Volker turned to crime to make his money was beyond me. He had that certain acumen when it came to business, he was meticulous, tenacious and honest. The very things needed to run a successful corporation. At the convention center I also saw for the first time the one-man water ski towing device. A person could have attained the rights to market that item in North America, and all that had to be done was to get it approved by the Underwriters Lab. I saw the device advertised on TV about five years ago so I'm assuming that someone did just that.

We were there all day and managed to see only two floors, we would have to return the next day to view the rest.

On the way back to our room we stopped at the Asia hotel, the last word in luxury in Taipei, to check the menu out at their restaurant. They were the only hotel in the city that catered to an American clientele, and therefore the only hotel to have knives and forks; what a pleasure it would have been to use those utensils. We checked the menus and dinner was $20. "I guess I'll just have to rough it on this trip," I told my pal, "because there is no way that I'm going to pay 20 times more for the same thing, but in a different atmosphere." I would much sooner sit with the native Taiwanese, who seemed to be a rather friendly lot, than to sit with my fellow countrymen in posh surroundings eating food that could be obtained at a fourth of the cost back home. It was these North American customers that kept the price of the meals artificially high.

So it was to be the little "buffet" that we had eaten at the night before for 75 cents. The people there seemed more than accommodating, and greeted us with enthusiasm, I guess they rarely get Americans entering places where the "commoners" eat and strangers "fear to tread." After dinner we went back to our room to try to shake off that nagging jet lag.

During my clean up ritual after waking, I couldn't help notice the ingenious way that their showers were built. There are no curtains or obvious dividers of any sort. There is just one room with a shower, water closet and basin, with the entire room top to bottom covered in ceramics. In the middle there is a floor drain that drains the shower and also facilitates the cleaning of the entire bathroom; a damn nifty design. If I were still in real estate I would build such a house to cater to Chinese clientele. I'm sure it would go over like "gang busters" for whites as well.

After breakfast we again made our way back down to the trade center to view all that there was to see in the form of new and wonderful items that could be either purchased or cornered to market in North America. Although I personally found this practice to be abhorrent because of the damage that it caused our economies, it was a fact of life. Perhaps in some way it would hasten the demise of the present system, and could then be replaced with a more nationalistic business format; a North America first policy.

Much of the items on display were inventions originating in western countries, but due to over priced manufacturing costs, were sent to places like Taiwan to be produced for resale back in our own markets. This in the long run would have a disastrous effect on our economy, taking jobs away from our own work sector, robbing them of the buying power to buy North American products. It doesn't take a Ph.D. in economics to figure out that if you paid your own workers enough money as a wage they would be able to afford the products that you produce.

Once one company started manufacturing its product overseas, others started to do likewise to remain competitive. All this stuff about "be patriotic, buy American" is a bunch of crap. When the worker is put up against the wall he is likely to purchase the best value for the buck. That's why free trade can't work. Our economy is fragile, too fragile and has to be protected, sometimes with heavy tariffs. If our guys are making $25/hr, how can one compete with someone making that much every week?

Our economy is also "exclusive" to our various regions and countries. Otherwise why would there even be a need for different currency and currency exchange rates. Think of a country like an "exclusive country club." There have to be requirements to gain entry. In this day and age that requirement is usually money. If everyone would be given membership in this moneyed club, then where is the exclusivity? You have to keep the rates high to protect the other high paying members investments. It is our elected representatives job to make sure that our country's border is safe from "cheap labor incursions," whether in the form of immigration or imported goods. If they abrogate their responsibilities they should be put in a stockade and severely lashed, instead of being given a luxurious pension and allowed to retire without the shame of incompetence.

Free trade is just another form of foreign aid; the problem is that now we are being made to pay twice. In 1992 Douglas Casey once wrote, "Foreign aid might be defined as a transfer (of money) from poor people in rich countries, to rich people in poor countries." Free trade now puts twice the buying revenue at the disposal of the "fat cats," while at the same time making the lives of the dying middle class much more miserable.

Forgetting the fundamentals that made the free enterprise system great, we now condone the exploitation of third world labor. In so doing we are in reality facilitating unemployment in our own country. Look and see what has happened. We make an inferior automobile, our steel industry is a joke, and the "good" jobs have been sent overseas for less than the minimum wages in our own country. Jobs that we took on when we were teenagers to purchase our first car or to have spare cash for that Saturday night outing to "score" with a date, are now considered "real jobs." Places like MacDonald's, Taco Bell and Wendy's were all manned mainly by pimply-faced kids who attended school or university; struggling to keep ahead of their limited finances so they wouldn't be chained to a debt-ridden society.

Think about it for a minute, how in the world can a person attain the so called "American Dream" of living in their own house, raising their own families and molding the future generation of responsible North Americans, and paying them with paltry wages. The greed and materialism of the "International Capitalist" has brought us to a gray land, devoid of hope for a better life. Instead we are faced with endless work for limited pay.

Both couples now have to work to make ends meet, while their children are left at home to be tended to by the "electric babysitter," spewing its inane message of "at least in America we know that we are free." Maybe you could get away with saying that in the 50's but now it is really wearing thin. Let's face it. No country is so free as to allow all freedoms, just as no country, even under the most brutal totalitarian regime, is so "total" as to remove all freedoms. The very qualities that were prized on the frontier, qualities like bravery, innovativeness and entrepreneurship are now shunned at all levels. The qualities that won the West have been shelved and sure as the sun will rise in the morning, another nation will take up where we left off and leave us scratching our heads.

So here congregate the businessmen of the world, in Taiwan, a country once deemed to be in the thralls of the "third world," doing commerce with an industrious people while our own workers are left languishing in a "sea of heartache." Can we not hear their cries or have we become used to them. Or more sinister, have we just turned off a switch and found that the suffering of foreign people is in some way more worthy of our sympathy than the suffering of our own? Isn't the government that we have elected, and given a mandate to run our affairs on a national and international level, supposed to act to the benefit of the people that have elected them? If these elected officials have acted contrary to the best interests of those people who elected them to office, they should be held to account. Worse, if they were aiding some corporation or some foreign entity, in the pursuit of their own selfish goals, disregarding the welfare of the public, then would that not constitute treasonable behavior? Isn't it time to stop "pussy footing" around with these "untouchable criminal elements," and if they are guilty of incompetence then replace them with people that are more able. And if they are guilty of treason then we should perhaps take a lesson from the Mainland Chinese by not only removing the head culprits, but also remove their heads?

They all seem inflicted with the disease of "political correctness," but is it not "correct" to be an asset to your own nation first? Family, community, city, state and the world are all obligations but an obligation that is in an order of importance that starts at the family level and gradually ascends the scale, without jumping the queue.

We sure have strayed wide and far from people like Davy Crocket who were virile representatives of a virile population. It almost seems that we have become effeminate, or certainly a great deal more passive. We think with the organs below our necks rather than the one above. Before a female will don a pair of pants, their male counter part must first have put on a skirt. This self-castration or "gender swapping" occurs because as men, we don't have the "balls" to oppose political correctness with plain old political sanity. Thinking with the heart, instead of the mind may have doomed the West.

A classic pet mania for the political correctness crowd is desegregation. I read the other day that a proponent for this policy, opted to send his kids to a private, "lily white" school after ensuring that kids, both black and white, had to be bussed "helter skelter" to meet racial quotas. Why can't a child go to school in his own neighborhood, more important why don't proponents of this kind of "legislative hypocrisy" be called to account? Both black and white constituents should have a say about where their children get an education. Perhaps that is too much to ask.

People with the narrowest shoulders seem to get the widest praise. Not from the ordinary citizen that have to live with insane laws, but from equally narrow minded "back slappers" of a "mutual admiration cult" intent on implementing some sort of a secret agenda. If they lauded the benefits of a "culturally diverse" education to us, surely one would have to ask the question why they didn't grasp at the same "wonderful opportunity" that they forced on us?

It is this elitist attitude that has got us into the "pickle" we are presently in. We have become the laughing stock of the entire world, not that we are rapidly slipping into a "third rate nation" status, but that we gleefully "greased" up our own rope to accommodate the slide. Don't get me wrong I can't blame the Chinese who are a business oriented people, for outdoing us because their respective governments assist the workers. That is one of the roles that governments should play. I put the blame squarely at the feet of our own government, which wasn't doing the job that we hired them to do for us. Perhaps there is a lot of truth in the old adage that "North Americans have the best politicians that money can buy," selling their services to the highest bidder, "doing unto others" that which should have been done for us. Teddy Roosevelt once said, "When they call the roll in the Senate, our legislators don't know whether to answer present or not guilty." This is even truer now than in his day, at the turn of the twentieth century.

Volker and I viewed the remainder of the items on display at the trade center, and came away in wonderment at the profits to be had in dealing with the Republic of China. Let me give just one example. After market automobile fenders for five bucks a piece that could fetch about $150 in the US. But you were required to buy a container load, possibly a thousand units.

Being white, the Chinese seem to be prejudiced in their outlook on us. They prejudge all of us as being wealthy and as a result we were invited to an exclusive unveiling on the main floor of the building of Madam Chiang Kai-Shek's (wife of the deceased strongman, thus perhaps "strong woman") pet project; a car made in Taiwan called the "Feelung." There they treated us to juice, coffee, tea, champagne and an assortment of appetizers and sandwiches. The sales teams were also present to offer helpful hints at franchise availabilities in various countries.

All in all I was quite impressed with the professionalism that the trade complex showed to potential investors from all over the globe. They were every bit as aggressive as any American entrepreneur that I had come across in my travels. They would go to great lengths to facilitate a deal.

If there was something that caught your eye the process that had to be followed was to hire a "trading company," usually Chinese, and they would handle all the paper work involved with the proposed transaction. Generally deals could be had only by the "container" load (a box deemed to be of a standard size to fit on a transport ship). Anything less, and the costs would escalate. Also, these trading companies were informed as to what was available for immediate shipment if some overseas purchaser company did not following up with final payment for a product. These I suppose could be classified as a "steal of a deal."

Volker found one such container full of "soft toys" (a trade name in the toy industry for stuffed animals) for $7000. He said that translated to about fifty cents per critter. I think companies put deposits on these things and then go back to their countries and try to market the product. After getting X number of sales they then make the final payment and have the containers that were saleable sent over. If the sales weren't what they anticipated, then they would just forfeit their deposits and go with the ones that are selling.

The jet lag had still not released its grip on us so we went back to our hotel to get some rest and somehow readjust our "body clocks." No need to stop to eat anywhere because we had filled up at the auto exhibit.

Upon awakening, we found that we have at last conquered our eternal drowsiness. Volker informed me that he was going to take me to a place that will either fill me with awe or will totally disgust me. We were to go to a place called the Huashi Jay, translated to English that literally means Snake Alley. This is where people drink fresh drained blood from cobras, and a place where it is said that live monkeys are positioned into the center of a table with just their heads protruding. Then with small hammers, provided to each patron they smash into the monkey's head and spoon out the brain matter eating it "while it's hot."

The place didn't open till the evening so we just kicked around till seven o'clock and then left.

I immediately notice that it was like a "farmer's market" Chinese style. Things are alive and slain on the spot for you. For instance a chicken's throat is cut and thrown into a barrel, which is lying on a slant, so the blood can be drained from the bird. At the bottom of this barrel a hole is cut to collect the accumulated fluid that has amassed as the miserable creature thrashes in its final throes of death, gasping for the air that it had been so callously deprived. As the thrashing subsides to a flutter I heard the vendor and the purchaser laughing and chatting, probably talking about the most mundane of things. The fluttering ceased. The merchant then picked up the bird and placed it into a vat of scalding water and in a flash it was stripped of its plumage. The once proud and fully feathered fowl now lay in a naked heap of flesh, subjected to its last humiliation. Oh the indignity of it all.

In relating this I have an inkling that this method is a lot more sanitary than what we have in North America. Also marketing products in this fashion comes with one huge advantage, you are guaranteed freshness. I suppose like many North Americans we are not used to eating that which was just killed, therefore this looked very unappetizing, but with time I'm sure we could acclimatize. The suffering of the various animals slain in this fashion was not taken into account. I did have other concerns that were haunting me. Questions like, what "macabre" meal was to be made from all that blood that has been drained off the various birds? This thought was high on my list.

We strolled farther inside Snake Alley and noticed restaurants catering to all sorts of tastes. I had already lost my appetite viewing the chicken transaction, but Volker was intent on eating. We stopped and he ordered a "squab" (pigeon) roasted with some sort of delicious sauce. He wolfed it down and in no time we continued our stroll.

We walk past the place called "The Snake Lady." Her specialty was the draining of blood from "live and wriggling" honest to goodness cobras. She secures the tail with some kind of clip overhead and stretched the poor creature out by pulling it down maintaining a firm grip just below the head. She then took a knife and slit the snake's neck vertically and still holding the reptile gingerly by the head with one hand, drained the blood slowly into a glass while the "King Cobra" unceremoniously writhed in agony. The glass was then handed to an eagerly waiting customer who took it, muttered some incoherent incantation, and downed it in one smooth gulp. I was left with the impression that the gentleman in question was putting on a show for us, showing his bravery or proving to the onlookers that he is a man. Or maybe it was to enhance his sexual potency by way of some "Ancient Chinese Secret," I can never know for sure. I do know that the entire ritual was branded in my memory and will stay there forever.

I started chatting with the "Snake Lady" and she asked me if I was interested in watches. She then brought out some excellent specimen for me to view. There were all kinds of brand name watches such as Omega, Cartier, Ferrari and of course Rolex. The one that impressed me the most was the Rolex "Presidential" model. It was a fake a "genuine fake" as they like to say, but it was done so well that it was hard to distinguish from the real McCoy. All the watches had a quartz movement and Rolex, like most Swiss timepieces, had a wind up mechanism causing the second hand to perform a sweeping motion. This was the ultimate give away that the piece was a fake. Although the quartz kept more accurate time, all the fakes had the patented pulsating second hand.

So this was the other side of business in Taipei, Volker sure knew his way around, and how to get things that seemed to be taboo. With little negotiation I picked up fifteen of the timepieces to sell to curiosity seekers back home. With the transaction complete we maintained our steady pace through the ever-narrowing streets.

My buddy tugged at my shirt in a beckoning, excited way, like someone who had a forbidden secret, and could barely hold it in. "Lets go this way," he said, in an agitated voice. We took a left and then another left into a narrow alley, the width of which was about eight feet. It was lined with cages on either side. Once we were in the midst of these, I noticed half crazed people sitting on chairs, motioning that we stop. Then the most depressing of all sights became apparent. There were girls in these cages, reaching out as if begging us to save them from an unimaginable doom. I looked at Volker with a quizzical wide eyed stare and he just looked at me with his analytical gaze, his eyes flashing with just a hint of a smirk, checking out my reaction to these unheard of conditions. I stopped and asked him if what I was viewing was in fact real. His answer was, "Yes Al, they really are sex slaves." The half crazed man sitting on the chair noticing our interest uttered, "two dalla." I almost got sick and couldn't get out of there fast enough. As we walked away, the drugged up pimp yelled "one dalla" in a loud voice, thinking that it was due to the steep price that we opted to walk. This alerted the rest of his "stable." Thus Volker and I had to walk a gauntlet of pawing and groping hands attached to the most forlorn faces that I had ever seen. What desperation was exhibited in those eyes of "the damned."

Volker was showing me the other side of life, a life, if had to be lived, would certainly have been akin to a hell, and a hell that one wasn't soon to forget. I now understood why the people called it Snake Alley. It was rife with snakes of the two-legged kind as well, and it was they that were the most dangerous animals of all. He later told me that those girls were from Thailand and sold to these "people merchants" who would in turn have them "servicing" tourists to recoup their investment. The girls were evidently kept well stocked in drugs. You would have to be high on something to endure those beastly conditions. Hell, I was happy when we left the Huashi Jay, a hangout for Mephistopheles himself.

My self-appointed tour guide then took me to a club frequented by well-healed tourists. There was disco music and plenty of women milling about, but all I really wanted at the time was a stiff drink to wash down the disgust from the previous scene. A pretty lady asked me to dance and I complied. When she asked me to buy her a drink, I told her that I was married and would rather be by myself. I wanted nothing to do with women for a while, I just wanted to digest and expel the "downloaded data of disgust" in my brain. The "mama san" came over to see if I wanted to hire one of her girls for the night. Volker asked me to intercede on his behalf for a girl that he had his eye on. I did and after some negotiation the price was "ten dalla." About an hour later he came back with a smile on his face and I had one on mine as well, as a result of several drinks.

We made it back to our room in the wee hours of the morning, finally free of that hounding jet lag. Just in time too, next day we had to rise early for our trip to Hong Kong. I can only wonder what things this "man of the world" still had in store for me.

Our flight seemed to last about an hour. Approaching Hong Kong and dropping altitude, one gets an eerie feeling of landing on top of the ocean. You see, the runway is a long thin man made peninsula jutting out to the sea. There is so little land available in this area that practical solutions such as these have to be improvised.

As it was with the airport, so it was with the housing situation. Every square inch of space was utilized for buildings. All the way up steep hills, buildings clung precariously on their man made perches carved out with "great prejudice" from the surrounding rock. The harbor too was full of "junks" (small fishing boats) used by fishermen as living accommodations.

So we had finally arrived at the city that held so much mystery for me. Growing up I read books based on adventures with Hong Kong as a backdrop. Memories of movies showing the landmarks of this huge "dynamo" of commerce, depicted in James Bond thrillers and countless martial arts flicks were now being recalled. The well-lit Chinese signs, and right hand drive automobiles, it was as if one was transported to a strange British city in which no Anglos were present. Oh, and let's not forget the cities tax free status, an inducement which has made Hong Kong one of the most desired shopping destinations in the world.

Volker instructed the driver to a hotel in the downtown area of Kowloon, a city across the bay from Hong Kong. The hotel was $50 a night, quite a deal. In Hong Kong the rooms run about $200 per night.

With nothing planned for that evening we went out for a beer in one of their many pubs. These English version pubs dotted the area to make the tourists feel right at home. The problem was, in the evening they became the hangouts for Chinese gangs. This could have been one of the reasons that no tourists were to be found in these places at night. The beer was the same anyway and at a fraction of the cost that they would have charged us at the local "tourist trap."

Later we went for a stroll and I stopped at a sidewalk vendor displaying silk ties. Now silk ties were $25 a-piece back home and this fellow was asking three dollars a-piece. I struck a deal with him and bought 25 of them for $35. What great gifts they were going to make. I bought another suitcase for ten dollars anticipating filling it with tax-free goodies purchased on this trip. After returning to the hotel, we "crashed" for the night.

An unpleasant surprise awaited us when we awoke. The bathroom plumbing was backing up. These displeasing events could be dealt with at home by asking for, and getting, a free night's lodging, given to people back home as a normal perk to mollify them for abnormal occurrences. However, in a strange land with an equally strange culture, this wasn't about to happen. Somehow my friend and I dealt with the problem of the deluge and we went about our business.

Volker went to a travel agent and purchased some tax-free airline vouchers for Air Canada at a cost of $800. I don't know exactly how it worked but he received ten vouchers that would take him anywhere Air Canada flew in North America. The stipulation was that he couldn't land in the same airport, other than Calgary twice. The tickets had to be used up in a one-year period, and had only standby status. It seemed like a heck of a deal to me. This guy sure knew his way around "the block;" you might say that he had made the world his "personal oyster."

We then went to a computer software company where he gave the proprietor ten discs to copy. Keep in mind that this was at a time when you couldn't get anything copied here in North America, because it was deemed "illegal."

Just looking around the shops we were constantly propositioned by tailors (you could tell that they were tailors because they all had their limp measuring tapes draped around their necks) that wanted to sell us pure wool suits for $120, custom fit, ready in one hour. In retrospect, I should have bought one because at the time the same suit would have cost $500 back home.

After that we went to the boat terminal and got the schedule, and some tickets for the boat ride to Macao for the next day, and then returned to our hotel.

Volker was having a wonderful time eating up a storm while I was still feeling a bit woozy from the Taiwan experience. Precisely when a person could enjoy good food at a reasonable price my appetite had deserted me. Such was my luck. I hoped that had not deserted me as well, for our appointment at the casino in Macao was for the following day. We retired early in order to be up in time to catch the boat.

Waking to the usual flood in the form of sewage backup, we somehow managed to cope with this minor disaster again and made our way to the terminal.

Hong Kong has a very efficient rapid transit system as it should have, to transport the high volumes of people that the city contains. For the first time, I noticed how elegantly the girls are dressed as they are queuing up to gain entry into the underground system. The style then was the liberal use of shoulder pads for female attire. It complimented their slim subtle features. However, to the American male and Volker in particular, who has a lurid imagination anyway, thought that those shoulder pads could have been better utilized, and "sexier" yet, had they been instead worn as kneepads.

With little fan fare we arrived at the station and were loaded on to the boat to take us to our destination.

I am delighted to find out that we were on a boat called a "hydrofoil." Hydrofoils contribute to the boat's speed by getting the hull out of the water. A foil is a kind of a large water ski that assumes the drag on itself rather than the hull. They lift the hull out of the water so that you only have to overcome the drag on the foils instead of all of the drag on the entire hull, making the journey faster and more fuel-efficient.

It took about an hour for us to make it to Macao. We arrived at low tide, and the harbor, which was basically dry, was full of large fishing boats lying beached on their sides. Because so many of them are "marooned" in this fashion, I assume that it is a recurring problem, which creates little concern. Our drop off point was okay, because it was regularly dredged.

There are two casinos in Macao, but only one of them was open. We went straight there to commandeer a room and managed to get one for $70. We then hired a cab to get a feel of the city. We noticed that the roads were in disarray, many with "no entry" signs. All in all the nicest building that we saw was the ruins of an Old Portuguese church. The church was so interesting that we let the cab go, and took a closer look at it.

At one time the huge structure must have been a beautiful centerpiece to the city. It was erected on a small hill with a commanding view of the area. It was of sand stone construction with a solid foundation. They certainly built it to last and why it was in such a dilapidated state I was unable to find out. My guess is that the catholic religion no longer was the corner stone of local worship. The Portuguese, along with the Spanish, had a policy of impregnating as many people as they could to capture more "souls" for "the church" and their empire. In the end, this very policy led to their total collapse, with no obvious racial identification with the original empire, the region eventually slipped back to it's former self.

It is obvious to me what resulted, the intermixing of the Chinese and Portuguese population. At first glance you notice a hint of the Chinese eye features, but then the nose, the most prominent feature of the face, protrudes out as in the European physiognomy, instead of a flatter feature, as we would expect to find in the Chinese. These Sino-Europeans are seen everywhere as further evidence of the extent of the miscegenation. One may venture to ask, "Is this the road that passes the present to the future?"

Macao reverted back to Chinese rule in 1999 and will, from the racial point of view, offer no obvious roadblocks to total assimilation. The British who were a lot more "stingy" in the scattering of their "seed" posed a greater problem when Hong Kong reverted back to Chinese rule that same year, because they don't look anything like the inhabitants.

After soaking up the sights, we readied ourselves to leave by hiring a rickshaw for the short journey back to the casino. My guy is quite old but in remarkably good shape. However, he did have an oddity about him. I asked him to show me his hands, and each one had two thumbs. The second thumb grew out of the main thumb, just below the first joint, like a cactus at right angles. Anthropology is one of my main interests and these mild mutations are of great curiosity to me. The Homo Sapien thumb, for instance, is regarded by many people in the craft as the main reason that we humans attained greatness. I personally think they are wrong. I think it's our larger brain, but hey, I'm open to new input of ideas. In the mean time I'm willing to explore other theories. When we arrive back to our hotel we got something to eat and went to the tables to test our luck.

We grabbed the first seats that we could, at a table that was empty; it filled up quickly once the shuffle was complete. On my very first hand, I got a soft four card twenty against a six. I waved off the hit, and was subjected to a round of verbosity from not only the players, but also the dealer. I didn't know what they were saying but I kept waving off the dealer who arbitrarily took it upon herself to hit the hand anyway, giving me a face card, and therefore not altering the value. She reached into her tray and paid me. Only then did I realize what all the fuss was about. With five cards, (in North America this is called a five-card Charlie) you automatically got paid if you didn't break. Several hands later I wanted to surrender my sixteen against the face card. I was sitting in the second position and was told I couldn't. One could only surrender after the initial two cards were dealt to the players, and before any more hits were given. Hmm, another good reason to sit at first base.

These were some of the problems faced when playing in a land were you didn't speak the language, but there were to be many more surprises. At the end of the deal, we were in wonderment as to why everyone "evacuated" the table. Couldn't they wait till the shuffle took place? There were two casino employees at each table, one would stand and deal, the other would just sit by the discard tray. They would alternate positions after each deal. The one that sat by the tray would use some "hokey" shuffle machine to mechanically shuffle one deck at a time. It was also her designated job to fetch the tea after each deal, and then they would take a ten-minute break. That was why the players knowing the routine would leave the table for one that was in play, while us "silly round eyes" would sit and watch in amazement at what was transpiring as we sat. In reflecting, the dealers from Macao must be the envy of dealers around the world; taking a ten-minute break after each shuffle. Hmm, I wonder if that is incentive to "up cut" the shoe to make their shift even shorter? Not a very good scenario for the aspiring card counter.

The dealers in Macao are unlike any I have encountered elsewhere in the world. They demand tips; one of them actually reached for a five-dollar equivalent to the Hong Kong dollar and went to put it into her tip tray. I got rather irate at the cheekiness of the gesture, and told her to immediately put it back. In North America a dealer can get "canned" for pulling a stunt like that.

It wasn't long before Volker and I were jumping from table to table like the regulars. It was simply impossible to remain at one table due to the long intervals between shuffling and dealing. We played for about four hours, and I made close to a $1000, while my buddy scored a $400 win.

In the evening we went to the lounge to check out the "scene." The place was crawling with hookers. There were no available single chicks mainly due to cultural differences. Imagine if you will for a moment, the impossibility of a single girl who is used to going out chaperoned, mixing with prostitutes and guys on the make for a one-night stand. In a place like China, the object of dating is eventual mating for life, and you can't achieve that purpose cavorting with whores and whoremongers.

In Asia, unions are often arranged by family members and thereby, by definition, marriage remains an "institution." In the Occident on the other hand, we usually bump into our future mates by accident, removing all aspects of planning. By removing parental genetic intuitional knowledge of what is best for the offspring, we then expose ourselves to hidden obstacles resulting in an abnormally high divorce rate.

Volker was again in his glory. He asked me to act as his intermediary to procure for him a lady. I was starting to feel like a "second," in a duel. Negotiating was of course done through a "mama san." Here I was again introduced to differentiation in pricing. Why would a typical Chinese lady fetch less of a price than for instance, a Korean? The answer was in fact quite simple. Although there are plenty of pretty Chinese gals, the ones that typically became involved in prostitution were inclined to be plain looking. Due perhaps to American involvement in the Korean conflict, the taboos of "the oldest profession" had been erased in the East. In China, the prettier women were the first to be married off, leaving the less attractive ones single, and more susceptible to the lure of what is perceived to be easy money.

The highest priced women came from Shanghai. This was once a German colony prior to the First World War, and was an area filled with a large garrison to protect their interests. Quite obviously the typical German soldier had a problem "keeping his fly done up." The off spring of these adventurers stood much taller than the typical Oriental and took on some of the facial tones of the European. Nearly a hundred years later, after Europe's two suicidal wars, genes truly speak louder than words. There in front of me stood a tall good-looking girl, although unable to speak English, she was my choice for Volker.

The good-looking girl from Shanghai that I was arranging on behalf of my friend was $30. The Korean was $20 and the Chinese lady was $15. The price reflected the quality of the product. I was shocked to hear that he wanted the Chinese lady whom I eventually acquired for $12, for an hour's worth of services. Volker asked for the exclusive use of our room for the time that he would be spending with his choice of playmate.

I remained steadfast at my station drinking gin and tonic, watching an excellent show featuring four dancing girls from England. They had an act "a la Las Vegas" bare from the waist up. Now these were the type of ladies with whom a guy like myself could strike up a conversation. At the end of their routine, they came to the lounge to get a cooling, refreshment prior to retiring backstage. We engaged one another in small talk, and they told me that they were on contract with the casino for six weeks, and in that time they were not allowed to date any of the patrons. I guess conversing with them a short time was allowed. This was fine by me because a short time was all I had. We talked about the entertainment business in Asia, and evidently female English performers are much in demand in this area, especially if they happen to be blonde. Just maybe the misconception is that they are more permissive, ergo the stipulation, "no fraternizing with the cliental." As for being blonde, thank god for "Revlon."

One more interesting thing that I learned was that Macao has a Formula Grand Prix race that was to be staged in the area. That's why some of the roads were cordoned off.

After about an hour my friend returned to the lounge allowing me to retire for the evening. I asked him why in the world he would choose that "lady" instead of the one that I had earmarked for him. He told me that she was too stuck up. I think she reminded him of his ex wife, and to him that must have been very unnerving.

Waking up around 11:00 am next day got us to the tables close to 1:00 pm. At the table where we were playing, a chap had put himself all in, on a slight high count. We bet $50 apiece, and both of us got what seemed to be great hands, against the dealer's seven. The guy who put himself all in, was dealt a pair of aces. He couldn't split because he didn't have any more money. He asked Volker if he would like the "action" on the split. Volker called over the pit boss and asked him if it was okay to get involved in another man's bet. They informed him that it would be fine, but that he should pick the hand on which he wanted the wager placed, in case a problem were to occur. He chose the second ace, and after the split the man received an eight on the first ace, and a ten on Volker's hand. The dealer made twenty-one, and took Volker's $100 and split it between the man and my buddy, giving them each $50. Volker was furious. That contravened the deal they had arrived at with the pit boss who was now gone on a lunch break. Volker had not listened to reason, and had lent money to a complete stranger, a taboo to be avoided when it comes to 21.

We played for another 30 minutes, but he was just too worked up to continue. We went down to lodge a formal complaint at the cage. In no time at all, the shift boss came over, and after hearing Volker's story and corroborating it with the pit boss at our table at the time, gave him back his $100. Also to appease his rage, we were given a comp to a great restaurant for dinner. The lesson learned is that if you feel that you have a legitimate complaint, go and pursue it. Don't "take it on the chin," if you do then perhaps you will take it in other parts of your anatomy. A philosopher once said, "Knowledge has made you unfit to be a slave, so let not the ass harness you to 'his' plough."

Learn the rules of engagement so you won't be caught short. If nothing else is gained, the casino will at least know that you won't take it lying down, and they will be more apt to straighten out the matter rather than let the situation fester and take a chance at you creating a disturbance. If they are not familiar with your play, they won't chance losing your business.

We ate a light lunch after our confrontation with the management. We decided to save the comp for the big meal for later in the evening. Volker felt a hell of a lot better after his refund, and we returned to the tables for another engagement.

The Chinese are the most superstitious people that I have ever met. I doubled an ace-seven against a six and although it is a "basic" double, another player at our table decided not to hit his ace five so as to bring back the rightful order of cards. I guess he had never read the basic double down charts, or perhaps his decision would have been different. I suppose his thinking was that the "mysterious powers" that rule over us would somehow get even, if we disturb the natural flow of the cards. So in accordance with the Asian laws of yin and the yang, the balance had to be brought back to the game. A postscript, we did win, but we would have anyway. Our Oriental tablemate was unconvinced. He still thought it was his superior play that cost the casino dearly. After I hit my stiff a few times against the six, and after he repeated his no hit strategy, of "balance," the outcome was that the dealer made his hand. Only then did he swallow his pride, leaving the table, seeking greener "yin, and or yang."

After about an hour of play at another table, I saw an opportunity for spreading to an extra square due to a fairly strong count with extra aces. The dealer unfortunately ended up with the ace. The player at the end was shaking his head, and told me in his broken English that wouldn't have happened, had I not gone to two squares. And it indeed wouldn't have happened, but what he didn't know was that the ace was easier to get than the face card, or so it seemed. He bought the insurance and we didn't, because of the multitude of aces left in the shoe. The dealer matched his ace with the face for the blackjack, and I looked over at the chap with the helpful advice and he said, "I toad you so."

A while later the same thing happened at a different table with another Oriental chap. I had spread to two squares, and the dealer dealt himself an ace. The same shaking of the head but this time he didn't know how to speak a word of English. In sign language he pointed to my two spots giving an involuntary "ah jah," and faithfully putting in his insurance bet. Sure enough, the dealer again placed a face card next to his ace. He seemed to gloat as he pulled back his winning insurance bet. After that a name was coined for just that occurrence. "The new man rule" had been born. Every time a new player joins the table, or if someone opens up two squares the new man rule is in the process of being invoked. Of course it is all superstition, but the reason it happens is that if the deck is strong, or at least strong in aces, and when somebody new sits down, they unknowingly sit down amidst a rich deck. Superstition kicks in when the cause is wrongfully ascribed to the new player sitting down or when a new spot is opened.

If a person is watching a table intently, and notices the count escalate, and opens up a new square to take advantage of the rich situation, large cards will in all probability manifest themselves equally at positions around the table including that of the dealer. Let us say for instance that three aces are to appear on a particular deal, and there are six spots being played including the dealer's hand. He will have a fifty percent chance of getting one of those aces, but so will everyone else. On a really high count, consider the exposed ace as a God send, because at least you have an opportunity to buy insurance, thereby nullifying the effect of a likely blackjack.

Later that day on a "sizzling" count with four players at the table, we were all dealt blackjacks. Everybody opted to take even money after the dealer was showing the ace. I had the largest bet and therefore the most to gain and still refused "even money." Although the count warranted the insurance bet I said "nay" for only one lousy reason. I had never seen five blackjacks, essentially the entire table in my life. After he made a believer out of me, I have never seen a repeat performance of that rarity. In retrospect, I should have taken insurance but the circumstances were a way too uusual.

Volker wanted to go and spend the dinner comp that he had earned, so we went up to our rooms to shower and change. Being the true connoisseur that he was, he insisted ordering the meal for us "pair of jokers." When it came, it was instead fit for a "pair of kings." Shark fin soup, squab roasted with some kind of liquor sauce, seafood of all kinds and an exotic dessert.

And truly, I did feel like a king. I was up about $2000 and everything was paid for including flight and trinkets. Hmm, maybe I could sell the watches to achieve some sort of profit for my time. Then it would really be a paid vacation.

We headed back to Hong Kong the following morning on the hydrofoil. We stayed at the same hotel but got a different room; this time without a plumbing problem.

We spent the evening carousing around Kowloon and I picked up a few things for Cindy as gifts. I purchased a large piece of jade carved into a smiling Buddha, and a miniature electronic chess set. I knew she enjoyed playing chess because shortly after we met she challenged me to a game, and after I implied that I was a chess "matador," she gave me that "your full of shit" smile as she proceeded to "wax" me in about ten minutes. The jade, well what a better memento to bring from china, after all weren't the two synonymous.

We boarded a plane that took us directly to San Francisco, where my pal and I parted company. I boarded a flight to Las Vegas, and he continued on to Calgary. It was a strange feeling, landing "yesterday," about 11 hours after our flight left the Asian continent. From the "jet lag" perspective, living that which we have already lived is easier on the body than living that which we have not. In reality, we were just getting back the time that we had "banked" at the start of our trip. Anyway, if was good to be back in the land of the "knife and fork."

I had given much thought to the situation regarding exchange with the Far East and how long that charade of free trade could last before it all came falling on to our collective heads. All goods purchased with cheap labor have little or no value because it doesn't propel "our" people up the financial ladder; in fact it has the opposite effect. It makes the poor poorer and the rich richer, promoting fertile ground for class struggle; with ideologies such as Marxism rearing their ugly heads. It has the immediate effect of exporting jobs to third world countries where labor is cheap, and therefore the profits made are extremely high. Yes the product is less expensive thus more affordable. We can't afford to purchase our own, more costly products due to the meager wages earned by our own labor force. This was caused by the exportation of jobs by the International Capitalists to third world economies. But here is the crusher. Jobs that pay fairly well like those in construction drive prices higher in the housing market. The guy making fewer wages can't support his family and the purchase of the necessary housing because he just doesn't make enough of a wage. Therefore he is confronted with the dilemma whether or not to have children.

In the sixties and seventies any tradesman could buy a house with one year's wages. Now it's the 25-year mortgage in Canada, and 30-year mortgage in the USA. That is the norm. Is this the, much heralded "North American Dream" that we hear so much about. Basically the pinnicle that we are aspiring to is a roof over our heads and a place to sleep. Something that was attainable in the 60s and 70s when normalcy reigned, now is only a dream? Or maybe it has become a nightmare of economic bondage, one lasting 25 or 30 years, sometimes paying three times the value of the home. Is this the dream? Maybe from the banker's point of view. Where else could one achieve unbelievable profits on the life of a loan, a life that often exceeds the life of the person taking out the loan?

Instead of looking to our own country for the manufacturing capabilities that we had, we are now looking to the third world to supply us with their cheap labor. But of course, this won't last, as their wages will also rise and eventually the cycle will come full circle again. The cheap labor will now be supplied by us once more. There are no national loyalties among the International Capitalists. Their loyalties are to the "Esperanto" of the international cartels, universally known as "CASH."

So if the insanity is already present with no immediate hope of change, you might ask yourself, "What's the harm in helping the economy end its suffering by aiding and abetting the administration in it's final plunge into the abyss of "third worldism;" of course all this with the approval of the captains of our ship of state, floundering without a rudder in this sea of global economic turmoil. Their motto of late has been, "If we can't get the economy to fly, then let's help it plunge." Isn't plunging after all a form of flying, only realizing after the sudden stop at the bottom, that it wasn't after all?

To help the plunge, the government even has tax breaks for companies leaving the USA. That is economic suicide and will eventually lead to a nation of bottle pickers as more and more opt out of a bad situation. Living off fringe economies looks more and more inviting. Pay no taxes, work minimally just enough to afford some good books, a place out of the rain, and the cold weather. Enjoy your free time because let's face it you will have a lot of it.

Getting out of the mind numbing job market that has us working till the end of June, traditionally called tax freedom day, the day earmarked before we start earning for ourselves, is a diabolical form of slavery. But they tell us that it is for the common good. "Rubbish." It is for their-own good. It is they, our own leaders that enjoy healthy wages, great pensions, and the best of schools. All the while they squander the country's wealth, and mortgage the country's future.

What ever happened to direct taxation? Gasoline taxes were a form of direct taxation that went to maintain roads and highways, but are now part of the general revenue. The government is looting financial assets from everywhere and spending it nowhere, feeding the black hole of foreign aid. And perhaps the "meanest cut of all," they spend on themselves lavishly, leaving the rest of us in relative squalor. Hmm, maybe a plebiscite on stuff like this would make them look bad. Imagine a question asking, "Do you feel that your government deserves a raise?" That is why "direct democracy" will never be implemented. Imagine giving an employee who is always screwing up a raise. Thus democracy in its present form is an illusion for the "politically naive."

If we were smart, we would boycott things that are super taxed such as cigarettes and liquor. Now that would really put a scare into our "spendthrift" politicos. Like a brat being deprived of his allowance, they would cry foul and seek other means of "cash flow" to appease their greed, perhaps even taxing food. Like nicotine, the indulgence in food is also addicting.

Already they are casting an eager eye at garage sales as a potential revenue source to increase their "allowance." They are after contractors that work for ten percent off because although they make less money they find that the cash incentive is a powerful tool, and ends up saving the end user a pile of "dough" as well as putting more money into their own families' revenues.

The government is like the person who invites himself to dinner bringing nothing, just his appetite, and we are to endure their presence "with tight jaws and clenched fists suffering their intrusion, in silence."

They lecture us about the illegality of not paying our "fair share", and the criminality of going outside the structured form of business. They berate us for venturing into a "fringe economy" because we wish to lighten the load from their heavy hand.

I wonder how they still find the courage to call this a free country. What are we free from anyway? Do we have freedom of religion? Not likely, have a look at what happened in Waco. Do we have freedom of speech? Look and see what they did in Ruby Ridge. We are all regarded as potential terrorists while the real terrorists are terrorizing us from their "seats of power from atop their ivory tower." We are living in a police state bent on "policing" a world that doesn't bend to its will. Now there is talk of citizens carrying ID cards, when in fact the only people that need to identify themselves for our own protection are the very same people that we have elected to manage our affairs. Their motto seems to be, "If at first you don't succeed, lie, lie, and lie again."

What road shall we choose to take us from the present to the future? Is it to be more of the same? Going from one war to the next with "Orwellian" precision, propounding the insane doctrines written by a gang of charlatans spinning the line of "eternal war for eternal peace," all in the name of "democracy." If a democracy is only democratic for one day out of every four years, and entitles the winner a mandate to "dictate" policy for the rest, can we not stand back and say to ourselves, "Hey, maybe this isn't a democracy." Why can't we vote on policy in a plebiscite every few months, airing our views on proposed laws, amendments to laws, immigration and where our tax dollars are to be spent. Isn't that true democracy or maybe we would prove to be too unmanageable. After all we are only "sheeple," in dire need of guidance from above.

We don't need to prop up or roll back the system to it's former "grandeur," the system is too easily hi-jacked by people with a lot of money, and that is precisely what should be avoided. Jettison the system totally and replace it with a revolutionary council. Why should a doctor even be sent to oversee the putrefaction of a rotting economic corpse? Wouldn't their time be better spent on tending the curable?

The dollar is declining so rapidly that it will soon be in the same circumstances as the old peso. Politically, economically and racially North America has become a cesspool managed by "democratically elected yes men," who don't have the balls to turn and point the nation in the "other" direction, and this is what we hold up as the benchmark when forming a government?

The Chinese seem to be working for the improvement of their respective economies. How I envy them. Imagine a government working for the people, and they weren't even elected democratically. Imagine what we could do here on this side of the world if we could make our leaders accountable for their actions, or for that matter, their inactions. Paying them bonuses for running surpluses, and firing them for running deficits. We could take a lesson or two from the Chinese. I salute them for making the best out of a bad situation.

Chapter Fourteen: Back in the USA

It was December of 1988, and being a homeowner in the southern USA, I discovered that fall arrives about the middle of November. In Calgary I was used to the trees shedding their leaves around mid September, so the advent of a late fall is a pleasant surprise. The leaves were in abundance in Las Vegas; especially noticeable were the leaves under, and around our fig trees, of which we had three. Their leaves are particularly large, and as a result quite bulky, and rapidly covered the entire periphery of our back yard, also inundating the pool area.

The weather around the Calgary area in mid to late November is relatively cold when compared to a place like Las Vegas. I guess the same could be said about many places in the US as well. This inhospitable climate inherent in many places around North America brought to the desert areas a phenomenon known as the "snow bird." These "avians" of the colder climes flock to Vegas not only for its milder temperatures, but also for its great deals on food and lodging.

Snowbirds basically are made up of the older retirement set, intent on living out their lives in relative comfort. They tend to congregate in an environment free of the extreme weather that can be experienced in a place like Fargo, N. Dakota in the late fall and winter, or the dreariness of unending rain that is the norm for a place like Vancouver, British Columbia. These snowbirds enjoy the best of both worlds, the mild weather of the summer at their home base, and the fairly mild winters that are the trademark of the desert climates.

Many hotels seeing a potential profit from these folks had the vision to make available parking places for the huge motor homes that these retirees, who somehow, only by "the will of God" it would seem, successfully navigated these huge "missiles" to our Las Vegas digs. With their large reserves of discretionary cash, these retirees were raised to the status of "honored guests" in these establishments.

Presumably grandparents, their obligations had all been met and as a result their cash reserves were hungrily ogled as a welcome addition to the "corporate coffers." Rents on these parking pads could be had for as little as seven dollars per night, and some of these had enticements such as free buffets. For the retirement crowd this was to be, if not a permanent haven, then certainly a must stop-over on their way to even warmer temperatures. Some of these people even felt that there was value in setting up permanent residence in our fair city.

At first there was just a trickle, but then when Hong Kong's lease was beginning to mature and the British rule was to be eclipsed by the mainland communists in the year 1999, there was a flood of "moneyed" people from Asia putting extreme pressure on the coastal real estate markets, especially in California. This influx of people had the effect of driving up the prices there and also all along the entire American and Canadian west coast, particularly in their respective major cities. Vegas had, "de facto" become a destination of preference for white retirees.

To me, this was a blessing in disguise because with the advent of people pouring into the city came the need to build more casinos, which in turn meant more sources of income. By attending the same casinos all the time you get "burned out." In other words, you become too familiar to the casino staff, thereby limiting your effectiveness as a winning player. The more you would play, the more you would win, and therefore the more often you would get kicked out. Having an abundance of casinos meant that you could frequent each establishment less regularly, in effect giving you less "exposure" to the elements as they say. More to the point, the hazards that go hand in hand in doing business on a daily basis as a card counter are reduced.

Another "spin off" of the casino building boom was competition. Players would frequent places where the rules were more liberal. Perhaps it was by instinct or word of mouth, but players that didn't even know how to count were in attendance at the "loosest" 21 tables in town. Whether they were given the advantage of a deeper cut, or re-splitting of aces, the tables at those gaming halls seemed to flourish. The other hotels had to match the "good" rules or be left vacant. Like the person with the least amount to say having the loudest voice, so it was with the casino. They had to make their pitch to either outdo, or at least match the other casino's competitive edge.

With every major establishment that opened, I was there arranging for credit at the cage for $10,000. The reason for this was to make sure that they knew I was from out of town, and perhaps worthy of being treated as a "valued" customer, giving me the "bundle of rights" that came with that title. Besides, that way I could still utilize the "multiple flight coupon reimbursement scenario" to put more cash into my jeans.

Everything seemed to be going along quite smoothly until one day, later that December, I was driving to "work" heading East on Tropicana Avenue in front of the Thomas and Mack Center. Staged inside was an event called the National Finals Rodeo, complete with cowboys, "wannabees" and drunks. Outside was a traffic tie up that would not abate. Events such as these turn people from Vegas into "white knuckled" neurotics, devoid of all patience and common courtesy. I was traveling in the center lane when a lady driving a Porsche pulled out in front of me making a U turn and I "whacked" her driver's side door. This in effect ripped my bumper off and demolished my passenger side fender with some minor damage to the hood area.

A quick trip to the body shop next day gave me the bad news, $2300 damage. Or was it bad news? I quickly opted for the cash settlement for the above amount, bought a fender and a bumper for $110, and I was back on the road in style after a couple of hours of work. The only real difference was that the fender was unpainted, and I had a bit of primer where some body repair was done. The good feeling was that I was now into the car for just a couple of bucks, and not just a car but a car that was a real joy to drive. A $200 paint job at Earl Schieb's and the car looked better than when I had purchased it.

So this was yet another way to capitalize on a misfortune; kind of like turning lemon into lemonade. And that wasn't all. I was in touch with a lawyer friend of mine before I endorsed any papers and he advised me to only sign off on the car and to keep the personal injury part separate. This worked out quite well because he ended up getting me a further $15,000 on the injury side of that claim. So, "where the rubber met the road," I had a free ride with fifteen grand in my jeans, less the $3000 that I paid him to act on my behalf.

The National Finals Rodeo has been staged in Las Vegas since 1985. This is the time of year that people trade in their "Armani" suits for the more fitting attire of jeans, boots and cowboy hats. It is always fun to dress up and play the part of cowboys, but the real cowboys that I used to hang out with usually wore baseball hats and hiking boots. Sure the jeans were still part of their wardrobe, but the boots and cowboy hats were "passé" because they were deemed to be too bulky. If four of you in "Stetsons" ever had to pile into a standard pickup truck, you would know what I was talking about.

Also the guys that I knew were in pretty good physical condition from hard work and plenty of unsolicited exercise. Usually their faces were like leather from exposure to the relentless sun, and their hands were hard and rife with calluses and blisters gained from the endless tasks faced by the average farmer or rancher.

During the ten days of the rodeo, the "urban cowboys" would descend onto the town beset in all their rural finery. Many would be rather wide in girth, yielding their secret as to their origins and could often be seen jostling for positions at one of the many excellent buffets that the town had to offer. These cowboys, often referred to as "chowboys," would then frequent the tables, forcing the minimum bets to be raised. Needless to say, for people who took blackjack seriously like myself, this was a mixture of good news and bad news. On the other hand the casinos loved it, cowboys and chowboys alike had certain expectations when it came to gaming. They were expected to gamble and gamble with a daring, doing things that only the foolhardy would do. They would do this to either impress their ladies or their friends who would usually be behind them goading them on. At their side was the omni present drink.

This is the only time that I would recommend the use of the "extreme play," that is the splitting of ten valued cards or doubling on the ace-nine. These patrons do that all the time, and you too can join in the fun, only on the high count of course. Make sure that you have on your cowboy hat and are in possession of a down home country boy drawl. If so you will be "In like Flynn," one of the boys as it were. If you are "folksy" enough and the staff take a liking to you, they may offer you a "helpful tip" such as not to split face cards, because you probably have a sure winner. They would be right of course, were it not for the high count.

After the big whoop up, the cowboys leave town and the place becomes quiet till the arrival of the new year, at which time the town again explodes with party seekers from all over the world; some with a lot of money, and some with less. The one thing that they have in common is the need to be in a place where they can let their hair down, and let loose with a few cheers and maybe even a few dollars. If you come to town for any of the above reasons you will have no problem in finding people to share the moment with you. If it's the latter that is of interest to you, there awaits a casino that is custom made to be of service to you, or if you don't count cards their well oiled machinery is geared up to "service" you in a totally different way.

Early in January I had to return to Calgary on business, so I again made arrangements with Ike to be on his plane on the reverse leg of his Golden Nugget junket in Vegas. This could enable me to do my thing, and return the very next week with him to Reno. Before returning I purchased the mandatory ticket, Calgary to Vegas return and Calgary Reno return so I could "work" the reimbursement game. I then phoned Harrah's in Lake Tahoe to book me on a three day junket at that hotel a day after the one with Ike's was over. With everything arranged, I was on my way to Reno with my brother.

All went very smoothly on the flight till we were approaching the Reno airport. I happened to be in the cockpit chatting with Ike and the pilot. As we descended we noticed that we had entered into a snowstorm. The pilot indicated that if the blind condition persisted he would have no option but to abort the landing at Reno, and instead fly to Sacramento from where we could have been bussed back to our target. Ike urged the pilot to descend a little further and finally we broke though the clouds allowing us a landing at the airport.

Once on the ground the weather was miserable with huge flakes the size of the Eisenhower "silver" dollar coins (given at the tables in lieu of one-dollar chips). We stayed at our hotel the entire weekend not wanting to leave and brave the extreme elements that prevailed.

The snow would not let up and our return flight was delayed till the afternoon. Then still showing no sign of abating, the flight was cancelled still further till the following day. A sort of "cabin fever" mentality gains hold of one's mind, not being able to leave the huge complex.

The hotel footed the entire bill for the rooms and the extra gourmet delights we had amply used along with any bar charges incurred due to the stay. It seemed that the hotel had been through this drill many times before and in a classy, though somewhat begrudging manner, they bit the bullet again as they did on those many previous occasions.

In a fit of desperation and monotony, I phoned up Harrah's in Lake Tahoe and asked them to include my brother Kevin for the pre-arranged three day junket at their hotel, which was originally only to include me. They said that they would pick us up at the MGM in two hours to be their guests for the agreed stay.

The long black limo with its darkened windows could be seen lumbering menacingly slowly around and up the ramp as it approached MGM's huge front main canopy. The steady whir of the tires' chains could be heard. The familiar sound of the tires squeaking as they compressed the snow under the vehicle's weight was absent, instead the sound reminded one of a badly oiled tank tread. Then it came to a halt at the valet drop off zone. The chauffer, complete with black uniform and hat, sprang out of the front seat and noticing that we were approaching, opened the trunk and said, "Mr. Simon I presume;" a fitting thing to say, as I noted his name was "Stanley." I nodded to the affirmative, and he then proceeded to put our suitcases into the trunk. He motioned to enter as he opened the back door and closed it after we were in.

The storm did indeed vent its fury on the area. Just passing Carson City we noticed the snowfall was in excess of three times the height of our luxury ride's roof. On the higher climbs the snow had still not let up but due to the relentless efforts of the road crews they were made passable. In just over two hours we had reached our destination and checked into our room.

With little else to do but gamble we went straight away to the tables to put in our time. I had the idea that I would put in a twelve-hour shift in one go round. After a very lucky session I was up $3000 in six hours of play. My brother broke out even, so we decided to break off the engagement and have dinner. We would resume our play after.

Having consumed a $500 meal we returned to the same table we had been playing before. There was a different dealer standing there alone, with his arms folded in that now familiar, waiting for action stance. We walked over and sat down. The deal continued where we had left off, but unfortunately this time it was all in favor of the house. I lost the $3000 within three hours, and had now to play the count in a blatant manner as well as "table hop" to remain at even. Then it happened. I just made a $100 bet when the floor man came running up to the table and pushed my bet out. He "read me my rights" saying, "You can play craps, roulette, or baccarat, but you can't play 21 at this casino anymore."

I've never been barred on a junket before, so I added two and two together and came up with an answer, or more pointedly a question. How could they bar me from play? First I was a guest at their hotel with their blessing, and had basically traveled 1200 miles to be there. Now they informed me, when it doesn't suit them, that my play was no longer welcome.

There was only one thing to do and that was to siphon off some credits by playing craps. We went to the crap table and got a $1000 marker and played till I was down about $100 then left. I did this three more times till I had just under $4000 in markers that were outstanding, and then went to Caesar's next door to patronize their blackjack game. We made the rounds at every casino, but Harrah's, until it was time to go.

On Thursday morning I went to the cage to straighten out accounts, that is to say to get my airfare refunded and to straighten out the $4000 marker that I had accumulated playing craps. They gave me back my markers, returned my airfare, and then I wrote them a check for the $4000. We then jumped into the limo and drove off to the Reno airport for the flight to Vegas.

Naturally, I had absolutely no intention what so ever of honoring that check as they had not honored their role as host. A host has the obligation to allow you to play at the game of your choice. If they don't like your play for one reason or another they will simply refrain from re-inviting you in the future. The way it was, they invited me down, not being quite sure whether I was a card counter or not. They were very willing to take my cash just in case I wasn't, but when it seemed that would be difficult to do, they simply said that I couldn't play. Again I have to stress that counting cards is never about how much you've won, it's all about how much you could have won. If I wouldn't have played further the casino could have refused my flight refund. I then would have had to pay for all the other comps as well.

Once in Vegas I phoned a friend at my bank who happened to be the manager there, filling him in on the situation. He promptly put a stop payment on that check. So now it was I who had them over the "barrel," so to speak.

They contacted me a few weeks later and reminded me that the check had not cleared and then I told them that it never would. Reminding them of the shoddy treatment given me at their casino, I reiterated that a check would not be reissued by me. They advised me that they would then take me to court to recover damages. "Good luck," I told them, "firstly in Alberta, a gambling debt is not collectable, and in Nevada they would laugh them out of the courtroom." Imagine bringing a guy 1200 miles to play cards with the stipulation that if he played his allotted time he would be given full comp, including R F B plus airfare, then denying him the right to play in order to earn those same privileges. Add to that the possibility that the case may make the newspaper; then that would be catastrophic, for not just Harrah's but for every casino. The worst-case scenario for them would be if the event, once aired, would become a precedent setting one. Harrah's, and perhaps the entire "junket" industry as a whole, would be inundated with delinquent accounts by people that have been emotionally man-handled like I was.

Cooler heads seemed to prevail as they appointed a mediator to come to terms with me, bringing the matter to a close. I offered them $500 to clear off the debt entirely, if they furnish me with a "paid in full" receipt to be given so as not to tarnish my AAA credit at all the other casinos. To my total surprise they accepted the offer. Who could blame them? In retrospect if word had gotten to the media of a law suit of this nature, it may have gotten out of hand entirely, causing an avalanche of similar cases. Let's face it I couldn't have been the only one, or for that matter the first one to be given that kind of treatment.

At Harrah's I was "persona non grata" from that point on. Not that I couldn't ever play there again, but I couldn't play there again as "a cherished guest," and that was just fine by me.

It became more and more apparent to me that there were many roads to the pay wicket other than simply playing B J at the tables. If you would let yourself be taken advantage of, the casinos would trample you. If you would stand up for your rights, you might gain the respect of the establishments, which in many instances meant the gaining of cash in your pocket.

There was an incident at the Horseshoe about this time involving two card counters. They were playing with a fairly large stake, and horror upon horror they happened to be winning. They were rushed to one of the "back rooms," accused of cheating, resulting in a severe beating administered by the casino's security staff.

The case subsequently was slated for trial, but the casino wisely opted for an out of court settlement for $250,000. All this due to an over zealous management, too quick to cast an accusing finger against two run of the mill card counters. They may otherwise have run out of money, forcing them to seek meaningful employment at some other occupation.

My wife Cindy was showing more and more. Pregnancy made her brim with beauty and femininity. I couldn't have loved anyone more than I did her. Her natural loveliness wasn't marred by any make up, she was more that attractive without it.

On April 16th she woke me up to inform me that her "water had broke." After much pain she gave birth to my son Beau at 5:00 pm. He looked great, a little bit like me, a little bit like Cindy and a whole lot like himself.

He gave me a totally new direction in life. From that moment on he was my ward. I would painstakingly teach him the things that he had to know, important things like smiling at the age of ten days, swimming underwater in our outdoor hot tub at the age of two weeks, walking at seven months, using the toilet at nine months and in general doing the things that a father would do when the wife was working.

Rarely did I go out to hit the tables, only if we had friends that would occasionally come in from out of town, then making the trip almost obligatory. But that was maybe twice a month. Other than that, I was the doting father in a matron role. Cooking, pureeing food and tending to the yard and the pool; I had become a total domestic over night.

To add to this I was presented with a second gift on the 17th of December in 1990 with the birth of a second son, Dylan. He was a mischievous little rascal, taking great delight in driving his walker down the two steps into our conversation pit. He too was given the total devotion that only a father starting out late in life could give them. They were two bundles of energy and required my undivided attention. Without a doubt I had my hands full, forcing me to take a sabbatical from the tables for an indefinite period.

Chapter Fifteen: Back in Business

In my endeavors to be a great father, my duties as a husband were left wanting. After an ugly divorce, an agreement was reached over custodial rights of the children. It was agreed that the two boys would live with me for one year, and then live with their mother for the following year. Needless to say in the years that they would be with their mom, I would have a lot of time on my hands. "Love is the real gamble, you pay with pieces of your life."

So it was on October of 1994 that Kevin and I found ourselves in Atlantic City checking out the action, more or less at the invitation of Joey L. He had invited us down to consult him on some renovations on his recently purchased home in Ventnor N.J., a district close to the famous Boardwalk. We could also be coerced into some gaming, as there were a lot of casinos dotting the area.

On our arrival we made arrangements to meet Joey at the Irish Pub located at St. James Place, a few doors from the Boardwalk, which in turn borders the Atlantic Ocean. Atlantic Avenue is the main road that travels north and south, two blocks from the Boardwalk. St James intersects to the east toward the ocean. It was a long couple of blocks from there to the Irish Pub.

Those two blocks were rife with old buildings boarded up for what seemed to be ages. Years ago, stripped of their paint, the boards displayed a brownish color laid naked to further ravages by the relentless elements. We heard a door creaking open and shut aided by a gentle breeze from the sea. Although the windows and doors had been nailed shut on these relics from a bygone age, you could hear strange scurrying sounds emanating from the inside. We walked by a group of five young blacks loitering about on the street doing their drug deals, unconcerned with any repercussions that might occur as a result. The Police have long ago grown numb to the problem as a direct result of the revolving door justice handed down by the system. The more skeptical cops that I have met say that they no longer implement a justice system, but merely feed a legal industry, one that is heavy with crooked lawyers, and over paid incompetent judges.

A car slows down and draws close to the curb. Its tire crushes an empty can of Colt 45 just before it comes to a halt. Colt 45 is the "beer down here," preferred for its high alcohol content and highly prized by the dwellers in these haunts. One of the dealers is alerted upon hearing this and is roused into action. He goes over to the passenger window, passes a small package to the occupant and he in turn passes him what is obviously money. The drug deal done the young thug, in the making goes back to his circle of friends.

We passed another condemned building and from within, a man stuck his head out of the window and yelled, "Get yo mutha f**ken ass in here and lay some o dat mutha f**ken bread on me sucka;" Strange how these two legged denizens can infest a building, indeed an entire city without any citizen reaction. More important was my concern with Joey's frame of mind. How could he knowingly invest in a city overflowing with the lower stratum of society?

We made it to the Irish Pub after "walking a gauntlet" of unbelievable misery. We were relieved to find that it just happened to be a police hangout, and not some place that was frequented by "brothas." I guess this is how Joey wanted to introduce us to AC.

Atlantic City was at one time the playground for affluent Easterners with lots of time and money on their hands. They used to bask on the beaches, while their not so well off countrymen sweltered in the hot humid heat that dogged those eastern summer months. The beaches in AC were prime, and in the summer months hotel rates would skyrocket making the rental business prosper. Stately old homes, once haunts of the well to do, were now affordable by those that were not so rich, or those that didn't have access to "old money." Mere mortals like us could buy these homes and partition off, once stately living quarters for the "budget" vacationers to rent at a far cheaper rate than those "top heavy" commercial competitors.

In the 30's the depression meandered through the economy of USA doing a considerable amount of damage, but when it hit AC it absolutely decimated the town. It hit so hard in fact that it might be said that the place is still in recovery mode. The squalor is immediately evident the moment you take your first step out of the lavish casinos that occupy the "Boardwalk." The most opulent of these is the billion-dollar Taj Mahal. It is neighbor to some of the most despicable slums in the entire country.

As all who have played the Fat Cat game of "monopoly" can attest, Baltic and Mediterranean avenues are the cheapest on the board, gradually rising in value till one reaches Park Place and the Boardwalk. AC's depression, which inspired the game, using the town as its backdrop, catches your eye immediately. One encounters familiar names such as Atlantic Avenue, Marvin Gardens, St. James Place and a smattering of other recognizable locations appearing on the game board.

Baltic is just a few blocks from the "Taj." This monument to Donald Trump's vanity was inspired to separate Americans and foreigners alike from their money. The blackjack rules in this mammoth structure are as bad as the casino is huge. The eight-deck shoe, which is the standard fare for blackjack, laid down by the New Jersey Gaming Commission, is routinely cut, leaving only five decks in play. Some say that the eight-deck game was a negotiated settlement made between Ken Uston, a card counter and the casinos. The deal theoretically would allow the card counter freedom to ply his craft without the fear of getting kicked out. Also there was to be a Gaming Commission representative placed in all casinos to air complaints that may arise from time to time between player and casino.

The eight-deck shoe, which in effect looks like a thinly sliced loaf of Wonder bread, shouldn't be a deterrent to play with one important caveat. Some difficulties arise using the eight-deck, especially on the first shuffle. Cards are very slippery. New dealers or lady dealers, especially those with petite hands, find that loading the shoe with that many cards can at times be very difficult. You must have heard of a game called 52-card pick up. Well, you haven't lived unless you were a witness to the 416 version of the same game. I can't tell you how many times I've seen those cards explode just as they were being inserted into the shoe. Other than that there is very little difference between the six-deck shoe and the eight when it comes to advantage.

It is the cut that is rather bothersome. If in a four-deck shoe one deck is cut off, simple division tells you that you are playing with 75% of the cards. In a six-deck shoe, if the cut off is two decks, the same math tells you that you are playing with 66% of the cards. Simple arithmetic tells us that three decks cut from the eight deck shoe gives us only 62.5% of the cards left to play with. After a couple of hours play I was pining for the six-deck shoe at the Las Vegas Club. They cut off half the shoe but the rules, as they say on their marquee, are the best rules in the world.

If you are experiencing a bad cut on the eight-deck game then it should be avoided. Go to a casino that offers the six-deck game instead. Either that, or play at the casino that gives you a better cut.

As strange as this may sound, after playing an eight-deck shoe the six deck looks skinny in comparison. Most casinos offered the odd game of six decks at a limited number of their tables. One such casino was Caesar's.

We met Joey sitting at the Irish Pub bar drinking his customary glass of orange juice. He greeted us with his usual reserved smile and we settled down for a conversation. When it came time to order food, Joey told us that he would "buy" us lunch but we would have to go to one of the casinos. He was a master when it came to full utilization of things that the gaming hall offered as lures to attract you to their respective establishments.

Our first stop was Caesar's. There he took us through to the main casino and from there he led us to the high limit slot machine area. People that play at those machines are pampered, as well they should be, because they generate a large part of the casino's revenue. Once there he took us into a back area where we drank gourmet coffee and partook in sandwiches and chocolates offered as perks to these clientele. I was surprised that we weren't challenged. After all we didn't dress in the fashion that was the norm for people that frequented that particular venue.

We then went to an area that had blackjack tables near their Sport Book section and settled down to some BJ action at one of their six deck tables. Meanwhile, Joey attended to some other business for about an hour.

While we were playing, a most unusual event was unfolding. The dealer, a pretty black lady, was talking to a floor man while she was administering to her game. I took a hit and broke, but my cards remained on the table. She broke and paid everyone, including me. Next round she hit a hard seventeen and broke, paying everybody again. This went on for about 20 minutes until she was relieved. Although the count was minus, my bet was $50 because it was paying no matter what I had. Once, she even paid me on my eighteen when she had twenty. Even stranger was the fact that the floor man was, seemingly, watching the game and not saying a word. But the oddest thing of all was that not one of us, six players all told, even uttered a peep. I felt as if we were being used as guinea pigs in some clandestine experiment on mass human behavior. The only thing one could attribute the strange conduct of the dealer, and indeed the floor man to was that they were both high on "coke." The classic feeling of being in total control was quite evident in their conduct. They were very talkative, seemingly self-assured, and yet to people that were not under "the influence," they were acting noticeably unnatural.

Someone once said that if you are doing cocaine it is evidence that you have too much money. Whoever made that comment was probably right, but the over abundance of money that she was shelling out was not hers, but the casino's.

The cocaine at the time was being sold for about $100 per gram. That was about ten times more than what I paid for bulk eighteen-carat gold.

Little did I know then just how bizarre this trip was going to be. That dealer, strung out on drugs, was just the harbinger of still more off the wall occurrences that we were to encounter during our trip.

Joey picked us up and we related the story to him. The only thing that he had to say was, "I hope you nailed the bastards, they got me for $200 yesterday." We got to his car in the casino garage and I noticed that he had one of those anti theft devices on the steering wheel of his latest love affair, a 1982 rabbit diesel pickup truck. I thought to myself, "What self respecting thief would even consider stealing a vehicle like that?" The truck was a two seater and there were three of us so I volunteered to jump in the back. Luckily there was a canopy on it with a window that opened to the cab so we could all carry on a conversation. He then drove us over to his new property located in Ventnor.

Atlantic City property was worth less due to the undesirable people that live there. Jackson Avenue is the dividing line between the two districts. Unfortunately for Joey he was in Ventnor just in name, as he lived right on Jackson Ave., across the street from AC.

The house was a three-story building that he picked up for $90,000. A similar house next door was listed at $140,000. When we entered the place Kevin and I just looked at each other in disbelief.

We were lead to believe the place just needed a little paint and some mild carpentry work, but this was a major renovation. There were holes in the walls, the ceilings and in the floors. To make matters worse there was the unmistakable smell of decaying flesh, presumably that of a rat, the four legged kind. We told him the bad news that short of an incendiary device the place was not worth the cost of repair. It was in such poor condition that one was pressed at where to even start the repairs.

By now it was close to supper, so Joey drove us to the Trump Plaza where he got us into Diamond Jim's for a little snack before we took on Caesar's six deck game one more time.

Diamond Jim's is a place reserved for the high betting, high risk high casualty game of high limit slots. How the hell he got this VIP card was a mystery to me, but one thing is certain, the staff always referred to him as mister. Up to that time, as far as I knew, he had shunned the game calling it what it was; a black hole of endless loss. This place offered unlimited smoked salmon, oysters on the half shell, soups and other delights. But most important, they served mocha chinos, a refreshing "wake me up," after a boring session. It was only after this dining interlude, that we went to play some 21 at Caesar's.

The evening brings out the best and the worst in a town with which you are not at all too familiar. As gambling is the main stay of AC, the casinos fill up with gamers of all sorts. The sweet little old ladies pumping quarters into machines that never pay, con artists trying to sell you one carat diamonds for a couple of hundred dollars, gamblers on a roll, gamblers down on their luck, and then of course you also get to see a lot of card counters.

In every walk of life you meet a hierarchy of people in their chosen fields. Card counters seem to be no different. They too have an intrinsic hierarchy from the down and out, to the "big player," the "klutz," the loud mouth and finally the soft-spoken but very efficient player. This night I was to see the most intriguing pair of card counters ever to grace a casino. Their names were Freddie and Ace.

These two chaps were unique in many ways. They were both about the same age; I would guess that to be around 35. Freddie was close to six feet tall, with a moustache and wore glasses that were held together with some kind of white first aid tape. Ace on the other hand, challenged the height bar at five feet on his tiptoes. He too wore glasses, but the feature that stood out the most, was his Harris Tweed jacket. Whenever we saw him out and about he was wearing this English style semi-formal apparel. It wasn't at all a bad looking piece of attire, but he seemed to wear it like an overcoat. The jacket, made to wear with dress pants, was several sizes too big for him. As a consequence of his slight stature it looked like one of those three quarter length coats that were popular in the sixties. For Ace, Wonging would certainly have been a chore. His height severely handicapped his field of vision. I can't remember whether or not Ace had one of those collapsible mini two step stools, the kind that house wives use for accessing the upper cabinets in the kitchen. If he didn't, he sure could have used one.

These two workhorses were yoked together like a team, pooling their money with only one person playing at any one time. When Freddie was playing, Ace could be seen bobbing and weaving behind Freddie's chair, trying to catch a glimpse at the outcome of a particular hand. Had he been carrying his stepstool, his work would have been so much easier. When Ace was in the player's seat, Freddie would scan the other tables looking for a rich card opportunity. If one would appear, he would give Ace a tap on the shoulder, and the two of them would high tail it to the rich table. Ace's long hair could be seen bouncing up and down in a choppy fashion due to his short strides; two steps to every one of Freddie's. Compared to Ace, Freddie's gait was as smooth as a sixteen hands high bay. Ace would seemingly have to climb the chair in order to sit down. Often the croupier would start the deal without giving him an opportunity of placing a bet; this would evoke a shrill protest from him. In his high pitched voice he would say to the dealer, "Damn it, you could see that I was about to sit down, why didn't you wait for me?" They could often be seen coaching some well dressed gambler on the finer points of counting, getting a free meal out of him to boot.

This overt system was totally foreign to guys like me, who were trained in the Vegas style of stealth. Walking around flaunting the fact that you were a counter, had already heralded in rules such as no mid-shoe entry on the high limit tables. These rule changes were both good and bad. They were bad because you couldn't do the "Walkabout," trawling for high-count opportunities. They were good, because the casinos obviously considered counting to be a threat, even in the eight-deck game. But because of the open style of AC counters, further restrictions in play would seem to be inevitable.

Another chap that was introduced to me was Frank. He was a high-spirited individual who would yell out loud the number of aces that were left in the shoe, basically alerting everyone to the fact that he was a card counter. To my way of thinking even though counting is tolerated, if you let the casino know who you are, you will be the first one to get punted when or if the rules change. So it's always best to fly where you can't be detected, under the radar. He went two squares once on a hot shoe, and they dealt him out of the extra square because technically that would have been mid-shoe entry. He got so mad that he "wrote the casino up" in the book at the Gaming Commission's office. Two or three of these complaints and the Commission had to do some investigating into the validity of the offence against the player.

These complaints weren't to be taken too lightly. Mike Daily, a very competent New Jersey lawyer, who I was destined to meet on an unrelated matter, sued the Claridge Hotel on behalf of a professional gambler who had a shoe pulled prior to the cut card coming out. This because the casino was afraid of losing a big bet. The amount of damages awarded to his client came to a whopping one million. The chap proved to the court that he was a professional gambler and as a consequence the casino interfered with his form of employment. As you can see, lodging a complaint against a casino wasn't just any small matter.

There were other people that sued a casino for $30,000.00 in a combined action for some tort that a casino pulled on them on more than one occasion. But in general, damages were awarded in the amount of about $10,000.00 for violations on a player's right to play without being harassed.

Of course harassment is very subjective. What is harassment to me is possibly not harassment to the guy sitting at the seat next to me. If they want to kick my butt out of a casino, all they have to do is "up cut" the deck, in other words cut the shoe in half. This very thing did happen to me on a few occasions, but unlike a lot of players I did bring it to the attention of the dealer and the floor man, if he happened to be hanging around the table. I made sure that the folks at the table realized that, "The sheep were being led to the slaughter." They were made aware of the fact in a language that they could understand. Luck! If the shoe was "bestowing" its benefits on to the player, then they would "up cut" the shoe to about the middle position. If on the other hand, the shoe was benefiting the establishment it would be "down cut" to two decks or less, leaving six decks for the player to struggle through. Isn't that also a form of harassment; a form that is virtually never challenged. Hmmm, this might be a great gig for a guy like me who hates bullies, and enjoys getting even.

In New Jersey, another way a casino has to remove undesirables is to raise the table minimum. When it gets busy the floor person walks up to a five-dollar table and nonchalantly tells everyone that the shoe we are presently playing will be the last one at that minimum. And, if we choose to remain there, we would have to up our minimum to twenty-five dollars. At least in Nevada you could remain at the original five dollars until you left the table for good.

Joey took us to the Sands Hotel, and to yet another place, which wined and dined the "high rolling slot players," those that played the $5 or greater slot machine. How the heck does the guy get all these freebies when he doesn't even play slots? Then he finally "spilt the beans." He has hundreds of Most Valuable Player (MVP) cards. These cards have your personal ID on them, to which only the casino is privy. You place these cards into the slot machines, and you start to play; gaining credits with every pull. He has about fifteen cards for each casino and, like a trap-line set with bait, he inserts them into strategic machines in the high limit slots area, preferably the $50 machines. Many Orientals, direct from Asia, play in New Jersey and are not aware of, and probably couldn't care a rat's ass about gaining points for future freebies and comps. After all, if they are playing the $50 slots they probably are "well heeled." Secondly, they are probably not very well versed in the English language and don't want to ask for their own MVP card to garner these same points. And most importantly, neither they nor the staff is aware that Joey's card is inserted into the machine on which the points are accumulating, win or lose, for "Trapper" Joe. To Joey, who lived not far away in New York City, these "trap line" comps not only got him meals at fancy restaurants and accommodations at the best suites in the finest hotels for his friends or himself, but were also money generators for him. Yes, the casinos do actually send checks to players who work the high limit machines or any machine for that matter. It is just that the high limit machines produce these gains a lot quicker.

A small percentage of your total bet is reimbursed because you play the slots. They don't know that it's not you plunking in those coins; they only go by the personal data on the card. In this case there are a lot of unwitting Oriental accomplices named "Joey." Although the casinos reimburse only a small percentage of your play, Joey has a great many cards at the best machines, and as world demographics show there is a lot of Orientals on this planet. If on the off chance, somebody notices that someone else's card is already in the MVP slot they will merely pull it out and place it with the attendant, who in turn will promptly return it to you if you can produce ID matching the name on the card.

He put us up at Bally's for the night with one of his many comps, and treated us to steak and lobster at a restaurant high up in its tower. In the morning he picked us up, bought us breakfast and went to handle the check out. After checking out he said with a smile, "I don't know if you realize it or not, but porn movies aren't comped at any casino." We told him that we didn't watch any as we had went straight to bed. So those hotels do try to slip the odd one by; if your not careful at checkout they can pad your bill. He promptly went back and got a refund for those videos that we hadn't watched, yet were charged steeply for.

We went directly to Joey's "new" old house in Ventnor and decided to rip apart a bedroom on the main floor. He couldn't believe the mess. By late afternoon we were putting it back together again much to his relief. The following day it was taped and after a few of coats of dry wall compound, it was ready to paint.

Next came the living room. There was a huge hole in the floor from a long time leak that wasn't patched until recently. We made general repairs to it, and to other areas that needed tending. Naturally, all the while Kevin and I would attend to casino business in the evenings then returning to Ventnor, since by this time the place had become livable.

It was on one of these nights, October 8th to be exact, that we paid a dollar boarding the jitney from Ventnor to Park Place by the Boardwalk. The nights were starting to get cool. The damp air blowing in from the ocean definitely had a bite to it, easily penetrating our light outerwear.

The Boardwalk at night brings out a different crowd than in the daytime. The sunshine brings out the joggers, the strollers and the cyclists. There are also plenty of pretty Eastern Europeans girls of every nationality, walking arm in arm with their mom or other chaperones, as is the custom back in their homeland. Their recent immigration is revealed by the wide-eyed stares at the opulence of their surroundings. The posh casinos seem to beckon the strollers to stop and make a statement, by making a bet. Souvenir shops are sprinkled along the Boardwalk, all of them advertising "salt water taffy," a nearly inedible form of toffee. One can hear the gentle peal of laughter from the children, drowning out the steady roar of the mighty ocean in its endeavor to make landfall.

The night crawls with the "inline" skate crowd, skate boarders, rickshaw drivers, hustlers, hookers that you wouldn't touch with a ten foot pole, and other people of dubious character. It is a nerve-wracking experience walking around with a large bankroll with no security immediately noticeable. Vegas always had a high visibility of law enforcement in rougher areas frequented by tourists; one never worried about getting mugged in "Sin City."

My brother and I entered the Wild West Casino to play some six-deck 21. Finding it packed to the brim with eager patrons, even more eager to invest in "blackjack futures," we decided to try the Claridge Hotel.

That place was also packed, so we went up a flight of stairs that led to the mezzanine floor where we eventually found a ten-dollar minimum table. We sat down in two empty seats and started to play. The session seemed to be going quite well; everyone was making money. I was basically flat betting the table minimum, occasionally raising the bet when warranted by the count, earning me two stacks of reds (five dollar value chips).

Then a very strange thing happened. I again had a minimum bet, and was dealt a thirteen. Sitting in the third spot, I waited till the players on the first and second spots were finished taking their cards. I then motioned for a card, and instead of hitting me the dealer took my card and put it on the guy's hand that was sitting in the fourth spot. He too had thirteen. The card was a four and he said that he didn't want that card because I had motioned for it, therefore it should be mine. He was quite correct of course and getting quite mad at the same time because the dealer was insisting that the card was his. I tried to quell the argument by reaching over, sliding the card back to my spot. "Don't touch the cards please," was the dealer's response to my action. "Okay, then call the pit boss and let's get on with the game," I said.

Finally, after about five minutes, the floor man came over inquiring what the problem was. We naturally told him. He laid down his judgment, saying that the guy sitting at number four had to take the card. The guy just so happened to be Italian. When he heard that, he flipped out. He started to cuss at the pit boss in his uniquely New York accent. "Get ahddah hee you dumb f**k, I didn't ask fo the caad and I don't want it now." Security was called and I then said, "Look, this is stupid, I want you to cash me out." I took my bet out of the square and slid the entire stack to the dealer to give me blacks. The pit boss grabbed my chips, fumbled them spilling them all over the table and the floor. Now I was pissed off. I told them that they had broken "the contract" and that the hand was null and void.

When you place a bet at a casino you are entering into a silent contractual agreement with your wager. By putting a bet into the square you agree that if you lose you will pay that amount. The agreement also states that if you win, you win that amount. Unless you have a BJ of course, because that nets you one and a half times your bet. The contract goes further and states, if you want a card the dealer has to supply you with one, if they don't provide you with a card, they haven't lived up to their end of the agreement. Therefore, the contract was broken as it was in my case. The boss, obviously new at the job, insisted that I put back the bet. I told him to forget about that, as I was putting on my jacket to leave. He kept on insisting that my bet be put back. I then requested a Gaming Commissioner. They would hear none of it, instead four security guards attacked me and roughed me up. They arrested me, took me in the basement and chained me to a garbage dumpster. There I sat for about a half an hour then a nurse came over to look at me. In the mean time I was thinking to myself. "Boy, one of those 'get out of jail free' cards from the monopoly game would sure come in handy about now." Down here the jails are notorious for making "wide receivers out of tight ends."

From what I had seen of AC, I suspected that the jails would be no picnic. Then a plainclothes detective, a muscular black man, made his appearance. I was pretty nervous until he said, "unchain that guy." The chief of security said that I hadn't as yet been searched. The cop said, "Give me a break, I just viewed the tape, and the altercation had nothing to do with any criminal intent by this man. He was merely reacting to a screw up by your staff." All of a sudden I felt great again. Maybe the hellhole that they call a jail wouldn't be my accommodation that evening after all.

He led me upstairs and there I was reunited with my brother. He too was arrested for disturbing the peace but wasn't subjected to the indignity of being shackled to a dumpster. The cop wanted the matter dropped, but the head of security insisted that they charge me with theft and disturbing the peace. The cop said, "What? You're going to charge him with stealing his own money?" The chief of security said, "He took it out of the square so it wasn't his." "Look, I'll charge him with whatever you want but making it stick is an entirely different situation."

So we were formally charged, but he declined to take us into custody for something so trivial. Instead we were kicked out of the casino and told that we were barred for life. Wow, so this is what a life sentence was like. We couldn't show our faces at their hotel or we would be charged again, this time with trespassing.

As we were walking away I realized that I was ten dollars light. They claimed that I was the one that stole the ten off them, but as it turned out they were the ones that stole the ten off me.

We were back on the street amidst the dregs of society once again. I was re-evaluating my former anxiety at being there. It seemed that we were at our most vulnerable inside a casino, not outside. Four thugs had just rolled me for ten bucks in front of hundreds of witnesses, inside a casino, and nobody would lift a finger to help me. Later an attorney, after viewing the tape of the altercation said to me that the only crime Kevin was guilty of was "not coming to your assistance."

I was really upset. I had to hire a lawyer to get back at those bastards. The problem was that I didn't know any local ones. Joey opened up a copy of Gambling Times magazine and pointed out a lawyer advertising his services. His name was Tom D. We asked several card counters if they had anything good to say about this guy, and those that knew him said that he had helped them out. We were new in town so on the following workday we paid this "legal beagle" a visit. His office was located in a suburb of AC called Absecon, famous for a lighthouse.

He seemed to really know his stuff about the rules pertaining to the gaming industry. We arranged to see a doctor who prescribed x rays and sent me to a hospital at Somers Point. While I was waiting at the hospital I scanned the local phone book to see if I could locate Darryl P., the guy I had met in Monte Carlo years ago. He wasn't listed; I guess everybody moves on.

After the x rays, the lawyer told me to leave matters in his good hands; he would take care of everything. Thinking that we had a competent attorney, we left AC with a good feeling. We were going to sue that casino for a fair hunk of change.

A casino after all is not an industry per se; it doesn't produce anything. It plays on the whims of the people who go there. A friend of mine, Dave I. once said, "It's like a big bag of gas, the more people that play there, the bigger it gets, one prick and that over inflated bag of gas goes bang; let me be that prick." Well according to the casino I am dirty enough to sue them and if that means that I am a prick, then so be it. They can call me "Du Prix," and I will try to fornicate them out of some of their cash.

Just about two years later, prior to the expiry date for filing a judgment, I gave lawyer Tom a call and asked him if all was going well. It seemed that he had forgotten about us, and gave me a song and a dance saying that it was good to wait till the last minute before filing a claim against the casino, that way, it will catch them off guard. This gave me concern as to the man's competence.

After entering our claim, we were recharged with the misdemeanors. Since we were starting a lawsuit against the casino, and they had by this time "shelved" the charges against us, they had to demonstrate "Just Cause" in using force to quell the disturbance. Answering these charges would of course be an annoyance but the problem of distance could be mitigated due to our interest in gaming. We could combine a visit to AC and an appointment with our lawyer; a working holiday, as it were.

So the new date was set to air charges against Kevin and myself for causing a disturbance, and an additional charge of theft against me for stealing my own money. The trial was set for the 24th of June 1997, at the Atlantic City Municipal Court. To be tried at 1:30 pm; Judge Weekes presiding.

We met our lawyer at the courthouse and to my surprise he started talking to me about making a deal. They would drop the theft charge, if I plead guilty to the disturbance charge. He and I argued in the hallway for a couple of hours, till he finally convinced me that we had a strong case regardless and this would free up time for him to go for the "jugular" of the Claridge. I finally relented, pleading guilty on the disturbance charge and appeared as a witness for my bro's trial on his disturbance charge.

To our horror Tom was like the lawyer for Stanley Rothstein on the show "My Cousin Vinny," starring Joe Pesci. Tom couldn't get his computer working and more importantly he couldn't talk. I suppose it could have been worse, he could have stuttered as well, as did the character in the movie. Thank God that was not the case, but they found Kevin guilty as charged never the less, fining him $100. It was almost like Tom was on the payroll of the Claridge rather than working for us. He blamed it all on his computer but gave us assurances that he would win on the appeal. We left town talking to ourselves.

A couple of months later, he got the appeal set for November 97. He also arranged for the lawyer representing the Claridge to depose us at the same time we were down there.

I made arrangements with my friend Peter in Toronto to get us two "partner" passes (partner passes were Air Canada's answer to gays who cried "discrimination" over the use of spousal passes for employees) direct to Philadelphia, Pa. the closest point to AC serviced by regular air carriers.

In Absecon, my brother and Tom were in his office discussing strategy for the upcoming appeal. The articling student walked in on them mentioning to Tom that he was looking over the case and that it would be a cinch to win. "If you're nervous at all about it Tom I'll go down and do it for you," he said. This gave courage to our fearless lawyer it seems. When he went down to the Court of Appeals, following the guidelines of his student attorney, he won the case. All he had to submit was the tape as evidence. The judge ruled in favor of my brother.

Now the stage was set for the lawsuit to follow. The case was to be heard in Camden, New Jersey, the place where Campbell's set up their big soup plant close to the Delaware River, truly one of the dirtiest places in the "land of the free and the home of the brave." I haven't been able to look at a can of Campbell's since. Run down buildings, one just as ugly as the next. A place out of one of your worst nightmares. Right across the Delaware River is Philadelphia, a city that has a more pleasant curb appeal shall we say.

The courthouse in Camden is one of the newest buildings in the city. It was positioned as an island in a sea of garbage. How could they let their cities go like that? No one in the justice system lives in Camden they merely commute to Camden. If they had to live there they would find a way to beautify it and to keep it clean and crime free. What a farce it all is. The judges and the lawyers come in to town to mete out justice, then go galloping out of town as fast as they can for fear of getting mugged. The US sends troops all over the world to keep foreigners safe, but when it comes to their own cities no one will do anything. I wonder what the citizens would say in a democratic free vote asking the question "Should we clean up our own streets or should we instead go 10,000 miles away to clean up someone else's," making it safe for democracy.

We entered the court only to find out that it was to be held a week later. I felt like strangling the asshole that called himself a lawyer. I'd just about had it with him. I told him that we were going to Washington DC, about a 100 miles away, to visit my aunt. We would meet him back here next week

When we returned a week later we rented a motel room near his Absecon office, one that he recommended, so we could confer with him in the morning before we went to court. He phoned the motel on the off chance that he may catch us and said that he would be right over. When he arrived he told us that he had arbitrarily moved the date up another week. "You did what?" I threw down what I had been reading and the snake could be seen running down the stairs in stark terror. I told him that in any case we would be there and if he didn't show, we would drag his "sorry ass" in front of the New Jersey Bar Association.

In the mean time I had been conferring with Joey. He told us that there was an attorney that he had read about in the papers by the name of Mike Daily. He seemed to be an excellent lawyer and as mentioned, got a card counter a lot of money. I had decided to fire Tom and hire this guy if he was available.

Once in the courtroom I appeared in front of the judge and said that I wasn't satisfied with my attorney as I thought he was derailing my case. The judge then said "shouldn't you fire Mr. D then." I looked at Tom and I said "Thomas D. your fired."

We went straight to Mike Daily's office and had a chat with him. He reviewed the tape and said that "You have got a pretty good case here, too bad you had hired a guy that mishandled it." He said that I would have to hire an expert witness to translate the tape into a blow by blow, in layman's terms, of the ensuing struggle to make sure that I wasn't taking a "fall" (faking it). I signed a contract with, him and he said "I'll take it from here." I asked him if I could possibly take Tom and sue him for malpractice. He said that he would look into it for me.

God it felt good to be rid of a nincompoop and get teamed up with a proven winner. On the way back to Canada I couldn't help but mention my good luck over and over to Kevin in hiring Mike. True to his word Mike attacked the casino like a pit bull.

Three weeks after returning he had written me a letter. In it he stated tdhat he had succeeded in entering the expert witnesses testimony. We were given the green light to fight for a large settlement. He also told me that Tom didn't carry malpractice insurance, therefore a lawsuit in that direction would be pointless.

About a year later he phoned me with the good news that the casino had agreed to pay me $28,000 US. A week after that, he phoned me with the bad news, the casino had filed for chapter eleven-bankruptcy protection.

My fears had been realized. Had it not been for Tom, this matter would already have been "laid to bed." Mike did the only thing that could be done; he filed a claim for $150,000.00 on my behalf. The claim had to be over $100,000.00 because anything under that amount didn't have to be addressed by the trustee.

It turned out that the Hilton Corporation bought out the Claridge and as a result, Mike again called to tell me that they offered to pay 60% of their original settlement. This came to $16,800. Mike said to jump on it; it's like finding that money on the street. We were basically dead in the water with the hotel going broke, so I accepted the offer.

A lesson was learned the hard way. Research the attorney situation well. The one that is nearest at hand is not always the best. Sure Tom knew the law but couldn't communicate his ideas. He conducted the case so shoddily that I thought he was in the casino's pocket. How he ever won a case is beyond me. Why he got those kudos from the card counters is incomprehensible. Had I been aware of Mike Daily prior to meeting Tom D., the lawsuit may well have ended in a $100,000 US payday. At least by paying that amount the casinos would think twice about roughing someone up who has a "legitimate beef."

So it would seem that this was yet another way of extracting money from the gaming institutions. All one had to do was to stick up for ones self. Many people would have just "rolled over," letting the chips fall where they may, pardon the expression. But by being assertive, a person can open up new horizons in his or her chosen career whatever that may be.

Chapter Sixteen: Count Dracula's Domain

Casinos in Eastern Europe have come into their "own," especially in more modern cities. I have already related some material on a few of them in Budapest. The ones in Prague deserve honorable mention.

After watching an exhibition hockey game at Prague's Sparta Sports Plex one hot July day, some of the dads and I went for a beer. Czechoslovakia vs. Canada always proves to be a physically keen, although not clean, match. We discussed the poor officiating provided by the Czechs, along with the unbelievable antic pulled by our coach. He basically threw in the towel by not allowing our team to go back onto the ice after a bad call by the referee. We went back to the hotel, which seemed to be a fair distance from the downtown area. We had lunch and I wanted to go back to the city center to look at the sights. Unbelievably everyone wanted to go for a nap. So, I decided to go it alone.

Most European cities including Prague have excellent subway systems. I boarded the car and sat down. I was facing a pretty girl about 25 years old who refused to look me square in the eye. You know they are looking, but they have a problem with eye contact. There were several stops along the way and at every one a loudspeaker would chime; a female voice would indicate the station. Some English tourists came on board carrying on a conversation. At the next stop the chime sounded; the voice indicated the station, "Stacionitza Muzium" (Museum Station). The car slowed down and I looked at the pretty girl who was still just staring straight ahead. I was wondering what was going through her mind, what kind of thoughts she was thinking? Did she perhaps think of us as noisy intruders, upsetting the peaceful equilibrium of this beautiful city? Or did she think of us as "ugly Americans," spoiled by too many material things; seemingly able to have enough funds on hand to travel at a moment's notice?

These good looking people, who wore little if any make up, had to make it with their natural attributes and personalities. Their clothes were simple but clean, and to look at them was absolutely refreshing.

I don't know what it was, but I instinctively knew that something was going to happen, a sort of an ESP sensation, making everything and everyone clearer. The senses seemed to be at "high focus." The train stopped and all of a sudden there was a commotion right there in front and to the side of me. All I saw was a strap worn around the shoulder of one of the tourists being stretched out and taut in the crowded subway car. I reached out and grabbed the strap from my sitting position putting a vise like grip on it; a grip that wouldn't release short of cutting off the hand. I could then feel the strap go limp as the door slammed shut. Looking back as the subway train left the station, you could see a scuffle between three or four people as we sped off to our next stop. I relaxed my grip as the chap thanked me for helping out. "What was that all about," I asked. He said, "The son of a bitch tried to steal my travel pack." I just smiled. I looked back at the girl who hadn't changed her stare one bit. She must have been a regular witness to this sort of thing.

The purse-snatcher was a "Gypsy" but here like in North America the police have been over run by political correctness and can't use that term. Colored "etnikum" (ethnic) is the "correct" way to refer to them. These bands of nomads have invaded Europe from points further east than Romania. They temporarily set down roots in large cities and commit the majority of the crime in that locality. They are the moneychangers on the streets. They are also the pimps, the "fences" and the thieves. When they change money they cheat the tourists who, mainly from their own greed, think they are getting a deal but end up with a fraction of what they could have received from a government sanctioned "cashier." The pimps are sleazy and their girls even sleazier. In Eastern Europe the big craze is "hooking" on the hi-way. If they see that you are by yourself these girls will lift their sweater and flash you a tit to entice you to stop. If you do, you are a likely-candidate to get mugged, usually by some Gypsies waiting close by, where the "tricks" are played out.

Prague is a beautifully laid out city with the ornate St. Karoy (St. Charles) Bridge providing the centerpiece for tourist traffic. The bridge is full of street entertainers that work their act for tips. One such act had a huge boa as a prop. We in the West know these creatures to be rather tame, but in Eastern Europe big reptiles were somewhat of a novelty. The entertainer wanted a volunteer to hold the snake while he wrapped it around himself. No one came forward, so he went into the crowd coming back with a tall, pretty blonde. She held the snake's tail as he coiled the serpent around his thin frame. Later on, this same lady passed me on route to Wenceslas Square, the heartbeat of the city. I couldn't resist complementing her on her composure in handling the snake. She was very receptive and we chatted at length over a coffee in one of the many excellent cafes that dotted the square. We walked by a shop where many puppets and marionettes were on display. There she stopped. Admiring one wearing a wizard's hat complete with stars and a half moon holding a royal flush. She turned to me and said in her New Zealand accent, "Seventy five dollars US. I love it but can't afford that." I told her that I would see what I could do for her, "Price is always determined through negotiation." Entering the shop, I tried to do just that but the proprietor was not there. "Do try again for me later would you," she said. We made arrangements to meet for supper that evening; I would attempt to get her that puppet then.

About a block from the St. Karoy Bridge there is a youth hostel. There, young people could "crash" for the night, or for several nights at a reasonable rate. Sarah P. fit in nicely in this crowd of young people from all over the world. At age 25 she was older than the rest, but with her charm and warm personality there were no walls erected around her and her roommates accepted her totally.

I knocked on the door about 6:00 pm and was allowed into a foyer. There, young people were engaged in various activities. I guess at age 50 the over use of the word "youth" is quite natural. Sarah came out and introduced me to some Swedes that she was hanging around with and engaged them in some small talk until we were about to eat.

We exited the place a half hour later, went down a few blocks to a Chinese restaurant and ordered enough food for the two of us, including two bottles of wine for ten dollars, including tip.

The streets around Prague are virtually bare of tourists in the evening hours. Taxicabs are the wiser alternative for that reason. Also the streets become slightly more dangerous due to the multitude of Gypsies that are out and about in the dark hours. Both Sarah and I are tall otherwise I would counsel due care and diligence when it comes to strolling the streets at night. Also be aware that the lack of vowels in the Czechoslovakian language made recognizing street names very difficult.

Finding it impossible to locate a casino even with explicit directions, we hailed a cab. It took us to Caesar's; again no ties to the famous one in Nevada. We settled down to a six-deck shoe, only to find out after several rounds that it was a "Spanish 21" game. No tens in the deck. We looked around and found one seat available at a regular six-deck game. We have all made mistakes, especially when drinking. You have just got to look at the rules. When you're "pie eyed" you may not notice those little signs that say "Spanish 21." Take the time to scan the area to make a note of the rules; maybe then you won't be caught off guard like I was.

We kind of staggered over and I insisted that Sarah sit down to play with some coaching from me.

I love playing with people that have never gambled before. Luck seems to hang all over them like a "Golden Halo." The table was full of "macho males," who rolled their eyes when Sarah sat down. I got her to hit a stiff a couple of times when the count was low, which seemed to confirm in their minds that she was merely another "bimbo," unable to follow the basic tenants of the game.

Then when we had a 100 mark bet with splits and double downs, we managed to score a 600 marks profit (the German mark at the time was the foreign currency of choice in Eastern Europe). She even managed to get a natural 21 in spades a few hands later, netting us a bottle of champagne. This we shared with everyone. Then, I leaned over and whispered into her ear that the puppet was hers, and the time to leave was now.

We were each ahead by two hundred dollars US. When we decided to cash in, the table protested her departure. They liked the way she played after all.

By now we were really "looped." She insisted on staying at my hotel, a kind of repayment for a great evening, and if that was the case it would be a very memorable one for me too.

    *   *   *   *   *

Eastern European casinos have their seedier venues as well. A girl friend and I had occasion to go to Europe in the summer of 2001. We did Austria, Germany and Hungary. These places were highly refined compared to our last stop. As soon as we crossed the border from Hungary to Transylvania, a province in Romania, we were immediately made acutely aware of the abject poverty and the squalor of the place.

The frontier between Hungary and Romania is much like many other borders in Eastern Europe. But when you reach the Romanian side of "no man's land" you get a little taste of North America, more to the point a little taste of Mexico. This is not because the people are dressed in serapes or wear sombreros, it's because the border guards all want tips to speed you on your way past no man's land. If paradise awaited us on the other side one would be glad to pay the tithe, but what awaits the unwary traveler is instead something quite different.

After leaving the domain of the border, one enters a sort of a "twilight zone." As our vehicle gropes down the hi-way, the reality of the situation only manifests itself when you set out to pass one of the countless horse drawn wagons that clog up the roads. It is surrealistic to say the least. Like being in the theatre that uses some twenty-first century "wrap around circle vision," and "smell a vision" to capture the environment in its totality.

"Jesus Christ! I thought we just lost a wheel," Kathy said to me as we hit an enormous divot in the road. I was brought back to reality after that bone jarring collision with the pothole.

Kathy S., with whom I had been tripping with around the world for the last five years, loved adventure. It was due to her prompting that we were now on our way to Sebis, a little town about 200kms east of Hungary in Transylvania (formerly part of Hungary).

While visiting a cousin of mine in Gyomro, a small town about twenty kilometers east of Budapest, I was told about a distant cousin living in Sebis. His name was Pubi L. He was a highly respected retired schoolmaster whose reputation was spread far and wide. Gyula (Julius) suggested that Kathy and I go there to start a liaison with him for future reference. After a few phone calls the trip was set. A few days later we found ourselves on the road, dodging those craters in the asphalt.

Reaching the first large town in Transylvania, south of our border entry point. we noticed the "roadside" hookers. Oradea was a main crossroads used by truckers for other conveniences besides truck stops, it would seem. The hookers would make themselves plentiful on all the roads leading out of town. We then turned toward Sebis on secondary roads. I thought that the main road was bad, that was before going down hi-way 726A. Encountering small towns with geese running wild on the streets was not the exception, but the norm. Being held up by, an evening cattle drive was to be expected when traveling around 6:00 pm.

One could finally see the formation of hills, which in turn herald in their younger relatives, the mountains. Then finally, we were there. We stopped at a service station and fueled up for a mere 60,000 leis (in Romanian currency, $100 US will get you a quarter of a million). I asked to use the phone but it was useless, communication was futile so I gave the lady service station attendant his name and number written on a piece of paper. All of a sudden she seemed to know who he was, made the call and passed me the phone. Pubi told me to stay where I was, and he would "pick" us up.

A rickety old bike with a heavy basket bolted on to the front could be seen turning up the main road and heading for the station where we held our post. It shook and rattled, as it made it's way along the cobble stone streets. I presumed it was Pubi, but couldn't be certain. I felt like hailing him by name, but considering the language problems encountered in Romania I decided against it.

Although he spoke many languages, (luckily for Kathy English was one of them), he looked like a typical Romanian while remaining Hungarian to the core. His deep wrinkles yielded evidence of a hard life. At one time his family was considered the elite of Transylvania. His uncle flew the first serious mono-wing aircraft from Sebis to the Paris air show in the twenties. The uncle ultimately went mad fighting patent infringements from around the world, finally dying in a mental institution.

He went to the service station attendant. After speaking with her she pointed him to our direction. He walked over to where we were parked. The closer he got the wider became his smile, exposing rifts that were only wrinkles before. "Welcome to Sebis," as we grasped one another in a hug, mutually kissing on either cheek. "This is my girlfriend Kathy," I said. Another round of hugs and kisses followed. He then said, "If you're not offended following an old man on a bicycle, I'll show you to my home." "Only if you keep to the speed limit, I wouldn't want to risk winding up in one of your Romanian jails," I replied.

True to his word he didn't ride with excessive speed and reached his stately house in about five minutes. He unlocked a wrought iron gate in front, and as it slowly creaked open you could see a Daccia parked inside.

The national car of Romania was much like many national autos of a lot of East European countries; they were ugly, but more important they were unreliable. Parking our car and walking into the courtyard we were greeted by his charming and lovely wife, Victoria. Immediately drinks and sweets were brought out in typical European fashion, a prelude to a much larger feast.

She then ushered us to a modest room, but classy by Romanian standards. It was well appointed with century old furniture. We showered up, and by then supper was ready.

Pubi reminisced about his uncle who he loved dearly, telling me how he had taught him to catch fish with his bare hands. His grandson now watches Pubi fish with his bare hands, massaging the fish on its stomach, slowly mesmerizing it into a false security, only then snatching it from the water. "Pubi you have become your uncle, and your grandson is you," I said. "Quite true, the circle is complete," he added, beaming with pride.

In the Transylvanian mountains, the nights are dark and the air is cool. The lack of street lamps, add to the desolation. Going to bed very late we had every intention of also arising very late. We slept with our window open, letting in the sweet air that flows off the hills, regenerating the little village every morning with a fragrant bouquet.

With the open windows one also hears the early morning sounds of the peasants about to start their day. The clopping of the horses hoofs, the cracking of the whip and the corresponding increase in the horse's gait, are all sounds that tired travelers incorporate into their dreams to stretch them out, using any excuse to extend their fantasy rather than be aroused into the world of the awakened. The dream seemed to heighten the sound of the leather tack as it draws tight around the animal's coat. A snapping sound is emitted as the animal, covered in sweat, hits at its neck yoke, causing the wagon to lurch in step with the rhythm of its stride. There is a heavy gasping and snorting as the horse nears our window. Is it a dream? Is it reality? Once asleep we wish not to be roused. Once awake we wish not to sleep. In the larger scope of things perhaps once alive we wish not to die. And once we are dead we wish not to be reborn. I hear the protest in the screams of a newborn babe.

Suddenly the sweet goddess of sleep releases me from her grasp. Yes we are in a strange bed, in a strange land, ancient and ancestral Transylvania. I am made rudely aware of the real world by the loud roar of a lorry and by the curse of it's driver, irritated at being held up by the slow pace of an animal, straining as it pulls it's load, driving the tips of its hoofs deep into the crevices of the cobble stones to gain traction.

Victoria rapped gently on our door to see if we would care to have breakfast. "We just ate it seems but if the coffee is on, we would love a cup." "Alright," was her reply, "it will be ready in five minutes." In Europe when ordering coffee you better specify American coffee or a brew will appear in front of you so thick you could stand your spoon up in it.

Pubi then announced that he was going to take us to the ancient marble quarries at a place called Menyesi. After coffee we embarked on the 30 km trek to the mine.

Not much has changed in two thousand years. Traveling on the same roads used by the Romans to get to the quarry, we arrived 40 minutes later. As there are many dormant volcanoes in the area, so are there many spas previously built by the Romans. There was one such spa built at the foot of Menyesi. A stark reminder of communist rule stood near the spa. A hotel that was as bland as any that I had ever seen in all my travels, dominated the small area. The first job of any responsible touristry minister would be to dynamite that "windowed box," and erect something akin to a hotel with a European personality.

As we neared the top of our assent we could hear the whirl of an electric motor. Getting nearer we approached a shack housing this source of power. The shack had several wires protruding from it, going in all directions. Besides the wires that powered the motor the other wires turned out to be the drives for the cutting devices used to harvest the marble from the mountain. Virtually the same technology that was used by the ancients. In those times, however horses were used to turn pulleys, which in turn were geared up to give speed to these carbon coated wires.

We stopped at a summer camp on our way back to have lunch. Being a respected man in this area is an honorarium that travels with you for a lifetime. Therefore lunch was free for Pubi and all that were in his party.

From here we went to Brad. There a friend of his, Ocsi, a retired professor at one of the universities, gave us a private tour of the Museum of Geology. There was more gold there than in any museum in the world. Had the communist regime known about it that too would have been looted along with the other treasures stolen from the people?

From there Ocsi took us to Baia de Cris, a small town with one of the most opulent accommodations that I have ever seen. We stopped at the newly built Hotel Phoenix constructed from stones, native to the area. There recently built was a five star hotel complete with spa, thermal baths and therapeutic massages, listing their services for $1.75 per hour. That's right folks a buck seventy-five for those of you that think the numerals are a typing error. To top it all off every one of the masseuses were blind. They tell me that this is because their sense of touch is greater than those others that ply the craft and can see.

Ocsi then insisted that we go for supper at the hotel restaurant. Four of us ate, had beer except for Ocsi, he had a double vodka, a habit he acquired while in Leningrad attending university. The bill came to four dollars US, including tip. The good news was that a casino was being contemplated for the area. Hmm, "maybe" if that happens we just "might be" regular customers.

On the way back to Sebis, Pubi convinced us to visit his daughter in Timosoara, a big city about two hours from his house. An excellent idea I thought, we can meet one of my long lost cousins along with an opportunity to check out one of the city's casinos.

After arriving back to his place, Pubi phoned his daughter and made arrangements for her to meet us at the outskirts of the city, under the "Welcome to Timosoara" sign. He and Victoria gave us directions, and we were off.

It was around 8:30 in the evening when we entered Arad, a large city on the way to our destination. We had just experienced a slight drizzle, which made the cobblestone roads shine like small mirrors, making driving and searching for road signs nearly impossible. On one of the main roads near a subway station there appeared the usual array of hookers, laying in wait for their next trick. Now there are aggressive hookers, and some that are out and out desperate. One came right out onto the road, diagonally heading for our vehicle. We had to swerve to miss hitting her. It was a totally unnerving experience. To top it all off she looked like an extra brought in by "Central Casting" to film "The Brides of Dracula," complete with a widow's peak. And if that wasn't enough, we missed our turn off, necessitating us to retrace our path only to be accosted by the same girl all over again, in the identical fashion. At last we found road E671, which took us directly to Timosoara.

We pulled over to the shoulder, by the sign welcoming us to the city. There we saw the Peugeot station wagon that we were to meet. Carmen, Pubi's daughter, jumped out of her car and greeted us with hugs and kisses. She was a good-looking 30 year old with flashing intelligent eyes. She was very personable with a broad smile just like her dad. Shyly waiting beside the car was Puiu, her boyfriend. He was probably the lightest skinned Romanian that I have ever met. With his blonde hair, and blue eyes, he stood out like some kind of alien in a strange land. Carmen introduced us and we embrace but did not kiss.

I thought I was finally learning the delicate nuances of etiquette and conduct in this Eastern European "meeting game." If you're related and have never met, you hug and kiss. If you are related to the person who has a friend and they are close to that person, you just hug. If that friend is merely a friend, you shake hands. On the other hand if you meet a person who is a comrade, or is of the same mind set as you, it's hugs and kisses all over again.

We were an hour late, but as a sign of their dedication they said they would have slept in their car till we arrived. We followed them as they coursed their way through several concentric circles, till we arrived at their home. I was amazed. The city had taken on a capitalistic look. Signs on buildings, in huge neon letters spelled it all out for me. Sony, Motorola, and Volkswagen were just a few. The town looked a little like Munich (Munchen); all this only thirteen years after the uprising to overthrow communism.

The problem of course was that the same gang that were the Communists were now running the show for capitalism. And really, after all, it was a show. How bloody nicely the gang fit in with the capitalists. Maybe these two economic systems were one and the same from inception; the state aspiring to monopolize, or a company with the same aspirations; what really was the difference to the middle class. If either succeeds, it spells disaster for the guy in the middle. A classic example of this would be the case of Enron in Texas.

At least, in China, heads literally rolled when a company stole money out of the workers pension fund. In North America if they don't punish, the translation is that they don't care. If they don't care then why the hell should we.

We arrived at their apartment close to the center of town and parked. We went upstairs to find a place without any furniture. They needlessly apologized for this, insisting that at bedtime we sleep on a mattress that they normally slept on. They would sleep on makeshift accommodations in the second bedroom.

We then crossed our legs on the "naked" living room floor and "rapped" like a bunch of hippies; nibbling on the goodies that Carmen and Puiu had made for us.

They had just purchased the apartment for 30,000,000.00 leis. That's about $12,000.00 US. The furniture had to be ordered, and generally took a few months to custom make. That would set them back another 3,000,000.00 Leis, about $1200 US. In the mean time, it was box crates for chairs and sleeping bags for beds.

Carmen is a lady with an Electrical Engineering Degree. Instead of plying her craft she chooses to work at a bank where they take advantage of her mastery of four languages. She gets paid twice as much there than she could ever make working at her chosen profession. Such are the ways in a revolutionary system. One day you are a respected professional; the next day you get respect only if you have money. Like the lyric in the Ray Charles song "Hit the Road Jack," one line depicts all that is wrong with a system that places too high a value on cash, "If you got no money you just ain't no good."

Puiu, a nickname meaning little chicken, hasn't got the derogatory connotation that it has in North America. He looked like a chap who could handle himself and any trouble that came his way or Carmen's. He was a very religious man but instead of making water into wine, his job was making bourbon out of corn. He related to us the big problem that they had in Romania, the subdivision of land. They couldn't get large enough farms on track to produce the corn because foreigners were buying up 100-acre parcels at eleven dollars an acre, such a deal. As a result, much of the corn had to be imported from Hungary.

Before the inflation that drove the prices up to eleven dollars, the land could be purchased even cheaper. At that price I wonder if the land would be less costly through speculation than through war.

Let's see, W. Bush's war in the gulf is projected to cost two hundred billion dollars, but let's face it, a trillion is a lot more realistic. Eleven into two hundred billion is eighteen point eight billion. That's how many acres one could purchase. Hell you could maybe buy the entire country of Romania, perhaps making a deal on the old Ploesti oil reserves to boot, thus eliminating the need for war. Don't forget that Alaska was purchased for around $50,000,000.00. Imagine if Alaska would have still been in Russian hands during the cold war. The Korean War could well have been fought out on Canadian soil.

On we gabbed till well after midnight. Carmen told us that she would take off early from work and show us around the city. We "crashed" on the mattress, provided for us and slept rock solid till 10:00 am.

We woke up to a smorgasbord of salamis and other delicacies. Much to our surprise, they even had an "American" style coffee maker with the coffee already made. The unfortunate thing was that they had filled the machine to the very top with grounds, making it the strongest American coffee that we ever had. They just can't get it through their minds, that in North America java is merely a beverage. It was never intended as a drink to jolt the system instantly; causing a caffeine rush to surge through your body, creating alertness and in some cases the jitters.

At eleven, Carmen showed up droving us to the downtown area. There was a mall in the center of town much like many cities in Europe. It was broad and well planned out in the modernistic sense, lots of room for expansion in buildings and roads.

At one end of the mall stood the enormous Romanian Orthodox Church. That building easily dominated the mall. Entering the basilica through enormous doors, one is struck immediately by its size, and then by the absence of pews. Perhaps they too were waiting the necessary two months for their furniture. Carmen assured us that austerity is part and parcel of the Orthodox religion. She told me how in 1989, during the overthrow of Nicolae Ceausescu, the patriarchs in the basilica slammed the door on the students who were clamoring to get in, out of the line of fire from the Romanian army, basically sentencing them to death. What a bunch of craven sycophants. I was proud to hear that the Hungarian protestant preacher did no such thing. Not only did he house the rebellious students, but stood out in front of the army defying them to shoot at him. After the rebellion was over with the ouster of Ceausescu, only then did the patriarchs apologize for their actions. This cost them a lot of sympathy as well as a large part of their congregation.

Walking to the other end of the mall, one could see that the buildings around the city were in the process of getting renovated. The opera house was one of the strangest buildings that I have ever seen. It seemed oddly unfinished, but Carmen again reassured us that the original plan for the structure is exactly the way we see it. It had a square finish with a definite lack of statues. There were plenty of bullet holes around the mall where the army and the freedom fighters engaged in pitched battles. This is of course what happens when the government loses touch with the people.

These same battles are just around the corner for us, right here in North America. As we get taxed more and more, as we bail big companies out of financial misadventures in strange lands, as the mounting body bags of our youth start piling up, a few hardy souls will say "enough." George Washington shook off the shackles placed there by an oppressive regime on the American people, and we are again destined to do the same thing.

Puiu joined us and we went to the university campus to enjoyed a light lunch. He ordered the national dish, which is served at virtually every restaurant in Romania, "tripe." Admittedly I had never tried it only because there were always things on the menu that interested me more. After lunch Carmen and Puiu went back to work, and Kathy and I carried on exploring the city. She popped into a MacDonald's to use the washroom as I waited outside for her.

While I was waiting, a Roma (Gypsy) came sidling up to me, eyes darting everywhere but refusing to fixate on mine. "Do you want to f**k," he asked? He motioned toward a shy looking teen about fourteen to sixteen years old. It was almost more than I could stand. There were some tourists milling around and I wanted to make sport to this "Roma." I said, "I don't think I heard you, you'll have to speak up." Again he said, "Do you want to f**k." "You're disgusting," I said, "You want me to f**k you." "No, no, f**k girl," he said. By now I just wanted to get rid of him so I said to him, "F**k off you disgusting Cigany before I get mad." Cigany means Gypsy all across Europe, a name that they don't like to be called.

After Kathy came out we ended our tour, and had a beer in one of their outdoor restaurants, then we went back to Puiu and Carmen's apartment. They came home shortly afterward and made a call to order pizza. The Romanian style of pizza is quite different from ours. They put an egg right in the middle so all can "enjoy" the extra protein. We found it to be unpalatable, but to be sociable we had a slice.

I asked Puiu if there were any casinos in the vicinity. He nodded to the affirmative. "Well let's go visit one while the girls gab." He had trouble understanding, so I got Carmen to interpret.

It was raining again as we made our way to the casino. The one that we went to first was closed and only open during the weekend. We drove about two blocks before reaching the other one. As we pulled up to the building we noticed a lot of cabs around with the drivers chatting amongst themselves. They looked to be all "Roma" types. Puiu and I are both well muscled and blonde, perhaps the kind of men that make up the Timosoara police force. As we made our way into the building they cast upon us their suspicious leers, as if admitting some guilt as yet undiscovered. We got into a dingy elevator, making our way to the tenth floor and into an equally dingy gaming area. After entering the premises, one could see the dregs of humanity that frequented the place. A swarthy morass of humanity glared at us as we made our way to the tables. Upon sitting down and pulling out some US dollars, you could visibly see a unanimous sigh of relief from not only the management, but also the patrons. This "gaggle" of potential felons must rarely see two light skinned guys enter their "territory" other than to make an arrest

There was no game in session, so I motioned for a dealer and within a minute a lady came over and started shuffling. We played by ourselves for about a half an hour before we were joined by "one of the boys." By now they were not too uncomfortable, realizing that we were probably not the police.

The rules were Standard English rules, with no surrender. The shift boss, who by the way also looked shifty, came over and offered to incorporate the rule. This was great you could negotiate your own terms. I forgot about the re-split of aces because I would have surely made it a point to put that one in there as well. They cut off two decks, but I talked them into cutting just over one.

Other than the fact that the tables were old and grungy along with the patrons and the personnel, the game turned out to be quite honest. Although I could see some latitude for cheating, I'm sure that they didn't pull that one on us. Maybe because we looked like cops and they didn't want to chance it; just in case.

The maximum bet was 50,000.00 leis, about twenty bucks. The chap that sat down at our table was getting his "clock cleaned," max betting on low counts. Before he came over we were down about $50. When he showed up all of a sudden it was him that was getting stuck with our bad hands. After an hour of play Puiu and I were up $75 a piece. He was beaming from ear to ear, in disbelief; a week's wages in just an hour. He said he thought it was a game for suckers and that gamblers could only lose playing the game. I filled him in on the facts. Playing in a two-casino town was really a "one way street to the cleaners." If you were a steady winner, they would either bar you from play, or in this town they were more likely to cheat you out of your money. Only in a regulated casino were your chances of walking out a winner in any way considered even. Where we were at, it looked like a "free enterprise" concern at best, a mafia one at worse.

The following day we bought our hosts an almost cost prohibitive item to complement their much-awaited new furniture; a fitted set of matched bed ware. With this complete, we were ready to depart Romania and ultimately Europe.

After making the acquaintance of two of the finest people in town we have cemented a friendship that will last a long time. The next time we meet, etiquette allows hugs and kisses for both.

Chapter Seventeen: Cruising

When all is said and done, subsidized trips are all right but going to the same old destinations can get rather stale. The deserts around Las Vegas are a sightseers delight, but if you have been there 30 or 40 times there is only so much that a person can see. With this in mind, Kathy and I set our sights on taking in the other venue offered to gamblers.

With the advent of computers, arranging for hotels at cheap rates has become a snap. You register your name with a couple of discount travel clubs, and before you know it you're on their list getting the necessary information on modestly priced trips, car rentals, accommodations and flights. On occasion, they also send you the odd sale on cruise ships. You should be made aware that cruise liners offer gaming on board most of their ships, except for some of the vessels sailing off Hawaii. There are many states that don't offer gambling, but if you are near an ocean, that shouldn't be a deterrent. On land there are governments and laws that dissuade people from opening establishments for gaming, but once you're a couple of miles off shore, those laws are no longer in effect.

Largely as a result of the 9/11 scare, cruising as a pastime was severely curtailed. As a result, clearing houses for cheap fares were loading "junk email" into as many computers that they could reach, trying to sell off their excess cruise tickets. As luck would have it, my computer also was filled with the same sort of mail.

It had unbelievable prices. There were fares being advertised from $300, for a seven day Caribbean cruise. That's less than $50 per night; that's got to be what a hotel room would cost without the gourmet food that they said was the norm on these excursions.

Kathy and I were doing Mexico for the last five years, to get away from the Canadian weather in December and January. Come to think of it, after all that time, five years in total, the only Spanish phrase I felt comfortable with was one used every so often by John Wayne himself. "Greetings senorita," would roll off my lips so fluently that it would have made the "Duke" proud. Mexico was however, getting to be old hat so we decided to make a detour to Florida to check out the cruise scene. We booked three of them, two one-week excursions and a three-day excursion. The total per person was about $800.

So the itinerary was set. We would drive down to Florida in Kathy's car, motoring straight through to Key West, Florida. There we would spend a few days in the quaint old part of town with a comrade with whom I recently struck up an acquaintanceship with. From there we would go and spend a few days sight seeing at Homestead, Fla., after which we would embark on our first cruise on Celebrity's ship, The Horizon, headed for the Western Caribbean. The second ship was The Norway, the oldest ship on the Norwegian Cruise Line's fleet, but newly renovated, being brought up to snuff with the new gadgetry, internet and computerized navigational devices. With this ship we were to see the Eastern Caribbean. The Ocean Breeze, on the other hand was a small ship, either owned or leased by a promotions company. They scheduled us for a three day cruise to the Bahamas, but the catch was that you had to sit in on one of their high pressure sales presentations, touting a time sharing venture. As I was basically "non-sellable," that would be a snap.

The long drive down was torturous, with Kathy and I taking turns at the wheel. After two days we had reached Nashville. The twenty dollar per night sign at the Howard Johnson was too tempting to pass up. We ended up staying there for the night.

In the morning, we made our way down through to Chattanooga making a stop at a battle memorial called Lookout Mountain. There one could view the various key battle sites that took the cream of the crop from both sides, in America's first civil war. Missionary Ridge and Chickamauga, two other battle sites, could also be seen from this lofty perch.

The quiet rolling hills with their green grass dare not speak of the massacre that befell the youth of America in holy sites like these. Abraham Lincoln, one of the USA's biggest "heroes" is responsible for this carnage of up to a half a million people. Some states in the South wanted to secede from the Union as guaranteed in the Constitution, but "Honest Abe" had other ideas. He wanted a larger federal system of government, as a result he reneged on the break away clause. If there is one thing more than any other that has caused the destruction of America, it is her interference in other nation's civil wars. Another "hero" president, Truman, interfered in someone else's civil war costing America the lives of 150,000 servicemen in Korea. Johnson with the staged Gulf of Tonkin incident got the US involved in Viet Nam costing the lives of another 50,000 Gis in that civil war. My, how uncivil of people when they shoot back at foreign occupiers.

It's hard to keep a dry eye walking those isolated fields around Georgia, imagining the pain and the suffering that went on; robbing the tomorrow by destroying the gene pool of yesterday. Satan must have been in his glory then. Each time there is a war like this it is the healthy that are made to suffer. The weak, or the 4-Fs, stay at home to spawn the next generation causing a kind of devolution, guaranteeing us "morons" for future presidents. And so, on it goes, until we get an "Alfred E. Newman" clone with his finger on the "hot button" threatening to use it.

Coming down off the mountain we continued on our trip through Georgia, down through the state of Florida, hopping from cay to cay, finally reaching Key West. After meeting with our contact we parked our belongings and went out to get a feel of the town.

Every morning you could see the fishing boats arrive with their bounty from the deep. The people would line up to purchase their vast and varied catch. Not just people who were tourists like us, but old timers, people who had lived there for half a century; people that have given up on the hustle of those other "big cities." These were the folks who didn't merely talk about change, but acted on it. They abandoned a system that valued hard work, with a nine to five existence, for something less mundane. That added a carnival feel to the town.

Every day you could see them and talk with them around Mallory Square, the main pier where the cruise ships dock. Some rode bikes predating the fifties. They had winged handlebars with bolted on heavy baskets on which they would carry their provisions facilitating the art of doing business. Some even carried a more precious cargo. Placing their pets in the basket, they would festoon them in all sorts of finery. A bull terrier with a kerchief around his neck wearing heart shaped sunglasses was a showstopper. A dog doing back flips with his partner asking for tips. A man juggling bowling balls while his dog would run about the periphery of the crowd with hat in mouth begging for tips; acts that challenged to ask, "Which is the performer and which is the shill?"

Key West is a sleepy little town, one time home of the great Ernest Hemmingway. Being an avid sportsman and fisherman, the town was not a disappointment to him. Bars were sprinkled liberally all along Key West's main street, Duval. For the price of a drink you might be able to find a Hemmingway look alike to engage in conversation. These people replicated the man not only in appearance, including his patented gray hair and beard, but also in the great author's insatiable love of bourbon. Key West, and "Papa" Hemmingway were synonymous.

Did Key West mold the character of the people that flocked to the town? Who knows? Maybe it was the eccentrics that migrated there, giving up their material life, maybe that's what gave the town that unique laid back flair. It's hard to say. Like a marriage of two people that complemented one another, making a whole where before only two gangly entities existed.

Mile Zero on the "Old Dixie Hi-way" is a landmark that has the distinction of being in Key West, the farthest southern point that one can be on the continental USA. From there, it makes the laborious trip up the east coast.

The ride back up is just as slow as the ride coming down. A two-lane hi-way liberally interspersed with small towns to slow the traffic to a near standstill. To make matters worse, there are still "other" things to make the journey even longer than it should be. A sign that reads, "Maximum 10 mph, Alligator crossing, vigorously enforced." Upon passing it you can see a Monroe County Highway Patrolman reach for his Stetson as he quickly jumps out of his car to stop a delinquent speeder. All the while another one is busily writing out a citation, enhancing the county coffers at the expense of an unwary tourist.

We reached Miami after a five-hour drive. Our departure for the first cruise wasn't to be until the next day, so we could do some tidying up of the car and buy the mandatory bottle of gin for the cruise. The security on the ship frowns on you bringing your own liquor on board. The price of their drinks are five bucks a piece, as you can see a large part of their profit is realized on the sale of drinks that can be quite costly to the consumer. For special occasions you can bring your own champagne or wine on board to be enjoyed by you after checking it in with the appropriate people that handle that sort of thing. The caveat is that there is an eight-dollar decanting fee involved with each bottle. You may choose to drink these with your meal in the dining room, or in the privacy of your own "digs."

We ran to the pharmacy to get a pack of "Bo-nine," an anti sea-sickness remedy that had been recommended as something that actually works. Kathy never gets seasick but I do, on all things that move on the oceans. With everything apparently ready, we turned in for the night at a roadside motel.

With nothing to eat we headed straight for the Port of Miami in the morning. We were directed to a parking garage, one that charges twelve dollars per day. We then stood in line, eventually boarding the vessel, but not before getting the mandatory "photo op" with a backdrop of the ship's logo, bedecked with palm trees and beaches. After that we enjoyed their "welcome aboard buffet," which also served as our breakfast.

First checking into our room. There we were pleasantly surprised. The $300/person fare only included an inner cabin. But perhaps due to the dismally low number of people on the boat they gave away some outside ocean view cabins; we were lucky enough to get one of these. Next we went to locate the on board casino. This is a must stop because the casino personnel are busy, prior to leaving, giving out two for one coupons as an inducement to come and play. These "perks" are only offered once, in port, the day you set sail, so amassing a collection of these coupons deserves your prompt attention. After that, we familiarized ourselves with the rest of the vessel.

Darkness falls on the city of Miami, with the December sun setting around 5:30 pm. The golden orb plays a serenade, reflecting its rays throughout the mirrored buildings that are plenty in the downtown core. Then it sinks from view in the west. The buildings can then be observed in their covert yet noticeable hue. Some are faintly purple, some blue and some even have a tinge of pink. Taken all together, these colors add to the underlying flair of the Latin tastes provided by the countless Cuban exiles that have sought refuge in this distinctly Spanish-speaking city.

The blast of the foghorn is heard and we slowly push away from our berth. Slowly we are being propelled out of the port. Every port has a "harbor pilot" who is quite familiar with his or her own respective ports. This is to minimize the problems that could occur as a result of some unfamiliar obstacles. Miami is no different and the "pilot" is the one that guides us out of Miami as well. A smaller boat follows us out and when we clear the port area the boat pulls along side our ship, still moving, plucking the pilot from the big ship; a hazardous maneuver but one that works. The entire ship is then called to the deck for a quick life jacket safety test, later we set out "steady as she goes," heading back to where we had just been, Key West.

We had put our names down for the early seating in the dinning room, at 6:00 pm. We are advised to change it to 8:00 pm, the ship's late seating, because at that time there would be far less kids to contend with. Predictably, we would play a few rounds of blackjack before the meal. A schedule outlining the dress code for the evening meals for the week was handed out when we boarded the ship, and is marked casual for the night. We would be able to go from the casino, directly to the dinning hall with the attire that we had on, after a quick trip to the lavatory to wash our hands. Casino chips are notoriously filthy with traces of urine and in some cases pathogens noticeable under a microscope. Washing is advisable at every opportunity.

The casino was nearly empty when we arrived. No one was at the 21 table so I called for a dealer to get things rolling. One was furnished for us immediately. The game was a standard six-deck shoe with English rules; most noticeably the dealer doesn't get a hole card. Tanya, the girl assigned to the table, cuts off two decks and starts dealing. Kathy is there, standing behind me being friendly to the dealer, sharing jokes and memories. In fact, she warmed up the dealer so much so that I asked her to cut the cards to make it a one deck cut. She gave a deck and a half, which is what is considered a great cut on a land-based casino. We had all the rules but for surrender. So as far as the game was concerned, I would have to call it quite good.

Most of the dealers ask you if you care to split your tens, or any other pair whether against a ten, or any other card that the dealer might be showing at the time. I was continually surprised at the response to these suggestions. A lot of the customers would split unsplitable hands to the casinos advantage. The dealers are taught this when they go to dealer's refresher classes at the ship's school.

They want every advantage. I heard of one ship's casino incorporating a rule of "prison" for half the bet that you make on a blackjack. You can't take the half bet out of jail, unless you win the following hand. Boy, I don't know about you but I think if I were confronted with a rule like that I would probably double down on my BJ to at least have a shot at instant gratification. Of course, they can get away with this kind of thing because they are the only "casino in town."

At dinnertime we went down to the dining room. The seating went rather smoothly, getting us seated a lot faster than we had anticipated, taking into consideration the long line. When on a cruise ship, you are made to sit with other couples, in our case three other couples. Keep in mind that in some cases obvious personality conflicts can arise. If this happens, it would be well advised to seek a different table. At our table there was Gail, a single Irish lady from the Buffalo, NY area. Teamed up with her was a lady named Lucy, a lively single Norwegian lady from Pennsylvania, she was the comic at our table, making us and the immediate tables within earshot of her loud voice, roar with laughter. Mitch and Michelle were from Boca Raton, Fla. They enjoyed ballroom dancing, also relishing shopping from the list of jewelers, keenly supplied by the company that owns the ship. They of course were unaware that the cruise ship people would in some way benefit from the purchases made by the people that had "discount" vouchers supplied by the ship. Then there was Diane and Gene, a "Right Wing" couple from the mid west who were always talking about money, trimming employee wages, and how wonderful President "Dubya" Bush was. His having a voice like "Mr. Magoo" didn't help to ingratiate himself to the rest of the table. I have an aversion to people that brag about their wealth. Imagine having the belief that class emanates from the wallet instead of the soul. That would put him closer to the philosophy of Karl Marx rather than that of his hero, Adam Smith. Needless to say, dining with Gene proved to be an interesting event. I would be the antagonist, deliberately taking the opposite view, no matter how hard he tried to find common ground.

We went back up to the casino shortly after 10:00 pm, only to find it packed. So I wasn't the only one to find the "risking" of money stimulating. Although my exposure to risk was considerably less than most of the people present, I still considered the casino the only place to spend "quality" time while confined for a week on board a ship.

Time spent with your spouse or in my case my girlfriend, was to be held as the paramount reason to go cruising. To let on that one enjoys gambling more than the excellent shows that were offered, or the nightclubs that were plenty on board any cruise ship, would have been an unforgivable tort. These are things better left mentioned in the hidden "cracks and crevices" of a book such as this.

Kathy was kept busy going back and forth from our cabin to the casino bringing us a steady stream of drinks. Drinks in casinos on cruise ships are not free, in fact they are notoriously expensive, thus the need for the shuttle service.

The full casino gave me an opportunity to have a conversation with the main supervisor. It seems that years ago the ships used to lease out the area that was presently being run as a casino to a company from England that specialized at that sort of thing. The liner company could then concentrate on what it did well, the running of the ship. The problem was that the casinos were taking such a swath of profits that the company slowly ended up hiring the same people that were running the "show" for the casinos. They are now taking that share of the market as well. There are still some smaller cruise companies that find it a lot less bothersome to lease out the space designated to be a casino to subcontractors, albeit for a lot more money than had been the case up till now. This was great information to take to bed.

In the morning we could feel the gentle bumping of the ship against the pier of our first stop, Key West. 6:00 am is pretty early especially when a person is on a vacation. Just a few minutes after that you could already hear the forklifts swing into action, drowning out the endless shrieking of the gulls as they fight for the orts of food cast over board by the fishermen from their boats. Ships are a far more economical way of sending freight than by truck. Many customers opt for this method, but cruise ships offer an added advantage. They are on a strict schedule. For the company that runs the cruises there is the added benefit of cutting the fuel expenses by handling some freight. Places like the Bahamas, Puerto Rico, and the Cayman Islands are surrounded by water. As a result they can only get supplied by sea or by air; the latter being the more costly choice. Cruise ships supply a lot of the manufactured products used on the islands as well as uploading products unique to the island's economy. Imagine a place like the Bahamas without a Coors' beer or a Pepsi.

Key West is of course "deja vous all over again," as the great Yogi Berra once said. But there were a few things a person could do. Like stock up on our gin supply. The night before, Kathy and I took a gouge out of our allotment, necessitating a foray to the liquor store. The next stop would be two days from now at the Grand Cayman Island, so we had to get plenty of gin. A good way to bring it on board is to put it into a water bottle such as Evion, or perhaps a local brand name. The important thing to remember is that they check your bags when you're boarding the ship so it's best to cover up the booze by not covering it up. No one has ever put their noses to my water bottle to check if it is liquor or not.

While on shore we stopped in at a local bar and noticed that our two on board casino dealers were there as well. I made it a point to buy Dawn and Tanya a couple of beers so they would remember us on the afternoon cruise to our next destination.

Tourism in Key West, as indeed many places around the "tourist belt," had been seriously curtailed as a result of the September 11th event. Due to this, prices were low on many of the items traditionally offered to tourists. Polo shirts with the Key West logo were selling three for ten dollars. I had never seen these items selling for fewer than ten dollars apiece before. The devastation to the travel industry has been immense, recovery seemed a long time into the future.

The ship's horn could be heard throughout the entire marina area, signaling our departure. Its side thrusters, one on the bow and one on the stern, were activated easing us away from the pier. When we are out far enough the command is finally given to turn the ship 180 degrees. To do this maneuver one of the side thrusters are shut down and the diagonally opposed one, on the other side was activated. After this tortuously slow procedure we were facing the correct direction and the main propellers kicked in, pushing us slowly away from port. There was a throng of people waving us "bon voyage." I suppose some of them were like we were years ago, watching the cruise ships leave Miami, thinking that this form of travel is too expensive; if they only knew. They couldn't live as cheap for a week on land as what we had spent on a cruise ship for a week at sea.

We stayed on deck till the city was too small to be seen, then rushed downstairs to shower up to prepare for some BJ action.

The afternoon session had Kathy and I "opening the doors" as they say. Dawn was present and also appreciative, thanking us for the earlier round of drinks in Key West. She gave me a one deck cut, but as the table filled up with "paying customers" she apologetically "up cut" it to a deck and a half. When I talked to her the next day, she told me that when the table filled up the pit boss kept a closer eye on things. Mitch came over and played for about an hour losing about $200. He flat bet ten or twenty at a time, pinning his hopes on basic strategy. He did notice that I went from five to fifty and up from there. He asked me about that at the table. I told him to keep that thought, to remind me at dinner that evening. I would try to explain it to him at that time.

One hears a lot of chatter by people who think they know something about the game. These people never play of course, they just chatter. They say stuff like "How can you possibly win at this table? They chase the aces." By that remark I think the guy meant that you shouldn't try to improve a hand against the dealer's ace. And the poetry is almost more than a person can endure. "Yes, faces always follow aces." Or is it the other way around? How about the guy giving advice to the person next to him on whether to hit a hand or not? If the dealer breaks, invariably he will say, "See I told you so." Luckily these folks are in the minority. They are losers venting out their frustrations at the only people to whom they can, the winners, or the people that still have money in front of them. "Ad captandum vulgus," Latin for "dazzle the mob" with their "fine tuned" knowledge of the game. One can only snicker to oneself by these egotistically appointed "experts." They should perhaps take heed in another Latin proverb that makes a lot more sense. "Scienta est Potentia," "Knowledge is Power." Thus we laugh at their vain attempt to gain respect by reciting "old wives tales" about events that have taken place on a blackjack table of "yore."

As if to lighten the mood a good-looking girl, of Eastern European descent came around with a tray of snack food in the middle of the deal. Quite unusual, maybe they don't want you to leave the casino for one of the many eateries on the ship. I was with Kathy, so naturally I couldn't devote all my time to the 21 game and had to spend some time with her. Besides, the smell of the food was too much for us to bear, so we opted to quit playing.

Food, food and still more food; it's enough to make you sick. On a cruise it seems that you are forever eating. The proof is in the pudding. A picture was taken of us after the third cruise and my face looks like a pizza pie (look in the picture section). If you go on one of these "ocean adventures" with the idea of losing weight you are already a "gainer." First you wake up confronting a gourmet breakfast in the dining room. Later on in the morning you can stroll up to the buffet, havng brunch, or a late breakfast. Of course all this wouldn't be complete without a wide assortment of decadent desserts. If you missed the buffet for some reason, you would be served pizzas in the afternoon from 2:00 pm till 5:00 pm. If you didn't like pizza, you could have a hamburger, fries or hotdogs at the outdoor barbeque slated for the same time. At 5:00 pm the buffet would open anew. You then could either dine early or late and if that wasn't enough they also had the midnight theme buffet. Every night was different. Rodeo night would have us eating ribs, steak and corn. Hawaii night would be roast pig, and so on. If you were still hungry after all that, you could order food to your room till 3:00 am.

There were also games played daily on the "promenade" deck. This day it was "name that tune." They would play a few bars of the song and you were supposed to guess the name of it. Whoever guessed the most correctly, would win champagne for the evening meal. These organized games are basically arranged with the older set in mind as most "cruisers" are largely made up from that age group. I'm sure that the same types of organized games are the rule for a retirement home.

Ever since I can remember I had this recurring nightmare of playing shuffleboard in a retirement home with a bunch of "old timers." To my horror, right there in front of me lay a shuffleboard. Somehow that was so "not me." I had always hoped for a speedier demise than to be put into isolation with a bunch of people "mentally mature." I may be close to 60, but my mind is a lot closer to 30, and nothing is more soothing to my ears as someone saying to me in a snit, "Grow up, why don't you." If you meet a young couple on the trip and if you get along, cherish them; they will help you from going mad. One can only talk about the weather for a limited time, before one absolutely "loses it." I did talk to another "casino dweller" that went on a different cruise, one sailing from San Juan. He described those cruisers to be only in the 40 to 50 year old range. So ultimately I guess it's the luck of the draw.

After doing some tanning by the pool, Kathy and I returned to the casino. Although it was still packed, we manage to find a spot at one of their five tables. It is obvious that the game enjoys tremendous popularity because the other games, roulette and craps, had a sparse crowd. The slot machines were also under used. The removal of them would enable the casino to install more 21 tables thus increasing their cash flow. And increase it they would because from what I could see, very few people could play basic strategy, let alone winning blackjack. A lot of people would fall prey to the dealer's suggestions of splitting all pairs. With more tables, there would be more opportunities to seduce more people to make even more errant plays.

Before dinner we went to our cabin getting ready for our 8:00 pm sitting. Many people are of the false impression that ships have truly "gourmet foods." Technically they offer interesting, gastronomically pleasing meals, but they are all mass-produced. They produce three or four meals well, but they have to do thousands of these everyday. It's the presentation that is classy. There are waiters, waiter assistants, headwaiters and then finally there is the maitre de. They are all there to make your meal as enjoyable as possible. They are also very professional, their courtesy is expressed knowing full well that they will be judged according to the service they provide when it comes time for the tip. This is usually given on the last night of the voyage.

Mitch and his wife were already at the table curious to know about betting variation and the amount of winning, if any. I told him that the system that I used depended on an abundance of face cards and aces. If these were in the majority, my bet would escalate. "How could you not notice that when I had a large bet out, not only you had received a blackjack," I said while reaching for a dinner roll. "But why did you make the bet when you did?" "Could you not hear them, could you not sense them? They were yearning to be set free," was my answer as the waiter opened the menu in front of me.

Just then Gene and his wife came and sat down. He had a smug look on his face. Gene reminded me of a guy that was sitting at a BJ table, years ago in Vegas, being rude to the dealer and in general just being a dork. Finally the dealer dealt him an ace and a king to which the guy blurted out, "Blackjack." She looked down at him with a scowl as she was paying him and said, "Not exactly a blackjack, because you're still one Jack off."

Gene said that he had been watching the news and the Taliban were getting their asses beat by the Americans in Afghanistan. "How naive you are Gene. It took al-qaeda, a CIA asset, and the Taliban ten long years to kick out the Soviets. Now the Russians are back and all that they lost in ten years has now been recovered in two weeks. The Russians are playing "Real Politik" and the Americans are being played as the patsies." "How can you say that? We're there fighting terrorism," he said. "Please Gene, save the theatrics, this wasn't the first time an American president sat on his hands knowing that an air strike was about to hit the shores of the USA." "What other time did the terrorists strike us," he asked. "Come on, it's not the biggest secret in the world that Roosevelt wrote his famous 'Pearl Harbor' speech a day before the attack."

I could sense that Gene was getting a little perturbed by my denial that the American leadership wasn't perhaps guiltless when it came to under the table international intrigues. He obviously read the news like I did and he also knew that the air force was made to "stand down" on September 11th. It was his denial that I found to be rather humorous. He was so out of touch and naïve that I figured his version of "de-Nile" held some reference to a large river in Egypt. I brought it to his attention that a golfer, Payne Stewart, had over flown an airport at which time a jet was scrambled to intercept it, and this was undertaken as a routine action within minutes of the ground control notifying them of the problem. The Lear 35 was 500 miles from the F-16, but flying at mach 2 the air force jet caught up to it in 30 minutes. That incident was about two years prior to the September events. In the golfer's case it was determined that all on board had succumbed to decompression and since the plane was not endangering any major city it was allowed to run out of fuel, and crash rather than be shot down. On September 11 why was there no similar F-16 or F-15 intercepts for over an hour and a half, although the Pentagon was being targeted? Andrews air force base was only fifteen miles away.

Gene couldn't even look at me after that. He knew that there was something fishy about the whole thing. The old argument that we get lots of false reports every month and we can't be fooled by all of them, just wouldn't cut it. The radar screen doesn't lie. If a passenger jet strays off course for even a minute without communicating the reason, the air force is immediately notified, and action is taken. The US, after all, doesn't maintain a state of the art, one trillion dollar defense system so that they could be attacked like some third rate country in Africa for instance. Hmmm, maybe only a twit could believe in T.W.A.T, short for "The War Against Terror."

Gail and Lucy were being seated, as I was about to relate the biggest "scoop" of all. Preceding our cruise I mentioned that we drove by a business, which stated on its window "We would rather serve 1000 al-qaeda than one American." Predictably Gene said, "That's bullshit, if a place put that on their window I would put a brick through it myself." "No you wouldn't Gene, the place was a funeral parlor."

Gene was an annoying bastard but the others were okay. I guess it could have been worse, a lot worse. Imagine getting stuck with a whole table of "jack offs" like Gene.

After two days at sea we reached our second destination, the Grand Cayman Island. There was no pier to facilitate large ocean liners so lifeboats, called "tenders," were lowered to take us to the main city of George Town. From there one could take an organized coach tour for $35, dollars or strike out on your own for $15 with one of the many freelance drivers waiting on shore with their private cars. We chose to do the latter, thus sidestepping the commission paid to the ship, instead giving the money directly to the people themselves.

Setting out from George Town, the capitol, a tour was given of the island, starting with the posh houses built by the rich. Prior to 9/11 the Grand Caymans used to be a tax haven, with banks that advertised anonymity much like that guaranteed by the Swiss. Pressure was brought to bear on those institutions and they are now functioning at the pleasure of the IRS.

Our first stop was made at a place that specializes in rum cakes. A faintest hint of rum can be detected after sampling a wide variety of these items. Certainly not like the rum cakes that "mom" used to make. As a child of seven I can remember getting "high" after just two slices of her version.

The next stop was a place called "Hell." It evidently got that name when the appointed governor from England hit a slice while playing golf, and the ball landed in an unusual corral formation, located more or less in the center of the island. Not being able to find his ball, he yelled the expletive "bloody hell;" the name stuck. There is even a fellow dressed up as the devil to give "realism" to the area. We then went back to George Town, to a jewelry shop, and were given a card by our driver. He asked us to submit the card if we bought anything. I presume he too gets a referral fee for items sold to us.

We were given a time when the last tender would be returning to the ship. We loaded up on another two bottles of gin and stood in line for the ride back. Once there we again had to wait for the captain to sail us out to international waters, so the casino could open anew. This night is to be set aside for tournament play. I have only been in three of these myself, losing one miserably, eking out a win on the other two. Because I play so sedom I readily admit that I watch from a distance, cheering on my favorite player.

Blackjack tournaments are a big thing onboard ship casinos. They draw a huge crowd, not only of players, but also onlookers. If the payoff wasn't so "paltry," I think that I might have joined in myself. The prize was $1000 with about 50 entrants at $35 a pop. Way too risky for me; more importantly, way too safe for the casino.

Tournaments have a strategy all their own. They are geared for a short run of luck. Timid players are usually not represented in the playoff rounds; this is the area set aside for the aggressive players. And they are aggressive at the right time. By that I mean they are well aware of the amount of money that is in play, and the amount of money that each player has in front of him. You are playing not only against the dealer, but also more importantly against all the other players at the table. If you are playing the last round and you have under bet, it isn't uncommon to see that error rectified by splitting tens against a ten up, or even doubling a hard seventeen against a ten.

There are a lot of people who are quite adept at tournament play, a lot better than I will ever be. The important thing to keep in mind is the payback percentage when entering a tournament. If the payback is only 50 percent, you will be in a losing situation. Get to near 100 percent payback as possible. You will never get that on a ship, because again they are the only game in town. In Nevada however, many casinos offer the 100% and sometimes more, in order to attract customers to their particular resorts. To keep abreast of these, one has to subscribe to magazines that list the upcoming tournaments. They will usually also include the maximum number of players allowed to enter. From this, you can calculate the percentage of "equity" in the game.

There are many players that don't believe the blackjack game is beatable; they call it the devil's game. These are the same people that incorrectly think Ed Thorpe's excellent book, titled "Beat The Dealer," explores various methods of martial arts. Their idea is to exact revenge from a loss by bad mouthing the person dealing to them. Little wonder that there are dealers who get great pleasure in taking from a person like that. Sometimes people get too involved in the game. Frustrated, they lash out at the only person that reaches into the square to take their money. To these emotionally charged people, the dealer is seen as an arch villain, one that is paid to take the abuse of the losing gambler. To this type of person, gambling shouldn't be included in his life style. Perhaps shuffleboard should be their game of choice.

At supper, Gene made a snide comment about the government that we have in Canada. He actually thought that I might take offense. "Oh what a person of small character he." Gene was quite taken aback when I told him that I couldn't agree with him more. "His best is so petty, and his worst is so petty." "You're right Gene, the Canadian government runs a close second to the USA when it comes to cheating people out of their hard earned money. Haven't you heard, both countries have laid siege on their old age security funds, placing them into their respective general revenues." Gene was the kind of guy you would just love to invite hunting, having him wear one of those hats with antlers protruding from them.

If the officers of a company were to tamper with their worker's pension plan, they would be sent to jail pronto, unless you happen to be chief executives of Enron of course. Because of their ties to the leadership in the "White House," a sacrificial lamb will be offered up as punishment, and the "big wigs" will be let off Scott free.

After dinner, Kathy and I took a walk out on the deck. The night sky was stripped of its clouds and spread above us shamelessly naked, revealing for us her hidden gems. It beckoned us to join hands and roam the darkness, using the stars as our guide; a view unspoiled by any artificial lights greeted us "star gazers" as we looked with awe on her unfettered beauty. The Big Dipper stood out, proclaiming dominance of the night. The only sound that could be heard was the ship, as it knifed through the gentle waves, propelling us forward to our next destination, Cozumel, Mexico.

The cruise was planned so the ship always slipped into port in the morning. We were gently aroused about 6:30 and prepare to leave. There was a trip offered where one could view some Mesoamerican ruins. They advertised Chichén Itza for a mere $135 per person. We chose instead to rent a jeep, and travel to a closer site called Coba, Mayan ruins smack dab in the middle of the jungle. This site is about thirty kilometers from Cozumel, and for us a lot more affordable than that charged by the people running the bus line in conjunction with the ship. Remember that they always take a fee for organizing these little escapades, therefore it is always cheaper to strike out on your own.

No matter what you do however, you will be gouged. The rental of the jeep for four hours is $35, no bargain from any point of view, but certainly a lot less than that planned for the people with deeper pockets. Again, coming back to the ship, we loaded up on liquor before our next stop at Progresso, Mexico.

Cruises are a relative novelty for Progresso. The internet-cafe charges one dollar per hour for use, a bargain compared to the nine dollars charged on board the ship. But in retrospect this too is a bargain compared with the eight dollars a minute that is charged for use of the telephone. Here in Progresso, you can still get a beer for a single dollar. Kathy and I followed Tanya and Dawn to a friendly little bar just off the main square. And oh what a small world it really is.

As we were drinking a "Cool Cervesa," I happen to glance over to an adjacent table and noticed a chap dressed in jungle khaki's, sitting with a "gringo" lady, having a beer. My but he looked familiar. Finally, I couldn't take the suspense any longer and walked up to the table and asked him if his name wasn't Dennis S. from Alberta. His eyes grew large and he said that he was. In the real estate business his house was the very first one that I had sold. We spent a few hours reminiscing, and he didn't want to let us go. I guess he felt lonely after the long drive from Edmonton. His ultimate destination was Cancun where he was to rendezvous with a friend. He had just met this particular "senorita" in town the day before, and was talking her ear off, along with other pieces of her attire I presumed. But alas, we had to part company to pick up our liquor rations for the two-day cruise back to our original port, Miami.

The Progresso pier is far from the city, and it seems that the cruise ship companies had spent a considerable amount of money dredging the area in order to facilitate the liners. A bus had to be supplied for us to go back and forth to the ship.

On the way back the omnipresent stench, of burning vegetation dominated our senses. It is the Mexican mode of doing things. Slash and burn, a quick and low-tech way to infuse nutrients back into the ground, at the expense of clean air.

As the ship slowly sidled out of the pier we went down to change and clean up for the casino. As soon as we reached the international boundary, it opened.

Unlike other casinos around the world, cruise companies don't find it in their best interests to offer "comps" for play. Again, this is a result of the lack of competition, the only game in town syndrome. Of course this is not the case in gaming houses in North America.

In a state like Nevada, the "comp" is the mainstay of customer relations. Needless to say if you're gambling, the drinks are supplied gratis. Whether you are sitting in a bar playing video poker, playing a table game or slot machine, the liquor is made available for free. A dollar tip ensures that the drinks are supplied at a regular pace, without the need to notify the pit crew to intercede on your behalf. It is the comp for food that some people may find problematic to acquire. This shouldn't be the case.

I know enough people in a town like Vegas for instance, to use my influence to gain the necessary freebies at various casinos. Casinos where you are an unknown, present the biggest problem. They are governed by a simple formula of money that you, as a casino client, put at risk. Depending on the number of people sitting at the $25 minimum table you can be putting at risk anywhere between 50 to 75 hands per hour. Taking the approximate average of 65 hands per hour, we derive at a total of 25x65=$1625. Let us assume that you play for two hours then your total risk exposure is 2x1625=$3250. The casino takes this figure and compiles a total comp payout for your particular play. They multiply $3250 by 2%, which gives them an edge of $65. They then divide this by two giving them the total amount of freebies that they are allowed to give. In our example, this amounts to $32.50. In spite of saying this, there are ways to enhance this process.

In gambling, like any other endeavor, there is no substitute for politeness. A great philosopher once said, "I can strike back with a sharp tongue when someone hurls an insult at me, but when someone gives me a compliment, how do I defend myself against that." It goes back to an earlier point made in the book about customer relations. How can you be rude to a customer, one that pays your wages and possibly even buy your dinner? The pit crew is always aware of the approximate bet that you are making, not the exact bet. If you are playing at the $25 dollar table, see a rich situation, and feel the need to put in $200, that's when you "politely" call over the pit person and ask him "nicely" if he can give you a comp for dinner. Also, make sure that you have a count strong enough to make a follow up bet, so he can appraise your play a bit closer. If the count drops, you may then want to exercise your option and go to the rest room. When you return to play again, don't call him over until you have a large bet. At that point you may want to ask him, "How is that comp coming?"

Can you see what I am getting at? He hasn't really seen you betting anything but $25. Every time he is scrutinizing you, however, you have a large bet out. If the count drops while he is talking with you, merely pull your bet as if engaged in thoughtful conversation. He is apt to rate your play at a $50 average bet, or higher. This of course means that you have upped your comp from $32.50 to $65, or if he rates you at $75 for an average bet, your comps have risen to almost $100. Although you only merit about $35 in freebies, you increased your level to almost three times that amount. If asked how long you have been playing at the table, don't be shy about inflating the time. After all, think about the times that you have been playing there without a comp.

The most important thing about comps, is to ask for them. You can't be introverted when it comes to dinners being given for free. You must ASK, or they WILL NOT be given. When talking to people who have been going to casinos for years, I am shocked to find that most of them don't ask. Perhaps it's an Anglo-Saxon thing, but for myself I have found that "It's the squeaky wheel that gets the oil." You have earned it, therefore it's yours. After all, is it not built in to the casinos' "give away" formula? For all the people that are too shy to ask, there is now an allotted give away fund that is untapped. As a consequence comps are often given out to friends and relatives who happen to "have juice" (knowing someone in a position to offer give a ways). I can't tell you the number of times that my ex and I were given shows and other comps just because she knew the shift boss. I would much sooner see a person who earned these things getting them, rather than someone who hasn't.

There was a time that Bob L., a shift boss at a casino that will remain unnamed, would ask me to bring down a box of "Cuban" cigars. For me the cost was well over $50 but well worth it from the public relations aspect. Because Cuba has been on "the evil empire list" for many decades, Americans have been forbidden to go there. That has not been the case for Canadians. As a result we have been importing Cuban goods into our country for years. Many citizens of the US that frequent Las Vegas, eagerly seek after cigars, especially the Cuban ones. If they are deemed to be sufficiently high betters a guy like Bob would naturally offer them one of the "Cabana's" (Havana's) delivered by me. Keep in mind that not everyone could obtain these treasured "gems." A big better was more apt to go to Bob's casino rather than one that didn't have that much desired "perk." Presidents and other important people could enjoy these taboo items, but by and large if you weren't real important you did without. This gave Bob a lot of "standing," and the way the trickle down effect works, it also ends up benefiting me. I have gotten rooms, shows and fancy restaurants without even having to wager a nickel.

They tell me that in the "old days" things were much better under mafia control. I'm sure they were. During the depression Al Capone himself would man the soup kitchens that he funded, helping to dole out the food. They knew how to create loyalties. On one of the interviews heard in Chicago, there was a chap that said, "I just want to let you know that it is Mr. Capone feeding us and not the government." Organized crime knew how to endear itself to the masses. It is surprising that the government, the largest band of organized criminals in the annals of history, have not taken some of the cues offered to them by the Cosa Nostra.

I've heard that merely cashing some money in for chips entitled you to food at either a coffee shop or buffet, during the "bad old days." Now it is the bottom line that dictates "freebies." Businessmen determine who gets the comps, and who gets the romps. An investor group now runs the show. Before, when the mob ran things, they answered to no one except perhaps "Mr. Big." They had a "family" that needed a certain return on their investments but they didn't have to pay large sums of money to individual shareholders in the form of yearly dividends.

Another important thing to keep in mind is that you can avoid long lineups by getting into the comp lane of a coffee shop or buffet. If you haven't yet put in enough time "gambling" and wanted to treat someone to a meal, ask the floor man for a "line pass" to circumvent the multitude. Often they will tell you that they don't have line passes. But if you have "oiled your way around the casino floor," done your homework, and have been courteous, he or she will, in all likely hood, write you out a comp for a buffet or other moderately priced cafes. To get comps for more expensive restaurants you of course have to be betting higher valued chips. My idea of a perfect cruise would be one that offers liquor incentives for gamblers, comps for wine and champagne for the evening meal, along with free drinks at the tables.

The session that we had was a successful one but alas it was a two-day trip, directly back to Miami with no more stops along the way. I was therefore pressured to get in some "deck time" of a different sort, and do some tanning with Kathy.

The nice thing about a ship is that one doesn't encounter pests such as mosquitoes and the like, making basking in the sun somewhat more pleasurable. If one is drinking on board, that is to say ordering at the bar, there are waiters and waitresses aplenty to supply you adequately in this department. They make most of their wages in this fashion, so it is to their benefit to "hustle" as many drinks as they can. Needless to say, thanks to Kathy's gin filled thermos mug, we were not their favorite people.

Later on we prepared for dinner. Kathy wasn't feeling too well at all, so she decides to forgo the evening "dining experience." Could it be that she is seasick? Nah! By her own admission, she never gets seasick. However, the ocean had a bit more motion than usual, but she laid the blame right where it ought to be, square on the shoulders of the Mexicans. They are the source for all ailments that have to do with the digestive tract. The deep fried corn chips with salsa that we had earlier at the bar in Progresso were deemed to be the culprit. I told her to order some chicken soup from the "eat in" menu, and I made my way up to the dining room.

Of all the meals to miss, the menu that night consisted of Kathy's favorite things. Lobster tails, crab salad and lobster bisque soup. The other spicy item on the menu was Gene's remarks, bragging about his money as usual. He asked about ages around the table. He probably did that to further brag, as he was eight years older than his wife. Kathy wasn't at the table so I took the liberty of exaggerating a little bit. I told him that I was 60 and that Kathy was 30. My, did he ever look dejected.

After dinner I went down to see if Kathy was all right. She said she had improved enough to order some consommé with matzo balls. Shortly after she had the soup, she became ill once more. I talked her into taking a Bo-nine and she felt fine for the rest of the trip. So much for "blame it all on the Mexicans" thing. My gal, the one that never got seasick, finally succumbed to the illness that only us landlubbers were supposed to be afflicted with.

The next day we tried out our luck at 21, and by the end of the last session we were up a total of $700 for the cruise. Let me see, that is a free cruise for Kathy and I with $100 left over after parking. After tipping that would be eroded to zero.

On cruises everybody, and I mean everybody is out for a tip; the cabin boy, the headwaiter, the assistant waiter, and the maitre de all had envelopes placed on our dresser with a gratuity guide on how much of a tip to place inside. These of course were astronomical, and $100 could only stretch so far. One must let his or her conscience be the guide. The most frequently used services and staff should obviously get the most tips if all was satisfactory. Without a doubt for us these were the dealers in the casino. They naturally got tipped during their act of service, that is to say, while dealing. When the place got packed they would give me the sign that they were told to "up cut the deck." We would then leave until I could have a more favorable situation. For this information alone, it was worthwhile tipping; not too much though, or one would end up gouging into ones own profit.

It was at 6:00 am when we felt a gentle nudge as we arrived at our berth in the Port of Miami. Our luggage had already been put out in the hallway for the disembarking procedure. The baggage people picked them up in the wee hours to speed up the process. After breakfast we started to queue up as per our color-coded luggage tags. The line diminished rapidly and in less than an hour we were at our car.

*　　　*　　　*　　　*　　　*

We had four days till the next cruise on the Norway. We decide to take a cruise to Freeport located on the Grand Bahamas Island. The cost was $150/per person. This included round trip to Freeport, an overnight stay at the Castaway Resorts, and buffets on board the ship. The ship sails out of Port Everglades, in Fort Lauderdale, the next big city up the beach from Miami. We stayed at a motel overnight and were at the pier for a 7:00am departure. On this boat we didn't have a cabin so we pack light and had one carry on bag apiece.

Like most ships there is a casino and it is open as soon as we were clear of Florida's legal off shore limit. I sat down at one of the tables and managed to eke out a $300 win by the time we called it quits having something to eat. We then watched on deck as we slowly got escorted to the Freeport pier by one of several tugs used for these older boats.

After arriving at our hotel an unbelievable occurrence had taken place. There was a mix up, and they didn't have our room. They had overbooked and now we had to stay at an exclusive hideaway some distance from any casino. I made sure that they issued us a letter stating that we had been forced to spend our mini vacation at a place other than the one that we had agreed to. This done, we insisted that they also pay for the cab fare that we would be out of pocket as a result of their oversight. After agreeing to this, we set out to try to enjoy ourselves the best we could.

We checked into our room, and there is no doubt about it, the place was magnificent. The problem was that there was no casino in the hotel. After all, that was the whole object of the trip. We had to cab it into the touristy area to enjoy some gaming action. After a break-even session, putting in two hours of play, we "limped" back to our home base ate and went to bed.

In the morning we packed and met at the Castaway for a pickup at 11:00am. On arriving back to Fort Lauderdale we march down to the travel agency and demand our money back, due to the circumstances. The broker complained a bit but eventually saw our side of the story refunding our money entirely.

So far we have been on two cruises and have yet to pay a thing. I wondered how the next cruise was going to treat us when we start playing there.

Driving across the Port of Miami Blvd., heading for Dodge Island and a rendezvous with the Norway, we noticed immediately an intensity of automobile traffic. The Norway was a huge ship built in 1960, originally called the SS France. It looked a little like the Titanic; hopefully we wouldn't be encountering any icebergs in the Caribbean. Its capacity was 1500-2100 passengers, (depending on who you talk to) and a crew of about 1000, with 1300 passengers on board for this, its maiden voyage after the refit in Germany. The Norway evidently suffered from an engineering "faux pas." When it was originally built, they made it one inch too wide. This extra inch prohibited the vessel from passing through Panama Canal. Talk about design follies, this was on a grand and irreparable scale.

Checking in was to be a major ordeal. Again, not only did we have to put up with the extortionate rates for car parking, we now were faced with a boat packed with people. The only bright spot was that it was 200-900 passengers under capacity, again depending on whom you spoke to. One has to make lemonade out of a lemon or be miserable the entire trip. We were shown to our quarters, this time they were inside cabins, very small and very Spartan. We then explored the ship till its departure at 5:00 pm.

Being a lot more experienced, we picked the late seating right away for supper due mainly to the number of kids being aboard this cruise. We took in the view and chatted with people till we finally "shoved off." Our first stop was to be St. Martaan, in two days.

When we cleared the port we wandered upstairs to get acquainted with the casino and it's staff. There were two dealers there from Romania, three from Hungary and one from Croatia. They all spoke fairly good English. Naturally there was only one person fluent in English, and that person was the shift boss. The dealers were all at their respective stations so I sat down to break the ice. They give me a two-deck cut, I protested strongly enough to reduce that to one and a half decks. After a few shoes, a tall Romanian took the deal and he too gave a decent cut, until I put a couple of big bets in at the end of the shoe. That was it for the decent cuts. He dealt a two-deck cut-off shoe, from that point on. And from that point on that was the end of the one-dollar tips that I gave him after each BJ. No other dealer seemed to have a problem with the one and a half decks, except him.

Tipping is the only "carrot" that one can use to modify the staff's behavior. If one tips regardless of cut, well, that doesn't do anyone any good. That in effect has the accumulative effect of taking away the dealers' incentive. Unfortunately, people don't know that they are getting "screwed," so they put in a tip, regardless. My holding back on mine was merely an isolated protest, a solitary gesture. About two hours after the place opened, it was standing room only at the blackjack tables. And the worst of it was that the management could move the minimum bet up and down at will, whether you were there first or not, forcing you to also raise your wager. In Nevada, you were assured the lower amount till you decided to leave. Needless to say the casino raised theirs as soon as it got crowded. Of course we quit play at that point, exiting for the dinning room.

We were seated with four older ladies in their seventies and eighties. There was one that complained about everything. The soup wasn't warm enough, the salad wasn't crispy, coffee too hot, and the taste of the food was off. All I could do was give our Filipino waiter a sympathetic look.

The casino on the Norway needed a larger area, or at least more 21 tables. When we returned, the place was still packed. All the tables were full, including the craps and the baccarat tables. Then I met a guy by the name of Jorgen, who was sporting a tie with a blackjack on it. He looked Norwegian, complete with accent. I told him that I liked his tie. He said, "You know what, after tonight's show I'm going to let you have it," the tie that is. True to his word that night, after an excellent "Las Vegas style" stage show, he came up to me and put the tie around my neck, gently of course. I wore that tie proudly every time we went to a formal dinner on that ship.

Finally, "dog ass" tired, we decided to go to bed. The ship was so large that Kathy and I never got fully oriented. Trying to find our way back down to our cabin was always an ordeal.

The steady groaning of the diesels, laboring as they turned the four massive propellers on the Norway could be heard on our tier, the forth level. Kathy was, by now, a fervent believer in Bo-nine. As the seas became rough, the Norway would buck, occasionally lifting the shallow screw out of the water, slightly speeding up the monotone drone. This was almost a relief; a sound that broke the tedium of the trip.

A few days later the steady droning stopped, thus awaking us. We were at St. Martaan, an island with a border, one side French and the other Dutch. Philipsburg, the big city in the Dutch section, beckoned to us as we were having our morning coffee before being loaded onto a tender that shuttled us to the island.

Once there I saw Jorgen. Again I thanked him for the tie. I saw that he is wearing a great looking hat and said to him with a smile, "I like your hat," thinking that it might net me yet another great "memento." He just looked at me and finally said with a smile, "If you think I'm going to give you my hat your crazy."

After setting foot on St. Martaan, we were accosted by an agent for a "time share" resort. She said that for one hour of our time we would be given $50 US a piece or $100 a piece in match play coupons at the Diamond Casino and a return trip to Oyster Bay. Since we were going to the beach at Oyster Bay anyway, here was an opportunity to save a couple of dollars on cab fare, plus receive some extra money. I must say that it was the coupons for match play at the casino that swung the deal for me. It did pose an interesting diversion from the regular play aboard the ship.

The presentation was the same old yada yada, "We're the number one destination, and all the others suck." After an hour of this, I looked at the clock and noted that we were a few minutes over that which was promised. I told the promoter that we were only asked to sit there for one hour and that time had now elapsed. I said we would like that which was promised, so that we might leave. They apologized, gave us our coupons and we walked to the beach to enjoy the solitude.

On the beach we met the juggler-comic that had performed the previous night in the show room. His name was John Barry, and he had a friend with him called Vinnie Marks. Vinnie was to be the featured comedy act for the show slated for that evening. They told us that they had just paid eight bucks a piece for a ride to the much-touted beach at Oyster Bay. That of course would mean that they still had to fork out an identical fare for the return trip. We told Vinnie that we would see him that night at the show. We then left to check out the town and of course the casino.

The driver dropped us off right at the front door. We entered a casino that was basically empty. There weren't any 21 tables open, so we asked for this to be arranged. The floor person sat high, as is the norm for European style table games; so they can observe more than one game in progress. We were the only patrons so her eyes would have been glued exclusively on our table. The very first hand out I was dealt a sixteen, and she had a seven up. Hitting it I got a three for a total of nineteen, the dealer had to hit hers and eventually got seventeen. She proceeded to scoop up my chips. I quietly let her do it hoping to get a protest from the lady sitting on high looking at the game. When no one realized the "mistake," I knew that I had been cheated. I looked at the pit boss and instructed her to inform the dealer that she had taken my money when I, in fact, had beaten her. She said that I had broke. If this happened, then she would not have taken a hit to make seventeen; they had blatantly tried to cheat us. Now there was no question of us staying in an empty casino, playing in ideal conditions. If they are cheating you or trying to cheat you, then playing at such a place is just plain not worth it. If you constantly have to look over your shoulders to see if your ass is covered, then it is no longer relaxing and therefore time to go.

We played the remainder of the chips and left. I wished the last double down I attempted would have been a winner. I had bet $50 getting a seven and a four pushing out another $50, I got an ace; the dealer got seventeen. We walked out with $90 instead of a guaranteed $100. Some may say, "See, you just can't win gambling." These people miss the whole point. I had lost ten dollars, the last bet meant a negative $200 turn around. In other words, I had a chance of making $200 or losing ten. If the chances were approximately even there isn't a person on this globe that wouldn't take that gamble.

Making a detour on our way back to the "pick up point," we checked out the sights and of course made a stop at the liquor store to top up on our dwindling supply of gin. All this complete, we were back in time to make the last tender to our ship.

There are some incredibly rich people around the world. On our way back, we saw several yachts anchored in the bay. The most impressive of these had all kinds of toys; a helicopter being the most eye-catching.

As the Norway steamed away from St. Martaan, or as the French call it St. Martin, many of us were still on deck watching as the charming island faded away from sight. Hopefully the more pleasant memory of that quaint little outpost will linger with us longer than that unpleasant episode at the Diamond Casino.

I got to the onboard gaming room early and managed to land a seat. There was a guy sitting there who was making some big bets, his name was CC. He asked why I would go from five dollars to one hundred. "Because I feel lucky," I said. "Yeah, but you sure do get a lot of blackjacks when you're feeling that way," he remarked, as the dealer paid me off $150. You can be rest assured that it isn't always that way, but for about a half an hour I was "in my zone" as they say in athletics.

CC's real name was Silvan. He said that he was from Salt Lake City, a place that has a lot of Mormons. It turned out that he too was a member of the Latter Day Saints. "Hey, isn't it against the tenets of your religion to gamble?" "Yeah," he said as he placed another $50 bet into the square, "But it's the only bad habit that I have." Well true enough, I guess there are a lot more habits that could be acquired that are worse than gambling. Smoking is one that I can think of right off. I don't know anyone who wouldn't give at least a month's wages to quit that addiction.

I told him that I used to live in Vegas and often cut through Salt Lake on my way to Calgary and back on Interstate 15. He said that next time, I would have to make it a point to stop over. He gave me his card and said to just call. I told him that I would make it a priority to do just that. I noticed on the card that he was a county sheriff. Well, it's probably safe at his house as there are sure to be a lot of guns around.

One thing for sure, criminals find it a lot safer to commit crimes against unarmed people than those that are armed. When one sees an effort by a government to disarm a population, that usually means that there are some bad economic times ahead; otherwise why bother? It almost seems that the authorities are protecting themselves against the "law abiding citizen." Surely they must know that any felon can readily get a hold of an illegal weapon. To deprive "Joe Citizen" of the opportunity to defend his family and property against these criminals is a felonious act in itself. In a "free" society all but criminals are allowed to have weapons. Unfortunately this brings a big question to the forefront. If the ordinary citizen in Iraq can have weapons, and they are governed by a "brutal dictatorship" then who exactly are we governed by? Dictatorships find it in their own best interests to disarm their populations to prevent any popular leader from assuming power via a popular revolt. Was Saddam Hussien not afraid of his people? If he wasn't, would that then really qualify him as a dictator? These questions on gun control seem to pose more problems than solutions.

My thirteen-year old boy asked an interesting question that had not occurred to me before. "Wasn't what was going on in the world arena between the USA and Iraq a global attempt at gun control?" Once you have disarmed, the criminals can break into your house unfettered. If, on the other hand, you do have weapons of mass destruction then no one will bother you. Hmm, smart boy. I wonder if there will be a global "home invasion" any time soon of North Korea, a country that has a verifiable arsenal of WMD. This more than any other thing may spark the proliferation of nuclear arms by all countries interested in securing their own borders from more powerful countries, that is to say, those countries that are eyeing up their respective natural resources.

There was another chap playing at our table, and betting big, but losing. His name was Billy B. He and his wife were on their honeymoon, and lived in a small place called Bay St. Louis in the beautiful state of Mississippi. He was a links pro at one of the biggest casino golf courses in the area. He was probably a good golfer, but he could sure have used some friendly advice in the 21 department. I took an instant liking to the guy, but there was nothing that I could do to persuade him to follow my bet. I saw him do a double down against a ten on a miserably low count and watched as a multi card twenty trumped his seventeen. Poor bastard had $100 out there plus his double, which meant that he had a $400 turn negative turn around. By that I mean the $200 that he had lost, plus the $200 that he could have won.

Later, as we were standing around, he asked me if I ever played golf before. "Yes I have," I said, "In fact the best two balls that I ever hit was when I was in a sand trap and stepped on a rake." On the golf course I am sure he could give me some tips on the game. I would of course know that he was a pro and therefore could feel comfortable in consulting him. He on the other hand, didn't know me from Adam. I could be just another "flake" giving him false counseling, advice that may harm him rather than help him. He had just pulled the biggest "boner" on the table. It was tantamount to stepping on a rake in golf. Doubling down eleven, playing with an anemic deck, is not the thing to do. In fact in an anemic deck there are a lot of double down situations due to a lot of small cards. I would have loved to tell him to the contrary but decided to wait till we were well away from our present "venue." He gave me his card insisting that we stop in the Biloxi area for cocktails and some lighthearted conversation on our the way back to Canada. I decided then not to interfere with his game and just hope that he got lucky recouping all his loses. Instead,

I would talk with him about the "finer points" of 21 when we were in Mississippi.

Kathy and I went on deck to take in some sun only to come back an hour later to find the casino half empty. Rather than go back to the cabin and get my bankroll, I decided to play with what I had. I cashed in a $100 for some chips and planned to wait until the start of a new shoe to commence play. There were four other people at the table when the dealer dealt a set of cards for everyone that contained no face cards. With the count soaring, I decided to put in only half of my cash, just in case I faced a double down situation. Sure enough, I was dealt "the bishop," a pair of twos against the dealers six (Bishop Tu Tu was a "sky pilot" from South Africa, thus the name). I put in my last $50, initiating the split. I then was dealt another deuce, but had no more money to re-split. I was now in a dilemma. Not having anymore cash on hand I couldn't re-split. I asked the floor man if he would mark the bet but he refused, (marking the wager is the "best bet in the house," because if you lose, you could put on your hat and leave. Not that I would personally do this, or for that matter recommend it, but it is a win win situation, nevertheless, for the player. Without any money he can be in on a win in conditions that wouldn't expose him to any further financial risk). If CC or Billy were present there wouldn't be a problem, but with four strangers at the table it didn't look very promising. Just then an Italian guy by the name of Tony flipped me a couple of green chips, allowing me to re-split again. I then was dealt a nine. Looking at him again, I said nothing. He again surrendered another $50 for the double. Receiving a five, I realized that I was in a "corrective stage of a low count." On the next card, I was again dealt a deuce. Asking for another $50 would have been the height of audacity. Slightly rolling his eyes, forcing a smile, Tony reached into his pocket and cashed in a hundred dollars; pushing the necessary amount over to me. The next card was a seven. This time without hesitation he slid over the last of his recent cash-in. If I had been getting great cards on my double downs I'm sure Tony would have been a little more at ease, but the way it was, I was getting nothing but junk. On the last deuce I was given an eight, and this time with a slight grunt he once again exhibited the "loser's lean" by reaching into his pocket. "You know, I've never bet more than about twenty dollars and here I am sticking my neck out for a guy that I don't even know, who is making bigger bets than my maximum." With a big smile I reached over and we introduced ourselves. "Tony, if I lose I want to let you know that we are going to go straight to my cabin so I can reimburse you for the money that you're out." Feeling a lot better and smiling once more, he passed me the last bet for the double down. This time I was given the ace. Well at least he wouldn't be out more than a $150, even if it turned out that I was nothing but a degenerate gambler. The dealer went on to break, using an unbelievable number of cards.

The strain melted from Tony's face. He was physically relieved and emotionally spent. He was, in all honesty, more relieved than I when the dealer broke. I called the waitress over to buy him a beer to relieve some of the stress that my play had put on his nerves. The moral of this event is to always bring enough money, in case you dig a hole for yourself. Hmm, or in case there is a dork like me playing that doesn't have enough money for the next bet.

There is an old blackjack adage, "When in doubt put it out;" if I can just add a small phrase of my own, "but only if you have the clout." If you see a lot of little cards, only two things are happening. The deck is either building up positive stress away from "zero," or it is releasing "laziness" on its way back to "zero." I thought the deck was building up stress and hence deciding to gamble. I was hoping to see a lot of face cards to give a confirmation to my bet. I was wrong, but came out smelling like a rose thanks to Tony. Casinos around Nevada and New Jersey have never refused me a marked double. But you can see where the casinos are sticking their necks out because if they lose to a total stranger they have no recourse.

Evening had us dining with the lady that whines, this truly gave new meaning to "whining and dining." It was very aggravating. Our Filipino "servant" was made to jump through hoops for this one old lady. I felt sorry for him but what can one do. Such is the nature of cruising. I was almost pining for Gene's company; at least I could raise my voice at him.

The Virgin Islands is to be our next port of call so we decided to retire early to do the island properly. There are no casinos there, so it would be sight seeing all the way.

The deafening silence is the first thing one noticed when we dropped anchor. You could only hear the murmur of the engines that gave us electrical power. The propeller shafts that drove the screws are put to rest. Maintenance resumes feverishly at our every stop. An old ship like the Norway is constantly in a state of repair. In her belly the Norway had a complete workshop with every imaginable tool to repair whatever break downs that may arise. Lathes of all sizes and shapes are supplied in the shop to facilitate the machinists in case of malfunction. There is also an array of spare parts to help the great ship complete her voyage without delays. In saying this there was a leak one floor below that had yet to remedied. Many people had their baggage soaked as a result. Naturally there are dry cleaning facilities onboard; the ship picking up the tab. No matter what eventuality they planned for, there was always something that popped up to make the crew's maintenance duties interesting. Since our cruise, there was an accident on board which created an explosion killing four crewmembers on that "Grand Dame of the Ocean."

As we started loading on to the tender that was going into St. Thomas, we realize that the sea was rough that day. Although bigger ships are subject to the same meteorological forces that govern smaller ships at sea, in the Norway one doesn't notice it as much due to the length of the vessel. It was built to span three waves, thus effectively smoothing out the ride a great deal. As the tender was being tossed about like a cork, the Norway stayed perfectly still. It was almost as if this huge vessel was bolted somehow to the ocean floor. It stood unmoved.

On the island we hired a cab for eight dollars per person to take us to Magens Bay, a trendy hangout for those who enjoy pristine beaches. We were transported over the summit of a mountain, which gave us a terrific view of Charlotte Amalie Harbor along with the bay with all its ships, boats and of course the city itself.

At the beach we went bathing finding the water quite pleasant. It wasn't as warm as San Andres, but here at St. Thomas we were at the fringe of the Caribbean where the Atlantic has a tremendous influence on the water temperature.

These port stops were great for restocking our liquor supply. It seemed that we drank a lot when the price is right. With "booze" in hand we returned to the Norway, "parked" waiting for us in the bay. After mixing a couple of drinks we laid ourselves out on the deck, awaiting the ship to steam out of the area.

Cruising

By the pool a chap started talking to me about the 9/11 ordeal that the Americans had recently endured. He asked me what I thought of the government's response. Using "the" philosopher's reasoning, I decided to answer his query with a question. "Do you really want to know what I think, what I feel? Are you sufficiently big enough or "bad" enough for my truth?" Looking at me like I was deranged he said, "You're not a member of al-qaeda are you?" "Let me tell you my thoughts, then you may tell me yours." "Okay," he answered." "Dubya is fighting terror by terrifying the people of the world." Looking rather displeased with me he responded by saying, "That sounds like an answer I would get from a conspiracy theorist." So that was his thought. It sounded like "responses one ought to give," thought out by some propaganda think tank in the basement of the White House. These "canned" responses that are in circulation are there to deprive a person of their own power of reason. If you don't conform to the status quo of what the good call good, then you are a "conspiracy monger." Of course some people fail to realize that every good homicide cop, worth his salt thinks "conspiracy." And why shouldn't he; very few people "fess" up to murders. Most slayings are committed by people close to the deceased, so if we are serious about solving this crime one should be firing these very questions at the people close to the trigger.

The Commander-In-Chief George "Dubya" Bush failed to scramble the air force for an hour and a half. NORAD also failed to respond. Yet they have the balls to blame a couple of guys sitting in a cave in Afghanistan for the dirty deed. "Hey Osama." "What is it Omar?" "You know what pisses me off about the Americans?" "No, what?" "They're free." "Omar." "What Osama?" "You know another thing that really picks my ass about those infidels?" "What's that?" "They get to cast a ballot." So it came to pass that I had yet another person that hates me for voicing my opinion in the "land of the free." "It is better to be hated for what you are than be loved for what you're not," as stated eloquently by Andre Gide. It's easier to say that you believe in free speech than it is to allow it. It's the "good" flock of sheep that baa in unison. When it comes to individuals committing crimes the "Columbo" attitude is an asset, but when nations do it, questioning is deemed inappropriate, but why? There were 3000 people that were murdered, among them a couple of hundred firemen whose families want answers and want their killers brought to justice.

Why can't we have these brazen touchy questions directed to the president about the whys and wherefores to solve this crime? Or is our "democracy" much too weak for that. Can't it withstand a barrage of questions aimed at coming to a truth?

Another thing that washed off the guy's back, was the curious coincidence that the "axis of evil," Iraq, Iran and North Korea all recently went from the American dollar to the "Euro," for use in international trade. Maybe I'm wrong but isn't a good cop supposed to ask these "icky" questions to get to the bottom of a felony. Maybe the US is covering its ass and bullying Iraq so that other countries won't abandon the "shaky" American dollar. In Canada, our dollar has recently gained twenty-five percent in an incredibly short time. I read the other day that the Russians are toying with the idea of adopting the Euro as their "international trade currency," another member of the "axis of evil" in the making? Cruising has indeed "sharpened" my tongue.

Gamblers, like us, with a lot of spare time for cruising are the main reason for the increase in popularity of the table games. This, as a result, caused them to fill up rapidly, resulting in over crowded conditions, again, good for the casino, bad for the player. Without a doubt the Norway could have stood a 25% increase in its table games, especially blackjack. The games would, in all likely hood, have been close to capacity. But for the players that don't particularly enjoy crowds, it would have given us more opportunity to play.

Playing alone at a table is the best of conditions. Or so I thought. It turns out that on a single deck game it is the play with four people that gives one the optimum penetration. Also when playing on a shoe with just you and the dealer, the cut card comes out, then you see a few more cards and that's it. Penetration is therefore negligible past the cut card. Therefore on the last few hands, it is a wise tactic to spread, if it is allowed to spread, to the four spots on a high count; that is, if it doesn't exceed the 3% ceiling of your bankroll. This will optimize the penetration on your "end game."

One ruse that I found beneficial for use while playing in packed quarters such as on the Norway was the old "I've got to go to the bathroom trick," on low counts. The constant washing of hands is essential anyway, especially in light of the recent viruses that haunt all cruises. If someone gets into contact with the virus, plays a table game, touching a chip, he or she is likely to contaminate the item. The only solution is to maintain a high level of hygiene by constantly washing your hands, and what better time to do this than on a low count. The problem was, on this ship anyway, that they ran out of soap about two days after we set sail. Even after my constant harping they didn't get around to rectifying the problem for two days. Little wonder why a short time later, the Norway was one of the first "cruisers" to be hit by the Norwalk virus.

The ship would make one more stop at "Stirrup Cay," a small islet owned by the Norwegian Cruise Lines, and from there, back to Miami.

        *   *   *   *   *

Our next ship, the Ocean Breeze, was much smaller and hopefully less packed. We had a few days wait and a timeshare promotion to attend before we could board this boat. We toured around the Miami area for a few days, taking in the Everglades, even getting a chance to fly on a 30's vintage bi-plane trainer called a "Waco."

The morning of the promotion we packed up our things to drive to Pompano Beach, to a resort where one of the big hotel chains was looking into sell off some of their available space. This is a great way to subsidize a vacation, especially if you are on a tight budget or just want to escape the high cost of hotels, fares or entertainment. Assuming of course that you are not a "plum," which is sales talk for easy pickings. For $199 we were to get a three day cruise to the Bahamas, three days at a Holiday Inn around the Fort Lauderdale area, and a ticket on the Jungle Cruise (a boat ride through the water ways of Fort Lauderdale which included a dinner and a show). Also included was a three-day stay at a Ramada Inn in Orlando, with tickets to Universal Studios. I couldn't even calculate what the retail cost of something like that would be. But at face value, $200 sounded like a hell of a deal.

Upon arrival at the hotel, we were assigned a salesman and he proceeded to take us to a cafe at the marina, located on the Inner waterway. This was "a warm up breakfast;" sales talk meant to lower our guard. Then it was back to the hotel to "put the squeeze on us," and to loosen up our wallets. He showed us the deal, which got better and better the more we hesitated. Then when he could not convince us, he brought in the heavy guns. The manager sat down throwing in a golf membership for "only" $1500 more per year. I said, "That doesn't sound like much of a deal." If we would be there for two weeks and golfed everyday, we might break even. But if we didn't, we would be better off paying by the round. After further futile efforts they saw that we were "non-buyers," thereby shuffling us to the next person, "the foot in the door" guy; last attempt to close. "If we can't convince you that you should buy here, would you be interested in a foreclosure that we are working on for a down the road investment." Kathy and I just smiled, looking at each other in disbelief. "I really don't think we would be interested in anything that you have to offer at this point." With that we were finally allowed to go, with all the necessary papers signed, and given the tickets for the various attractions. I guess most promotions are a little classier than the one to which we were a party to.

The big visual let down was getting to the bridge, which was part of the "Inner Coastal Waterway." There, the slums were still erect, with people inhabiting them. You just knew that the area was seething with crime. Why they didn't bus us in, to shield us from the sight was beyond me. They said that they were to be demolished, but like most buyers we held a healthy skepticism when it comes to "sales craft."

We used the facilities at the beach, which were very nicely tended and cared for, later returning to our hotel to prepare for the next cruise.

We drove the short distance to Port Everglade from Fort Lauderdale the next morning. Our ship was a "peanut" compared to the others that were resting in port. Word had it that there were only 300 passengers on board; the ship had room for 500. This might bode favorably as far as the BJ conditions were concerned. We were closely scrutinized as far as bringing liquor on board. But by now we were old hands at the camouflage.

As soon as the ship eased, out of port we went through the life vest drill and then we were free to explore the ship. Before you knew it we were out to sea and the casino was open. As usual I am the first one to be seated at the 21 table.

On the other two ships, it was the cruise ship line that ran their own casinos. On the Ocean Breeze it was subleased to a firm from England. They paid a healthy rate to the owners, but got to keep all the profits. Upon sitting, the dealer shuffled the cards, cutting the shoe in half. I protested and the shift boss came over, explaining to me that due to card counters, they used this cut to ascertain the play. Then if all was above board, they would then and only then, give us a proper cut. He said that it was imperative that they protect themselves from these "predators" because they were only a small casino and couldn't take the hit. He used an interestingly, typically English saying. "I know what I'm doing, they didn't send a 'Silly Billy, to run this casino."

I decided not to open the table although he pleaded with me to do so, to "act as a shill." By merely sitting there, with the deck already in the shoe, ready "for action," was enough to attract another player a few minutes later. I thought that I would wait out the first shoe to see precisely what he called a "decent cut." After the reshuffle the dealer, true to his word, didn't re-cut the cards in the middle; their "decent cut" consisted of well over two decks. It turned out that their cut was indeed decent; decently stacked, that is, in the casino's favor. I played off my "incentive coupons," and left.

"Man this is going to be a long trip," I thought to myself. I hope that I don't get cabin fever or go bonkers from lack of a diversion. There was no way that I was going to play a game that was fairly lopsided to the house's benefit. Beside our trips to Mexico we hadn't been on a non-working holiday in our lives; that is, a place where there wasn't some form of gaming to subsidize our vacation. Here on this boat I realized that I had to boycott the gaming area and do things that "others" do while on vacation. But I drew the line at shuffleboard.

The food was great like all the previous excursions and this time we were seated with only two other couples. They too had been a party to the timesharing "promo experience." The four of them were friends who came from Michigan to take in some sunshine, and get a much-needed break from the cold. I over heard them talking about the relentless pressure that the promotions people put on them to sign the contract. These are pressures that Kathy and I hadn't been exposed to because we didn't see any value in timeshare or in the latest sales spin called "fractional ownership." We thought that we would have a little fun with our new tablemates.

With a straight face I told them that the presentation doesn't end just, because they left the confines of the resort that "we" were marketing. With Kathy nodding her head as I went through my "ad lib" presentation I said, "You see all these people around you, well, they all have representatives at their respective tables too. Our company has asked us, one last time, to show you the advantages and to convince you to reconsider the timeshare offer presented the other day. I have been empowered by my company to sweeten the deal, giving you an 'opportunity' at timeshare ownership. I am prepared to reduce the price by $3000 if you will make a commitment right now." Then I stopped and watched them squirm. They were all real nervous, not knowing for sure whether I was on the "up and up." Meanwhile Kathy and I just sat there nodding our heads, not saying a word. The one guy started "humming and hawing," saying that it was not exactly the resort that they had in mind. Then we burst out laughing, unable to contain ourselves any further. We told them that we were just jesting. You could visibly see the relief on their faces. They told us that they were put through a lot of pressure, and the ruse of planting agents at all the tables as a last ditch effort to make a sale, was an approach that never occurred to them. But once it was brought up, they all thought that the promotion company was determined enough to do it.

Often, not realizing it, people put pressure on themselves. When, as in the case of the promoter, a scenario is presented that seems to make sense, these "plums" break into a sweat if they have no way of refuting the logic of the salesperson's presentation. They are scrambling to find a good argument that the sale's staff can't refute. Not realizing that a great team of professional promoters generally has thought out carefully all of the objections that may arise before hand, and have a "canned" come back to all potential questions. They find themselves without an argument as to whether to sign or not to sign, thus the perceived "pressure;" it emanates from within their own beings. The idea of simply telling them the truth did not occur to them. Just by saying, "Look, we're here "only" to take advantage of the great promotion that was offered us," would end the pressure, and effectively end the session.

For Kathy and I the matter is totally different. We come from the school of "fee simple." In other words we have a philosophy that if we are to purchase any real estate it is to be a free hold property with a lot or some other parcel of land on which one can erect a building if one doesn't already exist. We don't find any value in an undivided two weeks per year share of a building for the next 30 years. To be in a partnership with a thousand people, is to be in a venture with no interest at all. The fraction of 1/1000 equals zero. To be quit frank, throughout the entire presentation at Pompano Beach I was scheming as to how I could get a hold of a piece of property "spinning" it off, after purchasing it outright, along with a group of investors. Maybe even hiring a promotion company just like the one we were listening to as a marketer for our own time-share project. If people are willing to open up their wallets for a "perpetual vacation" we'd be willing to furnish them with the dream for a whack of their cash. Don't get me wrong, timeshare is okay for some people, but I can think of other ways to spend my money and time.

Some people miss the point of a vacation. If we go somewhere paying $300 per room, we're not exactly having fun. On the other hand if we entertain some people in our home, we haven't spent a whole lot of money supplying them with food and shelter, but we have made good contacts that usually span the course of a lifetime. Let us assume that we host a couple from Vegas in the summer time. We have cool air in the evening, without the air conditioning roaring all night. We have breathtaking scenery, which they can visit during the day, returning to comfortable and safe surroundings at night. And if we really get along with our guests we won't mind showing them around. With the computer age it's not that difficult to contact people from around the world who think along the same lines as you. Naturally reciprocating visits are the price. There are, however, some people that I would never have back again nor would I want to visit them on a reciprocating basis. But these instances are extremely rare.

By the time the main course arrived we were all laughing and in good humor. They because we were not promoters and we because, well just because. To get away with a joke that audacious without getting physically attacked was a relief. Anyway we became good "shipmates" to the end of our trip. They were a party to a gag that they could relate to their grand kids.

Not having too much to do after supper we took in their show. Surprisingly, it was quite good with dancers, singers and comedians. These entertainers were multi-talented in that they not only helped with the ships duties, but also did "yeoman" duty with performances to entertain us. This we found to be common practice amongst all the ships. On the way back to our quarters we bumped into a karaoke lounge. Not finding my favorite, James Brown's "I Feel Good" opus, I proceeded to sing to my gal, Elvis's "Heartbreak Hotel."

There was a little surprise when we went into our room. The steward arranged the towel in the form of a dog. He even put the sunglasses on the "soft sculptor" to give it some umpff. Every night there was a different critter that he arranged for us, the next night it was a rabbit and the last night on board it was to be a swan. Now that's what has to be classed as going that extra mile. This guy definitely got a tip. Doing that extra little bit when it came to turning down our bed will be appreciated at tithe time.

In the morning, after docking in Nassau we visited the Atlantis Casino and Hotel, truly a marvel of construction. Not the hotel itself nor the casino but the landscaping. They had countless pools housing various shark species throughout the property. There were water slides that would "zoom" through tubes that were surrounded by these creatures that gave a surreal view from our perspective. The casino was also decorated with flare. Exotic glass blown chandeliers hung throughout the gaming area. It must have made many people in the casino proud to know that their contributions had made all that possible.

Being deprived of gaming on the ship we sat down for about an hour session at a blackjack table just to say that we "did." Up $50, we "walked," with enough to pay for the cab and to replenish our supply of gin and Irish cream.

Back on board the ship we had a relaxing half-day building up to a relaxing dinner. On all cruise ships they have a gala ending to a voyage on the last evening. The entire dining room crew promenaded through the eating area accompanied by the "Hot Hot Hot" melody and song. This also occurred on every single blessed cruise that we were on. Understandably things wouldn't be "hot" unless there was fire. We were not to be disappointed. Our black waiter was balancing a cake aglow with candles atop his head as he led a formidable group of the staff. They snaked their way around the tables in the form of a "Conga" chain dance. After the grand finale, we wished our tablemates the best of luck and went our separate ways.

In the morning we had a hearty breakfast, to last us till we reached Orlando for the last part of the "promo" leg of our venture. We checked into our hotel about three miles from the Universal Studios complex, ate and had some R&R.

After touring Universal Studios the following day, we had two nights to kill in the area. What better way to spend it than at a casino? The problem was there are no casinos in or around the Orlando area. I picked up a couple of brochures at the front desk and noticed an ad for Sterling Casino Lines. The ship that they were advertising, the Ambassador II, sailed every day at 11:00 am and 7:00 pm. A well-appointed bus would pick you up from a prearranged stop at a shopping center in Orlando, taking you the 60 miles to Cape Canaveral, and from there to the boat. Everything is absolutely free of charge. Once on board the ship you can eat immediately at a so-so buffet, or wait until later as the crowd subsided. If you were gambling, the drinks too were to be free. Kathy and I were meaning to get lots of free drinks, free that is, but for the tip.

In the middle of the buffet, the ship started to move. In about fifteen minutes the tables were opened. After eating, we made our way to the 21 area to locate a five-dollar game. Much to our surprise, we located one a floor below the main casino. We sat down and on cue, the dealers started changing up our money. It was a six-deck game, with a typical one card up rule for the dealer. The cut was just under two decks, varying with different dealers. The table we were on was a non-smoking table, which was okay because we would leave when the count was low, so Kathy could have a cigarette. Betting very small amounts, we managed to eke out $50 for Kathy and $75 for me. One could also impress their family and friends with pictures on this perpetual cruise.

There is much to do in Orlando, an area with seemingly limitless attractions. Winter Haven was one such place located about 50 miles away. For the aviation buff there are vintage airplanes that a person can rent with the pilot in the rear seat. For a "mere" $800 per hour, you too can fly a powerful "war bird." Disney World and Epcot Center help make this part of the USA the "playground" of America.

We spread out our road map on the morning we were to leave. On the long road back home we were planning to make a detour to Mexico, and as we would be going through Mississippi anyway, the Biloxi area would be a definite stop to see Billy B. in Bay St. Louis. This is where the epicenter of hurricane Katrina hit in 2006, causing untold damage and hardship to the people located there.

I love the South, and always have. There is something charming, nay enchanting about the place. The women seem to be more feminine, and the gentry a tad more gallant. The friendly people, and the sweet "Southern Belles," with their Southern drawls captivate you with their natural poise and flair for things that are beautiful. The deep crimson color of the Southern clay, seemingly dyed by the blood of the innocent that took part in America's "first" civil war, catches your eye and imagination. The South spawned men like Robert E. Lee, a living testament that you don't need stature to have balls. And a man the likes of "Stonewall" Jackson and his band; although often out numbered ten to one, they withstood the armies of the North.

The Magnolia trees, interspersed on the lawns of stately houses, which in turn had magnificent facades held up by unique columns that always made me think of the South. The armies of Sherman, bent on destruction, couldn't destroy these things. Try as they did to destroy the will of the South, the people bounced back; the seedling that was the South remains. The Magnolia trees stand as a testimony to those who said "no." And if America ever achieves a "rebirth" from its slide into the abyss of its own making, surely the impetus for rejuvenation will come from the South. Despite insurmountable odds, Southerners said "no" to the decay that was the North, and are in the process of saying it again. Rebels to the end, a band of "rebels like my father before me." Truly I was in wonderful company in the South.

On arriving at Casino Magic in Bay St. Louis I dialed up Billy, and he put me in contact with the casino manager for that shift. He in turn invited us up to his office, and after a short chat booked us for a free three-day stay. Gambling would have gained me the comp, but in any case the free room in advance took the pressure off "the big bets." I was also supplied with a card so that they could track my play.

That night I sat down at the double deck game, which is the only game they really keep a close eye on. It was also a treat to have them deal a card down for themselves. Naturally it's just my perception, but it seems that they too get stiffed a lot more on the high count when we get stiffed. Possibly because they too are dealt from the same bad "clump" of cards as we are.

Not doing anything there, I went to the six-deck shoe and proceeded to drop $300 in short order. This prompted yet another move, this time to the eight-deck game where I regained all the losses suffered from the six-deck. The rules there were the same as the six but the cut was more advantageous. We were given a little under two-decks, allowing for a 75% + penetration. I don't know why I hesitated so long. I guess any game that requires a crane to lift its eight deck into the shoe makes me nervous. In the morning I tried the double deck again and found it to be quite easy going as far as surveillance was concerned. I made no money, but the penetration was praise worthy.

In the evening we went over to the pro shop where there was a lounge to sit and "shoot the shit" with Billy and a few of his fellow employees. They were a rather decent bunch. I promised Billy that if he taught me a few fine points in the game of golf I would reciprocate by teaching him a few pointers in the game of blackjack. With that we retired to our quarters to prepare for an early departure for New Orleans.

*   *   *   *   *

Fat City, some people call it, but the French Quarters is a far cry from being fat. Its narrow streets are not at all the images that were transposed to film. It is an area about eight blocks by about thirteen blocks, pressed against the Mississippi river on one side, and downtown New Orleans on the other. So narrow were the streets that they had to be alternately directed into one ways to prevent "grid lock." One couldn't visualize those huge floats traversing what looked to be lanes in some instances. But traverse them they did, manned be gaudy looking people wearing gaudy looking beads. Straining under massive head plumes they would toss their treasures called "throws." These would consist of plastic cups, beads, doubloons (coins) and general junk, which was eagerly sought by the teeming mob.

Mardi Gras! This is a time for the celebration of the flesh. Normally when men dress up in "drag" people look, and under their breath they are ridiculed. During Mardi Gras these same people are the stars. Folks tend to look the other way when men cross dress during "Carnival." There are so many of them that it has become common, "much too common," as a result some women find a need to pull up their tops to prove to people that they are the "real deal." In fact, others have taken up this method of identification, creating a lusty atmosphere in the streets of the French Quarters.

New Orleans, N'Awlins as the people that live and work there call it, is a thriving, bustling town. This city is purported to have the busiest port complex in the world. Served by no less than six class one railroads and an inland waterway system of 23,000 km., New Orleans is the port of choice for transportation of many goods. For the less faint of heart the city has one other attraction that brings in a lot of dough; casinos.

Not finding the time to stop and play, we did some looking around the Bourbon Street area and then make our way to Shreveport. We then proceeded to Dallas on our way to Mexico. In Dallas we stopped in to see Rick and Pauline L.. Rick, who I had met in Calgary, had made it in a big way financially, and the two of them were in the process of parleying there earnings into bigger and more interesting projects. He was also dabbling in the blackjack phenomenon, so much so in fact that he had a table set up in his office to practice 21 with a six deck shoe. He would practice on employees showing them "the evils of gambling" by putting their hard earned money down the table's drop box.

Rick happened to be a certified war hero from the Vietnam era, serving as a marine pilot with valor and distinction. He was now grounded, and needed a much-deserved infusion of adrenaline or excitement associated with risk to keep those old "pipes" from clogging up. Now, of course, risk was intended to mean risk of monetary assets rather than risking "your ass" for this highflying pilot.

His forays to Las Vegas were "legendary," if not in his own mind certainly in the casino marketers' minds where he was known to wager thousands of dollars on a single turn of cards. Various hotels would be in touch with him constantly, trying to coax him, and his lovely wife to stay at their particular venues. He didn't count cards therefore what I had to say was more or less a revelation for him. Being an intelligent man he realized quickly that his prior play was full of holes. As we worked the shoe you could see him grasping the concept more and more until he finally said that he was going to use it the next time they went to Vegas. It will be interesting to see how eagerly the casinos vie for his business after he applies his newfound skills to the game.

As you can see cruising does have its high points. It can afford you a chance to see a lot of the country, and visit with some of your friends. It also allows you to meet new people, and make lasting friendships. In some cases the game was "no hell" but most of the people that we met, aside from Gene and some "bitchy" ladies, were truly genuine and receptive. In saying that, I would have to offer one more thing though. I would never even entertain the thought of going on a cruise that didn't offer a 21 game.

On the way back from Mexico we went through Vegas and up Interstate 15 to Canada briefly stopping in Salt Lake City to visit CC (Silvan) and his family.

In the morning CC strapped on his gun, and he invited me out with him on a call involving a domestic mater. While in the car he mentioned that he and his son Cody often go to a place called Wendover, Nevada to gamble. It is two hours west of Salt Lake on Hi-way 80 just past the Bonneville Salt Flats. He asked if we were staying for the weekend at which time we could all go and enjoy couple of days relaxing and gambling. I had the urge, but we had to get back to Calgary to attend to some unfinished business.

We thanked them for a wonderful stay and departed for the snow blown reaches of Montana, and ultimately to our destination in Canada.

Once home I started going through the accumulation of mail received during our rather long absence. Much of the mail was from "on line" casinos in the form of checks. In the modern age of communication, one no longer has to leave home to enjoy the benefits of gambling. For sure I don't recommend playing in "cyberspace" because, for one thing, it really is a gamble. The only real reason that a person can make money playing casinos on the net is that they match your deposit, oft times up to a couple of hundred dollars.

Let's assume that you make a deposit of $100 into your account, in a particular casino. They then match it to give you a combined bankroll of $200. Let's say that their requirements are that you play the total amount ten times, for a total of $2000. Assuming that they have an extreme advantage of two percent you will lose $40 betting through the $2000. The total loss of $40 comes off the $200, giving you a profit of $60. Playing heads up against the dealer, flat betting shouldn't take more than fifteen minutes of your time. Combine the effect with the hundreds of casinos on the net, and you can see that there is some further money to be made using this medium. A fast server is required, however, to rapidly download the games into your computer.

Now there is no way whatever of counting cards with an "electronic dealer." It is my understanding that they use six decks, shuffling after each and every deal. Out of 312 cards you get to see about five cars before the cards are randomly shuffled again. Basic strategy rules this method of playing. There is only one play where the count can be employed, and that is hitting or standing on sixteen against the dealer's ten. For instance if you have two fives and have hit it with a six, you are now slightly positive. Surely this is a borderline play, but you do have the option of not hitting.

When downloading a casino game from the Internet there is a caveat that appears on many of them. "If you're from Denmark, you are not eligible for a bonus." This must mean that the people there, for the most part, play the bonuses and then cash out. Danes must be immune from the gambling bug. Like myself, and many like me, they play the "bonus game," that is "take the money and run." But in order to do this they must be incorruptible, and possess a non-addictive personality. If you are in any way a gambler, the best advice that I can impart to you is don't gamble on line. Remember, "You can lose your house with the click of a mouse."

Personally I have played about 75 casinos that offered high matching bonuses. Playing them through rapidly, I have at time doubled my deposit, plus bonus. Sometimes I've made as little as three dollars. At times I have lost five dollars and three times I got skunked totally, losing both my bonus and the deposit. In total I have won close to $4500US playing on line blackjack. The problem is that you are only allowed to receive a bonus once from any one casino. One rapidly goes through the casinos that give the best bonuses combined with the least number of play-through requirements.

There are also a number of casinos that cheat the unwary "surfer." These "rogue" casinos are listed on any number of web sites that deal with player issues relating to on line gaming. They should be noted, and avoided at all costs. I have been "burned" a few times myself. Excellent sites like the "Wizard of Odds" have these casinos listed along with casinos that are more reputable. If you are in doubt about a certain casino, email Michael Shakleford and I am sure that he can clear the air as to whether or not a certain casino is on the up and up.

Cruising

For those of you who have chosen BJ as a profession or for that matter as a profitable pass time, I do hope that you enjoy the above venues, but be careful. Remember I am only a teacher in the art of blackjack, after all that's my profession. If you have chosen BJ as a lively hood, I know that you can suffer the occasional set back because, after all, isn't that part of the game? As a player who dabbles in the game part time I would hate to have you on my conscience if you fall by the wayside. However, if you do, somewhere in that lofty casino up in the sky there is "The Big Pit Boss" that will offer me His forgiveness. After all, isn't that "His" profession?

Chapter Eighteen: Double Down, No Card

Many years ago, Las Vegas was just another uninhabitable tract of land. That was until late in the 1820s when Spaniards located a well, thus creating an oasis. They named it Las Vegas, Spanish for meadows. These "water miners" had no idea that the well they had dug wasn't really a well at all, in fact it turned out to be a huge underground lake. The oasis created on this "lake" was very important to the Spanish, as it shortened the trade route between Santa Fe and Los Angeles. Now they could cross the desert in a more direct route.

Miners of a different sort came to settle the Las Vegas area around 1860. These were the miners for souls. They were affiliated with the sect known as the Latter Day Saints, commonly called the Mormons. They settled the area in 1855, mainly due to the wells located there. Their stay was short lived and they "temporarily" left in 1857. It is obvious that their absence was brief. The allure of the town was irresistible. They make up a large part of the population to this day.

Mormons and gambling seem to go hand in hand. Although it is against the tenets of their religion to gamble, they kind of "turn the other cheek" the other way, as it were, to qualify their huge presents in the gaming industry.

When Jimmy Hoffa of the Teamsters got caught with his pants down swinging loans to the mob for casino acquisitions from their workers' own pension fund, the Mormons "muscled in on the action." They took over the loans, not because they were crooked but because they were sound investments. They didn't have a problem with the fact that gaming was "a sin." The Latter Day Saints were imbedded with the gangsters. But because it was good for business it was also good for Vegas. If it weren't for those investments, Vegas wouldn't be the gambling Mecca that it is at present. To this day some of the biggest banks, associated with casino development, are institutions with "old Mormon money" behind them.

Someone said that it wasn't the "thin blue line" of the law that leaned on the mob, forcing them out of town; it was the Mormons with their "bottom line." The town got too small for the both of them. The mob didn't have the nerve to hover around your pockets like the Mormons did; they had too much class for that. When the mob ruled, you were treated like royalty as a gambler. The "new mob" didn't care much if you gambled, the only thing they really cared about was that you lost. And losers were far more plentiful under the management of the "new overseers." Comps were cut dramatically and the "pomp" accorded to gamblers were seriously curtailed. From now on, only serious betters would be "wined and dined," or at least those that fell into their neatly defined calculations as "comp able."

Miners however come in all shapes and sizes. Some miners even mined things other than the precious metals that were buried deep in the ground. They mined the wealth that accumulated around the more than plentiful tables that graced the ever increasing number of casinos popping up on the "strip." In some ways these treasures were sought after more greedily than the gold and silver that ultimately gave rise to the state's motto. Even if for no particular reason, other than that they were there, shamelessly displayed for all to see. Everyone knows that the California gold rush produced some very rich people, but these were in the minority, and generally they were the ones with the rudimentary knowledge to become successful prospectors.

The "Silver State" has fomented a gold rush of its own. The legalization of gaming has given rise to an influx of people that is unprecedented for a desert community. Perhaps the reason for the rapid population increase is not for the most noble of reasons, but the outcome is the same. Like California, during their gold rush, the population in Nevada has also soared. In this population of new settlers, there exists a minority of people with the rudimentary knowledge to become successful "prospectors" in this new and latest "gold rush." For the majority of those "other" folks, well, let's just say that they supplied the mass which is, after all, the only currency used for demographic increase.

For those "latter day prospectors," there is a certain affinity that allows me to look at life, or more to the point, the life of gaming, from their particular perspective, Knowing the exhilaration of mining that "mother lode," and the agony of falling flat on your face.

In stalking the tables one runs across a most interesting cast of characters. Some of the most interesting of these haunt the casino scene in Calgary. Although the casinos there have a rule outlawing card counting, by stipulation of rule #24, it however, is rarely if ever invoked. It states, "Absolutely no card counting will be tolerated." The unwritten agreement stipulates that "counters" can only play a maximum of two squares. As a result, the "Usual Suspect" can be relied on to be there when you show up.

Joe "The Big Easy" W. is a classic. This retired "prospector" has been mining the table around North America since he removed himself from the work force years ago. His interest in "easy money" started out innocently enough, scouring the backcountry of Canada and the US in search of that illusive metal, gold. Accustomed as he was to disappointment and perpetual set backs in that field, his evolution to card counting wasn't to be a huge step. Experimenting in vain with "basic tragedy," which some people mistakenly call basic strategy, he was lucky enough to meet a fellow practitioner, Glenn "Whoa-ah" K. This mathematically keen minded individual acquired his name by shouting "whoa-ah," aptly excised from the Al Pacino flick titled "The Scent of a Woman," every time his "plan" came together resulting in a blackjack. Putting Joe under his wing, he finally convinced him to drop the basics of the blackjack game and taught him a simple counting method to avoid the pitfalls that bedevil the basic player, and which are built on folly. Since then he has amassed about $20,000 a year from that system. "The Smell of money" from this source is a subsidy that shouldn't escape any sharp-minded retiree. This of course doesn't include the revenues from his other hobbies, which still entail the relentless pursuit of the quest for that shinier metal. Whether he is panning for gold at some hidden creek, or chipping away at some of the assets from one of our more than bountiful casinos, he remains independent and free. A position that many of us talk about endlessly, but so very few of us achieve.

Then there is the "Heartbreak Kid," a guy who also answers to the name of Peter. He is an Asian who audibly blurts out "Heartbreak Hotel" when his well-laid plans get dashed by a string of uncooperative cards. It is rather comical to see "Whoa-ah" and the "Heartbreak Kid" playing at the same table on a high-count situation. They are often caught plagiarizing one another's particular antics. After the cars are dealt one has no need to looking to see what they had. Often Peter would say "whoa-ah" meaning that he got the "snapper," and Glenn would come out with Pete's patented jingle of "Heartbreak Hotel," if he was dealt the stiff.

"Fancy Fingers" Frank, another Asian chap, can cut the dealer a stiff with just a wee peek at the bottom card. Playing at the same table with him one day I noticed that he made a large bet. Asking him what the hell he was betting on, he answered, "The dealer's six." I quickly raised my bet too, and sure enough the dealer ended up with that six.

Arriving a "work," when one of us meet we give the "old rub of the nose" with our index finger, a move made famous by Paul Newman and Robert Redford, from their all time classic movie. We old timers just giggle, as the move basically means nothing else other than the that we all have watched too many reruns of that movie, "The Sting." The moral of the movie is not to be misconstrued; the little fish puts one over on the big one. The greed and the need for revenge of the latter is so overwhelming that he ends up taking the fall.

Blackjack, poker or any other game for that matter is not a platform to be launching a volley of emotions from. Usually when emotions are running high in gaming the take of revenues are low at best. A "cold blooded" determination is the approach that is best suited for 21 play. Over reaction to a string of loses by raising your bet to somehow rectify a losing proposition is an emotional response to an inanimate phenomenon. Like calling a hammer stupid because you accidentally hit yourself on the head with it, will only give cause to the mislaying of culpability. A hammer is in no way stupid or smart, it is only a tool. As in counting cards, a craftsman in the trade can rapidly realize what is transpiring in the deck. If he keeps hitting himself in the "melon" on the high count, he should then change tables. After all, isn't the best tool in the counter's bag the "stethoscope," as touched on earlier in the book, put there to study the health of the deck? As a "card carrying" card counter, I can't tell you how many times I have witnessed people pass on hitting a twelve against a six when the deck is running at a true minus five, or hit sixteen against a ten, when the deck is registering a plus. The reason for this is that they have yet to acquire that cold-blooded attribute that is necessary for the success of the "modern mercenary" in the battle that plays out on that semi circular table with the green felt. "You can only become winful a result of becoming sinful;" by learning how to count.

A friend of mine, Chris M., asked me if I would give him a few pointers in the game. He, being a typical gambler with all the baggage that goes along with it, was the type of guy that was after the "big win." Coincidentally, this is the same personality type that ends up being the "big loser." However, he does have an attribute of yearning for perfection in whatever he attempts. As a result I yielded to his request.

We entered the casino, a place where he had been many times before. I could see that he had been burned several times in a place just like the one we were in. He held the casino in too much "awe." Like going out horseback riding for the first time it's comforting to know that the person that is with you controls the animal with a tight grip on the reigns, and not the other way around. "Scienta est Potentia" (knowledge is power,) and if you have power the fear will evaporate. That queasy feeling of uncertainty, of not knowing whether you will win or lose doesn't enter into the equation at all. You know that in the long run you will be a winner. But to a "doubting Thomas" all this is new, and to Chris, playing winning blackjack was new.

We sat down and started our play. A reasonably good situation presented itself, and we each made a twenty-dollar bet. Losing that, I again placed a twenty-dollar bet into the square. "You're chasing your money," he said to me as I prodded him to put in the same bet as me. "You're chasing your money;" what a classic response, usually from a novice. Like the statement "aces follow faces" etc. I'm sure he would laugh at that one now, but back then he really believed all that stuff. He was going to be one tough nut to crack.

We played for several weeks and I recall seeing a glimmer of hope in his play. I decided then that he would be my protege. One day he phoned me to let me know that he was going to be there at a certain time. I informed him that I wouldn't be able to make it till much later, but we agreed to meet there nonetheless. Arriving several hours later, I looked for him at every 21 table but couldn't locate him. Phoning him on his cell, I could detect the gentle rhythm of his unique ring; it was coming from the "Let It Ride" table. Unbelievably, he had sat down there to actually try his luck.

I now knew the "pain" that Moses must have felt, descending from the Mount with calloused hands after days of chiselling "The Sacred Tablets," only to find that his beloved tribe had been seduced into worshiping "The Golden Calf." Confiding in me later he said that he would take some of the profits earned at 21 and apply them to a different game. Knowing that the odds lay strictly with the house didn't deter him in the least.

Imagine my protege being caught, eyes agape, at the Let It Ride table, perhaps in the attempt to trip the music device, controlled by the dealer to blare out its inane fan fare theme; alerting all in the casino that the player has just acquired a hand which is a straight or better. For us, the usual suspects, well, we merely look at those people and visualize them with four long legs and two long ears to match. I don't think I could bear to watch Chris in a win situation, gyrating to the "melody" with his toothy grin and long ears swaying in unison to the beat, as people often do that play that game. The gravity would be too much for even me to endure.

Being a professional racer he once told me that the mark of a "pro" on the racetrack circuit was not the one that constantly took chances; quite the contrary. As a professional he would gain one tenth of a second after every lap on the novice. After 100 laps he would presumably be ten seconds ahead of him. Like taking a man at the edge of an abyss, you try to shake some sense into him. Appealing to his "professionalism," I suggested that he apply some of that wise old racing know how to his blackjack game.

Admittedly I haven't caught him at the Let It Ride game since, but he now has a "bug" to play craps. Being in possession of an addictive personality, he is predisposed to this kind of self-destructive behaviour. He has told me that frankly he has lost thousands playing craps. The joke is that if anyone wishes to see him for any reason they would be wise to look for him anywhere but the BJ tables. This was my understudy, the person to whom I was supposed to pass the baton. He had picked up the theory of it all, and in some cases mastered certain facets of the game far more solidly than I. And why shouldn't he? Is not a teacher's work futile if none of his students have been taught sufficiently well that they may occasionally surpass the knowledge of their tutor? I would like for him, in essence, as a great sage once said, "to be a well of wine amongst empty buckets."

Cliff is another regular who has accounted for himself quite well. I remember the smile on his face one day as I was playing at a table opposite him. He alerted me, and looking down at his tray he said, "I finally did it, I won the $5000." There in his cup holder lay the evidence, or perhaps better put, the "trophy." He has augmented his income to such a degree that retirement has now become a pleasure. And isn't that what it's all about? Relaxing in one's twilight years, enjoying the ups and downs of the game, and also receiving monetary compensation at the same time. Walter S. is another one that has mastered all aspects of gambling. Like a social club with no fees he shows up regularly augmenting his meagre pension. Admittedly he doesn't count cards but rather uses meticulous money management techniques to stay above board.

Leon "The Machinist" C. has expertise working the automatic shuffle machine; a game that he claims has given him some excellent returns. "Swiss" John, who is also called "Mr. Blackjack" in his home country, has a claim to fame in loading up the deck and coming out when it's "there." Unfortunately he doesn't relate the information very well to his colleges; as a result, we usually miss out. Mark and Bea, on the other hand can be heard all over the casino cajoling people with their dry humour. There is also one guy that doesn't count cards and has made a lot more in twenty minutes than some will in ten years of play. Alex sat down at a Caribbean poker game on someone's lunch marker and got the Royal Flush for nearly $200,000. It took him only five hands after which he left. His remark was, "You know it only takes one hand." That was by far the most expensive lunch the guy ever took. He must be still talking to himself. By the way in Canada, like most reputable countries, one is not taxed on their gaming wins, unlike the USA.

Whether chatting with Alex or some other cohort it's always gratifying to know that they each have carved out a little niche in their particular field of expertise. And all this is good for the casinos as well. Due to winning players, the "suckers" keep coming. Most people just don't have the discipline to be winning players. They get into a bad run and either lose their BR, or revert back to their "losing" ways. You won't see any of the guys mentioned above, in a meeting at the "Wailing Wall" of the gambling genre because they are winners and only the losers fill the seats at G. A.

The losers will always be the multitude that will forever fill the casinos where bets are made, and more often lost than won. They will also be there giving their advice as to the way a particular hand should have been played, after the play of course.

At times these people refer to the genre of counters as guys who may have the "right stuff" but occasionally hit the "wrong stiff" causing the dealer to make his hand. Naturally it works both ways. "When you're right, no one remembers; when you're wrong, no one forgets." When you're wrong, and often you are, that's the time that sticks out in the gambler's mind.

At times a silly comment deserves an equally silly reply. Once I was watching a game where a "fellow traveler" hit a stiff, and the irate person sitting at third base doubled down on an eleven, and was subsequently stiffed. The dealer made his hand, and truly he would have broke had the counter not hit his stiff at that particular time. "He would have broke if you wouldn't have hit your hand," he said. "Hitting your hand was definitely not the correct play." Irritated at the person giving him his down home form of advice, my associate countered and said, "It was the correct play, it was your play that was incorrect." "How so," asked the player? My associate replied as he gathered up his multitude of chips, "Your correct play at that time should have been double down, no card."

Tables & Charts Section

The following section deals with various tables and charts that are essential in decision making for not only the basic player but also the card counter. These charts were supplied by Michael Shackleford from his excellent web site, "The Wizard of Odds."

Basic strategy table:

Your Hand	Dealer's Up Card									
	2	3	4	5	6	7	8	9	10	A
5,6,7,8	H	H	H	H	H	H	H	H	H	H
9	H	D	D	D	D	H	H	H	H	H
10	D	D	D	D	D	D	D	D	H	H
11	D	D	D	D	D	D	D	D	D	H
12	H	H	S	S	S	H	H	H	H	H
13,14	S	S	S	S	S	H	H	H	H	H
15,16	S	S	S	S	S	H	H	H	H	H
17,18,19,20	S	S	S	S	S	S	S	S	S	S
Soft 13,14	H	H	H	D	D	H	H	H	H	H
Soft 15,16	H	H	D	D	D	H	H	H	H	H
Soft 17	H	D	D	D	D	H	H	H	H	H
Soft 18	S	D	D	D	D	S	S	H	H	H
Soft 19,20	S	S	S	S	S	S	S	S	S	S
A-A	SP	SP	SP	SP	SP	SP	SP	SP	SP	SP
2-2,3-3	SP	SP	SP	SP	SP	SP	H	H	H	H
4-4	H	H	H	SP	SP	H	H	H	H	H
5-5	D	D	D	D	D	D	D	D	H	H
6-6	SP	SP	SP	SP	SP	H	H	H	H	H
7-7	SP	SP	SP	SP	SP	SP	H	H	H	H
8-8	SP	SP	SP	SP	SP	SP	SP	SP	SP	SP
9-9	SP	SP	SP	SP	SP	SP	SP	SP	S	S
10-10	S	S	S	S	S	S	S	S	S	S

H=Hit, S=Stand, D=Double down, SP=Split

Rule Variations	
Rule	Effect
Five card Charlie	+1.49%
Early surrender against ace	+.39%
Early surrender against ten	+.24%
Player may draw to split aces	+.19%
Six card Charlie	+.15%
Player may resplit aces	+.08%
Late surrender against ten	+.07%
Seven card Charlie	+.01%
Late surrender against ace	+.00%
Resplit to only 2 hands	-.01%
No-peek: ace showing	-.01%
Player may double on 9-11 only	-.09%
No-peek: ten showing	-.10%
Player may not resplit	-.10%
Player may not double after splitting	-.14%
Player may double on 10,11 only	-.18%
Dealer hits on soft 17	-.22%
Blackjack pays 6-5	-1.39%
Player loses 17 ties	-1.87%
Player loses 17,18 ties	-3.58%
Player loses 17-19 ties	-5.30%
Player loses 17-20 ties	-8.38%
Player loses 17-21 ties	-8.86%

Again, in the use of these tables and the previous ones, keep in mind these values for the count:

2 = plus 1	7 = zero	Ace =	minus 1
3 = plus 1	8 = zero	Ten =	minus 1
4 = plus 1	9 = zero	Jack =	minus 1
5 = plus 1		Queen =	minus 1
6 = plus 1		King =	minus 1

The deck is balanced, therefore it must start at zero and up at zero, unless you have made an error.

The following three pages have tables that have been excised from Stanford Wong's "Professional Blackjack" with his permission. The chart is only one, which deals with card counting and is tailored to meet the needs of the typical game in the Alberta casinos. That is, four decks, with the dealer hitting soft seventeen. In saying this, play strategy doesn't vary that much when more decks are added or taken away. More precise tables are offered in Wong's book dealing with one deck and multi decks, certainly a tome that the serious blackjack player would be remiss in not studying in greater detail. Keep in mind more precise play translates into greater profits.

Appendix A

Table A2
High-Low, Four Decks, H17

Player's Hand		Dealer's Upcard									
		2	3	4	5	6	7	8	9	10	ace
hit/stand	soft 18	-14	-15	-14	-15	-15		-15	h	h	h
	hard 17										-4
	hard 16	-9	-10	-11	-12	-14	9	7	5	0	3
	hard 15	-5	-7	-8	-9	-11	10	10	8	4	5
	hard 14	-3	-5	-6	-7	-9	17	h	h	h	9
	hard 13	0	-2	-3	-4	-7	h	h	h	h	15
	hard 12	3	1	0	-1	-3	h	h	h	h	h
double	11	-11	-12	-13	-14	-16	-9	-6	-4	-4	0
	10	-8	-9	-10	-11	-13	-6	-4	-1	4	3
	9	1	0	-2	-4	-6	3	7			
	8	13	9	5	3	1	14				
	7		16	12	9	8					
	6		20	15	11	12					
	5		20	15	12	13					
double	ace-9	10	8	6	5	4	14				
	ace-8	8	5	3	1	0	17				
	ace-7	0	-2	-6	-8	-13	20				
	ace-6	1	-3	-7	-10	-14					
	ace-5	15	3	-3	-6	-13					
	ace-4	18	6	0	-4	-10					
	ace-3	14	6	1	-1	-5					
	ace-2	12	7	3	0	-2					
split w/o double	ace-ace	-11	-12	-13	-13	-14	-9	-8	-7	-8	-4
	10-10	11	8	6	5	4	13	20	°		
	9-9	-1	-2	-3	-4	-6	6	-8	-9		2
	8-8	spl	spl	spl	spl	spl	spl	spl	17*	6*	-1
	7-7	-8	-10	-12	-14	-16	spl				
	6-6	1	-1	-3	-5	-7					
	5-5										
	4-4**		18	12	8	7					
	3-3	8	3	0	-2	-5	13*				
	2-2	7	3	0	-4	-7	spl				
split with double	ace-ace	-11	-12	-13	-13	-14	-9	-8	-7	-8	-4
	10-10	11	8	6	5	4	13	20			
	9-9	-2	-4	-5	-6	-8	3	-8	-9		1
	8-8	spl	spl	spl	spl	spl	spl	spl	18*	8*	-1
	7-7	-10	-11	-13	-14	-16	spl	5/19*			
	6-6	-2	-4	-6	-8	-10					
	5-5										
	4-4**	14	8	3	-1	-5					
	3-3	0	-3	-7	-9	-11	spl	4			
	2-2	-2	-5	-7	-9	-11	spl	5			

Table A2 (Continued)

Player's Hand	Dealer's Upcard									
	2	3	4	5	6	7	8	9	10	ace
10-7										-4
9-8										-4
10-6	-9	-10	-11	-12	-14	9	8	5	1	4
9-7	-9	-10	-11	-12	-14	10	8	5	0	4
8-8	spl	spl	spl	spl	spl	spl	spl	sp/-	sp/-	h/sp
10-5	-6	-7	-8	-9	-11	10	10	8	4	5
9-6	-6	-6	-8	-9	-11	11	10	8	4	5
8-7	-5	-6	-7	-8	-11	11	11	9	4	5
10-4	-3	-5	-6	-7	-9	17	h	h	h	10
9-5	-3	-4	-6	-7	-9	18	h	h	h	10
8-6	-3	-5	-6	-7	-9	18	h	h	h	9
7-7	h/sp	h/sp	h/sp	h/sp	h/sp	spl	20	h	11	8
10-3	0	-1	-3	-4	-6	h	h	h	h	16
9-4	0	-1	-3	-4	-6	h	h	h	h	16
8-5	-1	-2	-4	-5	-7	h	h	h	h	15
7-6	-1	-2	-4	-5	-7	h	h	h	h	14
10-2	3	2	0	-1	-2	h	h	h	h	h
9-3	3	1	0	-1	-3	h	h	h	h	h
8-4	3	1	0	-1	-3	h	h	h	h	h
7-5	2	1	0	-1	-3	h	h	h	h	h
6-6	h/sp	h/sp	h/sp	h/sp	h/sp	h	h	h	h	h
9-2	-11	-12	-13	-14	-15	-8	-6	-4	-4	0
8-3	-11	-12	-13	-14	-16	-9	-6	-4	-4	0
7-4	-11	-12	-13	-14	-16	-9	-6	-4	-4	0
6-5	-11	-12	-13	-14	-16	-9	-6	-4	-4	0
8-2	-8	-9	-10	-11	-13	-5	-3	-1	4	3
7-3	-8	-9	-10	-11	-13	-6	-4	-1	4	3
6-4	-8	-9	-10	-11	-13	-6	-3	-1	4	3
5-5	-8	-9	-10	-11	-13	-6	-4	-1	4	3
7-2	0	-1	-2	-4	-6	3	7			
6-3	1	0	-2	-4	-6	3	7			
5-4	1	0	-2	-4	-6	3	7			
6-2	13	9	5	3	1	14				
5-3	13	9	5	3	1	14				
4-4	13	9	5	2	1	14				
5-2		16	12	9	8					
4-3		16	11	8	8					
4-2		20	15	11	12					
3-2		20	15	12	13					

two-card hit/stand

two-card double

APPENDIX A

Table A2 (Continued)

Player's Hand	early		early & late			late	
	10	ace	7	8	9	10	ace
10-7	5	18*			13	11	
9-8	6	17*			13	12	
10-6	-5	-17	13	4	0	-2	-4/16*
9-7	-5	-18	10	4	0	-2	-4/14*
8-8	-2	-18/14*			7	1	-5/4*
10-5	-2	-14	10	6	2	0	-1/16*
9-6	-2	-14	11	7	2	0	0/15*
8-7	-2	-13	11	7	3	0	0/14*
10-4	0	-13	16	12	7	3	4/16*
9-5	0	-13	16	12	7	3	4/15*
8-6	0	-13	16	12	6	3	4/14*
7-7	-1	-14		11	5	2	2/13*
10-3	3	-11		20	14	8	
9-4	4	-10		20	14	9	
8-5	3	-11		19	12	7	
7-6	2	-11		18	12	7	
10-2	8	-7				14	
9-3	7	-8				13	
8-4	7	-8			20	13	
7-5	7	-8				13	
6-6	8	-8				14	
6-2		1/4*					
5-3		1/4*					
4-4		2/4*					
6-ace	18						
5-2	14	-6/12*				19	
4-3	14	-7/12*				19	
5-ace	15					19	
4-2	11	-4/15*			20	16	
3-3	11	-4/15*			20	16	
4-ace	16					20	
3-2	12	-2/14*				16	
3-ace							
2-2	15	0/11*				20	

surrender

A Book about Blackjack, Philosophy, and Politics.

How should a person confront a situation that has him in a venue where gambling is the main industry? Should he dive in, not knowing the first thing about gambling and its consequences? Should he sit down and take free advice from the other people "ruminating" at the same table? Or should he instead arm himself with the necessary tools to allow him to go to a destination such as Las Vegas with confidence and self-assurance? These questions are addressed quite early in the book, using the power of philosophy as a backdrop. The book takes the novice through the nerve wracking "first steps," faced by the typical gambler. The intimidation that some people may feel when first entering the environment of a casino, will be quickly overcome. The book talks about the pitfalls that are to be avoided and the classic mistakes made by the beginner. Slowly the reader is shown the way the casino looks at players and their behaviors, to ascertain whether or not they pose a threat to that casino.

Acknowledgements

This book offers a new and interesting insight on blackjack.
Stanford Wong. (Blackjack Authority)
It offers an introduction into a system that has gained the author the admiration of his peers and respectful wrath of the casinos.
Zoltan K. (Entrepreneur)
Al declares war on the casinos in his uniquely refreshing style.
Chris M. (Salesman)
A look at blackjack from the eyes of a truly modern day philosopher and political satirist.
Paul T. (Political Analyst)
A surprisingly light read considering the heavy philosophical overtones.
Keve S. (Businessman)